# Hands-On Full-Stack Web Development with GraphQL and React

Build scalable full-stack applications while learning to solve complex problems with GraphQL

**Sebastian Grebe**

**BIRMINGHAM - MUMBAI**

# Hands-On Full-Stack Web Development with GraphQL and React



**Commissioning Editor:** Kunal Chaudhari
**Acquisition Editor:** Larissa Pinto
**Content Development Editor:** Pranay Fereira
**Technical Editor:** Rutuja Vaze
**Copy Editor:** Safis Editing
**Language Support Editor**: Storm Mann, Mary McGowan
**Project Coordinator:** Pragati Shukla
**Proofreader:** Safis Editing
**Indexer:** Tejal Daruwale Soni
**Graphics:** Alishon Mendonsa
**Production Coordinator:** Jisha Chirayil

First published: January 2019

Production reference: 2200319

Published by Packt Publishing Ltd.
Livery Place
35 Livery Street
Birmingham
B3 2PB, UK.

ISBN 978-1-78913-452-0

`www.packtpub.com`

# Contributors

## About the author

**Sebastian Grebe** is a verified computer science expert for application development. He is a young entrepreneur working on a variety of products. He specializes in web development using modern technologies such as React and FeathersJS, traditional technologies such as PHP and SQL. He developed professionally by merging old and new applications, and developing cross-platform apps with React Native and Ionic.

Currently, he is actively working on his software agency, called Open Mind, which manages various software projects. He is also actively pushing a social network app that utilizes React, Apollo, and Cordova, which is called Coupled. He has worked for various companies as a software engineer and project manager, such as DB Netz AG.

*I thank my love, who has been able to give me the time I needed. Her support made every day better. Special thanks to my parents, who encourage me to take my own way in life.*

# About the reviewer

**Subhash Shah** works as a head of technology at AIMDek Technologies Pvt. Ltd. He is an experienced solutions architect with over 12 years of experience and holds a degree in information technology. He is an advocate of open source development and using it to solve critical business problems while reducing cost. His interests include microservices, data analysis, machine learning, artificial intelligence, and databases. He is an admirer of quality code and test-driven development. His technical skills include translating business requirements into scalable architecture, designing sustainable solutions, and project delivery. He is a co-author of *MySQL 8 Administrator's Guide* and *Hands-On High Performance with Spring 5*, both published by Packt.

# Packt is searching for authors like you

If you're interested in becoming an author for Packt, please visit `authors.packtpub.com` and apply today. We have worked with thousands of developers and tech professionals, just like you, to help them share their insight with the global tech community. You can make a general application, apply for a specific hot topic that we are recruiting an author for, or submit your own idea.

# Table of Contents

**Preface** 1

**Chapter 1: Preparing Your Development Environment** 7
- **Application architecture** 8
  - The basic setup 10
- **Installing and configuring Node.js** 11
- **Setting up React** 12
  - Preparing and configuring webpack 14
  - Render your first React component 18
  - Rendering arrays from React state 20
  - CSS with webpack 24
  - Event handling and state updates with React 26
  - Controlling document heads with React Helmet 30
  - Production build with webpack 30
- **Useful development tools** 32
  - Analyzing bundle size 34
- **Summary** 35

**Chapter 2: Setting up GraphQL with Express.js** 37
- **Node.js and Express.js** 37
  - Setting up Express.js 38
  - Running Express.js in development 39
- **Routing in Express.js** 40
  - Serving our production build 41
- **Using Express.js middleware** 42
  - Installing important middleware 43
  - Express Helmet 44
  - Compression with Express.js 45
  - CORS in Express.js 45
- **Combining Express.js with Apollo** 46
  - Writing your first GraphQL schema 49
  - Implementing GraphQL resolvers 50
  - Sending GraphQL queries 51
  - Using multiples types in GraphQL schemas 53
  - Writing your first GraphQL mutation 54
- **Back end debugging and logging** 56
  - Logging in Node.js 57
  - Debugging with Postman 58
- **Summary** 61

**Chapter 3: Connecting to The Database** 63
**Using databases in GraphQL** 63
Installing MySQL for development 64
Creating a database in MySQL 67
**Integrating Sequelize into our stack** 68
Connecting to a database with Sequelize 69
Using a configuration file with Sequelize 71
**Writing database models** 73
Your first database model 73
Your first database migration 75
Importing models with Sequelize 77
**Seeding data with Sequelize** 80
**Using Sequelize with Apollo** 82
Global database instance 82
Running the first database query 85
**One-to-one relationships in Sequelize** 86
Updating the table structure with migrations 87
Model associations in Sequelize 90
Seeding foreign key data 91
**Mutating data with Sequelize** 94
**Many-to-many relationships** 97
Model and migrations 97
Chat model 98
Message model 100
Chats and messages in GraphQL 101
Seeding many-to-many data 105
Creating a new chat 110
Creating a new message 112
**Summary** 113

**Chapter 4: Integrating React into the Back end with Apollo** 115
**Setting up Apollo Client** 115
Installing Apollo Client 116
Testing the Apollo Client 119
Binding the Apollo Client to React 122
**Using the Apollo Client in React** 122
Querying in React with the Apollo Client 124
Apollo HoC query 124
The Apollo Query component 126
**Mutations with the Apollo Client** 128
The Apollo Mutation HoC 129
The Apollo Mutation component 131
Updating the UI with the Apollo Client 133
Refetching queries 133
Updating the Apollo cache 134
Optimistic UI 135

Polling with the Query component 138
**Implementing chats and messages** 139
Fetching and displaying chats 139
Fetching and displaying messages 147
Sending messages through Mutations 152
**Pagination in React and GraphQL** 155
**Debugging with the Apollo Client Developer Tools** 160
**Summary** 164

**Chapter 5: Reusable React Components** 165
**Introducing React patterns** 165
Controlled components 166
Stateless functions 168
Conditional rendering 171
Rendering child components 172
**Structuring our React application** 173
The React file structure 173
Efficient Apollo React components 176
The Apollo Query component 176
The Apollo Mutation component 180
**Extending Graphbook** 185
The React context menu 185
FontAwesome in React 186
React helper components 187
The GraphQL updatePost mutation 190
The Apollo deletePost mutation 196
The React application bar 200
The React Context API versus Apollo Consumer 207
The React Context API 208
Apollo Consumer 210
**Documenting React applications** 212
Setting up React Styleguidist 212
React PropTypes 214
**Summary** 218

**Chapter 6: Authentication with Apollo and React** 219
**JSON Web Tokens** 219
**localStorage versus cookie** 221
**Authentication with GraphQL** 223
Apollo login mutation 225
The React login form 228
Apollo sign up mutation 233
React sign up form 235
Authenticating GraphQL requests 238
Accessing the user context from resolver functions 243
Chats and messages 243

CurrentUser GraphQL query 244
Logging out using React 246
**Summary** 249

**Chapter 7: Handling Image Uploads** 251
**Setting up Amazon Web Services** 251
Creating an AWS S3 bucket 253
Generating AWS access keys 257
**Uploading images to Amazon S3** 259
GraphQL image upload mutation 260
React image cropping and uploading 263
**Summary** 273

**Chapter 8: Routing in React** 275
**Setting up React Router** 275
Installing React Router 276
Implementing your first route 278
Secured routes 280
Catch-all routes in React Router 282
**Advanced routing with React Router** 283
Parameters in routes 284
Querying the user profile 290
Programmatic navigation in React Router 292
Remembering the redirect location 295
**Summary** 296

**Chapter 9: Implementing Server-Side Rendering** 297
**Introduction to server-side rendering** 297
**SSR in Express.js** 299
**Authentication with SSR** 314
**Running Apollo queries with SSR** 320
**Summary** 324

**Chapter 10: Real-Time Subscriptions** 325
**GraphQL and WebSockets** 325
**Apollo Subscriptions** 327
Subscriptions on the Apollo Server 328
Subscriptions on the Apollo Client 334
**Authentication with Apollo Subscriptions** 347
**Notifications with Apollo Subscriptions** 352
**Summary** 356

**Chapter 11: Writing Tests** 357
**Testing with Mocha** 357
Our first Mocha test 358
Starting the back end with Mocha 362

Verifying the correct routing 364
**Testing GraphQL with Mocha** 365
Testing the authentication 366
Testing authenticated requests 367
**Testing React with Enzyme** 369
**Summary** 374

**Chapter 12: Optimizing GraphQL with Apollo Engine** 375
**Setting up Apollo Engine** 375
**Analyzing schemas with Apollo Engine** 378
**Performance metrics with Apollo Engine** 380
**Error tracking with Apollo Engine** 383
**Caching with Apollo Server and the Client** 387
**Summary** 390

**Chapter 13: Continuous Deployment with CircleCI and Heroku** 391
**Preparing the final production build** 391
Code-splitting with React Loadable and webpack 392
Code-splitting with SSR 395
**Setting up Docker** 401
What is Docker? 402
Installing Docker 402
Dockerizing your application 404
Writing your first Dockerfile 404
Building and running Docker containers 408
Multi-stage Docker production builds 412
**Amazon Relational Database Service** 416
**Configuring Continuous Integration** 420
**Deploying applications to Heroku** 424
**Summary** 435

**Other Books You May Enjoy** 437

**Index** 441

# Preface

*Hands-On Full-Stack Web Development with GraphQL and React* is a hands-on book for web developers who want to enhance their skills and build complete full-stack applications using industry standards.

By the end of the book, you will be proficient in using GraphQL and React for your full-stack development requirements.

This book will help you implement a solid stack by using React, Apollo, Node.js, and SQL using best practices. We'll also focus on solving complex problems with GraphQL, such as abstracting a multi-table database architecture and handling image uploads.

## Who this book is for

This book is for web developers who want to enhance their skills and build complete full-stack applications using industry standards. The typical reader would be someone who wants to explore how to use GraphQL, React, Node.js, and SQL to write entire applications with this stack.

## What this book covers

`Chapter 1`, *Preparing Your Development Environment*, starts with the architecture for our application by going through the core concepts and preparing a working React setup. We will see how React and webpack fit together and cover some basic scenarios when working with React. We will also show the reader how to debug the frontend with React Dev Tools.

`Chapter 2`, *Setting Up GraphQL with Express.js*, focuses on setting up Express.js as the primary system to serve our backend. You will learn how to use Express.js' routing functionality to implement various APIs. Furthermore, at the end of the chapter, you will set up an endpoint that accepts GraphQL requests through the Apollo Server package. To guarantee that everything works, we will quickly go through using Postman to test and verify the functionality of the backend.

`Chapter 3`, *Connecting to the Database*, discusses how to use GraphQL to store and query data. As an example, traditional SQL is used to build a full application with MySQL. To simplify the database code, we are using Sequelize, which lets us query our SQL Server with a regular JavaScript object and also keeps it open if we use MySQL, MSSQL, PostgreSQL, or just a SQLite file. We will build models and schemas for users and posts in Apollo and Sequelize.

`Chapter 4`, *Integrating React into the Backend with Apollo*, explains how to hook Apollo into React and build entire frontend components. This chapter skips the introduction to basic React workflows but explains Apollo-specific configurations.

`Chapter 5`, *Reusable React Components*, dives deeper into writing more complex React components and sharing data across them.

`Chapter 6`, *Authentication with Apollo and React*, explains the common ways of authenticating a user on the web and in GraphQL and the differences between them. You will be guided through building the complete authentication workflow by using best practices.

`Chapter 7`, *Handling Image Uploads*, covers uploading images via Apollo and saving them in a separate object storage such as AWS S3.

`Chapter 8`, *Routing in React*, explains how to implement some more features for the end user, such as a profile page. We will accomplish this by installing React Router.

`Chapter 9`, *Implementing Server-Side Rendering*, explains that for many applications, server-side rendering is a must. It is important for SEO, but it can also have positive effects on your end users. This chapter will focus on getting your current application moved to a server-rendered setup.

`Chapter 10`, *Real-Time Subscriptions*, focuses on how to build a real-time chat functionality, including a notification system. Every second, a new message can come in and the user can be directly informed about it. This functionality will be implemented through a more or less experimental GraphQL and Apollo feature called subscriptions.

`Chapter 11`, *Writing Tests*, uses the Mocha and JavaScript unit testing framework. This chapter will primarily focus on testing the GraphQL backend and testing React applications properly.

`Chapter 12`, *Optimizing GraphQL with Apollo Engine*, answers the questions *how is our GraphQL API performing?*, *are there any errors?*, and *how can we improve the GraphQL schema?* We answer these questions using Apollo Engine in this chapter.

`Chapter 13`, *Continuous Deployment with CircleCI and Heroku*, is where we will look at how to set up our Heroku app and get the option to build and deploy Docker images through a continuous deployment workflow.

# To get the most out of this book

We recommend that you read the first chapter to make sure that you are up to speed with the basic concepts of React and webpack in general. After that, you can pretty much read any chapter you like. Each chapter is standalone, but the chapters are ordered by complexity and may require techniques explained in earlier chapters; the further you are into the book, the more complex the application is.

The application is adapted for real-world use, but some parts are left out, such as proper error handling, and other features that a real-world application would have, including analytics, since they are out of the scope of the book. This book aims to teach you the techniques behind everything. You should, get a good grasp of the building blocks of how to create a web application using React and GraphQL.

It does help if you have been a JavaScript and maybe a React developer for a while, or at least have experience with any other modern JavaScript framework, since many of the concepts are not application-specific but are good practices in general, such as reactive rendering.

But, most of all, it's a book you can use to kick-start your React and GraphQL development learning curve by focusing on the chapters that interest you the most.

# Download the example code files

You can download the example code files for this book from your account at `www.packt.com`. If you purchased this book elsewhere, you can visit `www.packt.com/support` and register to have the files emailed directly to you.

You can download the code files by following these steps:

1. Log in or register at `www.packt.com`.
2. Select the **SUPPORT** tab.
3. Click on **Code Downloads & Errata**.
4. Enter the name of the book in the **Search** box and follow the onscreen instructions.

Once the file is downloaded, please make sure that you unzip or extract the folder using the latest version of:

- WinRAR/7-Zip for Windows
- Zipeg/iZip/UnRarX for Mac
- 7-Zip/PeaZip for Linux

The code bundle for the book is also hosted on GitHub at `https://github.com/PacktPublishing/Hands-on-Full-Stack-Web-Development-with-GraphQL-and-React`. In case there's an update to the code, it will be updated on the existing GitHub repository.

We also have other code bundles from our rich catalog of books and videos available at `https://github.com/PacktPublishing/`. Check them out!

# Conventions used

There are a number of text conventions used throughout this book.

`CodeInText`: Indicates code words in text, database table names, folder names, filenames, file extensions, pathnames, dummy URLs, user input, and Twitter handles. Here is an example: "We pass our previously created `index.html` as a template."

A block of code is set as follows:

```
state = {
  posts: posts
}
```

Any command-line input or output is written as follows:

```
mkdir ~/graphbook
cd ~/graphbook
```

**Bold**: Indicates a new term, an important word, or words that you see onscreen. For example, words in menus or dialog boxes appear in the text like this. Here is an example: "After doing so, click on **Create**."

Warnings or important notes appear like this.

Tips and tricks appear like this.

# Get in touch

Feedback from our readers is always welcome.

**General feedback**: If you have questions about any aspect of this book, mention the book title in the subject of your message and email us at `customercare@packtpub.com`.

**Errata**: Although we have taken every care to ensure the accuracy of our content, mistakes do happen. If you have found a mistake in this book, we would be grateful if you would report this to us. Please visit `www.packt.com/submit-errata`, selecting your book, clicking on the Errata Submission Form link, and entering the details.

**Piracy**: If you come across any illegal copies of our works in any form on the Internet, we would be grateful if you would provide us with the location address or website name. Please contact us at `copyright@packt.com` with a link to the material.

**If you are interested in becoming an author**: If there is a topic that you have expertise in and you are interested in either writing or contributing to a book, please visit `authors.packtpub.com`.

## Reviews

Please leave a review. Once you have read and used this book, why not leave a review on the site that you purchased it from? Potential readers can then see and use your unbiased opinion to make purchase decisions, we at Packt can understand what you think about our products, and our authors can see your feedback on their book. Thank you!

For more information about Packt, please visit `packt.com`.

# 1
# Preparing Your Development Environment

The application we are going to build in this book will be a simplified version of Facebook, called **Graphbook**.

When developing an application, being well-prepared is always a requirement. However, before starting, we need to put our stack together. In this chapter, we will explore whether or not our techniques work well with our development process, what we need before getting started, and which tools can help us when building software.

This chapter explains the architecture for our application by going through the core concepts, the complete process, and the preparation of a working React setup.

This chapter covers the following topics:

- Architecture and technology
- Thinking critically about how to architect a stack
- Building the React and GraphQL stack
- Installing and configuring Node.js
- Setting up a React development environment with webpack, Babel, and other requirements
- Debugging React applications using Chrome DevTools and React Developer Tools
- Using `webpack-bundle-analyzer` to check the bundle size

# Application architecture

Since its initial release in 2015, GraphQL has become the new alternative to the standard SOAP and REST APIs. GraphQL is a specification, like SOAP and REST, that you can follow to structure your application and data flow. It is so innovative because it allows you to query specific fields of entities, such as users and posts. This functionality makes it very good for targeting multiple platforms at the same time. Mobile apps may not need all of the data displayed inside the browser on a desktop computer. The query you send consists of a JSON-like object defining which information your platform requires. For example, a query for a `post` may look like this:

```
post {
  id
  text
  user {
    user_id
    name
  }
}
```

GraphQL resolves the correct entities and data as specified in your query object. Every field in GraphQL represents a function that resolves to a value. Those functions are called **Resolver functions**. The return value could be just the corresponding database value, such as the name of a user, or it could be a date, which is formatted by your server before returning it.

GraphQL is completely database agnostic and can be implemented in any programming language.

To skip the step of implementing our own GraphQL library, we are going to use Apollo, which is a GraphQL server for the Node.js ecosystem. Thanks to the team behind Apollo, this is very modular. Apollo works with many of the common Node.js frameworks, such as Hapi, Koa, and Express.js.

We are going to use Express.js as our basis because it is used on a wide scale in the Node.js and GraphQL community.

GraphQL can be used with multiple database systems and distributed systems to offer a straightforward API over all your services. It allows developers to unify existing systems and handle data fetching for client applications.

How you combine your databases, external systems, and other services in one server back end is up to you.

In this book, we are going to use a MySQL server via Sequelize as our data storage.

SQL is the most well-known and commonly used database query language, and with Sequelize we have a modern client library for our Node.js server to connect with our SQL server.

HTTP is the standard protocol to access a GraphQL API. It also applies to Apollo Servers. GraphQL is not fixed to one network protocol, however.

We will build the front end of our **Graphbook** application with React. React is a JavaScript UI framework released by Facebook, which has introduced many techniques that are now commonly used for building interfaces on the web as well as on native environments.

Using React comes with a bunch of significant advantages. When building a React application, you always split your code into many components, targeting their efficiency and ability to be reused. Of course, you can do this without using React, but it makes it very easy. Furthermore, React teaches you how to update application states as well as the UI reactively. You never update the UI and then the data separately.

React makes rerendering very efficient by using a virtual DOM, which compares the virtual and actual DOM and updates it accordingly. Only when there is a difference between the virtual and real DOM does React apply these changes. This logic stops the browser from recalculating layout, Cascading Style Sheets, and other computations that negatively impact the overall performance of your application.

Throughout this book, we are going to use the Apollo client library. It naturally integrates with React and our Apollo Server.

If we put all this together, the result is the main stack consisting of Node.js, Express.js, Apollo, SQL, Sequelize, and React.

# The basic setup

The basic setup to make an application work is the logical request flow, which looks as follows:

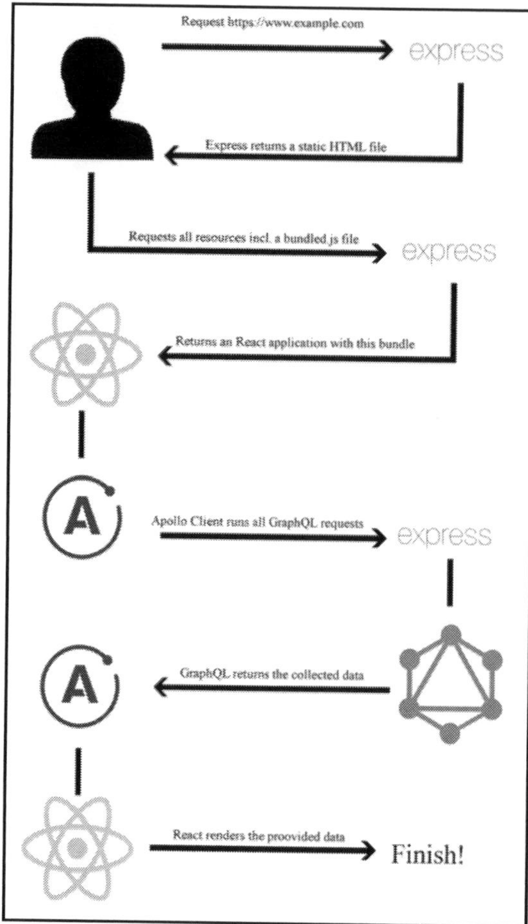


Here's how the logical request flow works:

1. The client requests our site.
2. The Express.js server handles these requests and serves a static HTML file.
3. The client downloads all necessary files, according to this HTML file. The files also include a bundled JavaScript file.

4. This bundled JavaScript file is our React application. After executing all JavaScript code from this file, all required Ajax alias GraphQL requests are made to our Apollo Server.
5. Express.js receives the requests and passes them to our Apollo endpoint.
6. Apollo queries all requested data from all available systems, such as our SQL server or third-party services, merges the data, and sends it back as JSON.
7. React can render the JSON data to HTML.

This workflow is the basic setup to make an application work. In some cases, it makes sense to offer server-side rendering for our client. The server would need to render and send all `XMLHttpRequests` itself before returning the HTML to the client. The user will save one or more round trips if the server sends the requests on the initial load. We will focus on this topic in a later chapter, but that's the application architecture in a nutshell. With that in mind, let's get hands-on and set up our development environment.

# Installing and configuring Node.js

The first step for preparing for our project is to install Node.js. There are two ways to do this:

- One option is to install the **Node Version Manager** (**NVM**). The benefit of using NVM is that you are easily able to run multiple versions of Node.js side by side and this handles the installation process for you on nearly all UNIX-based systems, such as Linux and macOS. Within this book, we do not need the option to switch between different versions of Node.js.
- The other option is to install Node.js via the package manager of your distribution if you are using Linux. The official PKG file is for Mac, whilst the MSI file is for Windows. We are going to use the regular Linux package manager for this book as it is the easiest method.

You can find the **Downloads** section of Node.js at the following link, `https://nodejs.org/en/download/`.

We are taking the second option above. It covers the regular server configurations and is easy to understand. I will keep this as short as possible and skip all other options, such as Chocolatey for Windows or Brew for Mac, which are very specialized for those specific operating systems.

I assume that you are using a Debian-based system for ease of use with this book. It has got the normal APT package manager and repositories to easily install Node.js and MySQL. If you are not using a Debian-based system, you can look up the matching commands to install Node.js at `https://nodejs.org/en/download/package-manager/`.

Our project is going to be new so that we can use Node.js 10 without any problems. You can skip the following installation of Node.js if you are running version 6 or higher:

1. First, let's add the correct repository for our package manager by running:

   ```
   curl -sL https://deb.nodesource.com/setup_10.x | sudo -E bash -
   ```

2. Next, install Node.js and the build tools for native modules, using the following command:

   ```
   sudo apt-get install -y nodejs build-essential
   ```

3. Finally, let's open a terminal now and verify that the installation was successful:

   ```
   node --version
   ```

The installation of Node.js via the package manager will automatically install npm.

Great. You're now set up to run server-side JavaScript with Node.js and install Node.js modules for your projects with npm.

All of the dependencies that our project relies on are available at `https://npmjs.com` and can be installed with npm or Yarn, if you are comfortable with these.

# Setting up React

The development environment for our project is ready. In this section, we are going to install and configure React, which is one primary aspect of this book. Let's start by creating a new directory for our project:

```
mkdir ~/graphbook
cd ~/graphbook
```

Our project will use Node.js and many npm packages. Create a `package.json` file to install and manage all of the dependencies for our project.

This stores information about the project, such as the version number, name, dependencies, and much more.

Just run `npm init` to create an empty `package.json` file:

```
npm init
```

Npm will ask some questions, such as asking for the package name, which is, in fact, the project name. Enter `Graphbook` to insert the name of your application in the generated `package.json` file.

I prefer to start with version number 0.0.1 since the default version number npm offered with 1.0.0 represents the first stable release for me. However, it is your choice which version you use here.

You can skip all other questions using the *Enter* key to save the default values of npm. Most of them are not relevant because they just provide information such as a description or the link to the repository. We are going to fill the other fields, such as the scripts while working through this book. You can see an example of the command line in the following screenshot:

```
This utility will walk you through creating a package.json file.
It only covers the most common items, and tries to guess sensible defaults.

See `npm help json` for definitive documentation on these fields
and exactly what they do.

Use `npm install <pkg>` afterwards to install a package and
save it as a dependency in the package.json file.

Press ^C at any time to quit.
package name: (graphbook)
version: (1.0.0) 0.0.1
description:
entry point: (index.js)
test command:
git repository:
keywords:
author:
license: (ISC)
About to write to C:\Users\sebig\Desktop\testit\graphbook\package.json:

{
  "name": "graphbook",
  "version": "0.0.1",
  "description": "",
  "main": "index.js",
  "scripts": {
    "test": "echo \"Error: no test specified\" && exit 1"
  },
  "author": "",
  "license": "ISC"
}
```

The first and most crucial dependency for this book is React. Use npm to add React to our project:

```
npm install --save react react-dom
```

This command installs two npm packages from `https://npmjs.com` into our project folder under `node_modules`.

Npm automatically edited our `package.json` file since we provided the `--save` option and added those packages with the latest available version numbers.

You might be wondering why we installed two packages although we only needed React. The `react` package provides only React-specific methods. All React hooks, such as `componentDidMount`, `componentWillReceivesProps`, and even React's component class, come from this package. You need this package to write React applications at all.

In most cases, you won't even notice that you have used `react-dom`. This package offers all functions to connect the actual DOM of the browser with your React application. Usually, you use `ReactDOM.render` to render your application at a specific point in your HTML and only once in your code. We will cover the rendering of React in a later chapter.

There is also a function called `ReactDOM.findDOMNode`, which gives you direct access to a `DOMNode`, but I hardly discourage using this since any changes on `DOMNodes` are not available in React itself. I personally have never needed to use this function, so try to avoid it if possible.

# Preparing and configuring webpack

Our browser requests an `index.html` file when accessing our application. It specifies all of the files that are required to run our application. We need to create the `index.html`, which we serve as the entry point of our application:

1. Create a separate directory for our `index.html` file:

   ```
   mkdir public
   touch index.html
   ```

2. Then, save this inside `index.html`:

   ```
   <!DOCTYPE html>
   <html lang="en">
     <head>
       <meta charset="UTF-8">
   ```

```
    <meta name="viewport" content="width=device-width, initial-
      scale=1.0">
    <meta http-equiv="X-UA-Compatible" content="ie=edge">
    <title>Graphbook</title>
  </head>
  <body>
    <div id="root"></div>
  </body>
</html>
```

As you can see, no JavaScript is loaded here. There is only `div` with the `root` id. This `div` tag is the DOMNode in which our application will be rendered by `ReactDOM`.

So, how do we get React up and running with this `index.html` file?

To accomplish this, we need to use a web application bundler. It prepares and bundles all our application assets. All of the required JavaScript files and `node_modules` are bundled and minified; SASS and SCSS preprocessors are transpiled to CSS as well as being merged and minified.

To name a few application bundler packages, there are webpack, Parcel, and Gulp. For our use case, we will use webpack. It is the most common module bundler, which has a large community surrounding it. To bundle our JavaScript code, we need to install webpack and all of its dependencies as follows:

```
npm install --save-dev @babel/core babel-eslint babel-loader @babel/preset-env @babel/preset-react clean-webpack-plugin css-loader eslint file-loader html-webpack-plugin style-loader url-loader webpack webpack-cli webpack-dev-server @babel/plugin-proposal-decorators @babel/plugin-proposal-function-sent @babel/plugin-proposal-export-namespace-from @babel/plugin-proposal-numeric-separator @babel/plugin-proposal-throw-expressions @babel/plugin-proposal-class-properties
```

This command adds all of the development tools to `devDependencies` in the `package.json` file that are needed to allow the bundling of our application. They are only installed in a development environment and are skipped in production.

As you can see in the preceding code, we also installed eslint, which goes through our code on the fly and checks it for errors. We need an `eslint` configuration file, which, again, we install from `https://npmjs.com`. The following handy shortcut installs the `eslint` configuration created by the people at Airbnb, including all peer dependencies. Execute it straight away:

```
npx install-peerdeps --dev eslint-config-airbnb
```

Create a `.eslintrc` file in the root of your project folder to use the `airbnb` configuration:

```
{
  "extends": ["airbnb"],
  "env": {
    "browser": true,
    "node": true
  },
  "rules": {
    "react/jsx-filename-extension": "off"
  }
}
```

In short, this `.eslinrc` file loads the `airbnb` config; we define the environments where our code is going to run, and we turn off one default rule.

The `react/jsx-filename-extension` rule throws a warning when using JSX syntax inside a file not ending in `.jsx`. Our files will end with `.js`, so we enable this rule.

If you aren't already aware, setting up webpack can be a bit of a hassle, There are many options that can interfere with each other and lead to problems when bundling your application. Let's create a `webpack.client.config.js` file in the root folder of your project.

Enter the following:

```
const path = require('path');
const HtmlWebpackPlugin = require('html-webpack-plugin');
const CleanWebpackPlugin = require('clean-webpack-plugin');
const buildDirectory = 'dist';
const outputDirectory = buildDirectory + '/client';
module.exports = {
  mode: 'development',
  entry: './src/client/index.js',
  output: {
    path: path.join(__dirname, outputDirectory),
    filename: 'bundle.js'
  },
  module: {
    rules: [
      {
        test: /\.js$/,
        exclude: /node_modules/,
        use: {
          loader: 'babel-loader'
        }
      },
```

```
        {
          test: /\.css$/,
          use: ['style-loader', 'css-loader']
        }
      ]
    },
    devServer: {
      port: 3000,
      open: true
    },
    plugins: [
        new CleanWebpackPlugin({
          cleanOnceBeforeBuildPatterns: [path.join(__dirname,
          buildDirectory)]
        }),
        new HtmlWebpackPlugin({
          template: './public/index.html'
        })
    ]
  };
```

The webpack configuration file is just a regular JavaScript file in which you can require `node_modules` and custom JavaScript files. This is the same as everywhere else inside Node.js. Let's quickly go through all of the main properties of this configuration. Understanding these will make future custom webpack configs much easier. All of the important points are explained below:

- `HtmlWebpackPlug`: This automatically generates an HTML file that includes all of the webpack bundles. We pass our previously created `index.html` as a template.
- `CleanWebpackPlugin`: This empties all of the provided directories to clean old build files. The `cleanOnceBeforeBuildPatterns` property specifies an array of folders which are cleaned before the build process is started.
- The `entry` field tells webpack where the starting point of our application is. This file needs to be created by us.
- The `output` object specifies how our bundle is called and where it should be saved. For us, this is `dist/client/bundle.js`.
- Inside `module.rules`, we match our file extensions with the correct loaders. All JavaScript files (except those located in `node_modules`) are transpiled by Babel, specified by `babel-loader` , so that we can use ES6 features inside our code. Our CSS gets processed by `style-loader` and `css-loader`. There are many more loaders for JavaScript, CSS, and other file extensions available.

- The `devServer` feature of webpack enables us to run the React code directly. It includes hot reloading code in the browser without rerunning a build or refreshing the browser tab.

If you need a more detailed overview of the webpack configuration, have a look at the official documentation here: `https://github.com/webpack/docs/wiki/configuration`.

With this in mind, let's move on. We are missing the `src/client/index.js` file from our webpack configuration, so let's create it as follows:

```
mkdir src/client
cd src/client
touch index.js
```

You can leave this file empty for the moment. It can be bundled by webpack without content inside. We are going to change it later in this chapter.

To spin up our development webpack server, we add a command to `package.json`, which we can run using `npm`.

Add this line to the `scripts` object inside `package.json`:

```
"client": "webpack-dev-server --devtool inline-source-map --hot --config
webpack.client.config.js"
```

Now execute `npm run client` in your console, and watch how a new browser window opens. We are running `webpack-dev-server` with the newly created configuration file.

Sure, the browser is still empty, but if you inspect the HTML with Chrome DevTools, you can see that we have already got a `bundle.js` file and our `index.html` file was taken as a template.

We have accomplished including our empty `index.js` file with the bundle and can serve it to the browser. Next, we'll render our first React component inside our template `index.html` file.

# Render your first React component

There are many best practices for React. The central philosophy behind it is to split up our code into separate components where possible. We are going to cover this approach in more detail later in `Chapter 5`, *Reusable React Components*.

Our `index.js` file is the main starting point of our front end code, and this is how it should stay. Do not include any business logic in this file. Instead, keep it as clean and slim as possible.

The `index.js` file should include this code:

```
import React from 'react';
import ReactDOM from 'react-dom';
import App from './App';

ReactDOM.render(<App/>, document.getElementById('root'));
```

The release of *ECMAScript 2015* introduced the `import` feature. We use it to require our `npm` packages, `react` and `react-dom`, and our first custom React component, which we must write now.

Of course, it is essential for us to cover the sample `Hello World` program.

Create the `App.js` file next to your `index.js` file, with the following content:

```
import React, { Component } from 'react';

export default class App extends Component {
  render() {
    return (
      <div>Hello World!</div>
    )
  }
}
```

This class is exported and then imported by the `index.js` file. As explained before, we are now actively using `ReactDOM.render` in our `index.js` file.

The first parameter of `ReactDOM.render` is the component that we want to render, which is the `App` class displaying the **Hello World!** message. The second parameter is the browser's `DOMNode`, where it should render. We receive `DOMNode` with plain `document.getElementById` JavaScript.

We defined our root element when we created the `index.html` file before. After saving the `App.js` file, webpack will try to build everything again. However, it shouldn't be able to do that. Webpack will encounter a problem bundling our `index.js` file because of the `<App />` tag syntax we are using in the `ReactDOM.render` method. It was not transpiled to a normal JavaScript function.

We configured webpack to load Babel for our JS file but did not tell Babel what to transpile and what not to transpile.

Let's create a `.babelrc` file in the root folder with this content:

```
{
  "plugins": [
    ["@babel/plugin-proposal-decorators", { "legacy": true }],
    "@babel/plugin-proposal-function-sent",
    "@babel/plugin-proposal-export-namespace-from",
    "@babel/plugin-proposal-numeric-separator",
    "@babel/plugin-proposal-throw-expressions",
    ["@babel/plugin-proposal-class-properties", { "loose": false }]
  ],
  "presets": ["@babel/env","@babel/react"]
}
```

You may have to restart the server because the `.babelrc` file is not reloaded when changes happen to the file. After a few moments, you should see the standard **Hello World!** message in your browser.

Here, we told Babel to use `@babel/preset-env` and `@babel/preset-react`, installed together with webpack. These presets allow Babel to transform specific syntax such as JSX, which we use to create normal JavaScript that all browsers can understand and that webpack is able to bundle. Furthermore, we are using some Babel plugins we installed too, because they transform specific syntax not covered by the presets.

# Rendering arrays from React state

`Hello World!` is a must for every good programming book, but this is not what we are aiming for when we use React.

A social network such as Facebook or Graphbook, which we are writing at the moment, needs a news feed and an input to post news. Let's implement this.

For the simplicity of the first chapter, we do this inside `App.js`.

We should work with some fake data here since we have not yet set up our GraphQL API. We can replace this later with real data.

Define a new variable above your `App` class like this:

```
const posts = [{
  id: 2,
  text: 'Lorem ipsum',
  user: {
    avatar: '/uploads/avatar1.png',
    username: 'Test User'
  }
},
{
  id: 1,
  text: 'Lorem ipsum',
  user: {
    avatar: '/uploads/avatar2.png',
    username: 'Test User 2'
  }
}];
```

We now render these two fake posts in React.

Replace the current content of your `render` method with the following code:

```
const { posts } = this.state;

return (
  <div className="container">
    <div className="feed">
      {posts.map((post, i) =>
        <div key={post.id} className="post">
          <div className="header">
            <img src={post.user.avatar} />
            <h2>{post.user.username}</h2>
          </div>
          <p className="content">
            {post.text}
          </p>
        </div>
      )}
    </div>
  </div>
)
```

We iterate over the `posts` array with the `map` function, which again executes the inner callback function, passing each array item as a parameter one by one. The second parameter is just called `i` and represents the index of the array element we are processing. Everything returned from the `map` function is then rendered by React.

We merely return HTML by putting each post's data in ES6 curly braces. The curly braces tell React to interpret and evaluate the code inside them as JavaScript.

As you can see in the preceding code, we are extracting the posts we want to render from the component's state with a destructuring assignment. This data flow is very convenient because we can update the state at any point later in our application and the posts will rerender.

To get our posts into the state, we can define them inside our class with **property initializers**. Add this to the top of the `App` class:

```
state = {
  posts: posts
}
```

The older way of implementing this—without using the ES6 feature—was to create a constructor:

```
constructor(props) {
  super(props);

  this.state = {
    posts: posts
  };
}
```

Upon initialization of the `App` class, the posts will be inserted into its state and rendered. It is vital that you run `super` before having access to `this`.

The preceding method is much cleaner, and I recommend this for readability purposes. When saving, you should be able to see rendered posts. They should look like this:

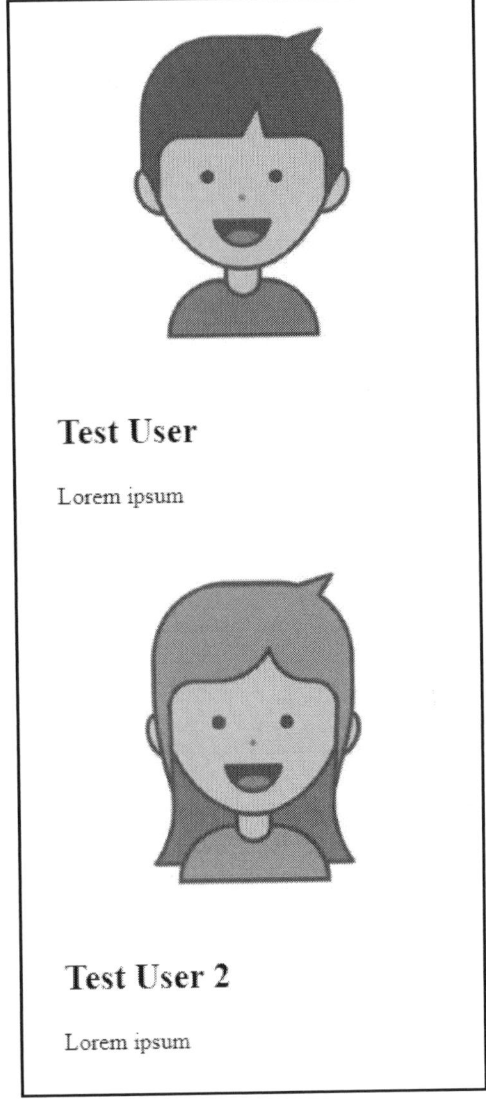


source: https://www.vecteezy.com/

The images I am using here are freely available. You can use any other material that you have got, as long as the path matches the string from the `posts` array. You can find those images in the official GitHub repository of this book.

# CSS with webpack

The posts from the preceding picture have not been designed yet. I have already added CSS classes to the HTML our component returns.

Instead of using CSS to make our posts look better, another method is to use CSS-in-JS using packages such as styled-components, which is a React package. Other alternatives include Glamorous and Radium, for example. There are numerous reasons why we do not switch to such a workflow and stay with good old CSS. With those other tools, you are not able to use SASS, SCSS, or LESS effectively. Personally, I need to work with other people, such as screen and graphics designers, who can provide and use CSS, but do not program styled-components. There is always a prototype or existing CSS that can be used, so why should I spend time translating this to styled-components CSS when I could just continue with standard CSS?

There is no right or wrong option here; you are free to implement the styling in any way you like. However, in this book, we keep using good old CSS.

What we've already done in our `webpack.client.config.js` file is to specify a CSS rule, as you can see in the following code snippet:

```
{
  test: /\.css$/,
  use: ['style-loader', 'css-loader'],
},
```

The `style-loader` injects your bundled CSS right into the DOM. The `css-loader` will resolve all `import` or `url` occurrences in your CSS code.

Create a `style.css` file in `/assets/css` and fill in the following:

```
body {
  background-color: #f6f7f9;
  margin: 0;
  font-family: 'Courier New', Courier, monospace
}
p {
  margin-bottom: 0;
}
.container {
  max-width: 500px;
  margin: 70px auto 0 auto;
}
.feed {
  background-color: #bbb;
  padding: 3px;
```

```
  margin-top: 20px;
}
.post {
  background-color: #fff;
  margin: 5px;
}
.post .header {
  height: 60px;
}
.post .header > * {
  display: inline-block;
  vertical-align: middle;
}
.post .header img {
  width: 50px;
  height: 50px;
  margin: 5px;
}
.post .header h2 {
  color: #333;
  font-size: 24px;
  margin: 0 0 0 5px;
}
.post p.content {
  margin: 5px;
  padding: 5px;
  min-height: 50px;
}
```

Refreshing your browser leaves you with the same old HTML as before.

This problem happens because webpack is a module bundler and does not know anything about CSS; it only knows JavaScript. We must import the CSS file somewhere in our code.

Instead of using `index.html` and adding a `head` tag, we can use webpack and our CSS rule to load it right in `App.js`. This solution is very convenient, since all of the required CSS throughout our application gets minified and bundled. Webpack automates this process.

In your `App.js` file, add the following behind the React `import` statement:

```
import '../../assets/css/style.css';
```

Webpack magically rebuilds our bundle and refreshes our browser tab.

You have now successfully rendered fake data via React and styled it with bundled CSS from webpack. It should look something like this:

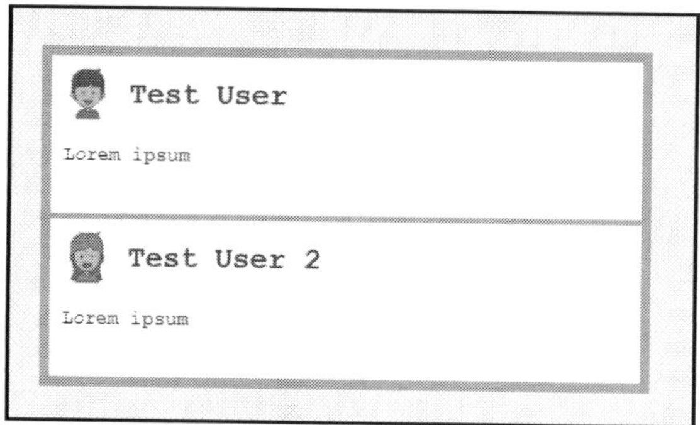


source: https://www.vecteezy.com/

The output looks very good already.

# Event handling and state updates with React

At the beginning of this project, it would be great to have a simple `textarea` where you can click a button and then have a new post added to the static `posts` array we wrote in the `App` class.

Add this above the `div` with the `feed` class:

```
<div className="postForm">
  <form onSubmit={this.handleSubmit}>
    <textarea value={postContent} onChange={this.handlePostContentChange}
      placeholder="Write your custom post!"/>
    <input type="submit" value="Submit" />
  </form>
</div>
```

You can use forms in React without any problems. React can intercept the submit event of requests by giving the form an `onSubmit` property, which will be a function to handle the logic behind the form.

We are passing the `postContent` variable to the `value` property of `textarea` to have what's called a **controlled component**.

Create an empty string variable at the `state` property initializer, as follows:

```
state = {
  posts: posts,
  postContent: ''
}
```

Then, extract this from the class state inside the `render` method:

```
const { posts, postContent } = this.state;
```

Now, the new state variable stays empty, although, you can write inside `textarea`. This issue occurs because you are directly changing the DOM element but did not bind the change event to an existing React function. This function has the task of updating the React internal state that is not automatically connected to the browser's DOM state.

In the preceding code, we already passed the update function called `this.handlePostContentChange` to the `onChange` property of `textarea`.

The logical step is to implement this function:

```
handlePostContentChange = (event) => {
  this.setState({postContent: event.target.value})
}
```

Maybe you are used to writing this a little differently, like this:

```
handlePostContentChange(event) {
  this.setState({postContent: event.target.value})
}
```

Both variants differ a lot. Try it out for yourself.

When using the second variant, executing the function will lead to an error. The scope inside the function will be wrong, and you won't have access to the class via `this`.

In this case, you would need to write a constructor for your class and manually bind the scope to your function as follows:

```
this.handlePostContentChange = this.handlePostContentChange.bind(this);
```

You easily end up with five more additional lines of code when writing the constructor to bind the scope correctly.

The first variant uses the ES6 arrow function, which takes care of the right scope for you. I recommend this variant since it is very clean and you save time understanding and writing code.

Look at your browser again. The form is there, but it is not pretty, so add this CSS:

```
form {
  padding-bottom: 20px;
}
form textarea {
  width: calc(100% - 20px);
  padding: 10px;
  border-color: #bbb;
}
form [type=submit] {
  border: none;
  background-color: #6ca6fd;
  color: #fff;
  padding: 10px;
  border-radius: 5px;
  font-size: 14px;
  float: right;
}
```

The last step is to implement the `handleSubmit` function for our form:

```
handleSubmit = (event) => {
  event.preventDefault();
  const newPost = {
    id: this.state.posts.length + 1,
    text: this.state.postContent,
    user: {
      avatar: '/uploads/avatar1.png',
      username: 'Fake User'
    }
  };
  this.setState((prevState) => ({
    posts: [newPost, ...prevState.posts],
    postContent: ''
  }));
}
```

The preceding code looks more complicated than it is, but I am going to explain it quickly.

We need to run `event.preventDefault` to stop our browser from actually trying to submit the form and reload the page. Most people coming from jQuery or other JavaScript frameworks will know this.

Next, we save our new post in the `newPost` variable that we want to add to our feed.

We are faking some data here to simulate a real-world application. For our test case, the new post id is the number of posts in our state variable plus one. React wants us to give every child in the ReactDOM a unique id. By counting the number of posts, we simulate the behavior of a real back end giving us unique ids for our posts.

The text for our new post comes from the `postContent` variable from the component state. Furthermore, we do not yet have a user system by now, that our GraphQL server can use to give us the newest posts, including the matching users with their avatars. We simulate this by having a static user object for all the new posts we create.

Finally, we update the component state again. This is where it gets a bit complicated. We are not passing an object as if we are doing it inside the `handlePostContentChange` function; we are passing an `update` function.

This approach gives us the current state reliably. Generally, I recommend using a function instead of using just an object. It automatically protects you against problems of race condition, where multiple functions manipulate the state. Always have in mind that the `setState` function is asynchronous.

The return value of the function is the state object we would normally have used directly. Thanks to the ES6 spread operator, we can prepend the `newPost` variable before the old posts, which will render the latest post at the top of our list. The `textarea` is cleared by passing an empty string into `setState` for the `postContent` field.

Now go ahead and play with your working React form. Do not forget that all posts you create do not persist since they are only held in the local memory of the browser and not saved to a database. Consequently, refreshing deletes your posts.

# Controlling document heads with React Helmet

When developing a web application, it is crucial that you can control your document heads. You might want to change the title or description, based on the content you are presenting.

React Helmet is a great package that offers this on the fly, including overriding multiple headers and server-side rendering.

Install it with the following command:

```
npm install --save react-helmet
```

You can add all standard HTML headers with React Helmet.

I recommend keeping standard `head` tags inside your template. They have the advantage that, before React has rendered, there is always the default document head. For our case, you can directly apply a title and description in `App.js`.

Import `react-helmet` at the top of the file:

```
import { Helmet } from 'react-helmet';
```

Add `Helmet` itself directly above `postForm` `div`:

```
<Helmet>
  <title>Graphbook - Feed</title>
  <meta name="description" content="Newsfeed of all your friends on
    Graphbook" />
</Helmet>
```

If you reload the browser and watch the title on the tab bar of your browser carefully, you will see that it changes from `Graphbook` to `Graphbook - Feed`. This behavior happens because we already defined a title inside `index.html`. When React finishes rendering, the new document head is applied.

# Production build with webpack

The last step for our React setup is to have a production build. Until now, we were only using `webpack-dev-server`, but this naturally includes an unimproved development build. Furthermore, webpack automatically spawns a web server. In a later chapter, we introduce Express.js as our web server so we won't need webpack to host it.

A production bundle does merge all JavaScript files, but also CSS files into two separate files. Those can be used directly in the browser. To bundle CSS files, we will rely on another webpack plugin, called `MiniCss`:

```
npm install --save-dev mini-css-extract-plugin
```

We do not want to change the current `webpack.client.config.js` file, because it is made for development work. Add this command to the `scripts` object of your `package.json`:

```
"client:build": "webpack --config webpack.client.build.config.js"
```

This command runs webpack using an individual production webpack config file. Let's create this one. First, clone the original `webpack.client.config.js` file and rename it `webpack.client.build.config.js`.

Change the following things in the new file:

1. The `mode` needs to be `production`, not `development`.
2. Require the `MiniCss` plugin:

   ```
   const MiniCssExtractPlugin = require('mini-css-extract-plugin');
   ```

3. Replace the current CSS rule:

   ```
   {
     test: /\.css$/,
     use: [{ loader: MiniCssExtractPlugin.loader,
       options: {
         publicPath: '../'
       }
    }, 'css-loader'],
   },
   ```

   We no longer use the `style-loader` but instead use the `MiniCss` plugin. The plugin goes through the complete CSS code, merges it in a separate file, and removes the `import` statements from the `bundle.js` we generate in parallel.

4. Lastly, add the plugin to the plugins at the bottom of the configuration file:

   ```
   new MiniCssExtractPlugin({
     filename: 'bundle.css',
   })
   ```

5. Remove the entire `devServer` property.

When running the new configuration, it won't spawn a server or browser window; it only creates a production JavaScript and CSS bundle, and requires them in our `index.html` file. According to our `webpack.client.build.config.js` file, those three files are going to be saved to the `dist/client` folder.

You can run this command by executing `npm run client:build`.

Look in the `dist/client` folder, and you will see three files. You can open the `index.html` in your browser. Sadly, the images are broken because the image URLs are not right anymore. We accept this for the moment because it will be automatically fixed when we have a working back end.

You are now finished with the basic setup of React.

# Useful development tools

When working with React, you will want to know why your application rendered in the way that it did. You need to know which properties your components received and how their current state looks. Since this is not displayed in the DOM or anywhere else in Chrome DevTools, you need a separate plugin.

Facebook has got you covered. Visit `https://chrome.google.com/webstore/detail/react-developer-tools/fmkadmapgofadopljbjfkapdkoienihi` and install React Developer Tools. This plugin allows the inspection of React applications and components. When opening Chrome DevTools again, you will see that there is a new tab at the end of the row.

If you are unable to see this tab, you may need to restart Chrome completely. You can also find React Developer Tools for Firefox.

This plugin allows you to view, search, and edit all of the components of your ReactDOM.

The left-hand panel looks much like the regular DOM tree (Elements) in Chrome DevTools, but instead of showing HTML markup, you see all of the components you used inside a tree. ReactDOM rendered this tree into real HTML, as follows:

```
▼<App>
  ▼<div className="container">
    ▼<div className="postForm">
      ▼<form onSubmit=fn()>
          <textarea value="" onChange=fn() placeholder="Write your custom post!"></textarea>
          <input type="submit" value="Submit"></input>
        </form>
      </div>
    ▼<div className="feed">
      ▼<div key="2" className="post">
        ▼<div className="header">
            <img src="/uploads/avatar1.png"></img>
            <h2>Test User</h2>
          </div>
          <p className="content">Lorem ipsum</p>
        </div>
      ▼<div key="1" className="post">
        ▼<div className="header">
            <img src="/uploads/avatar2.png"></img>
            <h2>Test User 2</h2>
          </div>
          <p className="content">Lorem ipsum</p>
        </div>
      </div>
    </div>
  </App>

App
```

The first component in the current version of Graphbook should be `<App />`.

By clicking a component, your right-hand panel will show its properties, state, and context. You can try this with the `App` component, which is the only real React component:

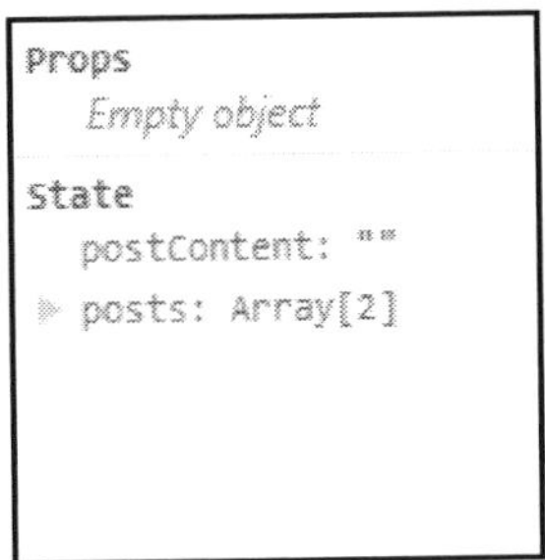

The `App` class is the first component of our application. This is the reason why it received no props. Children can receive properties from their parents; with no parent, there are no props.

Now test the `App` class and play around with the state. You will see that changing it rerenders your ReactDOM and updates the HTML. You can edit the `postContent` variable, which inserts the new text inside the `textarea`. As you can see, all events are thrown, and your handler runs. Updating the state always triggers a rerender, so try to update the state as little as possible.

# Analyzing bundle size

People that are trying to use as little bandwidth as possible will want to keep their bundle size low. I recommend that you always keep an eye on this, especially when requiring more modules via npm. In this case, you can quickly end up with a huge bundle size, since npm packages tend to require other npm packages themselves.

To protect us against this, we need a method to analyze the bundle size. Only the production build is worth checking. As previously mentioned, the development build includes React in a development release with source maps and so on.

Thanks to webpack, there is a simple solution for analyzing our bundle. This solution is called `webpack-bundle-analyzer`, and it does exactly what it sounds like.

Install this with the following:

```
npm install --save-dev webpack-bundle-analyzer
```

You then need to add two commands to the `scripts` object in the `package.json`:

- `"stats": "webpack --profile --json --config webpack.client.build.config.js > stats.json"`
- `"analyze": "webpack-bundle-analyzer stats.json"`

The first command creates a production build as well as a `stats.json` file in the root folder. This file holds the information we need.

The `analyze` command spins up the `webpack-bundle-analyzer`, showing us how our bundle is built together and how big each package that we use is.

Do this as follows:

```
npm run stats
npm run analyze
```

You can visually see our bundle and package sizes. Remove unnecessary packages in your projects and see how your bundle is reorganized. You can take an example from the following screenshot:

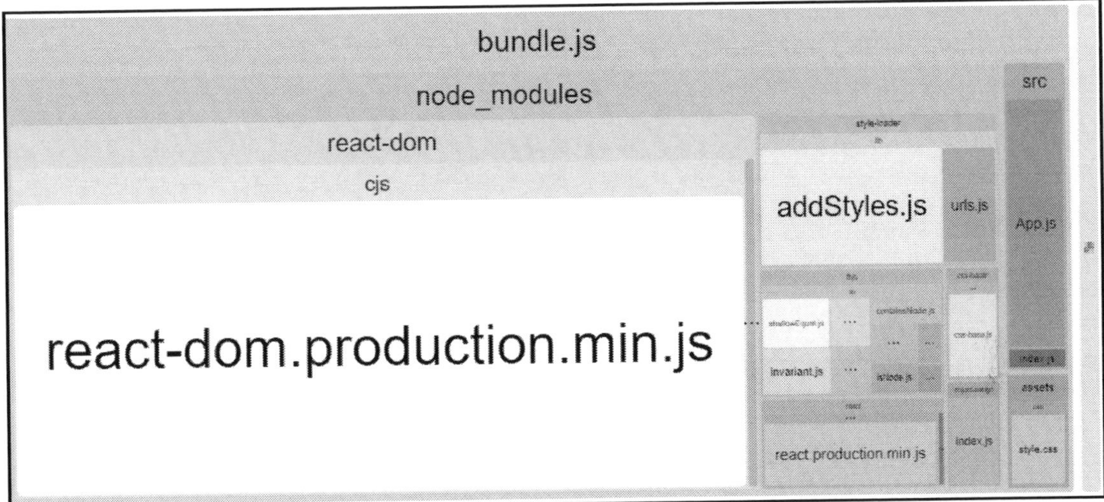


This diagram looks a lot like WinDirStat which is a software to display the disk usage of your computer. We can identify the packages that make up the majority of our bundle.

# Summary

In this chapter, we completed a working React setup. This is a good starting point for our front end. We can write and build static web pages with this setup.

The next chapter primarily focuses on our setup for the back end. We will configure Express.js to accept our first requests and pass all GraphQL queries to Apollo. Furthermore, you will also learn how to use Postman to test your API.

# 2
# Setting up GraphQL with Express.js

The basic setup and prototype for our front end are now complete. Going further, we need to get our GraphQL server running to begin implementing the back end. Apollo and Express.js are going to build the basis for our back end.

This chapter explains the installation process for Express.js, as well as the configuration of our GraphQL endpoint. We will quickly go through all the essential features of Express.js and the debugging tools for our back end.

This chapter covers the following points:

- Express.js installation and explanation
- Routing in Express.js
- Middleware in Express.js
- Binding Apollo Server to a GraphQL endpoint
- Serving static assets with Express.js
- Back end debugging and logging

## Node.js and Express.js

One primary goal of this book is to set up a GraphQL API, which is then consumed by our React front end. To accept network requests (especially GraphQL requests), we are going to set up a Node.js web server.

The most significant competitors in the Node.js web server area are Express.js, Koa, and Hapi. In this book, we are going to use Express.js. Most tutorials and articles about Apollo rely on it.

Express.js is also the most used Node.js web server out there and explains itself as a Node.js web framework, offering all the main features needed to build web applications.

Installing Express.js is pretty easy. We can use npm in the same way as in the first chapter:

```
npm install --save express
```

This command adds the latest version of Express to `package.json`.

In the first chapter, we created all JavaScript files directly in the `src/client` folder. Now, let's create a separate folder for our server-side code. This separation gives us a tidy directory structure. We will create the folder with the following command:

```
mkdir src/server
```

We can now continue with the configuration of Express.js.

# Setting up Express.js

As always, we need a root file loaded with all the main components that combines them to a real application.

Create an `index.js` file in the `server` folder. This file is the starting point for the back end. Here's how we go about it:

1. First, we import `express` from `node_modules`, which we just installed. We can use `import` here since our back end gets transpiled by Babel. We are also going to set up webpack for the server-side code in a later in `Chapter 9`, *Implementing Server-Side Rendering*.

```
import express from 'express';
```

2. We initialize the server with the `express` command. The result is stored in the `app` variable. Everything our back end does is executed through this object.

```
const app = express();
```

3. Then, we specify the routes that accept requests. For this straightforward introduction, we accept all HTTP `GET` requests matching any path, by using the `app.get` method. Other HTTP Methods are catchable with `app.post`, `app.put`, and so on.

```
app.get('*', (req, res) => res.send('Hello World!'));
app.listen(8000, () => console.log('Listening on port 8000!'));
```

To match all paths, you use an asterisk, which generally stands for `any` in the programming environment, as we have done it in the preceding `app.get` line.

The first parameter for all `app.METHOD` functions are the path to match. From here, you can provide an unlimited list of callback functions, which are executed one by one. We are going to look at this feature later in the *Routing with Express.js* section.

A callback always receives the client request as the first parameter and the response as the second parameter, which the server is going to send. Our first callback is going to use the `send` response method.

The `send` function sends merely the HTTP response. It sets the HTTP body as specified. So, in our case, the body shows `Hello World!`, and the `send` function takes care of all necessary standard HTTP headers, such as `Content-Length`.

The last step to make our server publicly available is to tell Express.js on which port it should listen for requests. In our code, we are using `8000` as the first parameter of `app.listen`. You can replace `8000` with any port or URL you want to listen on. The callback is executed when the HTTP server binding has finished, and requests can be accepted on this port.

This is the easiest setup we can have for Express.js.

# Running Express.js in development

To launch our server, we have to add a new script to our `package.json`.

We will add the following line to the `scripts` property of the `package.json` file:

```
"server": "nodemon --exec babel-node --watch src/server
src/server/index.js"
```

As you can see, we are using a command called `nodemon`. We need to install it first:

```
npm install --save nodemon
```

Nodemon is an excellent tool for running a Node.js application. It can restart your server when the source changes.

For example, to get the above command working follow the steps below:

1. Furthermore, we must install the `@babel/node` package, because we are transpiling the back end code with Babel, using the `--exec babel-node` option. It allows the use of the `import` statement:

    ```
    npm install --save-dev @babel/node
    ```

    Providing `--watch` as the option following a path or file will permanently track changes on that file or folder and reload the server to represent the latest state of your application. The last parameter refers to the actual file being the starting execution point for the back end.

2. Start the server now:

    ```
    npm run server
    ```

When you now go to your browser and enter `http://localhost:8000`, you will see the text **Hello World!** from our Express.js callback function.

`Chapter 3`, *Connecting to the Database*, covers how Express.js routing works in detail.

# Routing in Express.js

Understanding routing is essential to extend our back end code. We are going to play through some simple routing examples.

In general, routing stands for how an application responds to specific endpoints and methods.

In Express.js, one path can respond to different HTTP methods and can have multiple handler functions. These handler functions are executed one by one in the order they were specified in the code. A path can be a simple string, but also a complex regular expression or pattern.

When using multiple handler functions—either provided as an array or multiple parameters—be sure to pass `next` to every callback function. When you call `next`, you hand over the execution from one callback function to the next function in the row. Those functions can also be middleware. We'll cover this in the next section.

Here is a simple example. Replace this with the current `app.get` line:

```
app.get('/', function (req, res, next) {
  console.log('first function');
  next();
}, function (req, res) {
  console.log('second function');
  res.send('Hello World!');
});
```

When you look at the server logs in the terminal, you will see both `first function` and `second function` printed. If you remove the execution of `next` and try to reload the browser tab, the request will time out. This problem occurs because neither `res.send` nor `res.end`, or any alternative is called. The second handler function is never executed when `next` is not run.

As previously discussed, the **Hello World!** message is nice but not the best we can get. In development, it is completely okay for us to run two separate servers: one for the front end and one for the back end.

# Serving our production build

We can serve our production build of the front end through Express.js. This approach is not great for development purposes but is useful for testing the build process and seeing how our live application will act.

Again, replace the previous routing example with the following:

```
import path from 'path';

const root = path.join(__dirname, '../../');

app.use('/', express.static(path.join(root, 'dist/client')));
app.use('/uploads', express.static(path.join(root, 'uploads')));
app.get('/', (req, res) => {
  res.sendFile(path.join(root, '/dist/client/index.html'));
});
```

The `path` module offers many functionalities for working with the directory structures.

We use the global `__dirname` variable to get our project's root directory. The variable holds the path of the current file. Using `path.join` with `../../` and `__dirname` gives us the real root of our project.

Express.js provides the `use` function which runs a series of commands when a given path matches. When executing this function without a path, it is executed for every request.

We use this feature to serve our static files (the avatar images) with `express.static`. They include `bundle.js` and `bundle.css`, created by `npm run client:build`.

In our case, we first pass `'/'` with `express.static` following it. The result of this is that all files and folders in `dist` are served beginning with `'/'`. Other paths in the first parameter of `app.use`, such as `'/example'`, would lead to the result that our `bundle.js` would be downloadable under `'/example/bundle.js'` instead.

For example, all avatar images are served under `'/uploads/'`.

We are now prepared to let the client download all necessary files. The initial route for our client is `'/'` specified by `app.get`. The response to this path is `index.html`. We run `res.sendFile` and the file path to return this file—that is all we have to do here.

Be sure to execute `npm run client:build` first. Otherwise, you will receive an error message that these files were not found. Furthermore, when running `npm run client`, the `dist` folder is deleted, so you have to rerun the build process.

Refreshing the browser now presents you with the *post* feed and form from `Chapter 1`, *Preparing Your Development Environment*.

The next section focuses on the great functionality of middleware functions in Express.js.

# Using Express.js middleware

Express.js provides great ways to write efficient back ends without duplicating code.

Every middleware function receives a request, a response, and `next`. It needs to run `next` to pass control further to the next handler function. Otherwise, you will receive a timeout. Middleware allows us to pre- or post-process the request or response object, execute custom code, and much more. We previously covered a simple example of handling requests in Express.js.

Express.js can have multiple routes for the same path and HTTP method. The middleware can decide which function should be executed.

The following code is an easy example showing what can generally be accomplished with Express.js:

1. The root path `'/'` is used to catch any request.

   ```
   app.get('/', function (req, res, next) {
   ```

2. We randomly generate a number with `Math.random` between 1 and 10.

   ```
   var random = Math.random() * (10 -1) + 1;
   ```

3. If the number is higher than `5`, we run the `next('route')` function to skip to the next `app.get` with the same path.

   ```
   if (random > 5) next('route')
   ```

   This route will log us `'second'`.

4. If the number is lower than `0.5`, we execute the `next` function without any parameters and go to the next handler function. This handler will log us `'first'`.

   ```
     else next()
   }, function (req, res, next) {
     res.send('first');
   })

   app.get('/', function (req, res, next) {
     res.send('second');
   })
   ```

You do not need to copy this code as it is just an explanatory example. This functionality can come in handy when covering special treatments such as admin users and error handling.

# Installing important middleware

For our application, we have already used one built-in Express.js middleware: `express.static`. Throughout this book, we continue to install further middleware:

```
npm install --save compression cors helmet
```

Now, execute the `import` statement on the new packages inside the server `index.js` file so that all dependencies are available within the file:

```
import helmet from 'helmet';
import cors from 'cors';
import compress from 'compression';
```

Let's see what these packages do and how we can use them.

# Express Helmet

Helmet is a tool that allows you to set various HTTP headers to secure your application.

We can enable the Express.js Helmet middleware as follows in the server `index.js` file:

```
app.use(helmet());
app.use(helmet.contentSecurityPolicy({
  directives: {
    defaultSrc: ["'self'"],
    scriptSrc: ["'self'", "'unsafe-inline'"],
    styleSrc: ["'self'", "'unsafe-inline'"],
    imgSrc: ["'self'", "data:", "*.amazonaws.com"]
  }
}));
app.use(helmet.referrerPolicy({ policy: 'same-origin' }));
```

We are doing multiple things here at once. We add some **XSS(Cross-Site-Scripting)** protection tactics and remove the `X-Powered-By` HTTP header and some other useful things just by using the `helmet()` function in the first line.

You can look up the default parameters, as well as other functionalities of Helmet, at, `https://github.com/helmetjs/helmet`. Always be conscious when implementing security features and do your best to verify your attack protection methods.

Furthermore, to ensure that no one can inject malicious code, we are using the `Content-Security-Policy` HTTP header or, in short, CSP. This header prevents attackers from loading resources from external URLs.

As you can see, we also specify the `imgSrc` field, which tells our client that only images from these URLs should be loaded, including **Amazon Web Services** (**AWS**). We will see how to upload images to it in `Chapter 7`, *Handling Image Uploads*, of this book.

Read more about CSP and how it can make your platform more secure at, `https://helmetjs.github.io/docs/csp/`.

The last enhancement is to set the `Referrer` HTTP header only when making requests on the same host. When going from domain A to domain B, for example, we do not include the referrer, which is the URL the user is coming from. This enhancement stops any internal routing or requests being exposed to the internet.

It is important to initialize Helmet very high in your Express router so that all responses are affected.

# Compression with Express.js

Enabling compression for Express.js saves you and your user bandwidth, and this is pretty easy to do. The following code must also be added to the server `index.js` file:

```
app.use(compress());
```

This middleware compresses all responses going through it. Remember to add it very high in your routing order so that all requests are affected.

Whenever you have middleware like this, or multiple routes matching the same path, you need to check the initialization order. The first matching route is executed unless you run the `next` command. All routes that are defined afterward will not be executed.

# CORS in Express.js

We want our GraphQL API to be accessible from any website, app, or system. A good idea might be to build an app or offer the API to other companies or developers so that they can use it. When using APIs via Ajax, the main problem is that the API needs to send the correct `Access-Control-Allow-Origin` header.

For example, if you build the API, publicize it under `https://api.example.com`, and try to access it from `https://example.com` without setting the correct header, it won't work. The API would need to set at least `example.com` inside the `Access-Control-Allow-Origin` header to allow this domain to access its resources. It seems a bit tedious, but it makes your API open to cross-site requests which you should always be aware of.

Allow **CORS (Cross-origin resource sharing)** requests with the following command to the `index.js` file:

```
app.use(cors());
```

This command handles all of the problems we usually have with cross-origin requests at once. It merely sets a wildcard with `*` inside of `Access-Control-Allow-Origin`, allowing anyone from anywhere to use your API, at least in the first instance. You can always secure your API by offering API keys or by only allowing access to logged-in users. Enabling CORS only allows the requesting site to receive the response.

Furthermore, the command also implements the `OPTIONS` route for the whole application.

The `OPTIONS` method or request is made every time we use `Cross-origin resource sharing`. This action is what's called a **preflight request**, which ensures that the responding server trusts you. If the server does not respond correctly to the `OPTIONS` preflight, the actual method, such as `POST`, will not be made by the browser at all.

Our application is now ready to serve all routes appropriately and respond with the right headers.

We can move on now and finally set up a GraphQL server.

# Combining Express.js with Apollo

First things first; we need to install the Apollo and GraphQL dependencies:

```
npm install --save apollo-server-express graphql graphql-tools
```

Apollo offers an Express.js-specific package that integrates itself into the web server. There is also a standalone version without Express.js. Apollo allows you to use the available Express.js middleware. In some scenarios, you may need to offer non-GraphQL routes to proprietary clients who do not implement GraphQL or are not able to understand JSON responses. There are still reasons to offer some fallbacks to GraphQL. In those cases, you can rely on Express.js, since you are already using it.

Create a separate folder for services. A service can be GraphQL or other routes:

```
mkdir src/server/services/
mkdir src/server/services/graphql
```

Our GraphQL service must handle multiple things for initialization. Let's go through all of them one by one:

1. We require the `apollo-server-express` and `graphql-tools` packages.

```
import { ApolloServer } from 'apollo-server-express';
import { makeExecutableSchema } from 'graphql-tools';
```

2. We must combine the GraphQL schema with the `resolver` functions. We import the corresponding schema and resolver functions at the top from separate files. The GraphQL schema is the representation of the API, that is, the data and functions a client can request or run. Resolver functions are the implementation of the schema. Both need to match 100 percent. You cannot return a field or run a mutation that is not inside the schema.

```
import Resolvers from './resolvers';
import Schema from './schema';
```

3. The `makeExecutableSchema` function of the `graphql-tools` package merges the GraphQL schema and the resolver functions, resolving the data we are going to write. The `makeExecutableSchema` function throws an error when you define a query or mutation that is not in the schema. The resulting schema is executable by our GraphQL server resolving the data or running the mutations we request.

```
const executableSchema = makeExecutableSchema({
  typeDefs: Schema,
  resolvers: Resolvers
});
```

4. We pass this as a `schema` parameter to the Apollo Server.
The `context` property contains the `request` object of Express.js. In our resolver functions, we can access the request if we need to.

```
const server = new ApolloServer({
  schema: executableSchema,
  context: ({ req }) => req
});
```

5. This `index.js` file exports the initialized server object, which handles all GraphQL requests.

```
export default server;
```

Now that we are exporting the Apollo Server, it needs to be imported somewhere else, of course. I find it convenient to have one `index.js` file on the services layer so that we only rely on this file if a new service is added.

Create an `index.js` file in the `services` folder and enter the following code:

```
import graphql from './graphql';

export default {
  graphql,
};
```

The preceding code requires our `index.js` file from the `graphql` folder and re-exports all services in one big object. We can define further services here if we need them.

To make our GraphQL server publicly accessible to our clients, we are going to bind the Apollo Server to the `/graphql` path.

Import the services `index.js` file in the `server/index.js` file as follows:

```
import services from './services';
```

The `services` object only holds the `graphql` index. Now we must bind the GraphQL server to the Express.js web server with the following code:

```
const serviceNames = Object.keys(services);

for (let i = 0; i < serviceNames.length; i += 1) {
  const name = serviceNames[i];
  if (name === 'graphql') {
    services[name].applyMiddleware({ app });
  } else {
    app.use(`/${name}`, services[name]);
  }
}
```

For convenience, we loop through all indexes of the `services` object and use the index as the name of the route the service will be bound to. The path would be `/example` for the `example` index in the `services` object. For a typical service, such as a REST interface, we rely on the standard `app.use` method of Express.js.

Since the Apollo Server is kind of special, when binding it to Express.js, we need to run the `applyMiddleware` function provided by the initialized Apollo Server and avoid using the `app.use` function of Express.js. Apollo automatically binds itself to the `/graphql` path because it is the default option. You could also include a `path` parameter if you want it to respond from a custom route.

Two things are missing now: the schema and the resolvers. The schema is next on our to-do list.

## Writing your first GraphQL schema

Let's start by creating a `schema.js` inside the `graphql` folder. You can also stitch multiple smaller schemas to one bigger schema. This would be cleaner and would make sense when your application, types, and fields grow. For this book, one file is okay and we insert the following code into the `schema.js` file:

```
const typeDefinitions = `
  type Post {
    id: Int
    text: String
  }

  type RootQuery {
    posts: [Post]
  }

  schema {
    query: RootQuery
  }
`;

export default [typeDefinitions];
```

The preceding code represents a basic schema, which would be able to at least serve the fake posts array from `Chapter 1`, *Preparing Your Development Environment*, excluding the users.

First, we define a new type called `Post`. A `Post` type has `id` as `Int` and `text` as `String`.

For our GraphQL server, we need a type called `RootQuery`. The `RootQuery` type wraps all of the queries a client can run. It can be anything from requesting all posts, all users, or posts by just one user, and so on. You can compare this to all `GET` requests as you find them with a common REST API. The paths would be `/posts`, `/users`, and `/users/ID/posts` to represent the GraphQL API as a REST API. When using GraphQL, we only have one route, and we send the query as a JSON-like object.

The first query we will have is going to return an array of all of the posts we have got.

If we query for all posts and want to return each user with its corresponding post, this would be a sub-query that would not be represented in our `RootQuery` type but in the `Post` type itself. You will see how it is done later.

At the end of the JSON-like schema, we add `RootQuery` to the `schema` property. This type is the starting point for the Apollo Server.

Later, we are going to add the mutation key to the schema where we implement a `RootMutation` type. It is going to serve all of the actions a user can run. Mutations are comparable to the `POST`, `UPDATE`, `PATCH`, and `DELETE` requests of a REST API.

At the end of the file, we export the schema as an array. If we wanted to, we could push other schemas to this array to merge them.

The last thing missing here is the implementation of our resolvers.

# Implementing GraphQL resolvers

Now that the schema is ready, we need the matching resolver functions.

Create a `resolvers.js` file in the `graphql` folder as follows:

```
const resolvers = {
  RootQuery: {
    posts(root, args, context) {
      return [];
    },
  },
};

export default resolvers;
```

The `resolvers` object holds all types as a property. We set up `RootQuery`, holding the `posts` query in the same way as we did in our schema. The `resolvers` object must equal the schema but recursively merged. If you want to query a subfield, such as the user of a post, you have to extend the `resolvers` object with a `Post` object containing a `user` function next to `RootQuery`.

If we send a query for all posts, the `posts` function is executed. There, you can do whatever you want, but you need to return something that matches the schema. So, if you have an array of `posts` as the response type of `RootQuery`, you cannot return something different, such as just one post object instead of an array. In that case, you would receive an error.

Furthermore, GraphQL checks the data type of every property. If `id` is defined as `Int`, you cannot return a regular MongoDB `id` since these ids are of type `String`. GraphQL would throw an error too.

GraphQL will parse or cast specific data types for you if the value type is matching. For example, a `string` with the value of `2.1` is parsed to `Float` without any problems. On the other hand, an empty string cannot be converted to `Float`, and an error would be thrown. It is better to directly have the correct data types, because this saves you casting and also prevents unwanted problems.

Our `posts` query will return an empty array, which would be a correct response for GraphQL. We will come back to the `resolver` functions later, but it is okay for the moment. You should be able to start the server again.

# Sending GraphQL queries

We can test this query using any HTTP client, such as Postman, Insomnia, or any you are used to. This book covers HTTP clients in the next section of this chapter. If you want to send the following queries on your own, you can read the next section and come back here.

You can test our new function when you send the following JSON as a `POST` request to `http://localhost:8000/graphql`:

```
{
  "operationName": null,
  "query": "{
    posts {
      id
      text
    }
  }",
  "variables": {}
}
```

The `operationName` field is not required to run a query, but it is great for logging purposes.

The query object is a JSON-like representation of the query we want to execute. In this example, we run the RootQuery posts and request the id and text fields of every post. We do not need to specify RootQuery because it is the highest layer of our GraphQL API.

The variables property can hold parameters such as user the ids by which we want to filter the posts, for example. If you want to use variables, they need to be defined in the query by their name too.

For developers who are not used to tools like Postman, there is also the option to open the GraphQL endpoint in a separate browser tab. You will be presented with a GraphQLi instance made for sending queries easily. Here, you can insert the content of the query property and hit the play button. Because we set up Helmet to secure our application, we need to deactivate it in development. Otherwise, the GraphQLi instance is not going to work. Just wrap the Helmet initialization inside this if statement:

```
if(process.env.NODE_ENV === 'development')
```

This short condition only activates Helmet when the environment is in development. Now you can send the request with GraphQLi or any HTTP client.

The resulting answer of POST should look like the following code snippet:

```
{
  "data": {
    "posts": []
  }
}
```

We received the empty posts array as expected.

Going further, we want to respond with the fake data we statically wrote in our client to come from our back end. Copy the posts array from App.js above the resolvers object. We can respond to the GraphQL request with this filled posts array.

Replace the content of the posts function in the GraphQL resolvers with this:

```
return posts;
```

You can rerun the POST request and receive both fake posts. Apparently, the response does not include the user object we have in our fake data. We must define a user property on the post type in our schema to fix this issue.

# Using multiples types in GraphQL schemas

Let's create a `User` type and use it with our posts. First, add it somewhere to the schema:

```
type User {
  avatar: String
  username: String
}
```

Now that we have a `User` type, we need to use it inside the `Post` type. Add it to the `Post` type as follows:

```
user: User
```

The `user` field allows us to have a sub-object inside our posts with the post's author information.

Our extended query to test this looks like the following:

```
"query":"{
  posts {
    id
    text
    user {
      avatar
      username
    }
  }
}"
```

You cannot just specify the user as a property of the query. Instead, you need to provide a sub-selection of fields. This is required whenever you have multiple GraphQL types stacked inside each other. Then, you need to select the fields your result should contain.

Running the updated query gives us the fake data, which we already have in our front end code; just the `posts` array as it is.

We have made good progress with querying data, but we also want to be able to add and change data.

# Writing your first GraphQL mutation

One thing our client already offered was to add new posts to the fake data temporarily. We can realize this in the back end by using GraphQL mutations.

Starting with the schema, we need to add the mutation as well as the input types as follows:

```
input PostInput {
  text: String!
}

input UserInput {
  username: String!
  avatar: String!
}

type RootMutation {
  addPost (
    post: PostInput!
    user: UserInput!
  ): Post
}
```

GraphQL inputs are not more than types. Mutations can use them as parameters inside requests. They may look weird, because our current output types look almost the same. However, it would be wrong to have an `id` property on `PostInput`, for example, since the back end chooses the id and the client cannot give it. Consequently, it does make sense to have separate objects for input and output types.

The `addPost` function receiving our two new required input types—`PostInput` and `UserInput`, is a new feature here. Those functions are called mutations, since they mutate the current state of the application. The response to this mutation is an ordinary `Post` object. When creating a new post with the `addPost` mutation, we will directly get the created post from the back end in response.

The exclamation mark in the schema tells GraphQL that the field is a required parameter.

The `RootMutation` type corresponds to the `RootQuery` type and is an object that holds all of our GraphQL mutations.

The last step is to enable the mutations in our schema for the Apollo Server:

```
schema {
  query: RootQuery
  mutation: RootMutation
}
```

Usually, the client does not send the user with the mutation. This is because the user is authenticated first, before adding a post, and through that, we already know which user initiated the Apollo request. However, we can ignore this for the moment and implement authentication later in `Chapter 6`, *Authentication with Apollo and React.*

The `addPost` resolver function needs to be implemented now in the `resolvers.js` file.

Add the following `RootMutation` object to the `RootQuery` in `resolvers.js`:

```
RootMutation: {
  addPost(root, { post, user }, context) {
    const postObject = {
      ...post,
      user,
      id: posts.length + 1,
    };
    posts.push(postObject);
    return postObject;
  },
},
```

This resolver extracts the `post` and `user` objects from the mutation's parameters, which are passed in the second argument of the function. Then, we build the `postObject` variable. We want to add our `posts` array as property by destructuring the `post` input and adding the `user` object. The `id` field is just the length of the `posts` array plus one.

The `postObject` variable looks like a `post` from the `posts` array now. Our implementation does the same as the front end is already doing. The return value of our `addPost` function is the `postObject`. To get this working, you need to change the initialization of the `posts` array from `const` to `let`. Otherwise, the array will be static and unchangeable.

You can run this mutation via your preferred HTTP client like this:

```
{
  "operationName": null,
  "query": "mutation addPost($post : PostInput!, $user: UserInput!) {
    addPost(post : $post, user: $user) {
      id
      text
      user {
        username
        avatar
      }
    }
```

```
    }",
    "variables": {
      "post": {
        "text": "You just added a post."
      },
      "user": {
        "avatar": "/uploads/avatar3.png",
        "username": "Fake User"
      }
    }
}
```

Here, we are using the `variables` property to send the data we want to insert in our back end. We need to pass them as parameters within the `query` string. We define both parameters with a dollar sign and the awaited data type inside the `operation` string. Those variables marked with a dollar sign can then be mapped into the actual action we want to trigger on the back end. Again, we need to send a selection of fields our response should have.

The result will have a `data` object including an `addPost` field. The `addPost` field holds the post, which we send with our request.

Query the posts again, and you will see that there are now three posts. Great, it worked!

As with our client, this is only temporary until we restart the server. We'll cover how to persist data in a SQL database in `Chapter 3`, *Connecting to the Database*.

Next, we'll cover the various ways to debug your back end properly.

# Back end debugging and logging

There are two things that are very important here: the first is that we need to implement logging for our back end in case we receive errors from our users, and the second is that we need to look into Postman to debug our GraphQL API efficiently.

So, let's get started with logging.

# Logging in Node.js

The most popular logging package for Node.js is called `winston`. Configure `winston` by following the steps below:

1. Install `winston` with npm:

```
npm install --save winston
```

2. We create a new folder for all of the helper functions of the back end:

```
mkdir src/server/helpers
```

3. Then, insert a `logger.js` file in the new folder with the following content:

```
import winston from 'winston';

let transports = [
  new winston.transports.File({
    filename: 'error.log',
    level: 'error',
  }),
  new winston.transports.File({
    filename: 'combined.log',
    level: 'verbose',
  }),
];

if (process.env.NODE_ENV !== 'production') {
  transports.push(new winston.transports.Console());
}

const logger = winston.createLogger({
  level: 'info',
  format: winston.format.json(),
  transports,
});

export default logger;
```

This file can be imported everywhere where we want to log.

In the preceding code, we defined the standard `transports` for `winston`. A transport is nothing more than the way in which `winston` separates and saves various log types in different files.

The first `transport` generates an `error.log` file where only real errors are saved.

The second transport is a combined log where we save all other log messages, such as warnings or info logs.

If we are running the server in a development environment, which we are currently doing, we add a third transport. We will also directly log all messages to the console while developing on the server.

Most people who are used to JavaScript development know the difficulty with `console.log`. By directly using `winston`, we can see all messages in the terminal, but we do not need to clean the code from `console.log` either, as long as the things we log make sense, of course.

To test this, we can try the `winston` logger in the only mutation we have.

In `resolvers.js`, add this to the top of the file:

```
import logger from '../../helpers/logger';
```

Now, we can extend the `addPost` function by logging the following:

```
logger.log({ level: 'info', message: 'Post was created' });
```

When you send the mutation now, you will see that the message was logged to the console.

Furthermore, if you look in the root folder of your project, you will see the `error.log` and `combined.log` files. The `combined.log` file should contain the log from the console.

Now that we can log all operations on the server, we should explore Postman to send requests comfortably.

# Debugging with Postman

Some time ago, **Postman** started as a Chrome app, which was installed through the Chrome Web Store.

Since Chrome apps will be deprecated, the guys behind **Postman** switched to a native implementation.

You can install **Postman** by downloading the appropriate file from the download section at, `https://www.getpostman.com/apps`.

There are numerous other HTTP client tools, such as Postman, that are useful for debugging your application. You are free to use your tool of choice. Some other great clients that I personally use are Insomnia, SoapUI, and Stoplight, but there are many more. In this book, we use Postman, as it is the most popular from my point of view.

When you have finished the installation, it should look something like this:

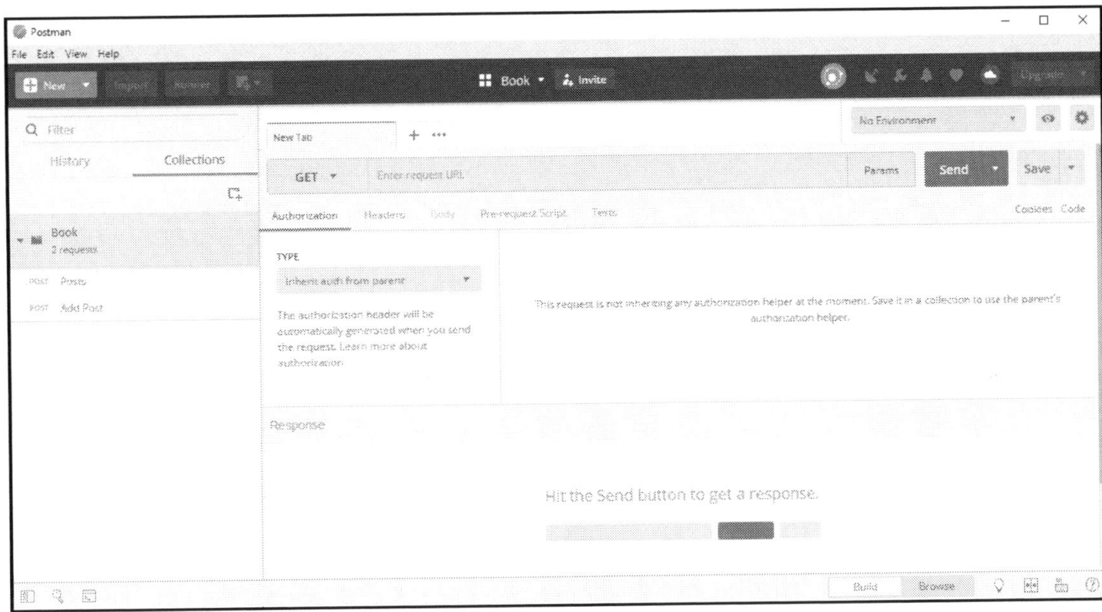


As you can see, I have already created a collection called **Book** in the left-hand panel. This collection includes our two requests: one to request all posts and one to add a new post.

As an example, the following screenshot shows you how the **Add Post** mutation looks in Postman:

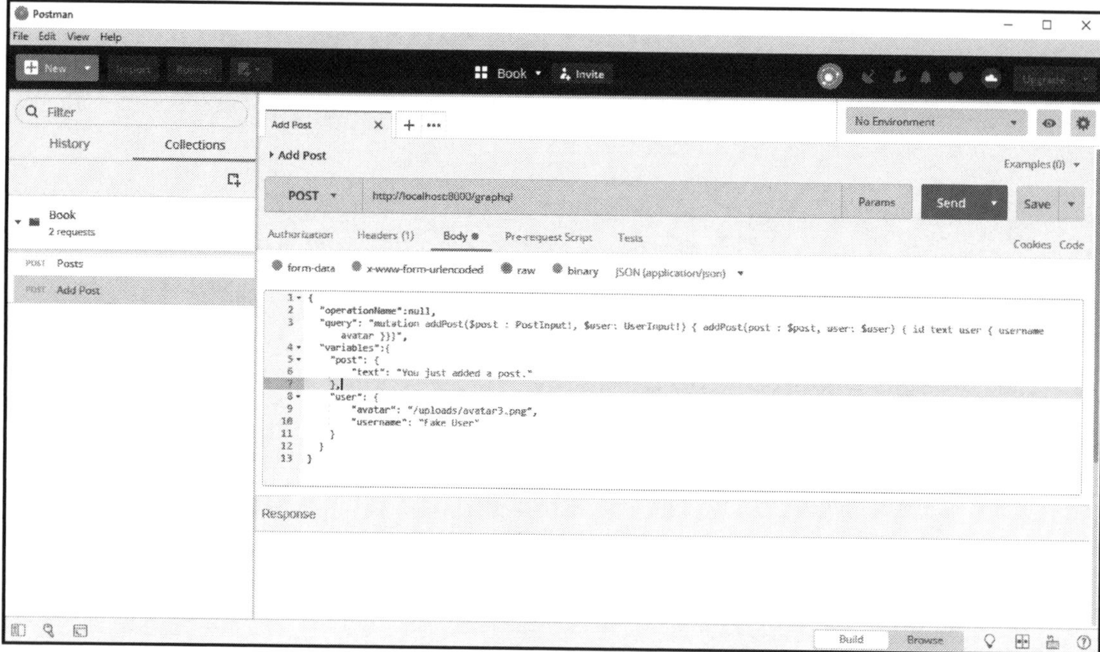

The request body looks pretty much like what we saw before.

In my case, I need to write the query inline because Postman is not able to handle multi-row text inside JSON. If this is not the case for you, please ignore it.

Be sure to select `application/json` as `Content-Type` next to the `raw` format.

The URL is localhost, including port `8000` as expected.

If you add a new request, you can use the `Ctrl + S` shortcut to save it. You need to select a collection and a name to save it. One major downfall of using **Postman** (at least with GraphQL APIs) is that we are, of course, only using `POST`. It would be great to have some kind of indication of what we are doing here, for example, a query or a mutation. We will also see how to use authorization in **Postman** when we have implemented it.

**Postman** also has other great features, such as automated testing, monitoring, and mocking a fake server.

In later chapters, it will become more complicated to configure Postman for all requests. In such cases, I like to use Apollo Client Developer Tools, which perfectly integrate into the front end and make use of Chrome DevTools. What's great about Apollo Client Developer Tools is that they use Apollo Client we configure in the front end code and therefore reuse the authentication we built into our front end.

# Summary

At this point, we have set up our Node.js server with Express.js and bound Apollo Server to respond to requests on a GraphQL endpoint. We are able to handle queries, return fake data, and mutate that data with GraphQL mutations.

Furthermore, we can log every process in our Node.js server. Debugging an application with Postman leads to a well-tested API, which can be used later in our front end.

In the next chapter, we will learn how to persist data in a SQL server. We will also implement models for our GraphQL types and cover migrations for our database. We need to replace our current `resolver` functions with queries via Sequelize.

There is a lot to do here, so read on for more.

# 3 Connecting to The Database

Our back end and front end can communicate, create new posts, and respond with a list of all posts while using fake data. The next step on our list will be to use a database, such as an SQL server, to serve as data storage.

We want our backend to persist data to our SQL database by using Sequelize. Our Apollo Server should use this data for queries and mutations, as needed. In order for this to happen, we must implement database models for our GraphQL entities.

This chapter will cover the following points:

- Using databases with GraphQL
- Using Sequelize in Node.js
- Writing database models
- Performing database migrations with Sequelize
- Seeding data with Sequelize
- Using Apollo together with Sequelize

## Using databases in GraphQL

**GraphQL** is a protocol for sending and receiving data. **Apollo** is one of the many libraries that you can use to implement that protocol. Neither GraphQL (in its specifications) nor Apollo work directly on the data layer. Where the data that you put into your response comes from, and where the data that you send with your request is saved, are up to the user to decide.

This logic indicates that the database and the services that you use do not matter to Apollo, as long as the data that you respond with matches the GraphQL schema.

As we are living in the Node.js ecosystem in this project and book, it would be fitting to use MongoDB. MongoDB offers a great client library for Node.js, and also uses JavaScript as its native choice of language for interactions and querying.

The general alternative to a database system like MongoDB is a typical SQL server with proven stability and enormous spreading. One case that I encounter more and more frequently involves systems and applications relying on older code bases and databases that need upgrades. A great way to accomplish this is to get an over-layering API level with GraphQL. In this scenario, the GraphQL server receives all requests, and, one by one, you can replace the existing code bases that the GraphQL server relies on. In these cases, it is helpful that GraphQL is database agnostic.

In this book, we will use SQL via Sequelize in order to see this feature in a real-world use case. For future purposes, it will also help you to handle problems with existing SQL-based systems.

# Installing MySQL for development

MySQL is an excellent starting point for getting on track in a developmental career. It is also well-suited to local development on your machine, since the setup is pretty easy.

How to set up MySQL on your machine depends on the operating system. As we mentioned in `Chapter 1`, *Preparing Your Development Environment*, we are assuming that you are using a Debian-based system. For this, you can use the following instructions. If you already have a working setup for MySQL or Apache, these commands may not work, or may not be required in the first place.

Do not follow these instructions when setting up a real SQL server for public and production use. A professional setup includes many security features to protect you against attacks. This installation should only be used in development, on your local machine.

Execute the following steps to get MySQL running:

1. First, you should always install all of the updates available for your system:

   ```
   sudo apt-get update && sudo apt-get upgrade -y
   ```

   We want to install MySQL and a GUI, in order to see what we have inside of our database. The most common GUI for a MySQL server is phpMyAdmin. It requires the installation of a web server and PHP. We are going to install Apache as our web server.

If, at any point in the process, you receive an error stating that the package could not be found, ensure that your system is Debian-based. The installation process is tested on Ubuntu 18.04, but can differ on other systems. You can easily search for the matching package for your system on the internet.

2. Install all dependencies with the following command:

```
sudo apt-get install apache2 mysql-server php php-pear php-mysql
```

3. After the installation, you will need to run the MySQL setup in the root shell. You will have to enter the root password for this. Alternatively, you can run `sudo -i`:

```
su -
```

4. Now, you can execute the MySQL installation command; follow the steps as prompted. From my point of view, you can ignore most of these steps, but be careful when you are asked for the root password of your MySQL instance. Since this is a development server on your local machine, you can skip the security settings:

```
mysql_secure_installation
```

5. We must create a separate user for development, aside from the root and phpMyAdmin user. It is discouraged to use the root user at all. Log in to our MySQL Server with the root user in order to accomplish this:

```
mysql -u root
```

6. Now, run the following SQL command. You can replace the `PASSWORD` string with the password that you want. It is the password that you will use for the database connection in your application, but also when logging in to phpMyAdmin. This command creates a user called `devuser`, with root privileges that are acceptable for local development:

```
GRANT ALL PRIVILEGES ON *.* TO 'devuser'@'%' IDENTIFIED BY
'PASSWORD';
```

7. You can install phpMyAdmin, since our MySQL server has been set up. You will be asked for a web server when executing the following command. Select `apache2` with the spacebar, and navigate to `ok` by hitting the *Tab* key. Select the automatic setup method for phpMyAdmin, when asked for it. You should not do this manually.

Furthermore, phpMyAdmin will want you to enter a password. I recommend that you choose the same password that you chose for the root user:

```
sudo apt-get install phpmyadmin
```

8. After the installation, we will need to set up Apache, in order to serve phpMyAdmin. The following `ln` command creates a symbolic link in the root folder of the Apache public `HTML` folder. Apache will now serve phpMyAdmin:

```
cd /var/www/html/
sudo ln -s /usr/share/phpmyadmin
```

We can now visit phpMyAdmin under `http://localhost/phpmyadmin` and log in with the newly created user. It should look like the following screenshot:

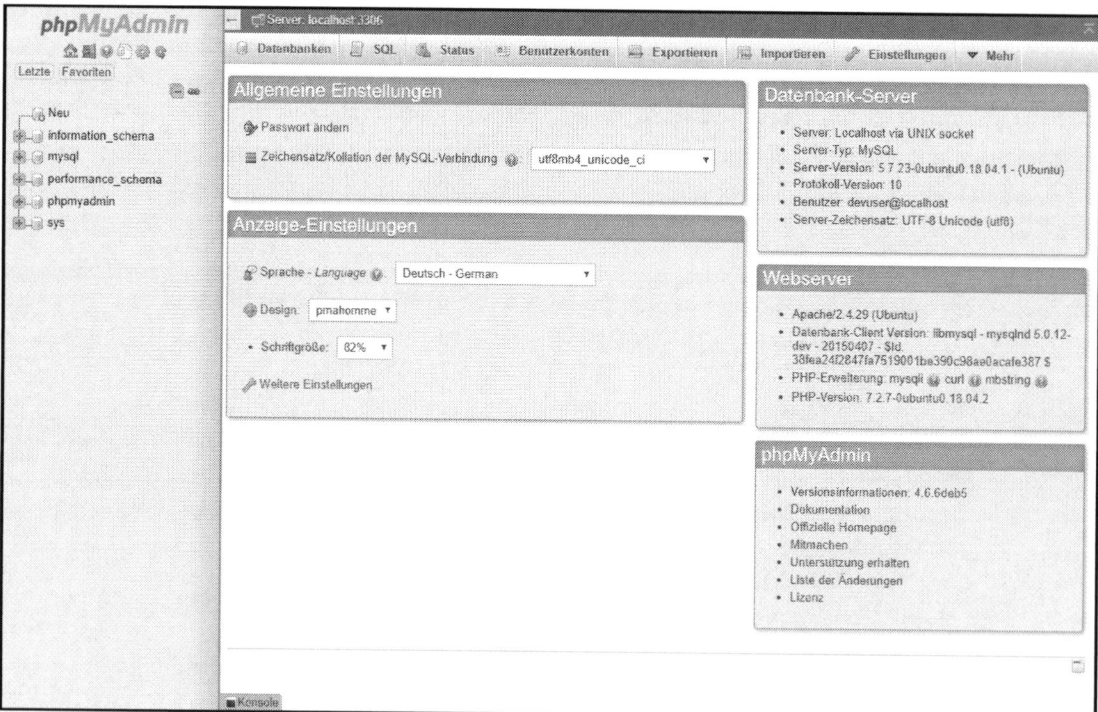


We have now finished the complete database installation for our development environment.

PhpMyAdmin chooses the language according to your environment, so it might differ slightly from the preceding screenshot.

For other operating systems, there are great prebuilt packages. I recommend that all Windows users use XAMPP, and that Mac users use MAMP. These offer an easy installation process for what we did manually on Linux. They also implement MySQL, Apache, and PHP, including phpMyAdmin.

# Creating a database in MySQL

Before we begin with the implementation of our back end, we need to add a new database that we can use.

You are free to do this via the command line or phpMyAdmin. As we have just installed phpMyAdmin, we are going to use it, of course.

You can run raw SQL commands in the **SQL** tab of phpMyAdmin. The corresponding command to create a new database looks as follows:

```
CREATE DATABASE graphbook_dev CHARACTER SET utf8 COLLATE utf8_general_ci;
```

Otherwise, you can follow the next steps to use the graphical method. In the left-hand panel, click on the **New** button.

You will be presented with a screen like the following. It shows all databases including their collation of your MySQL server:

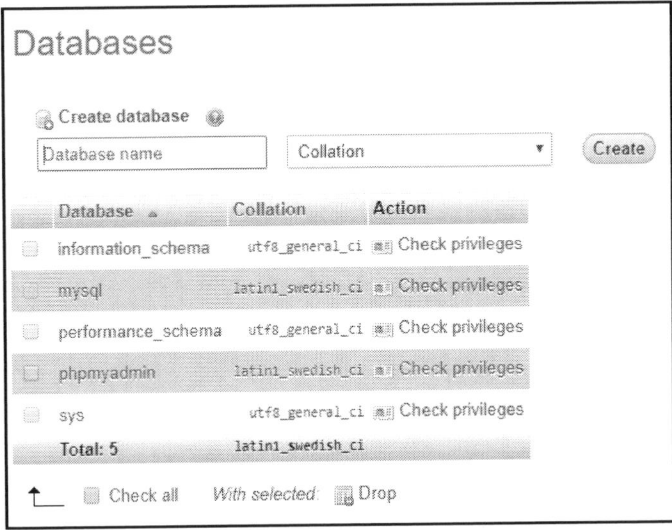

Enter a database name, such as `graphbook_dev`, and then choose the `uft8_general_ci` collation. After doing so, click on **Create**.

You will see a page that says, **No tables found in database**, which is correct (for now). This will change later, when we have implemented our database models, such as posts and users.

In the next chapter, we will start to set up Sequelize in Node.js, and will connect it to our SQL server.

# Integrating Sequelize into our stack

We have just set up a MySQL database, and we want to use it inside of our Node.js back end. There are many libraries to connect and query your MySQL database. We are going to use Sequelize in this book.

Alternatives include Waterline ORM and js-data, which offer the same functionalities as Sequelize. What's great about these is that they not only offer SQL dialects, but also feature database adapters for MongoDB, Redis, and more. So, if you need an alternative, check them out.

Sequelize is an ORM for Node.js. It supports the PostgreSQL, MySQL, SQLite, and MSSQL standards.

Install Sequelize in your project via `npm`. We will also install a second package, called `mysql2`:

```
npm install --save sequelize mysql2
```

The `mysql2` package allows Sequelize to speak with our MySQL server.

Sequelize is just a wrapper around the various libraries for the different database systems. It offers great features for intuitive model usage, as well as functions for creating and updating database structures and inserting development data.

Typically, you would run `sequelize init` before starting with the database connection or models, but I prefer a more custom approach. From my point of view, this is a bit cleaner. This approach is also why we are setting up the database connection in an extra file, and do not rely on boilerplate code.

You can take a look at the official tutorial in the Sequelize documentation if you want to see how it would usually be done. The approach that we are taking and the one from the tutorial do not differ much, but it is always good to see another way of doing things. The documentation can be seen at `http://docs.sequelizejs.com/manual/tutorial/migrations.html`.

Let's start by setting Sequelize up in our backend.

# Connecting to a database with Sequelize

The first step is to initialize the connection from Sequelize to our MySQL server. To do this, we will create a new folder and file, as follows:

```
mkdir src/server/database
touch src/server/database/index.js
```

Inside of the `index.js` database, we will establish a connection to our database with Sequelize. Internally, Sequelize relies on the `mysql2` package, but we do not use it on our own, which is very convenient:

```
import Sequelize from 'sequelize';

const sequelize = new Sequelize('graphbook_dev', 'devuser', 'PASSWORD', {
 host: 'localhost',
  dialect: 'mysql',
  operatorsAliases: false,
  pool: {
    max: 5,
    min: 0,
    acquire: 30000,
    idle: 10000,
  },
});

export default sequelize;
```

As you can see, we require Sequelize from the `node_modules`, and then create an instance of it. The following properties are important for Sequelize:

- We pass the database name as the first parameter, which we just created.

- The second and third parameters are the credentials of our `devuser`. Replace them with the username and password that you entered for your database. The `devuser` has all user rights, and can read and write all of the databases in our MySQL server. This makes development a lot easier.
- The fourth parameter is a general options object that can hold many more properties. The preceding object is an example configuration.
- The `host` of our MySQL database is our local machine alias, `localhost`. If this is not the case, you can also specify the IP or URL of the MySQL server.
- The `dialect` is, of course, `mysql`.
- The `operatorsAliases` property specifies which strings can be used as aliases by Sequelize, or whether they can be used at all. An example would look as follows:

```
[Op.gt]: 6 // > 6
$gt: 6 // same as using Op.gt (> 6)
```

This example is taken from the Sequelize documentation. Generally, it is discouraged to use operators aliases at all. This is why you should disable it, and should always sanitize user input, to avoid SQL injections.

If you want to read more about this topic and what possibilities Sequelize gives you for operator aliases, you can find more information at `http://docs.sequelizejs.com/manual/tutorial/querying.html#operators-aliases`.

- With the `pool` option, you tell Sequelize the configuration for every database connection. The preceding configuration allows for a minimum of zero connections, which means that Sequelize should not maintain one connection, but should create a new one whenever it is needed. The maximum number of connections is five. This option also relates to the number of replica sets that your database system has.
- The `idle` field of the `pool` option specifies how long a connection can be unused before it gets closed and removed from the pool of active connections.
- When trying to establish a new connection to our MySQL server, the timeout before the connection is aborted is defined by the `acquire` option. In cases in which a connection cannot be created, this option helps to stop your server from freezing.

Executing the preceding code will instantiate Sequelize, and will successfully create a connection to our MySQL server. Going further, we need to handle multiple databases for every environment in which our application can run, from development to production. You will see that in the next section.

# Using a configuration file with Sequelize

The previous setup for our database connection with Sequelize is fine, but it is not made for later deployment. The best option is to have a separate configuration file that is read and used according to the environment that the server is running in.

For this, create a new `index.js` file inside a separate folder (called `config`), next to the `database` folder:

```
mkdir src/server/config
touch src/server/config/index.js
```

Your sample configuration should look like the following code, if you have followed the instructions for creating a MySQL database. The only thing that we did here was to copy our current configuration into a new object indexed with the `development` or `production` environment:

```
module.exports = {
  "development": {
    "username": "devuser",
    "password": "PASSWORD",
    "database": "graphbook_dev",
    "host": "localhost",
    "dialect": "mysql",
    "operatorsAliases": false,
    "pool": {
      "max": 5,
      "min": 0,
      "acquire": 30000,
      "idle": 10000
    }
  },
  "production": {
    "host": process.env.host,
    "username": process.env.username,
    "password": process.env.password,
    "database": process.env.database,
    "logging": false,
    "dialect": "mysql",
    "operatorsAliases": false,
```

```
      "pool": {
        "max": 5,
        "min": 0,
        "acquire": 30000,
        "idle": 10000
      }
    }
  }
```

Sequelize expects a `config.json` file inside of this folder by default, but this setup will allow us a more custom approach in later chapters. The `development` environment directly store the credentials for your database whereas the `production` configuration uses environment variables to fill them.

We can remove the configuration that we hardcoded earlier and replace the contents of our `index.js` database file to require our `configFile`, instead.

This should look like the following code snippet:

```
import Sequelize from 'sequelize';
import configFile from '../config/';

const env = process.env.NODE_ENV || 'development';
const config = configFile[env];

const sequelize = new Sequelize(config.database, config.username,
 config.password, config);

const db = {
  sequelize,
};

export default db;
```

In the preceding code, we are using the `NODE_ENV` environmental variable to get the environment that the server is running in. We read the `config` file and pass the correct configuration to the Sequelize instance. The environmental variable will allow us to add a new environment, such as `production`, at a later point in the book.

The Sequelize instance is then exported for use throughout our application. We use a special `db` object for this. You will see why we are doing this later on.

Next, you will learn how to generate and write models and migrations for all of the entities that our application will have.

# Writing database models

After creating a connection to our MySQL server via Sequelize, we want to use it. However, our database is missing a table or structure that we can query or manipulate. Creating those is the next thing that we need to do.

Currently, we have two GraphQL entities: `User` and `Post`.

Sequelize lets us create a database schema for each of our GraphQL entities. The schema is validated when inserting or updating rows in our database. We already wrote a schema for GraphQL in the `schema.js` file used by Apollo Server, but we need to create a second one for our database. The field types, as well as the fields themselves, can vary between the database and the GraphQL schema.

GraphQL schemas can have more fields than our database model, or vice versa. Perhaps you do not want to export all data from your database through the API, or maybe you generate data for your GraphQL API on the fly, when requesting data.

Let's create the first model for our posts. Create two new folders (one called `models`, and the other, `migrations`) next to the `database` folder:

```
mkdir src/server/models
mkdir src/server/migrations
```

Creating each model in a separate file is much cleaner than having one big file for all models.

# Your first database model

We will use the Sequelize CLI to generate our first database model. Install it globally with the following command:

```
npm install -g sequelize-cli
```

This gives you the ability to run the `sequelize` command inside of your Terminal.

The Sequelize CLI allows us to generate the model automatically. This can be done by running the following command:

```
sequelize model:generate --models-path src/server/models --migrations-path
src/server/migrations --name Post --attributes text:text
```

Sequelize expects us to run the command in the folder in which we have run `sequelize init`, by default. Our file structure is a bit different, because we have two layers with `src/server`. For this reason, we specify the path manually, with the first two parameters: `--models-path` and `--migrations-path`.

The `--name` parameter gives our model a name under which it can be used. The `--attributes` option specifies the fields that the model should include.

If you are increasingly customizing your setup, you may want to know about other options that the CLI offers. You can view the manual for every command easily, by appending `--help` as an option: `sequelize model:generate --help`.

This command creates a `post.js` model file in your `models` folder, and a database migration file, named `XXXXXXXXXXXXXX-create-post.js`, in your `migrations` folder. The `X` is the timestamp when generating the files with the CLI. You will see how migrations work in the next section.

The following model file was created for us:

```
'use strict';

module.exports = (sequelize, DataTypes) => {
  var Post = sequelize.define('Post', {
    text: DataTypes.TEXT
  }, {});

  Post.associate = function(models) {
    // associations can be defined here
  };

  return Post;
};
```

We are using the `define` Sequelize function to create a database model:

- The first parameter is the name of the database model.
- The second option is the field configuration for this model.

There are many more options that Sequelize offers us to customize our database models. If you want to look up which options are available, you can find them at `http://docs.sequelizejs.com/manual/tutorial/models-definition.html`.

A post object has the `id`, `text`, and `user` properties. The user will be a separate model, as seen in the GraphQL schema. Consequently, we only need to configure the `id` and `text` as columns of a post.

The `id` is the key that uniquely identifies a data record from our database. We do not specify this when running the `model:generate` command, because it is generated by MySQL automatically.

The `text` column is just a MySQL `TEXT` field, which allows us to write pretty long posts. Alternatively, there are other MySQL field types, with `MEDIUMTEXT`, `LONGTEXT`, and `BLOB`, which could save more characters. A regular `TEXT` column should be fine for our use case.

The Sequelize CLI created a model file, exporting a function that, after execution, returns the real database model. You will soon see why this a great way of initializing our models.

Let's take a look at the migration file that is also created by the CLI.

# Your first database migration

Until now, MySQL has not known anything about our plan to save posts inside of it. Our database tables and columns need to be created, of course, and this is why the migration file was created.

A migration file has multiple advantages, such as the following:

1. Migrations allow us to track database changes through our regular version control system, such as Git or SVN. Every change to our database structure should be covered in a migration file.
2. It also enables us to write updates that automatically apply database changes for new versions of our application.

Our first migration file creates a `Posts` table and adds all required columns, as follows:

```
'use strict';

module.exports = {
  up: (queryInterface, Sequelize) => {
    return queryInterface.createTable('Posts', {
      id: {
        allowNull: false,
        autoIncrement: true,
        primaryKey: true,
        type: Sequelize.INTEGER
```

```
        },
        text: {
          type: Sequelize.TEXT
        },
        createdAt: {
          allowNull: false,
          type: Sequelize.DATE
        },
        updatedAt: {
          allowNull: false,
          type: Sequelize.DATE
        }
      });
    },
    down: (queryInterface, Sequelize) => {
      return queryInterface.dropTable('Posts');
    }
  };
```

By convention, the model name is pluralized in migrations, but it is singular inside of model definitions. Our table names are also pluralized. Sequelize offers options to change this.

A migration has two properties, as follows:

- The `up` property states what should be done when running the migration.
- The `down` property states what is run when undoing a migration.

As stated previously, the `id` and `text` column are created, as well as two additional `datetime` columns, to save the creation and update time.

The `id` field has set `autoIncrement` and `primaryKey` to `true`. The `id` will count upward, from one to nearly infinite, for each post in our table. This `id` uniquely identifies posts for us. Passing `allowNull` with `false` disables the feature to insert a row with an empty field value.

To execute this migration, we use the Sequelize CLI again, as follows:

```
sequelize db:migrate --migrations-path src/server/migrations --config
src/server/config/index.js
```

Look inside of phpMyAdmin. Here, you will find the new table, called `Posts`. The structure of the table should look as follows:

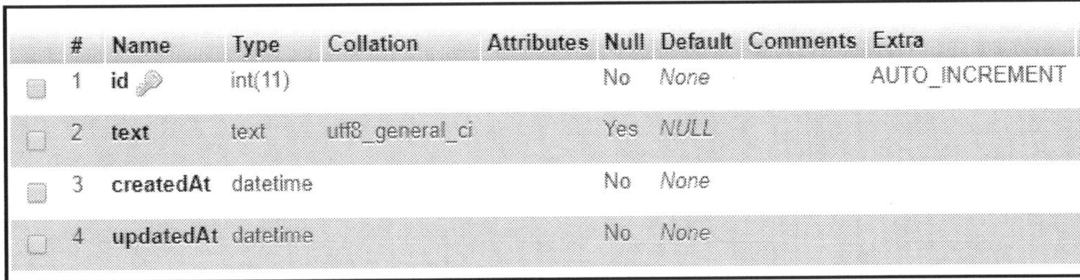

| | # | Name | Type | Collation | Attributes | Null | Default | Comments | Extra |
|---|---|---|---|---|---|---|---|---|---|
| | 1 | **id** | int(11) | | | No | *None* | | AUTO_INCREMENT |
| | 2 | **text** | text | utf8_general_ci | | Yes | *NULL* | | |
| | 3 | **createdAt** | datetime | | | No | *None* | | |
| | 4 | **updatedAt** | datetime | | | No | *None* | | |

All of the fields were created as we desired.

Furthermore, two additional fields, `createdAt` and `updatedAt`, were created. These two fields are what are called timestamps, and are used to tell when a row was either created or updated. The fields were created by Sequelize automatically. If you do not want this, you can set the `timestamps` property in the model to `false`.

Every time that you use Sequelize and its migration feature, you will have an additional table, called `SequelizeMeta`. The contents of the table should look as follows:

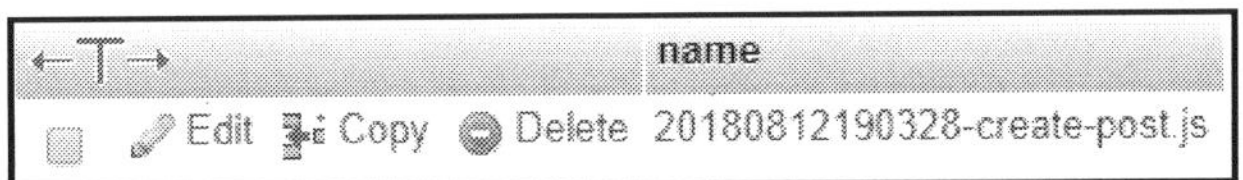

| ←T→ | name |
|---|---|
| Edit Copy Delete | 20180812190328-create-post.js |

Sequelize saves every migration that has been executed. If we add further fields in development or in a new release cycle, we can write a migration that runs all table alterings for us as an update. Sequelize skips all migrations that are saved inside of the meta table.

One major step is to bind our model to Sequelize. This process can be automated by running `sequelize init`, but understanding it will teach us way more than relying on premade boilerplate commands.

# Importing models with Sequelize

We want to import all of our database models at once, in a central file. Our database connection instantiator will then use this file on the other side.

Create an `index.js` file in the `models` folder, and fill in the following code:

```
import Sequelize from 'sequelize';
if (process.env.NODE_ENV === 'development') {
  require('babel-plugin-require-context-hook/register')()
}

export default (sequelize) => {
  let db = {};

  const context = require.context('.', true, /^\.\/(?!index\.js).*\.js$/,
   'sync')
  context.keys().map(context).forEach(module => {
    const model = module(sequelize, Sequelize);
    db[model.name] = model;
  });

  Object.keys(db).forEach((modelName) => {
    if (db[modelName].associate) {
      db[modelName].associate(db);
    }
  });

  return db;
};
```

This file will also be generated when running `sequelize init`, but I have split up the setup of the database connection and this part into different files. Usually, this would happen in just one file.

To summarize what happens in the preceding code, we search for all files ending with `.js` in the same folder as the current file, and load them all with the `require.context` statement. In development, we must execute the `babel-plugin-require-context-hook/register` hook to load the `require.context` function at the top. This package must be installed with `npm`, with the following command:

```
npm install --save-dev babel-plugin-require-context-hook
```

We need to load the plugin with the start of our development server, so, open the `package.json` file and edit the server script, as follows:

```
nodemon --exec babel-node --plugins require-context-hook --watch src/server
src/server/index.js
```

When the plugin is loaded and we run the `require('babel-plugin-require-context-hook/register')()` function, the `require.context` method is available for us. Make sure that you set the `NODE_ENV` variable to `development`; otherwise, this won't work.

In production, the `require.context` function is included in the generated bundle of webpack.

The loaded model files export a function with the following two parameters:

- Our sequelize instance, after creating a connection to our database
- The sequelize class itself, including the data types it offers, such as integer or text

Running the exported functions imports the actual Sequelize model. When all models are imported, we loop through them and check whether they have a function called `associate`. If this is the case, we execute the `associate` function, and, through that, we establish relations between multiple models. Currently, we have not set up an association, but that will change later in this chapter.

Now, we want to use our models. Go back to the `index.js` database file and import all models through the aggregation `index.js` file that we just created:

```
import models from '../models';
```

Before exporting the `db` object at the end of the file, we need to run the `models` wrapper to read all model `.js` files. We pass our Sequelize instance as a parameter, as follows:

```
const db = {
  models: models(sequelize),
  sequelize,
};
```

The new database object in the preceding command has `sequelize` and `models` as a property. Under `models`, you can find the `Post` model, and every new model that we are going to add later.

The database `index.js` file is ready, and can be used now. You should import this file only once, because it can get messy when creating multiple instances of Sequelize. The pool functionality won't work correctly, and we will end up with more connections than the maximum of five that we specified earlier.

We create the global database instance in the `index.js` file of the root server folder. Add the following code:

```
import db from './database';
```

We require the `database` folder and the `index.js` file inside this folder. Loading the file instantiates the Sequelize object, including all database models.

Going forward, we want to query some data from our database via the GraphQL API that we implemented in `Chapter 2`, *Setting Up GraphQL with Express.js*.

# Seeding data with Sequelize

We should fill the empty `Posts` table with our fake data. To accomplish this, we will use Sequelize's feature for seeding data to our database.

Create a new folder, called `seeders`:

```
mkdir src/server/seeders
```

Now, we can run our next Sequelize CLI command, in order to generate a boilerplate file:

```
sequelize seed:generate --name fake-posts --seeders-path src/server/seeders
```

Seeders are great for importing test data into a database for development. Our `seed` file has the timestamp and the words `fake-posts` in the name, and should look as follows:

```
'use strict';

module.exports = {
  up: (queryInterface, Sequelize) => {
    /*
      Add altering commands here.
      Return a promise to correctly handle asynchronicity.
      Example:
      return queryInterface.bulkInsert('Person', [{
        name: 'John Doe',
        isBetaMember: false
      }], {});
    */
  },
  down: (queryInterface, Sequelize) => {
    /*
      Add reverting commands here.
      Return a promise to correctly handle asynchronicity.
```

```
      Example:
      return queryInterface.bulkDelete('Person', null, {});
    */
  }
};
```

As you can see in the preceding code snippet, nothing is done here. It is just an empty boilerplate file. We need to edit this file to create the fake posts that we already had in our backend. This file looks like our migration from the previous section. Replace the contents of the file with the following code:

```
'use strict';

module.exports = {
  up: (queryInterface, Sequelize) => {
    return queryInterface.bulkInsert('Posts', [{
      text: 'Lorem ipsum 1',
      createdAt: new Date(),
      updatedAt: new Date(),
    },
    {
      text: 'Lorem ipsum 2',
      createdAt: new Date(),
      updatedAt: new Date(),
    }],
    {});
  },
  down: (queryInterface, Sequelize) => {
    return queryInterface.bulkDelete('Posts', null, {});
  }
};
```

In the `up` migration, we are bulk inserting two posts, through the `queryInterface` and its `bulkInsert` command. For this, we pass an array of posts, excluding the `id` and the associated user. The `id` is created automatically, and the user is saved in a separate table later on. The `QueryInterface` of Sequelize is the general interface that Sequelize uses to talk to all databases.

In our seed file, we need to add the `createdAt` and `updatedAt` field, since Sequelize does not set up default values for the timestamp columns in MySQL. In reality, Sequelize takes care of the default values of those fields by itself, but not when seeding data. If you do not provide these values, the seed will fail, because `NULL` is not allowed for `createdAt` and `updatedAt`.

The `down` migration bulk deletes all rows in the table, since this is the apparent reverse action of the `up` migration.

Execute all of the seeds from the `seeders` folder with the following command:

```
sequelize db:seed:all --seeders-path src/server/seeders --config
src/server/config/index.js
```

Sequelize does not check or save if a seed has been run already, as we are doing it with the preceding command. This means that you can run seeds multiple times if you want to.

The following screenshot shows a filled `Posts` table:

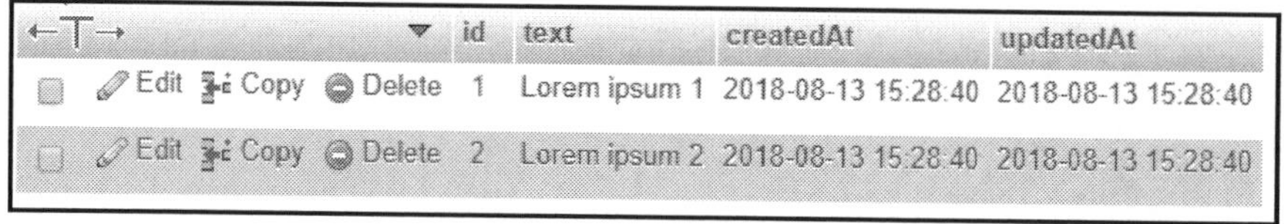

| ←T→ | | | | id | text | createdAt | updatedAt |
|---|---|---|---|---|---|---|---|
| ☐ | Edit | Copy | Delete | 1 | Lorem ipsum 1 | 2018-08-13 15:28:40 | 2018-08-13 15:28:40 |
| ☐ | Edit | Copy | Delete | 2 | Lorem ipsum 2 | 2018-08-13 15:28:40 | 2018-08-13 15:28:40 |

The demo posts are now inside of our database.

We will cover how to use Sequelize with our Apollo Server, and how to add the relationship between the user and their posts, in the next section.

# Using Sequelize with Apollo

The database object is initialized upon starting the server within the root `index.js` file. We pass it from this global location down to the spots where we rely on the database. This way, we do not import the database file repeatedly, but have a single instance that handles all database queries for us.

The services that we want to publicize through the GraphQL API need access to our MySQL database. The first step is to implement the posts into our GraphQL API. It should respond with the fake posts from the database we just inserted.

## Global database instance

To pass the database down to our GraphQL resolvers, we create a new object in the server `index.js` file:

```
import db from './database';

const utils = {
  db,
};
```

We create a `utils` object directly under the `import` statement of the `database` folder.

The `utils` object holds all of the utilities that our services might need access to. This can be anything, from third-party tools, to our MySQL, or any other database, such as in the preceding code.

Replace the line where we import the `services` folder, as follows:

```
import servicesLoader from './services';
const services = servicesLoader(utils);
```

The preceding code might look weird to you, but what we are doing here is executing the function that is the result of the `import` statement, and passing the `utils` object as a parameter. We must do this in two separate lines, as the `import` syntax does not allow it in just one line; so, we must first import the function exported from the `services` folder into a separate variable.

Until now, the return value of the `import` statement was a simple object. We have to change this to match our requirements.

To do this, go to the services `index.js` file and change the contents of the file, as follows:

```
import graphql from './graphql';

export default utils => ({
  graphql: graphql(utils),
});
```

We surrounded the preceding `services` object with a function, which was then exported. That function accepts only one parameter, which is our `utils` object.

That object is then given to a new function, called `graphql`. Every service that we are going to use has to be a function that accepts this parameter. It allows us to hand over any property that we want to the deepest point in our application.

When executing the preceding exported function, the result is the regular `services` object we used before. We only wrapped it inside of a function to pass the `utils` object.

The `graphql` import that we are doing needs to accept the `utils` object.

Open the `index.js` file from the `graphql` folder and replace everything but the `require` statements at the top with the following code:

```
export default (utils) => {
  const executableSchema = makeExecutableSchema({
    typeDefs: Schema,
    resolvers: Resolvers.call(utils),
  });

  const server = new ApolloServer({
    schema: executableSchema,
    context: ({ req }) => req,
  });

  return server;
};
```

Again, we surrounded everything with a function that accepts the `utils` object. The aim of all this is to have access to the database within our GraphQL resolvers.

To accomplish this, we are using the `Resolvers.call` function of JavaScript. The function allows us to set the owner object of the exported `Resolvers` function. What we are saying here is that the scope of the `Resolvers` is the `utils` object.

So, within the `Resolvers` function, accessing `this` now gives us the `utils` object. At the moment, the `Resolvers` are just a simple object, but because we use the `call` method, we must also return a function from the `resolvers.js` file.

Surround the `resolvers` object in this file with a function, and return the `resolvers` object from inside of the function:

```
export default function resolver() {
  ...
  return resolvers;
}
```

We cannot use the arrow syntax, as before. ES6 arrow syntax would automatically take a scope, but we want the `call` function to take over here.

An alternative way of doing this would be to also hand over the `utils` object as a parameter. I think the way that we have chosen is a bit cleaner, but handle it as you like.

# Running the first database query

Now, we want to finally use the database. Add the following code to the top of the `export default function resolver` statement:

```
const { db } = this;
const { Post } = db.models;
```

The `this` keyword is the owner of the current method, and holds the `db` object, as stated previously. We extract the database models from the `db` object that we built in the previous section.

The good thing about models is that you do not need to write raw queries against the database. You have already told Sequelize which fields and tables it can use by creating a model. At this point, you are able to use Sequelize's methods to run queries against the database within your resolvers.

We can query all posts through the Sequelize model, instead of returning the fake posts from before. Replace the `posts` property within the `RootQuery` with the following code:

```
posts(root, args, context) {
  return Post.findAll({order: [['createdAt', 'DESC']]});
},
```

In the preceding code, we search and select all of the posts that we have in our database. We are using the Sequelize `findAll` method and returning the result of it. The return value will be a JavaScript promise, which automatically gets resolved when the database is finished collecting the data.

A typical news feed, such as on Twitter or Facebook, orders the posts according to the creation date. That way, you have the newest posts at the top and the oldest at the bottom. Sequelize expects an array of arrays as a parameter of the order property that we pass as the first parameter to the `findAll` method. The results are ordered by the creation date.

There are many other methods that Sequelize offers. You can query for just one entity, count them, find them, create them if they are not found, and much more. You can look up the methods that Sequelize provides at `http://docs.sequelizejs.com/manual/tutorial/models-usage.html#data-retrieval-finders`.

As we are not using the demo `posts` array anymore, you can remove it from the `resolvers.js` file.

You can start the server with `npm run server` and execute the GraphQL posts query from `Chapter 2`, *Setting Up GraphQL with Express.js*, again. The output will look as follows:

```
{
  "data": {
    "posts": [{
      "id": 1,
      "text": "Lorem ipsum 1",
      "user": null
    },
    {
      "id": 2,
      "text": "Lorem ipsum 2",
      "user": null
    }]
  }
}
```

The `id` and `text` fields look fine, but the `user` object is `null`. This happened because we did not define a user model or declare a relationship between the user and the post model. We will change this in the next section.

# One-to-one relationships in Sequelize

We need to associate each post with a user, to fill the gap that we have created in our GraphQL response. A post has to have an author. It would not make sense to have a post without an associated user.

First, we will generate a `User` model and migration. We will use the Sequelize CLI again, as follows:

```
sequelize model:generate --models-path src/server/models --migrations-path
src/server/migrations --name User --attributes
avatar:string,username:string
```

The migration file creates the `Users` table and adds the `avatar` and `username` column. A data row looks like a post in our fake data, but it also includes an autogenerated ID and two timestamps, as you have seen before.

The relationships of the users to their specific posts is still missing as we have only created the model and migration file. We still have to add the relationship between posts and users. This is covered in the next section.

What every post needs, of course, is an extra field, called `userId`. This column acts as the foreign key to reference a unique user. Then, we can join the user relating to each post.

MySQL offers great documentation for people that are not used to foreign key constraints. If you are one of them, you should read up on this topic at `https://dev.mysql.com/doc/refman/8.0/en/create-table-foreign-keys.html`.

# Updating the table structure with migrations

We have to write a third migration, adding the `userId` column to our `Post` table, but also including it in our database `Post` model.

Generating a boilerplate migration file is very easy with the Sequelize CLI:

```
sequelize migration:create --migrations-path src/server/migrations --name add-userId-to-post
```

You can directly replace the content, as follows:

```
'use strict';

module.exports = {
  up: (queryInterface, Sequelize) => {
    return Promise.all([
      queryInterface.addColumn('Posts',
        'userId',
        {
          type: Sequelize.INTEGER,
        }),
      queryInterface.addConstraint('Posts', ['userId'], {
        type: 'foreign key',
        name: 'fk_user_id',
        references: {
          table: 'Users',
          field: 'id',
        },
        onDelete: 'cascade',
        onUpdate: 'cascade',
      }),
    ]);
```

```
    },

    down: (queryInterface, Sequelize) => {
      return Promise.all([
        queryInterface.removeColumn('Posts', 'userId'),
      ]);
    }
  };
```

This migration is a bit more complex, and I will explain it on a step-by-step basis.

In the `up` migration, we are using the `queryInterface` to first add the `userId` column to the `Posts` table.

Secondly, we add a foreign key constraint, with the `addConstraint` function. The constraint represents the relationship between both the user and the post entities. The relationship is saved in the `userId` column of the Post table.

I experienced some issues when running the migrations without using `Promise.all`, which ensures that all promises in the array are resolved. Returning only the array did not run both the `addColumn` and `addConstraint` methods.

The preceding `addConstraint` function receives the `foreign key` string as a `type` which says that the data type is the same as the corresponding column in the `Users` table. We want to give our constraint the custom name `fk_user_id`, in order to identify it later.

Then, we specify the `references` field for the `userId` column. Sequelize requires a table, which is the `Users` table, and the field that our foreign key relates to, which is the `id` column of the `User` table. This is everything that is required to get a working database relationship.

Furthermore, we change the `onUpdate` and `onDelete` constraints to `cascade`. What this means is that, when a user either gets deleted or has their user ID updated, the change is reflected in the user's posts. Deleting a user results in deleting all posts of a user, and updating a user's ID updates the ID on all of the user's posts. We do not need to handle all of this in our application code, which would be inefficient.

There is a lot more about this topic in the Sequelize documentation. If you want to read up on this, you can find more information at `http://docs.sequelizejs.com/class/lib/query-interface.js~QueryInterface.html`.

Rerun the migration, in order to see what changes occurred:

```
sequelize db:migrate --migrations-path src/server/migrations --config
src/server/config/index.js
```

The benefit of running migrations through Sequelize is that it goes through all of the possible migrations from the `migrations` folder. It excludes those that are already saved inside of the `SequelizeMeta` table, and then chronologically runs the migrations that are left. Sequelize can do this because the timestamp is included in every migration's filename.

After running the migration, there should be a `Users` table, and the `userId` column should be added to the `Posts` table.

Take a look at the relation view of the `Posts` table in phpMyAdmin. You can find it under the **Structure** view, by clicking on **Relation view**:

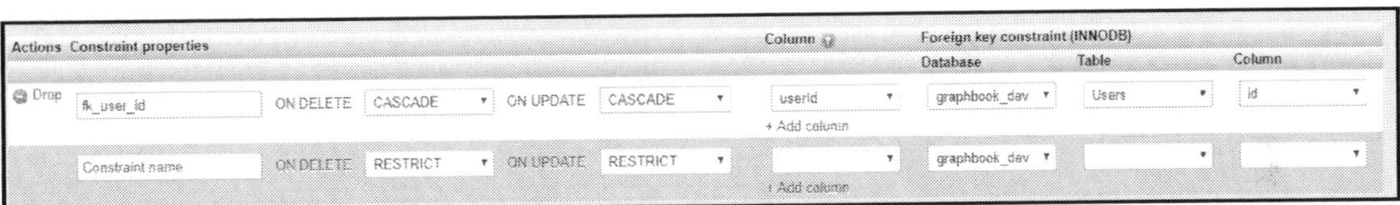


As you can see in the preceding screenshot, we have our foreign key constraint. The correct name was taken, and the cascade option, too.

If you receive an error when running migrations, you can easily undo them, as follows:

```
sequelize db:migrate:undo --migrations-path src/server/migrations --config
src/server/config/index.js
```

This command undoes the most recent migrations. Always be conscious of what you do here. Keep a backup if you are unsure whether everything works correctly.

You can also revert all migrations at once, or only revert to one specific migration, so that you can go back to a specific timestamp:

```
sequelize db:migrate:undo:all --to XXXXXXXXXXXXXX-create-posts.js --
migrations-path src/server/migrations --config src/server/config/index.js
```

Leave out the parameter `--to` to undo all migrations.

We have now established the database relationship, but Sequelize must know about the relationship, too. You will learn how this is done in the next section.

# Model associations in Sequelize

Now that we have the relationship configured with the foreign key, it also needs to be configured inside of our Sequelize model.

Go back to the `Post` model file and replace the `associate` function with the following:

```
Post.associate = function(models) {
  Post.belongsTo(models.User);
};
```

The `associate` function gets evaluated inside of our aggregating `index.js` file, where all model files are imported.

We are using the `belongsTo` function, which tells Sequelize that every post belongs to exactly one user. Sequelize gives us a new function on the `Post` model, called `getUser`, to retrieve the associated user. The naming is done by convention, as you can see. Sequelize does all of this automatically.

Do not forget to add the `userId` as a queryable field to the `Post` model itself, as follows:

```
userId:  DataTypes.INTEGER,
```

The `User` model needs to implement the reverse association, too. Add the following code to the `User` model file:

```
User.associate = function(models) {
  User.hasMany(models.Post);
};
```

The `hasMany` function means the exact opposite of the `belongsTo` function. Every user can have multiple posts associated in the Post table. It can be anything, from zero to multiple posts.

You can compare the new data layout with the preceding one. Up to this point, we had the posts and users inside of one big array of objects. Now, we have split every object into two tables. Both tables connect to each other through the foreign key. This is required every time we run the GraphQL query to get all posts, including their authors.

So, we must extend our current `resolvers.js` file. Add the `Post` property to the `resolvers` object, as follows:

```
Post: {
  user(post, args, context) {
    return post.getUser();
  },
},
```

The `RootQuery` and `RootMutation` were the two main properties that we had so far. The `RootQuery` is the starting point where all GraphQL queries begin.

With the old demo posts, we were able to directly return a valid and complete response, since everything that we needed was in there already. Now, a second query, or a `JOIN`, is needed to collect all necessary data for a complete response.

The `Post` entity is introduced to our `resolvers`, where we can define functions for every property of our GraphQL schema. Only the user is missing in our response; the rest is there. That is why we have added the `user` function to the resolvers.

The first parameter of the function is the `post` model instance that we are returning inside of the `RootQuery` resolver.

Then, we use the `getUser` function that Sequelize gave us. Executing the `getUser` function runs the correct MySQL `SELECT` query, in order to get the correct user from the `Users` table. It does not run a real MySQL `JOIN`, but only queries the user in a separate MySQL command. Later on, you will learn another method for running a `JOIN` directly, which is more efficient.

However, if you query for all posts via the GraphQL API, the user will still be `null`. We have not added any users to the database yet, so let's insert them next.

# Seeding foreign key data

The challenge of adding users is that we have already introduced a foreign key constraint to the database. You can follow these instructions to learn how to get it working:

1. We use the Sequelize CLI to generate an empty `seeders` file, as follows:

```
sequelize seed:generate --name fake-users --seeders-path
src/server/seeders
```

2. Fill in the following code to insert the fake users:

```
'use strict';

module.exports = {
  up: (queryInterface, Sequelize) => {
    return queryInterface.bulkInsert('Users', [{
      avatar: '/uploads/avatar1.png',
      username: 'TestUser',
      createdAt: new Date(),
      updatedAt: new Date(),
    },
    {
      avatar: '/uploads/avatar2.png',
      username: 'TestUser2',
      createdAt: new Date(),
      updatedAt: new Date(),
    }],
    {});
  },
  down: (queryInterface, Sequelize) => {
    return queryInterface.bulkDelete('Users', null, {});
  }
};
```

The preceding code looks like the `seeders` file for the posts, but instead, we are now inserting users with the correct fields. Every user receives an auto-incremented ID by our MySQL server when inserting a user.

3. We must maintain the relationships as configured in our database. Adjust the `posts` seed file to reflect this, and add a `userId` to both posts in the `up` migration:

```
return queryInterface.bulkInsert('Posts', [{
  text: 'Lorem ipsum 1',
  userId: usersRows[0].id,
  createdAt: new Date(),
  updatedAt: new Date(),
},
{
  text: 'Lorem ipsum 2',
  userId: usersRows[1].id,
  createdAt: new Date(),
  updatedAt: new Date(),
}],
{});
```

We created the `users` seed file after the `post` seeders file. This means that the posts are inserted before the users exist, because of the timestamps of the files. Generally, this is not a problem, but since we have introduced a foreign key constraint, we are not able to insert posts with a `userId` when the underlying user does not exist in our database. MySQL forbids this.

There is also another problem. The current posts in our table do not receive a `userId`, and we do not want to write a separate migration or seed to fix those posts.

There are two options here. You can either manually truncate the tables through phpMyAdmin and SQL statements, or you can use the Sequelize CLI. It is easier to use the CLI, but the result will be the same either way. The following command will undo all seeds:

```
sequelize db:seed:undo:all --seeders-path src/server/seeders --config
src/server/config/index.js
```

When undoing seeds, the tables are not truncated, and therefore, the `autoIncrement` index is not set back to one, but stays at the current index. Reverting seeds multiple times raises the user's or post's ID, and therefore, stops the seeds from working. The `userId` column in the post seed cannot be hardcoded when using the `down` migration.

You can fix this by selecting all users with a raw query in the `post` seed file. We can pass the retrieved user IDs statically. Replace the `up` property with the following:

```
up: (queryInterface, Sequelize) => {
  // Get all existing users
  return queryInterface.sequelize.query(
    'SELECT id from Users;',
  ).then((users) => {
    const usersRows = users[0];
    return queryInterface.bulkInsert('Posts', [{
      text: 'Lorem ipsum 1',
      userId: usersRows[0].id,
      createdAt: new Date(),
      updatedAt: new Date(),
    },
    {
      text: 'Lorem ipsum 2',
      userId: usersRows[1].id,
      createdAt: new Date(),
      updatedAt: new Date(),
    }],
    {});
  });
},
```

This way, we get all of the users first, and then select the ID manually. This solution is not great, but it fixes the problem with the static `userId` field in the seeds. You can undo and redo the seeds as often as you want. There is no need to truncate the table to get the correct `autoIncrement` index.

We have not gotten any further now, since the posts are still inserted before the users. From my point of view, the easiest way to fix this is to rename the seeder files. Simply adjust the timestamp of the fake user seed file to be before the post seed file's timestamp, or the other way around. Again, execute all seeds, as follows:

```
sequelize db:seed:all --seeders-path src/server/seeders --config
src/server/config/index.js
```

If you take a look inside your database, you should see a filled `Posts` table, including the `userId`. The `Users` table should look like the following screenshot:

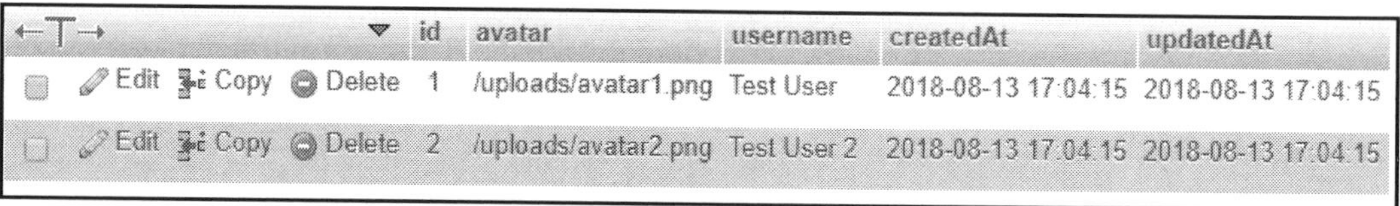

| ←T→ | | | | id | avatar | username | createdAt | updatedAt |
|---|---|---|---|---|---|---|---|---|
| | Edit | Copy | Delete | 1 | /uploads/avatar1.png | Test User | 2018-08-13 17:04:15 | 2018-08-13 17:04:15 |
| | Edit | Copy | Delete | 2 | /uploads/avatar2.png | Test User 2 | 2018-08-13 17:04:15 | 2018-08-13 17:04:15 |

You can now rerun the GraphQL query, and you should see a working association between the users and their posts, because the `user` field is filled.

We have achieved a lot. We can serve data from our database through the GraphQL API by matching its schema.

There are some ways to automate this process, through additional npm packages. There is a package that automates the process of creating a GraphQL schema from your database models for you. As always, you are more flexible when you do not rely on preconfigured packages. You can find the package at `https://www.npmjs.com/package/graphql-tools-sequelize`.

# Mutating data with Sequelize

Requesting data from our database via the GraphQL API works. Now comes the tough part: adding a new post to the `Posts` table.

Before we start, we must extract the new database model from the `db` object at the top of the exported function in our `resolvers.js` file:

```
const { Post, User } = db.models;
```

Currently, we have no authentication to identify the user that is creating the post. We will fake this step until the authentication is implemented in a later chapter.

We have to edit the GraphQL resolvers to add the new post. Replace the old `addPost` function with the new one, as shown in the following code snippet:

```
addPost(root, { post }, context) {
  logger.log({
    level: 'info',
    message: 'Post was created',
  });

  return User.findAll().then((users) => {
    const usersRow = users[0];
    return Post.create({
      ...post,
    }).then((newPost) => {
      return Promise.all([
        newPost.setUser(usersRow.id),
      ]).then(() => {
        return newPost;
      });
    });
  });
},
```

As always, the preceding mutation returns a promise. The promise is resolved when the deepest query has been executed successfully. The execution order is as follows:

1. We retrieve all users from the database through the `User.findAll` method.
2. We insert the post into our database with the `create` function of Sequelize. The only property that we pass is the post object from the original request, which only holds the text of the post. MySQL autogenerates the `id` of the post.

Sequelize also offers a `build` function, which initializes the model instance for us. In this case, we would have to run the `save` method to insert the model manually. The `create` function does this for us all at once.

3. The post has been created, but the `userId` was not set.

   You could also directly add the user ID in the `Post.create` function. The problem here is that we did not establish the model associations on the JavaScript side. If we return the created post model without explicitly using `setUser` on the model instance, we cannot use the `getUser` function until we create a new instance of the post model.

   So, to fix this problem, we run the `create` function, resolve the promise, and then run `setUser` separately. As a parameter of `setUser`, we statically take the ID of the first user from the `users` array.

   We resolve the promise of the `setUser` function by using an array surrounded by `Promise.all`. This allows us to add further Sequelize methods later on. For example, you could add a category on each post, too.

4. The returned value is the newly created post model instance, after we have set the `userId` correctly.

Everything is set now. To test our API, we are going to use Postman again. We need to change the `addPost` request. The `userInput` that we added before is not needed anymore, because the backend statically chooses the first user out of our database. You can send the following request body:

```
{
  "operationName":null,
  "query": "mutation addPost($post : PostInput!) { addPost(post : $post) {
    id text user { username avatar }}}",
  "variables":{
    "post": {
      "text": "You just added a post."
    }
  }
}
```

Your GraphQL schema must reflect this change, so remove the `userInput` from there, too:

```
addPost (
  post: PostInput!
): Post
```

Running the `addPost` GraphQL mutation now adds a post to the `Posts` table, as you can see in the following screenshot:

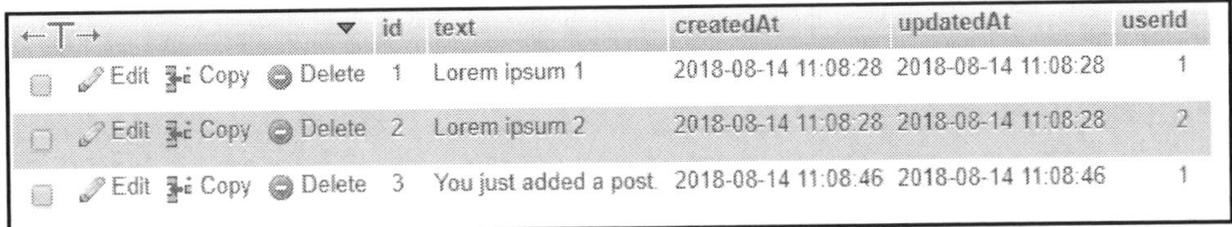

|  | id | text | createdAt | updatedAt | userId |
|---|---|---|---|---|---|
| Edit Copy Delete | 1 | Lorem ipsum 1 | 2018-08-14 11:08:28 | 2018-08-14 11:08:28 | 1 |
| Edit Copy Delete | 2 | Lorem ipsum 2 | 2018-08-14 11:08:28 | 2018-08-14 11:08:28 | 2 |
| Edit Copy Delete | 3 | You just added a post. | 2018-08-14 11:08:46 | 2018-08-14 11:08:46 | 1 |

We have rebuilt the example from the last chapter, but we are using a database in our backend. To extend our application, we are going to add two new entities.

# Many-to-many relationships

Facebook provides users with various ways to interact. Currently, we only have the opportunity to request and insert posts. As in the case of Facebook, we want to have chats with our friends and colleagues. We will introduce two new entities to cover this.

The first entity is called `Chat`, and the second is called `Message`.

Before starting with the implementation, we need to lay out a detailed plan of what those entities will enable us to do.

A user can have multiple chats, and a chat can belong to multiple users. This relationship gives us the opportunity to have group chats with multiple users, as well as private chats, between only two users. A message belongs to one user, but every message also belongs to one chat.

# Model and migrations

When transferring this into real code, we first generate the `Chat` model. The problem here is that we have a many-to-many relationship between users and chats. In MySQL, this kind of relationship requires a table, to store the relations between all entities separately.

Those tables are called **join tables**. Instead of using a foreign key on the chat or a user to save the relationship, we have a table called `user_chats`. The user's ID and the chat's ID are associated with each other inside of this table. If a user participates in multiple chats, they will have multiple rows in this table, with different chat IDs.

## Chat model

Let's start by creating the `Chat` model and migration. A chat itself does not store any data; we use it for grouping specific users' messages:

```
sequelize model:generate --models-path src/server/models --migrations-path
src/server/migrations --name Chat --attributes
firstName:string,lastName:string,email:string
```

Generate the migration for our association table, as follows:

```
sequelize migration:create --migrations-path src/server/migrations --name
create-user-chats
```

Adjust the `users_chats` migration generated by the Sequelize CLI. We specify the user and chat IDs as attributes for our relationship. References inside of a migration automatically create foreign key constraints for us. The migration file should look like the following code snippet:

```
'use strict';

module.exports = {
  up: (queryInterface, Sequelize) => {
    return queryInterface.createTable('users_chats', {
      id: {
        allowNull: false,
        autoIncrement: true,
        primaryKey: true,
        type: Sequelize.INTEGER
      },
      userId: {
        type: Sequelize.INTEGER,
        references: {
          model: 'Users',
          key: 'id'
        },
        onDelete: 'cascade',
        onUpdate: 'cascade',
      },
      chatId: {
        type: Sequelize.INTEGER,
        references: {
          model: 'Chats',
          key: 'id'
        },
        onDelete: 'cascade',
        onUpdate: 'cascade',
      },
```

```
        createdAt: {
          allowNull: false,
          type: Sequelize.DATE
        },
        updatedAt: {
          allowNull: false,
          type: Sequelize.DATE
        }
      });
    },
    down: (queryInterface, Sequelize) => {
      return queryInterface.dropTable('users_chats');
    }
  };
```

A separate model file for the association table is not needed, because we can rely on this table in the models where the association is required. The `id` column could be left out, because the row should be identifiable.

Associate the user to the `Chat` model via the new relation table in the `User` model, as follows:

```
User.belongsToMany(models.Chat, { through: 'users_chats' });
```

Do the same for the `Chat` model, as follows:

```
Chat.belongsToMany(models.User, { through: 'users_chats' });
```

The `through` property tells Sequelize that the two models are related via the `users_chats` table. Normally, when you are not using Sequelize and are trying to select all users and chats merged in raw SQL, you need to maintain this association manually, and join the three tables on your own. Sequelize's querying and association capabilities are so complex, this is all done for you.

Rerun the migrations to let the changes take effect:

```
sequelize db:migrate --migrations-path src/server/migrations --config
src/server/config/index.js
```

The following screenshot shows how your database should look now:

| Table | Action | Rows | Type | Collation | Size | Overhead |
|---|---|---|---|---|---|---|
| Chats | Browse Structure Search Insert Empty Drop | 0 | InnoDB | utf8_general_ci | 16 KiB | - |
| Posts | Browse Structure Search Insert Empty Drop | 3 | InnoDB | utf8_general_ci | 32 KiB | - |
| SequelizeMeta | Browse Structure Search Insert Empty Drop | 5 | InnoDB | utf8_unicode_ci | 32 KiB | - |
| Users | Browse Structure Search Insert Empty Drop | 2 | InnoDB | utf8_general_ci | 16 KiB | - |
| users_chats | Browse Structure Search Insert Empty Drop | 0 | InnoDB | utf8_general_ci | 48 KiB | - |
| 5 tables | Sum | 10 | InnoDB | utf8_general_ci | 144 KiB | 0 B |

You should see two foreign key constraints in the relation view of the `users_chats` table. The naming is done automatically:

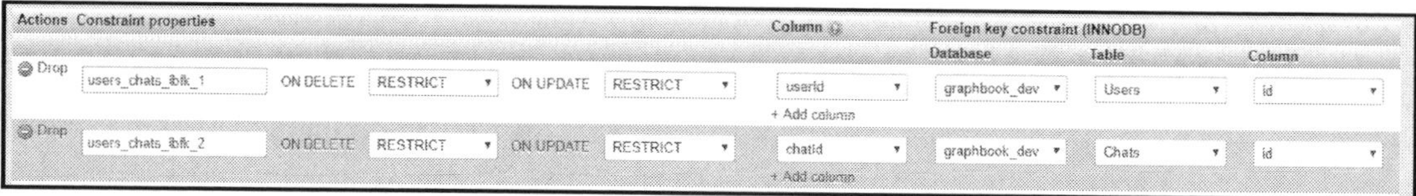


This setup was the tough part. Next up is the message entity, which is a simple one-to-one relationship. One message belongs to one user and one chat.

## Message model

A message is much like a post, except that it is only readable inside of a chat, and is not public to everyone.

Generate the model and migration file with the CLI, as follows:

```
sequelize model:generate --models-path src/server/models --migrations-path
src/server/migrations --name Message --attributes
text:string,userId:integer,chatId:integer
```

Add the missing references in the created migration file, as follows:

```
userId: {
  type: Sequelize.INTEGER,
  references: {
    model: 'Users',
    key: 'id'
  },
  onDelete: 'SET NULL',
  onUpdate: 'cascade',
```

```
},
chatId: {
  type: Sequelize.INTEGER,
  references: {
    model: 'Chats',
    key: 'id'
  },
  onDelete: 'cascade',
  onUpdate: 'cascade',
},
```

Now, we can run the migrations again, in order to create the `Messages` table using the `sequelize db:migrate` Terminal command.

```
{
  "operationName":null,
  "query": "mutation addPost($post : PostInput!) { addPost(post : $post) {
    id text user { username avatar }}}",
  "variables":{
    "post": {
      "text": "You just added a post."
    }
  }
}
```

The references also apply to our model file, where we need to use Sequelize's `belongsTo` function to get all of those convenient model methods for our resolvers. Replace the `associate` function of the `Message` model with the following code:

```
Message.associate = function(models) {
  Message.belongsTo(models.User);
  Message.belongsTo(models.Chat);
};
```

In the preceding code, we define that every message is related to exactly one user and chat.

On the other side, we must also associate the `Chat` model with the messages. Add the following code to the `associate` function of the `Chat` model:

```
Chat.hasMany(models.Message);
```

The next step is to adjust our GraphQL API to provide chats and messages.

## Chats and messages in GraphQL

We have introduced some new entities with messages and chats. Let's include those in our Apollo schema. In the following code, you can see an excerpt of the changed entities, fields, and parameters of our GraphQL schema:

```
type User {
  id: Int
  avatar: String
  username: String
}

type Post {
  id: Int
  text: String
  user: User
}

type Message {
  id: Int
  text: String
  chat: Chat
  user: User
}

type Chat {
  id: Int
  messages: [Message]
  users: [User]
}

type RootQuery {
  posts: [Post]
  chats: [Chat]
}
```

Take a look at the following short changelog of our GraphQL schema:

- The `User` type received an `id` field, thanks to our database.
- The `Message` type is entirely new. It has a text field like a typical message, and user and chat fields, which are requested from the referenced tables in the database model.

- The `Chat` type is also new. A chat has a list of messages that are returned as an array. These can be queried through the chat ID saved in the message table. Furthermore, a chat can have an unspecified number of users. The relationships between users and chats are saved in our separate join table, as stated previously. The interesting thing here is that our schema does not know anything about this table; it is just for our internal use, to save the data appropriately in our MySQL server.
- I have also added a new `RootQuery`, called `chats`. This query returns all of a user's chats.

These factors should be implemented in our resolvers, too. Our resolvers should look as follows:

```
Message: {
  user(message, args, context) {
    return message.getUser();
  },
  chat(message, args, context) {
    return message.getChat();
  },
},
Chat: {
  messages(chat, args, context) {
    return chat.getMessages({ order: [['id', 'ASC']] });
  },
  users(chat, args, context) {
    return chat.getUsers();
  },
},
RootQuery: {
  posts(root, args, context) {
    return Post.findAll({order: [['createdAt', 'DESC']]});
  },
  chats(root, args, context) {
    return User.findAll().then((users) => {
      if (!users.length) {
        return [];
      }

      const usersRow = users[0];

      return Chat.findAll({
        include: [{
          model: User,
          required: true,
          through: { where: { userId: usersRow.id } },
```

```
          },
          {
            model: Message,
          }],
        });
      });
    },
  },
```

Let's go through the changes, one by one, as follows:

1. I added the new `RootQuery`, called `chats`, to return all fields, as in our schema:
   - Until we get a working authentication, we will statically use the first user when querying for all chats.
   - We are using the `findAll` method of Sequelize and joining the users of any returned chat. For this, we use the `include` property of Sequelize on the user model within the `findAll` method. It runs a MySQL `JOIN`, and not a second `SELECT` query.
   - Setting the `include` statement to `required` runs an `INNER JOIN` and not a `LEFT OUTER JOIN`, by default. Any chat that does not match the condition in the `through` property is excluded. In our example, the condition is that the user ID has to match.
   - Lastly, we join all available messages for each chat in the same way, without any condition.
2. We added the `Chat` property to the resolvers object. There, we ran the `getMessages` and `getUsers` functions, to retrieve all of the joined data. All messages are sorted by the ID in ascending order (to show the latest message at the bottom of a chat window, for example).
3. We added the `Message` property to our resolvers.

It is important that we are using the new models here. We should not forget to extract them from the `db.models` object inside of the resolver function. It must look as follows:

```
const { Post, User, Chat, Message } = db.models;
```

After saving all of the files, you can start the backend (or, it should restart automatically).

You can send this GraphQL request to test the changes:

```
{
  "operationName":null,
  "query": "{ chats { id users { id } messages { id text user { id username
  } } } }",
  "variables":{}
}
```

The response should give us an empty `chats` array, as follows:

```
{
  "data": {
    "chats": []
  }
}
```

The empty array was returned because we do not have any chats or messages in our database. You will see how to fill it with data in the next section.

# Seeding many-to-many data

Testing our implementation requires data in our database. We have three new tables, so we will create three new seeders, in order to get some test data to work with.

Let's start with the chats, as follows:

```
sequelize seed:generate --name fake-chats --seeders-path src/server/seeders
```

Now, replace the new seeder file with the following code. Running the following code creates a chat in our database. We do not need more than two timestamps, because the chat ID is generated automatically:

```
'use strict';

module.exports = {
  up: (queryInterface, Sequelize) => {
    return queryInterface.bulkInsert('Chats', [{
      createdAt: new Date(),
      updatedAt: new Date(),
    }],
    {});
  },
  down: (queryInterface, Sequelize) => {
```

```
    return queryInterface.bulkDelete('Chats', null, {});
  }
};
```

Next, we insert the relation between two users and the new chat. We do this by creating two entries in the `users_chats` table where we reference them. Now, generate the boilerplate seed file, as follows:

```
sequelize seed:generate --name fake-chats-users-relations --seeders-path
src/server/seeders
```

Our seed should look much like the previous ones, as follows:

```
'use strict';

module.exports = {
  up: (queryInterface, Sequelize) => {
    const usersAndChats = Promise.all([
      queryInterface.sequelize.query(
        'SELECT id from Users;',
      ),
      queryInterface.sequelize.query(
        'SELECT id from Chats;',
      ),
    ]);
    return usersAndChats.then((rows) => {
      const users = rows[0][0];
      const chats = rows[1][0];

      return queryInterface.bulkInsert('users_chats', [{
        userId: users[0].id,
        chatId: chats[0].id,
        createdAt: new Date(),
        updatedAt: new Date(),
      },
      {
        userId: users[1].id,
        chatId: chats[0].id,
        createdAt: new Date(),
        updatedAt: new Date(),
      }],
      {});
    });
  },
  down: (queryInterface, Sequelize) => {
    return queryInterface.bulkDelete('users_chats', null, {});
  }
};
```

First, we resolve all users and chats by using `Promise.all`. This ensures that, when the promise is resolved, all of the chats and users are available at the same time. To test the chat functionality, we choose the first chat and the first two users returned from the database. We take their IDs and save them in our `users_chats` table. Those two users should be able to talk to each other through this one chat later on.

The last table without any data is the `Messages` table. Generate the seed file, as follows:

```
sequelize seed:generate --name fake-messages --seeders-path
src/server/seeders
```

Again, replace the generated boilerplate code, as follows:

```
'use strict';

module.exports = {
  up: (queryInterface, Sequelize) => {
    const usersAndChats = Promise.all([
      queryInterface.sequelize.query(
        'SELECT id from Users;',
      ),
      queryInterface.sequelize.query(
        'SELECT id from Chats;',
      ),
    ]);

    return usersAndChats.then((rows) => {
      const users = rows[0][0];
      const chats = rows[1][0];

      return queryInterface.bulkInsert('Messages', [{
        userId: users[0].id,
        chatId: chats[0].id,
        text: 'This is a test message.',
        createdAt: new Date(),
        updatedAt: new Date(),
      },
      {
        userId: users[1].id,
        chatId: chats[0].id,
        text: 'This is a second test message.',
        createdAt: new Date(),
        updatedAt: new Date(),
      },
      {
        userId: users[1].id,
        chatId: chats[0].id,
```

```
        text: 'This is a third test message.',
        createdAt: new Date(),
        updatedAt: new Date(),
      }],
      {});
    });
  },
  down: (queryInterface, Sequelize) => {
    return queryInterface.bulkDelete('Messages', null, {});
  }
};
```

Now, all of the seed files should be ready. It makes sense to empty all of the tables before running the seeds, so that you can work with clean data. I personally like to delete all tables in the database from time to time and rerun all of the migrations and seeds, in order to test them from zero. Whether or not you are doing this, you should at least be able to run the new seed.

Try to run the GraphQL `chats` query again, as follows:

```
{
  "data": {
    "chats": [{
      "id": 1,
      "users": [
        {
          "id": 1
        },
        {
          "id": 2
        }
      ],
      "messages": [
        {
          "id": 1,
          "text": "This is a test message.",
          "user": {
            "id": 1,
            "username": "Test User"
          }
        },
        {
          "id": 2,
          "text": "This is a second test message.",
          "user": {
            "id": 2,
            "username": "Test User 2"
```

```
            }
          },
          {
            "id": 3,
            "text": "This is a third test message.",
            "user": {
              "id": 2,
              "username": "Test User 2"
            }
          }
        ]}
      ]
    }
  }
```

Great! Now, we can request all of the chats that a user participates in, and get all referenced users and their messages.

Now, we also want to do that for only one chat. Follow these instructions to get it done:

1. Add a `RootQuery` chat that takes a `chatId` as a parameter:

   ```
   chat(root, { chatId }, context) {
     return Chat.findById(chatId, {
       include: [{
         model: User,
         required: true,
       },
       {
         model: Message,
       }],
     });
   },
   ```

   With this implementation, we have the problem that all users can send a query to our Apollo server, and in return, get the complete chat history, even if they are not referenced in the chat. We will not be able to fix this until we have implemented authentication.

2. Add the new query to the GraphQL schema, under `RootQuery`:

   ```
   chat(chatId: Int): Chat
   ```

3. Send the GraphQL request to test the implementation, as follows:

```
{
  "operationName":null,
  "query": "query($chatId: Int!){ chat(chatId: $chatId) {
    id users { id } messages { id text user { id username } } } }",
  "variables":{ "chatId": 1 }
}
```

We are sending this query, including the `chatId` as a parameter. To pass a parameter, you must define it in the query with its GraphQL data type. Then, you can set it in the specific GraphQL query that you are executing, which is the `chat` query, in our case. Lastly, you must insert the parameter's value in the `variables` field of the GraphQL request.

You may remember the response from the last time. The new response will look much like a result from the `chats` query, but instead of an array of chats, we will just have one `chat` object.

We are missing a major feature: sending new messages or creating a new chat. We will create the corresponding schema, and the resolvers for it, in the next section.

# Creating a new chat

New users want to chat with their friends. Creating a new chat is essential, of course.

The best way to do this is to accept a list of user IDs that also allows the creation of group chats. Do this as follows:

1. Add the `addChat` function to the `RootMutation` in the `resolvers.js` file, as follows:

```
addChat(root, { chat }, context) {
  logger.log({
    level: 'info',
    message: 'Message was created',
  });
  return Chat.create().then((newChat) => {
    return Promise.all([
      newChat.setUsers(chat.users),
    ]).then(() => {
      return newChat;
    });
  });
},
```

Sequelize added the `setUsers` function to the chat model instance. It was added because of the associations using the `belongsToMany` method in the chat model. There, we can directly provide an array of user IDs that should be associated with the new chat, through the `users_chats` table.

2. Change the schema so that you can run the GraphQL mutation. We have to add the new input type and mutation, as follows:

```
input ChatInput {
  users: [Int]
}

type RootMutation {
  addPost (
    post: PostInput!
  ): Post
  addChat (
    chat: ChatInput!
  ): Chat
}
```

3. Test the new GraphQL `addChat` mutation as your request body:

```
{
  "operationName":null,
  "query": "mutation addChat($chat: ChatInput!) { addChat(chat:
    $chat) { id users { id } }}",
  "variables":{
    "chat": {
      "users": [1, 2]
    }
  }
}
```

You can verify that everything worked by checking the users returned inside of the `chat` object.

## Creating a new message

We can use the `addPost` mutation as our basis, and extend it. The result accepts a `chatId` and uses the first user from our database. Later, the authentication will be the source of the user ID:

1. Add the `addMessage` function to the `RootMutation` in the `resolvers.js` file, as follows:

```
addMessage(root, { message }, context) {
  logger.log({
    level: 'info',
    message: 'Message was created',
  });

  return User.findAll().then((users) => {
    const usersRow = users[0];

    return Message.create({
      ...message,
    }).then((newMessage) => {
      return Promise.all([
        newMessage.setUser(usersRow.id),
        newMessage.setChat(message.chatId),
      ]).then(() => {
        return newMessage;
      });
    });
  });
},
```

2. Then, add the new mutation to your GraphQL schema. We also have a new input type for our messages:

```
input MessageInput {
  text: String!
  chatId: Int!
}

type RootMutation {
  addPost (
    post: PostInput!
  ): Post
  addChat (
    chat: ChatInput!
  ): Chat
  addMessage (
```

```
        message: MessageInput!
      ): Message
    }
```

3. You can send the request in the same way as the `addPost` request:

```
    {
        "operationName":null,
        "query": "mutation addMessage($message : MessageInput!) {
          addMessage(message : $message) { id text }}",
        "variables":{
          "message": {
            "text": "You just added a message.",
            "chatId": 1
          }
        }
    }
```

Now, everything is set. The client can now request all posts, chats, and messages. Furthermore, users can create new posts, create new chat rooms, and send chat messages.

# Summary

Our goal in this chapter was to create a working backend with a database as storage, which we have achieved pretty well. We can add further entities and migrate and seed them with Sequelize. Migrating our database changes won't be a problem for us when it comes to going into production.

In this chapter, we also covered what Sequelize automates for us when using its models, and how great it works in coordination with our Apollo Server.

In the next chapter, we will focus on how to use the Apollo React Client library with our backend, as well as the database behind it.

# 4
# Integrating React into the Back end with Apollo

Sequelize makes it easy to access and query our database. Posts, chats, and messages can be saved to our database in a snap. React helps us to view and update our data by building a user interface.

In this chapter, we will introduce Apollo's React client to our front end, in order to connect it with the back end. We will query, create, and update post data, using our front end.

This chapter will cover the following points:

- Installing and configuring Apollo Client
- Sending requests with GQL and Apollo's Query component
- Mutating data with Apollo
- Debugging with Apollo Client Developer Tools

## Setting up Apollo Client

We have tested our GraphQL API multiple times during development. We can now start to implement the data layer of our front end code. In later chapters, we will focus on other tasks, such as authentication and client-side routing. For now, we will aim to use our GraphQL API with our React app.

To start, we must install the React Apollo Client library. Apollo Client is a GraphQL client that offers excellent integration with React, and the ability to easily fetch data from our GraphQL API. Furthermore, it handles actions such as caching and subscriptions, to implement real-time communication with your GraphQL back end. Although Apollo Client is named after the Apollo brand, it is not tied to Apollo Server. You can use Apollo Client with any GraphQL API or schema out there, as long as they follow the protocol standards. You will soon see how perfectly the client merges with our React setup.

As always, there are many alternatives out there. You can use any GraphQL client that you wish with the current API that we have built. This openness is the great thing about GraphQL: it uses an open standard for communication. Various libraries implement the GraphQL standard, and you are free to use any of them.

The most well-known alternatives are Relay (which is made by Facebook), Lokka, and graphql-request (which is made by the people behind Prisma). All of these are great libraries that you are free to use. Personally, I mostly rely on Apollo, but Relay is highly recommended, as well. You can find a long list of packages related to the GraphQL ecosystem at `https://github.com/chentsulin/awesome-graphql`.

In addition to special client libraries, you could also just use the `fetch` method or `XMLHttpRequest` requests. The disadvantage is that you need to implement caching, write request objects, and integrate the request method into your application on your own. I do not recommend doing this, because it takes a lot of time, and you want to put that time into your business, not into implementing existing functionalities.

# Installing Apollo Client

We use `npm` to install our client dependencies, as follows:

```
npm install --save apollo-client apollo-cache-inmemory apollo-link-http
apollo-link-error apollo-link react-apollo
```

We need to install many packages just to get a simple GraphQL client, but fortunately each package is pretty small. Before we get started, let's introduce them one by one, as follows:

- `apollo-client` is the wrapping package for all of the packages that we installed. Apollo Client relies on all of the other packages.
- `apollo-cache-inmemory` is the package that manages all state and cache dynamics. This package no longer relies on Redux, unlike previous versions.

- `apollo-link-http` implements the methods to send your GraphQL request through HTTP. As mentioned in the previous chapters, you can also choose to use GraphQL with other transport layers.
- `apollo-link-error` handles all errors that occur during a request to Apollo. They can be network, schema, or other errors.
- `apollo-link` is an interface that the other link packages rely on. It allows them to adjust requests or responses according to your requirements.
- `react-apollo` manages the communication between the browser DOM and the virtual DOM of React. Any changes made to the what's called the shadow DOM of React are transferred to the real DOM. However, changes made to the real DOM are not transmitted to the React state.

You will see how these packages work together in this section. The great thing about this approach is that you can customize almost all parts of Apollo Client, according to your requirements.

An alternative approach is to use the `apollo-boost` package. By installing `apollo-boost`, you install all of the preceding packages at once. If you use this package, however, you can't customize your Apollo stack. It is more work to do it manually, but the benefits are worth it.

To get started with the manual setup of the Apollo Client, create a new folder and file for the client, as follows:

```
mkdir src/client/apollo
touch src/client/apollo/index.js
```

We will set up Apollo Client in this `index.js` file. Our first setup will represent the most basic configuration to get a working GraphQL client.

The following code was taken from the official Apollo documentation. Generally, I recommend reading through the Apollo documentation, as it is very well written: https://www.apollographql.com/docs/react/essentials/get-started.html

Just insert the following code:

```
import { ApolloClient } from 'apollo-client';
import { InMemoryCache } from 'apollo-cache-inmemory';
import { HttpLink } from 'apollo-link-http';
import { onError } from 'apollo-link-error';
import { ApolloLink } from 'apollo-link';

const client = new ApolloClient({
```

```
  link: ApolloLink.from([
    onError(({ graphQLErrors, networkError }) => {
      if (graphQLErrors) {
        graphQLErrors.map(({ message, locations, path }) =>
        console.log(`[GraphQL error]: Message: ${message}, Location:
        ${locations}, Path: ${path}`));
        if (networkError) {
          console.log(`[Network error]: ${networkError}`);
        }
      }
    }),
    new HttpLink({
      uri: 'http://localhost:8000/graphql',
    }),
  ]),
  cache: new InMemoryCache(),
});

export default client;
```

The preceding code uses all of the new packages, apart from `react-apollo`. Let's break down the code:

- First, at the top of the file, we imported nearly all of the packages that we installed.
- We instantiated `ApolloClient`. For this to work, we passed some parameters, which are the `link` and `cache` properties.
- The `link` property is filled by the `ApolloLink.from` command. This function walks through an array of links and initializes each of them, one by one:
    - The first link is the error link. It accepts a function that tells Apollo what should be done if an error occurs.
    - The second link is the HTTP link for Apollo. You have to offer a URI, under which our Apollo or GraphQL server is reachable. Apollo Client sends all requests to this URI. Notably, the order of execution is the same as the array that we just created.
- The `cache` property takes an implementation for caching. One implementation can be the default package, `InMemoryCache`, or a different cache.

There are many more properties that our links can understand (especially the HTTP link). They feature a lot of different customization options, which we will look at later. You can also find them in the official documentation, at `https://www.apollographql.com/docs/react/`.

In the preceding code we export the initialized Client using the `export default client` line. We are then able to use it in our React app.

The basic setup to send GraphQL request using the Apollo Client is finished. In the next section, we will send our first GraphQL request through Apollo Client.

# Testing the Apollo Client

Before inserting the GraphQL client directly into our React application tree, we should test it. This is also the next step in Apollo's official documentation. We will write some temporary code to send our first GraphQL query. After testing our GraphQL client, we will remove the code again. The easiest way to do this is to use the `graphl-tag` package:

1. First, install this package with `npm`, as follows:

```
npm install --save graphql-tag
```

2. Import the package at the top of the Apollo Client setup, as follows:

```
import gql from 'graphql-tag';
```

3. Then, add the following code before the client is exported:

```
client.query({
  query: gql`
    {
      posts {
        id
        text
        user {
          avatar
          username
        }
      }
    }`
}).then(result => console.log(result));
```

The preceding code is almost the same as the example from the Apollo documentation, but I have replaced their query with one that matches our back end.

Here, we used the `graphql-tag` package to parse a **template literal**. A template literal is just a multi-line string surrounded by two grace accents. The `gql` command parses this literal to an **abstract syntax tree (AST)**. Abstract syntax trees are the first step of GraphQL, they are used to validate deeply nested objects the schema and the query.

If you want to know more about ASTs, the people at Contentful wrote a great article about what ASTs mean to GraphQL, at `https://www.contentful.com/blog/2018/07/04/graphql-abstract-syntax-tree-new-schema/`.

The client sends our query after the parsing has completed. A great feature of `graphql-tag` is that it caches parsed queries and saves them for the next use.

To test the preceding code, we should start the server and the front end. One option is to build the front end now, and then start the server. In this case, the URL to browse the front end would be `http://localhost:8000`. A better option would be to spawn the server with `npm run server`, and then open a second terminal. Then, you can start the webpack development server by executing `npm run client`. A new browser tab should open automatically.

However, we have forgotten something: the client is set up in our new file, but it is not yet used anywhere. Import it in the `index.js` root file of our client React app, below the import of the `App` class:

```
import client from './apollo';
```

The browser should be reloaded, and the query sent. You should be able to see a new log inside the console of the developer tools of your browser.

The output should look like the following screenshot:

```
▼ {data: {…}, loading: false, networkStatus: 7, stale: false}
  ▼ data:
    ▼ posts: Array(2)
      ▼ 0:
          id: 1
          text: "Lorem ipsum 1"
        ▼ user:
            avatar: "/uploads/avatar1.png"
            username: "Test User"
            __typename: "User"
            Symbol(id): "$Post:1.user"
          ► __proto__: Object
          __typename: "Post"
          Symbol(id): "Post:1"
        ► __proto__: Object
      ▼ 1:
          id: 2
          text: "Lorem ipsum 2"
        ▼ user:
            avatar: "/uploads/avatar2.png"
            username: "Test User 2"
            __typename: "User"
            Symbol(id): "$Post:2.user"
          ► __proto__: Object
          __typename: "Post"
          Symbol(id): "Post:2"
        ► __proto__: Object
        length: 2
      ► __proto__: Array(0)
      Symbol(id): "ROOT_QUERY"
    ► __proto__: Object
    loading: false
    networkStatus: 7
    stale: false
  ► __proto__: Object
```

The `data` object looks much like the response that we received when sending requests through Postman, except that, now, it has some new properties: `loading`, `networkStatus`, and `stale`. Each of these stands for a specific status, as follows:

- `loading`, as you might expect, indicates whether the query is still running or has already finished.
- `networkStatus` goes beyond this and gives you the exact status of what happened. For example, the number seven indicates that there are no running queries that produce errors. The number eight means that there has been an error. You can look up the other numbers in the official GitHub repository, at `https://github.com/apollographql/apollo-client/blob/master/packages/apollo-client/src/core/networkStatus.ts`.
- `stale` is set whenever data is missing and is only partially available to the user.

Now that we have verified that the query has run successfully, we can connect Apollo Client to the React DOM. Please remove the temporary code that we wrote in this section before continuing. This includes everything except the import statement in the `App.js` file.

# Binding the Apollo Client to React

We have tested Apollo Client, and have confirmed that it works. However, React does not yet have access to it. Since Apollo Client is going to be used everywhere in our application, we can set it up in our root `index.js` file, as follows:

```
import React from 'react';
import ReactDOM from 'react-dom';
import { ApolloProvider } from 'react-apollo';
import App from './App';
import client from './apollo';

ReactDOM.render(
  <ApolloProvider client={client}>
    <App />
  </ApolloProvider>, document.getElementById('root')
);
```

As we mentioned in `Chapter 1`, *Preparing Your Development Environment*, you should only edit this file when the whole application needs access to the new component. In the preceding code, you can see that we import the last package that we installed at the beginning, with `react-apollo`. The `ApolloProvider` that we extracted from it is the first layer of our React application. It surrounds the `App` class, passing the Apollo Client that we wrote to the next level. To do this, we pass the `client` to the provider as a property. Every underlying React component can now access the Apollo Client.

We should be now able to send GraphQL requests from our React app.

# Using the Apollo Client in React

The Apollo Client gives us everything that we need to send requests from our React components. We have already tested that the client works. Before moving on, we should clean up our file structure, in order to make it easier for us later in the development process. Our front end is, at the moment, still displaying posts that come from static demo data. The first step is to move over to the Apollo Client and fetch the data from our GraphQL API.

Follow the instructions below to connect your first React component with the Apollo Client:

1. Clone the `App.js` file to another file, called `Feed.js`.
2. Remove all parts where React `Helmet` is used, and rename the class `Feed`, instead of `App`.
3. From the `App.js` file, remove all of the parts that we have left in the `Feed` class.
4. Furthermore, we must render the `Feed` class inside of the `App` class. It should like the following code:

```
import React, { Component } from 'react';
import { Helmet } from 'react-helmet';
import Feed from './Feed';
import '../../assets/css/style.css';

export default class App extends Component {
  render() {
    return (
      <div className="container">
        <Helmet>
          <title>Graphbook - Feed</title>
          <meta name="description" content="Newsfeed of all your
           friends on Graphbook" />
        </Helmet>
        <Feed />
      </div>
    )
  }
}
```

The corresponding `Feed` class should only include the parts where the news feed is rendered.

We imported the `Feed` class and inserted it inside of the `render` method of our `App` class, so that it is rendered. The next chapter focuses on reusable React components, and how to write well-structured React code. Now, let's take a look at why we split our `App` class into two separate files.

# Querying in React with the Apollo Client

There are two main approaches offered by Apollo that can be used to request data. The first one is a **higher-order component (HoC)**, provided by the `react-apollo` package. The second one is the `Query` component of Apollo, which is a special React component. Both approaches have their advantages and disadvantages.

## Apollo HoC query

A higher-order component is a function that takes a component as input and returns a new component. This method is used in many cases wherein we have multiple components all relying on the same functionalities, such as querying for data. In these cases, you extract the logic to query for data in a separate function, which extends the original components and enables them to fetch their data. The necessary properties are passed to the component by a higher-order function.

If you are not familiar with higher-order components, you should read up on them. The official React documentation provides you with the essential information at `https://reactjs.org/docs/higher-order-components.html`.

To see a real example of this, we use the `posts` feed. Follow these instructions to get a working Apollo Query HoC:

1. Remove the demo posts from the top of the `Feed.js` file.
2. Remove the `posts` field from the state initializer.
3. Import `graphl-tag` and parse our query with it, as follows:

```
import gql from 'graphql-tag';
import { graphql } from 'react-apollo';

const GET_POSTS = gql`{
  posts {
    id
    text
    user {
      avatar
      username
    }
  }
}`;
```

4. Replace everything in the `render` function, before the final `return` statement, with the following code:

```
const { posts, loading, error } = this.props;
const { postContent } = this.state;

if(loading) {
  return "Loading...";
}
if(error) {
  return error.message;
}
```

   Note that the `render` function is now very clean, as it was before. It only includes and renders the markup and the loop over the posts.

5. Remove the `export` statement from the `Feed` class. We will export the new component returned from the HoC at the end of the file. The export must look as follows:

```
export default graphql(GET_POSTS, {
  props: ({ data: { loading, error, posts } }) => ({
    loading,
    posts,
    error
  })
})(Feed)
```

Notably, we also imported the `graphql` HoC function from the `react-apollo` package. This function accepts the actual GraphQL query that we want to send as the first parameter. The second parameter allows us to map the result of the HoC to specific properties of the child component, which is our `Feed` class. The `posts`, `loading`, and `error` parameters are passed as properties to the `Feed` component, via the HoC. This separates the rendering logic from the data fetching. The last parameter is the `Feed` class (the component that is processed by the HoC). We pass it to a new function call, which is the result of the `graphql` function. We do not pass it as the third parameter of the `graphql` function.

This approach is my favorite solution to query data from a GraphQL API through Apollo. However, I would recommend that you use a different solution, which we will look at in the following section.

## The Apollo Query component

We will now take a look at the second approach, which is also the approach of the official Apollo documentation. Before getting started, undo the HoC implementation to send requests from the previous section. The new way of fetching data through the Apollo Client is via `render` props, or `render` functions. These were introduced to the Apollo Client in March 2018, and they replaced the good old HoC process.

Take a look at the official React documentation about render props, because this is not a particularly easy topic: `https://reactjs.org/docs/render-props.html`

Now, follow these instructions to get the `Query` component running:

1. Remove the demo posts from the top of the `Feed.js` file.
2. Remove the `posts` from the state and stop extracting them from the component state in the `render` method, too.
3. Import the `Query` component from the `react-apollo` package and `graphl-tag`, as follows:

```
import gql from 'graphql-tag';
import { Query } from 'react-apollo';

const GET_POSTS = gql`{
  posts {
    id
    text
    user {
      avatar
      username
    }
  }
}`;
```

4. The `Query` component can now be rendered. The only parameter, for now, is the parsed query that we want to send. Replace the complete `render` method with the following code:

```
render() {
  const { postContent } = this.state;

  return (
    <div className="container">
      <div className="postForm">
```

```
            <form onSubmit={this.handleSubmit}>
              <textarea value={postContent} onChange=
              {this.handlePostContentChange} placeholder="Write your
               custom post!"/>
              <input type="submit" value="Submit" />
            </form>
          </div>
          <div className="feed">
            <Query query={GET_POSTS}>
              {({ loading, error, data }) => {
                if (loading) return "Loading...";
                if (error) return error.message;

                const { posts } = data;
                return posts.map((post, i) =>
                  <div key={post.id} className="post">
                    <div className="header">
                      <img src={post.user.avatar} />
                      <h2>{post.user.username}</h2>
                    </div>
                    <p className="content">
                      {post.text}
                    </p>
                  </div>
                )
              }}
            </Query>
          </div>
        </div>
      )
    }
```

In the preceding code, you can see why I prefer not to use this approach. The `Query` component requires a function as its child. This function receives three properties—`loading`, `error`, and `data`—much like with the HoC approach. Inside of this function, you can handle whatever you want to render. If the `posts` request is successful, we render the posts feed as before.

You may think that you could render a component directly, as a child instead of as a function, as with the higher-order component, but this is not possible. Apollo requires us to specify a function, not a React component, as a child.

In my opinion, this is a dirty way of rendering and requesting data. It moves away from the standard component workflow of React. The React community, however, prefers render props, which is why it was implemented in Apollo Client. To improve this, you can write separate components for each `Query` or `Mutation` component that you use. Then, you can hand over all of the properties given by our Apollo components to our custom ones. This way, the `render` function is more readable when using the `Query` component. You will see this solution soon.

We will continue to use the `Query` and `Mutation` components, as this is the default way of writing GraphQL requests in the latest versions of Apollo Client.

There are some great comparisons between the solutions on Medium: `https://medium.com/@dai_shi/the-nice-query-component-in-react-apollo-2-1-688e50e03893`

No matter which approach you take, the rendered output should look like that in `Chapter 1`, *Preparing Your Development Environment*. The form to create a new post is not working at the moment because of our changes; let's fix this in the next section.

# Mutations with the Apollo Client

We have replaced the way that we get the data in our client. The next step is to switch the way that we create new posts, too. Before Apollo Client, we had to add the new fake posts to the array of demo posts manually, within the memory of the browser. Now, everything in our text area is sent with the `addPost` mutation to our GraphQL API, through Apollo Client.

As with GraphQL queries, there is a `Mutation` component that we are going to use. We are also going to compare it to the HoC method. To keep up the comparisons between them, we will start with the HoC method. Both approaches are valid ways to do this; there is nothing that is vastly different between them behind the scenes.

Let's start with the higher-order component approach.

# The Apollo Mutation HoC

The complete HoC workflow requires you to have the HoC `Query` method set up, too. Otherwise, you won't be able to see why this approach has some advantages over the other one.

So, if you have undone the `Query` HoC, you should insert the code again, in order to test the mutation HoC. You can also skip to the next section, where you will learn how to use the `Mutation` component.

Follow these instructions to set up the mutation HoC:

1. Import the `compose` method from the `react-apollo` package, as follows:

```
import { graphql, compose } from 'react-apollo';
```

2. Add the `addPost` mutation and parse it with `graphql-tag`:

```
const ADD_POST = gql`
  mutation addPost($post : PostInput!) {
    addPost(post : $post) {
      id
      text
      user {
        username
        avatar
      }
    }
  }
`;
```

3. We will adjust the way that the `Feed` class is exported. In the first HoC example, we had the `graphql` method, which sent the GraphQL query and inserted that response data into the underlying `Feed` component. Now, we will use the `compose` function of `react-apollo`, which takes a set of GraphQL queries, or mutations. These are run or passed as functions to the component. Add the following code to the bottom, and remove the old `export` statement:

```
const ADD_POST_MUTATION = graphql(ADD_POST, {
  name: 'addPost'
});

const GET_POSTS_QUERY = graphql(GET_POSTS, {
  props: ({ data: { loading, error, posts } }) => ({
    loading,
    posts,
```

```
      error
    })
  });

  export default compose(GET_POSTS_QUERY, ADD_POST_MUTATION)(Feed);
```

Instead of using the `graphql` method directly on the `Feed` component, we first save the mutation and query in two separate variables. The mutation takes a parameter, `name`, which says that the mutation can be run under the name `addPost`, inside of the `Feed` component. The query looks similar to the query that we used in the previous section. The `compose` method takes both variables and connects them with the `Feed` component. All of the queries are directly executed, if not specified differently. All mutations are passed as functions to the component to be run programmatically.

4. Our form works as expected. Every piece of text that you enter in the text area is saved to the state of the component. When submitting the form, we want to send the `addPost` mutation with the Apollo Client. The `addPost` function is available under the properties of the `Feed` component, as we specified it in the preceding code. When giving a `variables` object as a parameter, we can fill in our input fields in the mutation, as is expected by our GraphQL schema:

```
handleSubmit = (event) => {
  const self = this;
  event.preventDefault();
  const newPost = {
    text: this.state.postContent
  };
  this.props.addPost({ variables: { post: newPost }}).then(() => {
    self.setState((prevState) => ({
      postContent: ''
    }));
  });
}
```

The code looks very clean when using the HoC approach. We first parse all of the queries. Then, we define our class, including the `render` method, which we haven't touched at all. Finally, we define the two GraphQL requests that we are going to send, and export the constructed component. The code is very readable.

If you try to add a new post through the front end, you won't be able to see it immediately. The form will be empty, and everything will look as though it should have worked, but the new post will not be shown. This happens because the current state (or cache) of our component has not yet received the new post. The easiest way to test that everything has worked is to refresh the browser.

Of course, this is not the way that it should work. After the mutation has been sent, the new post should be directly visible in the feed. We will fix this after we have had a look at the second approach, which uses the `Mutation` component.

# The Apollo Mutation component

The `Mutation` component is very similar to the `Query` component. Be sure to undo the HoC solution changes before continuing. Follow these steps to get the `Mutation` component running:

1. Import the `Mutation` component from the `react-apollo` package, as follows:

```
import { Query, Mutation } from 'react-apollo';
```

2. Export the `Feed` component again, as we did in the previous `Query` component example. Remove the `ADD_POST_MUTATION` and `GET_POSTS_QUERY` variables when doing so:

```
export default class Feed extends Component
```

3. Next, add the `Mutation` component inside of the `render` function. We will surround the form with this component, as this is the only part of our content where we need to send a mutation:

```
render() {
  const self = this;
  const { postContent } = this.state;

  return (
    <Query query={GET_POSTS}>
      {({ loading, error, data }) => {
        if (loading) return <p>Loading...</p>;
        if (error) return error.message;

        const { posts } = data;

        return (
```

```
                <div className="container">
                  <div className="postForm">
                    <Mutation mutation={ADD_POST}>
                      {addPost => (
                        <form onSubmit={e => {
                          e.preventDefault();
                          addPost({ variables: { post: { text:
                            postContent
                          } } }).then(() => {
                            self.setState((prevState) => ({
                              postContent: ''
                            }));
                          });
                        }}>
                        <textarea value={postContent} onChange=
                        {self.handlePostContentChange} placeholder="Write
                        your custom post!"/>
                        <input type="submit" value="Submit" />
                      </form>
                    )}
                  </Mutation>
                </div>
                <div className="feed">
                  {posts.map((post, i) =>
                      <div key={post.id} className="post">
                        <div className="header">
                          <img src={post.user.avatar} />
                          <h2>{post.user.username}</h2>
                        </div>
                        <p className="content">
                          {post.text}
                        </p>
                      </div>
                    )}
                  </div>
                </div>
              )
            }}
          </Query>
        )
      }
```

The surrounded form now directly implements the `onSubmit` function. We could also extract this to a separate class method, but it is working this way. The `Mutation` component accepts the `mutation` property, which receives the GraphQL request that we want to send. The form can access the `addPost` function, which is exposed inside of the `render` prop function.

The `render` function is now more complex than it was before. In my opinion, the HoC solution looks much cleaner, despite the advantages that this solution might have. In the next chapter, we will look at how to make this more readable and reusable. No matter which approach you choose, the result will be the same.

You can now try out the `Mutation` component by submitting a new post. Our feed does not show the post until we refresh the browser again. In the next section, we will look at how to fix this issue.

# Updating the UI with the Apollo Client

After running the `addPost` mutation, the request goes through to the server and saves the new post in our database without any problems. However, we still cannot see the changes take effect in the front end immediately.

In this introduction to direct cache access and refetching, we will focus on the new standard `Query` and `Mutation` components. If you, like me, prefer HoCs, there are many tutorials that cover how to update the UI when using HoCs.

There are two different ways to update the UI after a mutation:

- **Refetching the dataset**: This is easy to implement, but it refetches all of the data, which is inefficient.
- **Updating the cache according to the inserted data**: This is harder to understand and implement, but it attaches the new data to the cache of the Apollo Client, so no refetching is needed.

We use these solutions in different scenarios. Let's take a look at some examples. Refetching makes sense if further logic is implemented on the server, which is hidden from the client when requesting a list of items, and which is not applied when inserting only one item. In these cases, the client cannot simulate the state of the typical response of a server.

Updating the cache, however, makes sense when adding or updating items in a list, like our post feed. The client can insert the new post at the top of the feed.

We will start by simply refetching requests, and then we'll go over the cache update implementation. The following sections (and chapters) will assume that you are not using the HoC method.

## Refetching queries

As mentioned previously, this is the easiest method to update your user interface. The only step is to set an array of queries to be refetched. The `Mutation` component should look as follows:

```
<Mutation
  refetchQueries={[{query: GET_POSTS}]}
```

Each object that you enter in the `refetchQueries` array needs a `query` property. Each component relying on one of those requests is rerendered when the response for its associated query arrives. It also includes components that are not inside of the `Feed` class. All components using the post's `GET_POSTS` query are rerendered.

You can also provide more fields to each query, such as variables to send parameters with the re-fetch request. Submitting the form resends the query, and you can see the new post directly in the feed. Refetching also reloads the posts that are already showing, which is unnecessary.

Now, let's take a look at how we can do this more efficiently.

## Updating the Apollo cache

We want to explicitly add only the new post to the cache of the Apollo Client. Using the cache helps us to save data, by not refetching the complete feed or rerendering the complete list. To update the cache, you should remove the `refetchQueries` property. You can then introduce a new property, called `update`, as shown in the following code:

```
<Mutation
  update = {(store, { data: { addPost } }) => {
    const data = store.readQuery({ query: GET_POSTS });
    data.posts.unshift(addPost);
    store.writeQuery({ query: GET_POSTS, data });
  }}
```

The new property runs when the GraphQL `addPost` mutation has finished. The first parameter that it receives is the `store` of the Apollo Client, in which the whole cache is saved. The second parameter is the returned response of our GraphQL API.

Updating the cache works as follows:

1. Use the `store.readQuery` function by passing a `query` as a parameter. It reads the data, which has been saved for this specific query inside of the cache. The `data` variable holds all of the posts that we have in our feed.
2. Now that we have all of the posts in an array, we can add the missing post. Make sure that you know whether you need to prepend or append an item. In our example, we want to insert a post at the top of our list, so we need to prepend it. You can use the `unshift` JavaScript function to do this. We just set our `addPost` as the first item of the `data.posts` array.
3. We need to save the changes back to the cache. The `store.writeQuery`.The function accepts the query which we used to send the request. This query is used to update the saved data in our cache. .second parameter is the data that should be saved.
4. When the cache has been updated, our user interface reactively renders the changes.

In reality, you can do whatever you want in the `update` function, but we only use it to update the Apollo Client store.

We wait for the response to arrive, and then push the new item to the list afterward. In the next section, we will be a bit more optimistic about the response of our server, and will add the item before the request's response successfully arrives.

# Optimistic UI

Apollo provides the great feature of being able to update the UI in an optimistic manner. An optimistic manner means that Apollo adds the new data or post to the storage before the request has finished. The advantage is that the user can see the new result, instead of waiting for the response of the server. This solution makes the application feel faster and more responsive.

This section expects the `update` function of the `Mutation` component to already be implemented. Otherwise, this UI feature will not work. We need to add the `optimisticResponse` property to our mutation, as follows:

```
optimisticResponse= {{
  __typename: "mutation",
  addPost: {
    __typename: "Post",
    text: postContent,
```

```
      id: -1,
      user: {
        __typename: "User",
        username: "Loading...",
        avatar: "/public/loading.gif"
      }
    }
  }}
```

The `optimisticResponse` can be anything from a function to a simple object. The return value, however, needs to be a GraphQL response object. What you see here is an `addPost` object that looks like our GraphQL API could return it, if our request is successful. You need to fill in the `__typename` fields, according to the GraphQL schema that you are using. That is why the type names `Post` and `User` are inside of this fake object.

The `id` of the optimistic response is set to minus one. React expects that every component in a loop gets a unique `key`. We usually use the id of a post as the key. Minus one is never used by any other post, because MySQL starts counting at one. Another advantage is that we can use this id to set a special class to the post item in our list.

Furthermore, the username and the user's avatar are set to `loading`. That is because we don't have built-in authentication. React and Apollo do not have a user associated with the current session, so we cannot enter the user's data into the `optimisticResponse`. We fix this once the authentication is ready. This is an excellent example of how to handle a situation in which you do not have all of the data until you receive a response from the server.

To set a particular class on the list item, we conditionally set the correct `className` in our `map` loop. Insert the following code into the `render` method:

```
{posts.map((post, i) =>
  <div key={post.id} className={'post ' + (post.id < 0 ? 'optimistic':
    '')}>
    <div className="header">
      <img src={post.user.avatar} />
      <h2>{post.user.username}</h2>
    </div>
    <p className="content">
      {post.text}
    </p>
  </div>
)}
```

An example CSS style for this might look as follows:

```
.optimistic {
  -webkit-animation: scale-up 0.4s cubic-bezier(0.390, 0.575, 0.565, 1.000)
    both;
  animation: scale-up 0.4s cubic-bezier(0.390, 0.575, 0.565, 1.000) both;
}

@-webkit-keyframes scale-up {
  0% {
    -webkit-transform: scale(0.5);
    transform: scale(0.5);
  }
  100% {
    -webkit-transform: scale(1);
    transform: scale(1);
  }
}

@keyframes scale-up {
  0% {
    -webkit-transform: scale(0.5);
    transform: scale(0.5);
  }
  100% {
    -webkit-transform: scale(1);
    transform: scale(1);
  }
}
```

CSS animations make your applications more modern and flexible. If you experience issues when viewing these in your browser, you may need to check whether your browser supports them.

You can see the result in the following screenshot:

Loading...

This is a test post!

The loading spinner and the username are removed once the response arrives from our API, and the `update` function is executed again with the real data. You do not need to take care of removing the loading post yourself; it is done by Apollo automatically. Any spinner component from an npm package or GIF file can be used where I have inserted the loading animation. The file that I am using needs to be saved under the `public` folder, with the name `loading.gif`, so that it can be used through the CSS that we added in the preceding code.

Everything is now set up for sending new posts. The user interface responds immediately, and shows you the new post.

However, what about new posts from your friends and colleagues? Currently, you need to reload the page to see them, which is not very intuitive. At the moment, we only add the posts that we send on our own, but do not receive any information about new posts from other people. I will show you the quickest way to handle this in the following section.

## Polling with the Query component

**Polling** is nothing more than rerunning a request after a specified interval. This procedure is the simplest way to implement real-time updates for our news feed. However, multiple issues are associated with polling, as follows:

- It is inefficient to send requests without knowing whether there is any new data. The browser might send dozens of requests without ever receiving a new post.
- If we directly send the initial request again, we will get all of the posts, including those that we are already showing to the user.
- When sending requests, the server needs to query the database and calculate everything. Unnecessary requests cost money and time.

There are some use cases in which polling makes sense. One example is a real-time graph, in which every axis tick is displayed to the user, whether there is data or not. You do not need to use an interrupt-based solution, since you want to show everything. Despite the issues that come with polling, let's quickly run through how it works. All you need to do is fill in the `pollInterval` property, as follows:

```
<Query query={GET_POSTS} pollInterval={5000}>
```

The `Query` component looks like the preceding code. The request is resent every 5 seconds (5,000 milliseconds).

As you might expect, there are other ways to implement real-time updates to your user interface. One approach is to use **server-sent events**. A server-sent event is as the name suggests: an event that is sent by the server to the client. The client needs to establish a connection to the server, but then the server can send messages to the client, in one direction. Another method is to use **WebSockets**, which allow for bidirectional communication between the server and the client. The most common method, however, is to use **Apollo Subscriptions**. They are based on Websockets, and work perfectly with GraphQL. I will show you how Apollo Subscriptions work in `Chapter 10`, *Real Time subscriptions*.

Let's continue and integrate the rest of our GraphQL API.

# Implementing chats and messages

In the previous chapter, we programmed a pretty dynamic way of creating chats and messages with your friends and colleagues, either one-on-one or in a group. There are some things that we have not discussed yet, such as authentication, real-time subscriptions, and friend relationships. First, however, we are going to work on our new skills, using React with Apollo Client to send GraphQL requests. It is a complicated task, so let's get started.

# Fetching and displaying chats

Our news feed is working as we expected. Now, we also want to cover chats. As with our feed, we need to query for every chat that the current user (or, in our case, the first user) is associated with.

The initial step is to get the rendering working with some demo chats. Instead of writing the data on our own, as we did in the first chapter, we can now execute the `chats` query. Then, we can copy the result into the new file as static demo data, before writing the real `Query` component.

Let's get started, as follows:

1. Send the GraphQL query. The best options involve Apollo Client Developer Tools, if you already know how they work. Otherwise, you can rely on Postman, as you did previously:

```
query {
  chats {
    id
    users {
```

```
            avatar
            username
          }
        }
      }
```

The request looks a bit different from the one we tested with Postman. The chat panel that we are going to build only needs specific data. We do not need to render any messages inside of this panel, so we don't need to request them. A complete chat panel only requires the chat itself, the id, the usernames, and the avatars. Later, we will retrieve all of the messages, too, when viewing a single chat.

Next, create a new file called `Chats.js`, next to the `Feed.js` file.

Copy the complete response over to an array inside of the `Chats.js` file, as follows. Add it to the top of the file:

```
const chats = [{
  "id": 1,
  "users": [{
      "id": 1,
      "avatar": "/uploads/avatar1.png",
      "username": "Test User"
    },
    {
      "id": 2,
      "avatar": "/uploads/avatar2.png",
      "username": "Test User 2"
    }]
  }
];
```

2. Import React ahead of the `chats` variable. Otherwise, we will not be able to render any React components:

```
import React, { Component } from 'react';
```

3. Set up the React `Component`. I have provided the basic markup here. Just copy it beneath the `chats` variable. I am going to explain the logic of the new component shortly:

```
export default class Chats extends Component {
  usernamesToString(users) {
    const userList = users.slice(1);
    var usernamesString = '';
```

```
    for(var i = 0; i < userList.length; i++) {
      usernamesString += userList[i].username;
      if(i - 1 === userList.length) {
        usernamesString += ', ';
      }
    }
    return usernamesString;
  }
  shorten(text) {
    if (text.length > 12) {
      return text.substring(0, text.length - 9) + '...';
    }

    return text;
  }
  render() {
    return (
      <div className="chats">
        {chats.map((chat, i) =>
          <div key={chat.id} className="chat">
            <div className="header">
              <img src={(chat.users.length > 2 ?
                '/public/group.png' : chat.users[1].avatar)} />
              <div>
                <h2>{this.shorten(this.usernamesToString(chat.users
                  ))}</h2>
              </div>
            </div>
          </div>
        )}
      </div>
    )
  }
}
```

The component is pretty basic, at the moment. In the `render` method, we `map` over all of the chats, and return a new list item for each chat. Each list item has an image, which is taken from the second user of the array, since we defined that the first user in the list is the current user, as long as we have not implemented authentication. We use a group icon if there are more than two users. When we have implemented authentication, and we know the logged-in user, we can take the specific avatar of the user that we are chatting with.

The title displayed inside of the `h2` tag at the top of the chat is the name (or names) of the user(s). For this, I have implemented the `usernamesToString` method, which loops over all of the usernames and concatenates them into a long string. The result is passed into the `shorten` function, which removes all of the characters of the string that exceed the size of the maximum-twelve characters.

4. Our new component needs some styling. Copy the new CSS to our `style.css` file.

To save the file size in our CSS file, replace the two `post header` styles to also cover the style of the chats, as follows:

```
.post .header > *, .chats .chat .header > * {
  display: inline-block;
  vertical-align: middle;
}

.post .header img, .chats .chat .header img {
  width: 50px;
  margin: 5px;
}
```

We must append the following CSS to the bottom of the `style.css` file:

```
.chats {
  background-color: #eee;
  width: 200px;
  height: 100%;
  position: fixed;
  top: 0;
  right: 0;
  border-left: 1px solid #c3c3c3;
}

.chats .chat {
  cursor: pointer;
}

.chats .chat .header > div {
  width: calc(100% - 65px);
  font-size: 16px;
  margin-left: 5px;
}

.chats .chat .header h2, .chats .chat .header span {
  color: #333;
```

```
    font-size: 16px;
    margin: 0;
  }

  .chats .chat .header span {
    color: #333;
    font-size: 12px;
  }
```

5. To get the code working, we must also import the `Chats` class in our `App.js` file:

   ```
   import Chats from './Chats';
   ```

6. Render the `Chats` class inside of the `render` method, beneath the `Feed` class inside of the `App.js` file.

The current code generates the following screenshot:

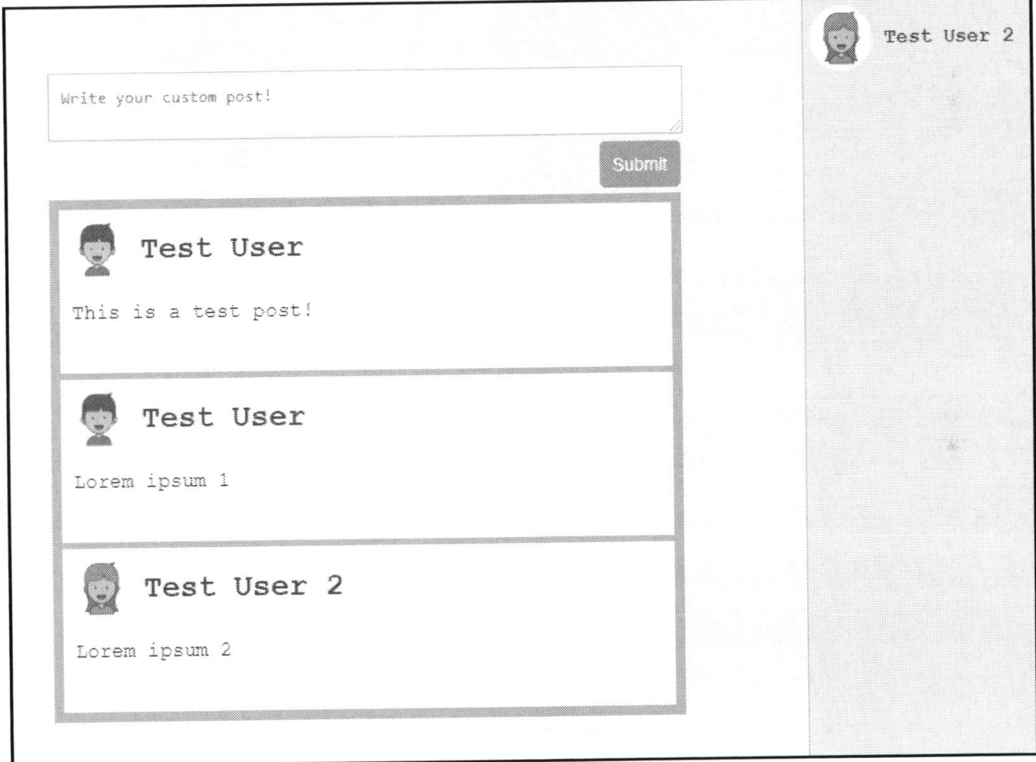


source: https://www.vecteezy.com/

On the right-hand side, you can see the chats panel that we have just implemented. Every chat is listed there as a separate row.

The result isn't bad, but it would be much more helpful to at least have the last message of every chat beneath the username, so that you could directly see the last content of your conversations.

Just follow these instructions to get the last message into the chats panel:

1. The easiest way to do this would be to add the messages to our query again, but querying all of the messages for every chat that we wanted to display in the panel would not make much sense. Instead, we will add a new property to the chat entity, called `lastMessage`. That way, we will only get the newest message. We will add the new field to the GraphQL schema of our chat type, in the back end code, as follows:

```
lastMessage: Message
```

Of course, we must also implement a function that retrieves the `lastMessage` field.

2. Our new `resolvers.js` function orders all of the chat messages by id, and takes the first one. By definition, this should be the latest message in our chat. We need to resolve the promise on our own and return the first element of the array, since we expect to return only one message object. If you return the promise directly, you will receive `null` in the response from the server, because an array is not a valid response for a single message entity:

```
lastMessage(chat, args, context) {
  return chat.getMessages({limit: 1, order: [['id',
'DESC']]}).then((message) => {
    return message[0];
  });
},
```

3. You can add the new property to our static data, inside of `Chats.js`. Rerunning the query (as we did in step 1) would also be possible:

```
"lastMessage": {
  "text": "This is a third test message."
}
```

4. We can render the new message with a simple `span` tag beneath the `h2` of the username. Copy it directly into the `render` method, inside of our `Chats` class:

```
<span>{this.shorten(chat.lastMessage.text)}</span>
```

The result of the preceding changes renders every chat row with the last message inside of the chat. This looks like the following screenshot:

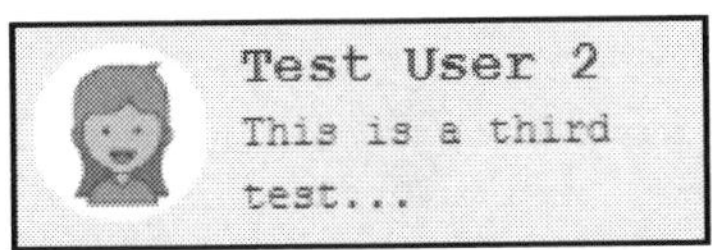


source: https://www.vecteezy.com/

If you are not that happy with the design, feel free to change it as you wish. As I am not a designer, I won't put too much effort into it.

Since everything is displayed correctly from our test data, we can introduce the `Query` component, in order to fetch all of the data from our GraphQL API. We can remove the `chats` array. Then, we will import all of the dependencies and parse the GraphQL query, as in the following code:

```
import gql from 'graphql-tag';
import { Query } from 'react-apollo';

const GET_CHATS = gql`{
  chats {
    id
    users {
      id
      avatar
      username
    }
    lastMessage {
      text
    }
  }
}`;
```

Our new `render` method does not change much. We just include the Apollo `Query` component, as follows:

```
<div className="chats">
  <Query query={GET_CHATS}>
    {({ loading, error, data }) => {
      if (loading) return <p>Loading...</p>;
      if (error) return error.message;

      const { chats } = data;
      return chats.map((chat, i) =>
        <div key={"chat" + chat.id} className="chat">
          <div className="header">
            <img src={(chat.users.length > 2 ? '/public/group.png' :
             chat.users[1].avatar)} />
            <div>
              <h2>{this.shorten(this.usernamesToString(chat.users))}
              </h2>
              <span>{chat.lastMessage &&
              this.shorten(chat.lastMessage.text)}</span>
            </div>
          </div>
        </div>
      )
    }}
  </Query>
</div>
```

Be sure to render the `div` with the `chats` class name first, and after that, the chat loop function. The reason for this is that we want to show the user the gray panel, with a loading indicator. If you do it the other way round, the gray panel will be displayed when the response is successfully received. You should have run the `addChat` mutation from the previous chapter through Postman. Otherwise, there will be no chats to query for, and the panel will be empty. You have to execute this mutation also for any following chapter because we are not going to implement a special button for this functionality.

One obvious question that you might have is as follows: How can we create new chats with other users? We will focus on this issue when we have implemented the authentication properly, and can visit users' profiles. Next, we want to display the chat messages after opening a specific chat.

# Fetching and displaying messages

We will start with the `Query` component from the beginning. First, however, we have to store the chats that were opened by a click from the user. Every chat is displayed in a separate, small chat window, like in Facebook. Add a new `state` variable to save the ids of all of the opened chats to the `Chats` class:

```
state = {
  openChats: []
}
```

To let our component insert something into the array of open chats, we will add the new `openChat` method to our `Chats` class:

```
openChat = (id) => {
  var openChats = this.state.openChats.slice();

  if(openChats.indexOf(id) === -1) {
    if(openChats.length > 2) {
      openChats = openChats.slice(1);
    }
    openChats.push(id);
  }

  this.setState({ openChats });
}
```

When a chat is clicked on, we will first check that it is not already open, by searching the id using the `indexOf` function inside of the `openChats` array.

Every time a new chat is opened, we will check whether there are three or more chats. If that is the case, we will remove the first opened chat from the array, and exchange it with the new one by appending it to the array with the `push` function. We will only save the chat ids, not the whole JSON object.

The last step is to bind the `onClick` event to our component. In the `map` function, we can replace the wrapping `div` tag with the following line:

```
<div key={"chat" + chat.id} className="chat" onClick={() =>
self.openChat(chat.id)}>
```

Here, we use `onClick` to call the `openChat` method, with the chat id as the only parameter. At this point, the new function is already working, but the updated state isn't used. Let's take care of that:

1. Add a surrounding wrapper `div` tag to the whole `render` method:

```
<div className="wrapper">
```

2. We insert the new markup for the open chats next to the chats panel. You cannot insert it inside the panel directly, due to the CSS that we are going to use:

```
<div className="openChats">
  {openChats.map((chatId, i) =>
    <Query key={"chatWindow" + chatId} query={GET_CHAT}
      variables={{ chatId }}>
      {({ loading, error, data }) => {
        if (loading) return <p>Loading...</p>;
        if (error) return error.message;

        const { chat } = data;

        return (
          <div className="chatWindow">
            <div className="header">
              <span>{chat.users[1].username}</span>
              <button className="close">X</button>
            </div>
            <div className="messages">
              {chat.messages.map((message, j) =>
                <div key={'message' + message.id} className=
                {'message ' + (message.user.id > 1 ? 'left' :
                'right')}>
                  {message.text}
                </div>
              )}
            </div>
          </div>
        )
      }}
    </Query>
  )}
</div>
```

Here, we are walking over the `openChats` variable by using the `map` function again. Every id in this array is given to the `Query` component as a variable for the GraphQL request. The rest can be understood easily.

Once the request arrives, we render a `div` tag with the `chatWindow` class name, in which all messages are displayed. Again, we are using the user id to fake the class name of the messages. We will replace it when we get authentication running.

3. As you can see in the preceding code, we are not only passing the chat id as a parameter to the `variables` property of the `Query` component, but we also use another query stored in the `GET_CHAT` variable. We must parse this query first, with `graphql-tag`. Add the following code to the top of the file:

```
const GET_CHAT = gql`
  query chat($chatId: Int!) {
    chat(chatId: $chatId) {
      id
      users {
        id
        avatar
        username
      }
      messages {
        id
        text
        user {
            id
        }
      }
    }
  }
`;
```

4. Because we rely on the `openChats` state variable, we must extract it in our `render` method. Add the following code before the `return` state, in the `render` method:

```
const self = this;
const { openChats } = this.state;
```

5. The `close` button function relies on the `closeChat` method, which we will implement in our `Chats` class:

```
closeChat = (id) => {
  var openChats = this.state.openChats.slice();
  const index = openChats.indexOf(id);
  openChats.splice(index,1),
  this.setState({ openChats });
}
```

6. The last thing missing is some styling. The CSS is pretty big. Every message from the other users should be displayed on the left, and our own messages on the right, in order to differentiate them. Insert the following CSS into the `style.css` file:

```
.chatWindow {
  width: 250px;
  float: right;
  background-color: #eee;
  height: 300px;
  margin-right: 10px;
  border-left: 1px solid #c3c3c3;
  border-right: 1px solid #c3c3c3;
}

.chatWindow .header {
  width: calc(100% - 10px);
  background-color: #c3c3c3;
  padding: 5px;
  height: 20px;
}

.chatWindow .header .close {
  float: right;
  border: none;
  background: none;
  color: #fff;
  cursor: pointer;
}

.chatWindow .header .close:focus {
  outline: none;
}

.chatWindow .messages {
  overflow-y: scroll;
  height: calc(100% - 50px);
}

.chatWindow .messages .message {
  width: 80%;
  border: 1px solid #4079f3;
  margin: 2px;
  border-radius: 5px;
  padding: 2px;
}
```

```
.chatWindow .messages .message.left {
  background-color: #78a3ff;
  color: #fff;
  float: left;
}

.chatWindow .messages .message.right {
  float: right;
  background-color: #E8F4FB;
  color: #000;
}

.openChats {
  position: fixed;
  right: 200px;
  width: calc(100% - 200px);
  bottom: 0;
}

.wrapper {
    height: 100%;
    right: 0;
    top: 0;
}
```

Take a look at the following screenshot:

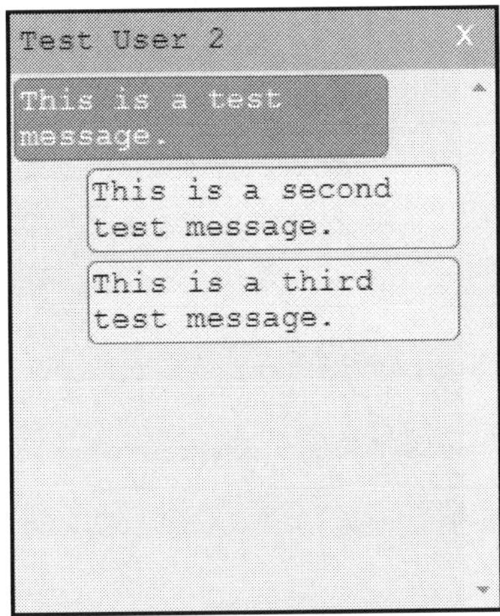

We have forgotten something important. We can see all of the messages from our chat, but we are not able to add new messages, which is essential. Let's take a look at how to implement a chat message form in the next section.

# Sending messages through Mutations

The `addMessage` mutation already exists in our back end, so we can add it to our `Chats` component. First, parse the mutation at the top, next to the other requests:

```
const ADD_MESSAGE = gql`
  mutation addMessage($message : MessageInput!) {
    addMessage(message : $message) {
      id
      text
      user {
        id
      }
    }
  }
`;
```

For each open chat, we will have one input where the user can type his message. There are multiple solutions to save all of the inputs' text inside the React component's state. For now, we will keep it simple, but we will take a look at a better way to do this in the `Chapter 5`, *Reusable React Components*.

Open a new object inside of the state initializer in our `Chats` class:

```
textInputs: {}
```

This object is indexed with the chat id. The current input value is saved under each key. If we open or close a chat, we need to either add the index to the object with an empty string, or remove the property again. You should not use this in a production-ready application, as it is an example implementation. We will rework this in the next chapter.

Import the `Mutation` component from the `react-apollo` package, as follows:

```
import { Query, Mutation } from 'react-apollo';
```

Replace the existing `openChat` and `closeChat` methods with the following code:

```
openChat = (id) => {
  var openChats = this.state.openChats.slice();
  var textInputs = Object.assign({}, this.state.textInputs);
  if(openChats.indexOf(id) === -1) {
```

```
        if(openChats.length > 2) {
          openChats = openChats.slice(1);
        }
        openChats.push(id);
        textInputs[id] = '';
      }
      this.setState({ openChats, textInputs });
    }

    closeChat = (id) => {
      var openChats = this.state.openChats.slice();
      var textInputs = Object.assign({}, this.state.textInputs);

      const index = openChats.indexOf(id);
      openChats.splice(index,1);
      delete textInputs[id];
      this.setState({ openChats, textInputs });
    }
```

The new functions in the preceding code include some logic to clear or create the input's state variable, once the chat is closed or opened.

Now, we must also handle the change event of the input by implementing a special function, as follows:

```
onChangeChatInput = (event, id) => {
  event.preventDefault();
  var textInputs = Object.assign({}, this.state.textInputs);
  textInputs[id] = event.target.value;
  this.setState({ textInputs });
}
```

We must prepare the markup needed to render a fully functional input. Put the input below the messages list, inside of the chat window. The `Mutation` component is rendered before the input, so that we can pass the mutation function to the input. The input inside receives the `onChange` property, in order to execute the `onChangeChatInput` function while typing:

```
<Mutation
    update = {(store, { data: { addMessage } }) => {
        const data = store.readQuery({ query: GET_CHAT, variables: {
         chatId: chat.id } });
        data.chat.messages.push(addMessage);
        store.writeQuery({ query: GET_CHAT, variables: { chatId: chat.id },
         data });
    }}
    mutation={ADD_MESSAGE}>
```

```
        {addMessage => (
        <div className="input">
            <input type="text" value={textInputs[chat.id]} onChange={(event
            ) => self.onChangeChatInput(event, chat.id)} onKeyPress={(event
             ) => {self.handleKeyPress(event, chat.id, addMessage)}}/>
        </div>
        )}
</Mutation>
```

We have already covered pretty much everything here in previous examples. To quickly sum it up, we are using the `update` method to insert the server response inside of our cache, instead of refetching all of the messages. The input saves all changes directly inside of the component state. Furthermore, we use the `onKeyPress` event to handle *Enter* key hits, so that we can send the chat message. To make it just a bit cleaner, we pass the `addMessage` mutation to the `handleKeyPress` function, so that the mutation is run if we hit the *Enter* key.

The implementation of the `handleKeyPress` method is pretty straightforward. Just copy it into our component, as follows:

```
handleKeyPress = (event, id, addMessage) => {
  const self = this;
  var textInputs = Object.assign({}, this.state.textInputs);

  if (event.key === 'Enter' && textInputs[id].length) {
    addMessage({ variables: { message: { text: textInputs[id], chatId: id }
     } }).then(() => {
      textInputs[id] = '';
      self.setState({ textInputs });
    });
  }
}
```

Every time you hit *Enter* inside of the input, if you have entered valid text, the message will be sent to the GraphQL API. The new message is pushed to our local cache, and the input is cleared.

Let's quickly add some CSS to our `style.css` file, to make the input field look good:

```
.chatWindow .input input {
  width: calc(100% - 4px);
  border: none;
  padding: 2px;
}
.chatWindow .input input:focus {
  outline: none;
}
```

The following screenshot shows the chat window, with a new message inserted through the chat window input:

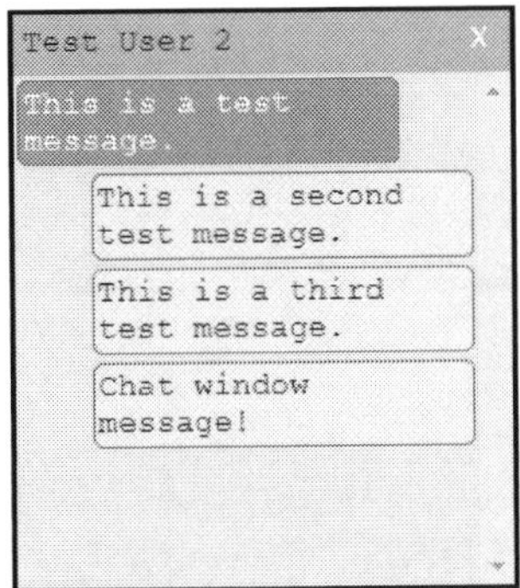


There are many features that we have not implemented, and that we won't cover in this book. For example, it would make sense to have the username next to the chat message if it is a group chat, to show the avatar next to the message, or to update the `lastMessage` in the chats panel once a new message is sent. The workload required to achieve a fully-fledged social network, such as Facebook, is impossible to cover in this book, but you are going to learn all of the required techniques, tools, and tactics, so that you can approach this on your own. The next important feature that we are going to cover is pagination.

# Pagination in React and GraphQL

By **pagination**, most of the time, we mean the batch querying of data. Currently, we query for all posts, chats, and messages in our database. If you think about how much data Facebook stores inside one chat with your friends, you will realize that it is unrealistic to fetch all of the messages and data ever shared at once. A better solution is to use pagination. With pagination, we always have a page size, or a limit, of how many items we want to fetch per request. We also have a page, or offset number, from which we can start to select data rows.

In this section, we're going to look at how to use pagination with the posts feed, as it is the most straightforward example. In the `Chapter 5`, *Reusable React Components*, we will focus on writing efficient and reusable React code. Sequelize offers the pagination feature by default. We can first insert some more demo posts, so that we can paginate in batches of 10.

We need to adjust the back end a bit before implementing it on our front end:

1. Add a new `RootQuery` to our GraphQl schema, as follows:

```
postsFeed(page: Int, limit: Int): PostFeed
```

2. The `PostFeed` type only holds the `posts` field. Later on, in the development of the application, you can return more information, such as the overall count of items, the page count, and so on:

```
type PostFeed {
  posts: [Post]
}
```

3. Next, we must implement the `PostFeed` entity in our `resolvers.js` file. Copy the new resolver function over to the `resolvers` file, as follows:

```
postsFeed(root, { page, limit }, context) {
  var skip = 0;

  if(page && limit) {
    skip = page * limit;
  }

  var query = {
    order: [['createdAt', 'DESC']],
    offset: skip,
  };

  if(limit) {
    query.limit = limit;
  }

  return {
   posts: Post.findAll(query)
  };
},
```

We build a simple `query` object that Sequelize understands, which allows us to paginate our posts. The `page` number is multiplied by the `limit`, in order to skip the calculated number of rows. The `offset` parameter skips the number of rows, and the parameter limit stops selecting rows after a specified number (which, in our case, is 10).

Our front end needs some adjustments to support pagination. Install a new React package with npm, which provides us with an infinite scroll implementation:

```
npm install react-infinite-scroller --save
```

Infinite scrolling is an excellent method to let a user load more content by scrolling to the bottom of the browser window.

You are free to program this on your own, but we are not going to cover that here. Go back to the `Feed.js` file, replace the `GET_POSTS` query, and import the `react-infinite-scroller` package, with the following code:

```
import InfiniteScroll from 'react-infinite-scroller';

const GET_POSTS = gql`
  query postsFeed($page: Int, $limit: Int) {
    postsFeed(page: $page, limit: $limit) {
      posts {
        id
        text
        user {
          avatar
          username
        }
      }
    }
  }
`;
```

Since the `postsFeed` query expects parameters other than the standard query from before, we need to edit our `Query` component in the `render` method. The changed lines are as follows:

```
<Query query={GET_POSTS} variables={{page: 0, limit: 10}}>
  {({ loading, error, data, fetchMore }) => {
  if (loading) return <p>Loading...</p>;
  if (error) return error.message;

  const { postsFeed } = data;
  const { posts } = postsFeed;
```

In the preceding code, we extract the `fetchMore` function from the `Query` component, which is used to run the pagination request to load more post items. According to the new data structure defined in our GraphQL schema, we extract the `posts` array from the `postsFeed` object. Replace the markup of the `div` tag of our current feed to make use of our new infinite scroll package:

```
<div className="feed">
  <InfiniteScroll
    loadMore={() => self.loadMore(fetchMore)}
    hasMore={hasMore}
```

```
        loader={<div className="loader" key={"loader"}>Loading ...</div>}
      >
        {posts.map((post, i) =>
          <div key={post.id} className={"post " + (post.id < 0 ?
          "optimistic": "")}>
            <div className="header">
              <img src={post.user.avatar} />
              <h2>{post.user.username}</h2>
            </div>
            <p className="content">
              {post.text}
            </p>
          </div>
        )}
      </InfiniteScroll>
    </div>
```

The only thing that the infinite scroll package does is run the `loadMore` function, as long as `hasMore` is set to `true` and the user scrolls to the bottom of the browser window. When `hasMore` is set to `false`, the event listeners are unbound, and no more requests are sent. This behavior is great when no further content is available, so that we can stop sending more requests.

It is important that we initialize the `hasMore` and `page` index state variable in our class first. Insert the following code:

```
state = {
  postContent: '',
  hasMore: true,
  page: 0,
}
```

Of course, we must also extract the `hasMore` variable in the `render` method of our class:

```
const { postContent, hasMore } = this.state;
```

We need to implement the `loadMore` function before running the infinite scroller. It relies on the `page` variable that we just configured. The `loadMore` function should look like the following code:

```
loadMore = (fetchMore) => {
  const self = this;
  const { page } = this.state;

  fetchMore({
    variables: {
      page: page+1,
```

```
    },
    updateQuery(previousResult, { fetchMoreResult }) {
      if(!fetchMoreResult.postsFeed.posts.length) {
        self.setState({ hasMore: false });
        return previousResult;
      }

      self.setState({ page: page + 1 });
      const newData = {
        postsFeed: {
          __typename: 'PostFeed',
          posts: [
            ...previousResult.postsFeed.posts,
            ...fetchMoreResult.postsFeed.posts
          ]
        }
      };
      return newData;
    }
  });
}
```

Let's quickly go through the preceding code, as follows:

1. The `fetchMore` function receives an object as a parameter.
2. We specify the `variables` field, which is sent with our request, in order to query the correct page index of our paginated posts.
3. The `updateQuery` function is defined to implement the logic to add the new data that needs to be included in our news feed. We can check whether any new data is included in the response by looking at the returned array length. If there are not any posts, we can set the `hasMore` state variable to `false`, which unbinds all scrolling events. Otherwise, we can continue and build a new `postsFeed` object inside of the `newData` variable. The `posts` array is filled by the previous `posts` query result and the newly fetched posts. At the end, the `newData` variable is returned and saved in the client's cache.
4. When the `updateQuery` function is finished, the user interface rerenders accordingly.

At this point, your feed is able to load new posts whenever the user visits the bottom of the window. We no longer load all posts at once, but instead, we only get the 10 most recent from our database. Every time you build an application with large lists and many rows, you have to add some kind of pagination, with either infinite scrolling or simple page buttons.

We have now created a new problem. We can submit a new post with the GraphQL mutation if the React Apollo cache is empty, but the `update` function of the `Mutation` component will throw an error. Our new query is stored not only under its name, but also under the variables used to send it. To read the data of a specific paginated `posts` request from our client's cache, we must also pass variables, such as the page index. Furthermore, we have a second layer, `postsFeed`, as the parent of the `posts` array. Change the `update` function to get it working again, as follows:

```
update = {(store, { data: { addPost } }) => {
  const variables = { page: 0, limit: 10 };
  const data = store.readQuery({ query: GET_POSTS, variables });
  data.postsFeed.posts.unshift(addPost);
  store.writeQuery({ query: GET_POSTS, variables, data });
}}
```

This approach is the same as the `addMessage` mutation, where we needed to pass the chat id as a variable.

Complex code like this requires some useful tools to debug it. Continue reading to learn more about Apollo Client Developer Tools.

# Debugging with the Apollo Client Developer Tools

Whenever you write or extend your own application, you have to test, debug, and log different things during development. In the `Chapter 1`, *Preparing Your Development Environment*, we looked at the React Dev Tools for Chrome, while in the `Chapter 2`, *Setting up GraphQL with Express.js*, we explored Postman for testing APIs. Now, let's take a look at another tool.

**Apollo Client Developer Tools** is another Chrome extension, allowing you to send Apollo requests. While Postman is great in many ways, it does not integrate with our application, and does not implement any GraphQL-specific features. Apollo Client Developer Tools rely on the Apollo Client that we set up very early on in this chapter.

Every request, either a query or mutation, is sent through the Apollo Client of our application. The Developer Tools also provide features such as autocomplete, for writing requests. They can show us the schema as it is implemented in our GraphQL API. Let's take a look at an example:

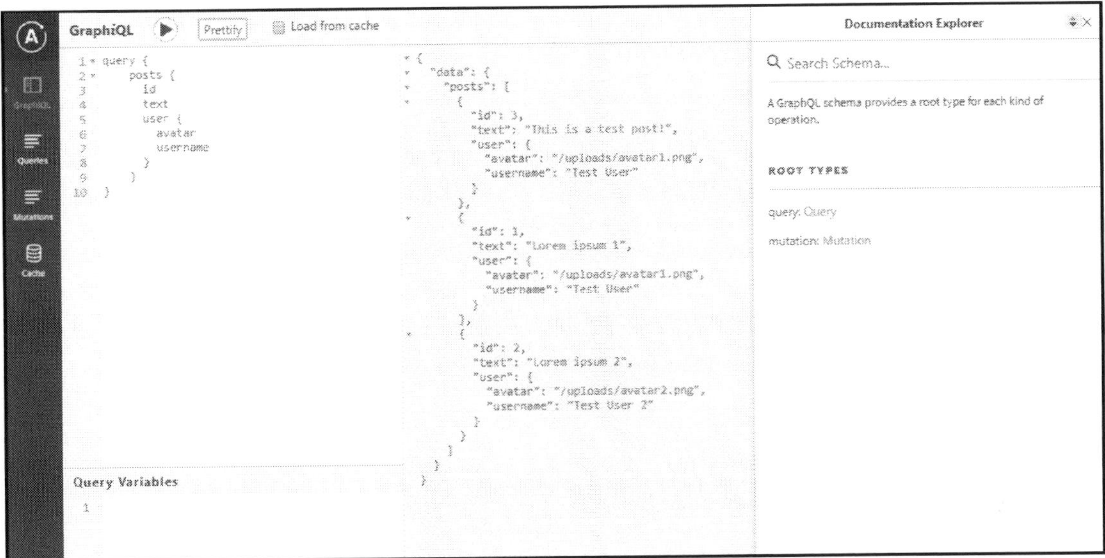

We will go over all four of the main windows offered by the extension.

The **GraphiQL** window is shown in the preceding screenshot. The three panels in the preceding screenshot are described as follows:

- You can enter the request that you want to send in the left-hand text area. It can be a mutation or query, including the markup for inputs, for example. It is the same as the `query` property in Postman. You can also enter the variables at the bottom.
- When sending the request, the response is shown in the middle panel.
- In the panel on the right, you can find the schema against which you will run the requests. You can search through the complete GraphQL schema, or manually step into the tree by clicking on the root types. This feature is useful when you forget what a specific field or mutation is called, or which parameters it accepts.

In the top bar, you will find the **Prettify** button, which tidies your query so that it is more readable. The **Load from cache** checkbox tries to retrieve any requested data directly from the cache, when possible. By clicking on the play button, you run the query. These are all tools to test our GraphQL requests properly.

Next, there is the **Queries** window, which is a helpful display. All of the queries that were ever run through the client are listed here, including the query string and variables. If you want to, you can rerun the query by clicking on the button at the top:

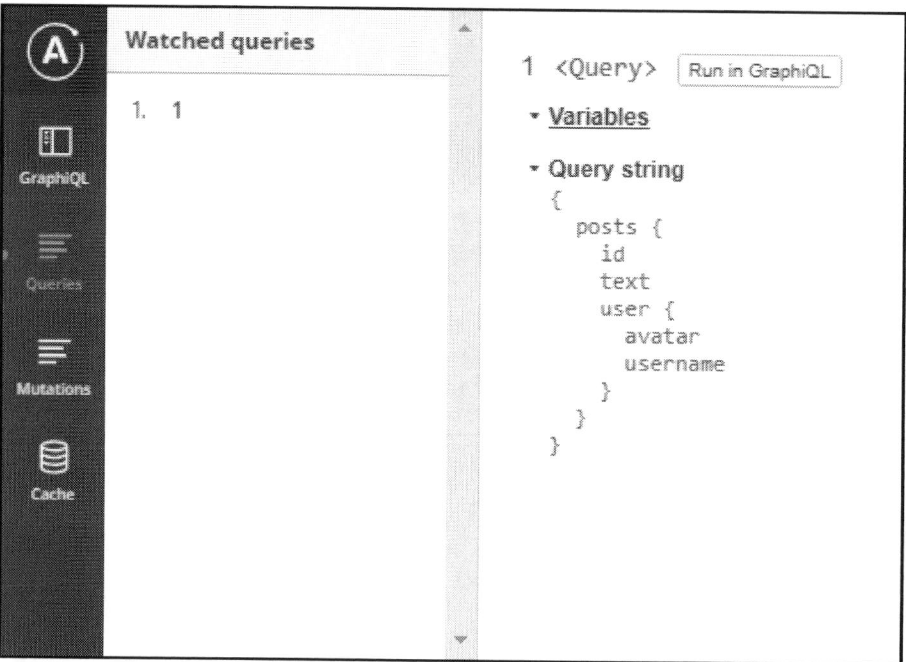


The **Mutations** window is actually the same as the **Queries** window, but for mutations. The list is empty, as long as you have not sent any mutations.

The last window is **Cache**. Here, you are able to see all of the data stored inside the Apollo cache:

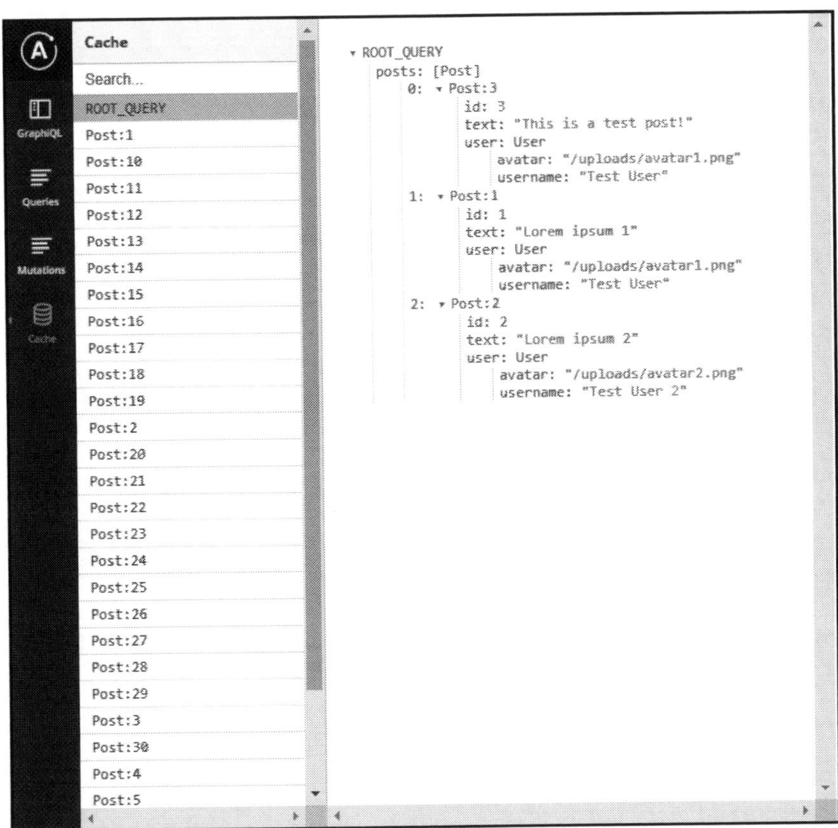


In the left-hand panel, you can search through your data. The right-hand panel shows you the selected object in JSON.

You can also see that I have tested the API a lot, as there are multiple **Post** objects in the left-hand panel. In the `ROOT_QUERY`, there are only three. For testing purposes, I submitted multiple posts via a mutation, but I deleted them, to make sure that the screenshots were clear. Apollo did not delete the old posts that were deleted in the database, so they are still inside of the cache. You should delete this data when a user logs out of your application, so that unauthorized users cannot access it.

That is everything that you need to know about Apollo Client Developer Tools.

# Summary

In this chapter, you learned how to connect our GraphQL API to React. To do this, we used Apollo Client to manage the cache and the state of our components, and to update the React and the actual DOM of the browser. We looked at how to send queries and mutations against our server in two different ways. We also covered how to implement pagination with React and Apollo, and how to use Apollo Client Developer Tools.

The next chapter will cover how to write reusable React components. Up to this point, we have written the code, but we haven't thought about readability or good practices very much. We will address these issues in the next chapter.

# 5
# Reusable React Components

We have done a lot to reach this point in the book, including saving, requesting, inserting, and updating data through the use of Apollo Client, in connection with our GraphQL API. Much of the code that we have written will also have to be reviewed many times. This is especially important because we are building an application so quickly. Everything is working for now, but we have not done a great job here; there are some best practices and tactics that need to be observed in order to write good React applications.

This chapter will cover everything you need to know in order to write efficient and reusable React components. It will cover the following topics:

- React patterns
- Structured React components
- Rendering nested components
- The React Context API
- The Apollo Consumer component

## Introducing React patterns

With any programming language, framework, or library that you use, there are always common tactics that you should follow. They present an understandable, efficient way to write applications.

In `Chapter 4`, *Integrating React into the Back end with Apollo*, we tackled some patterns, such as rendering arrays, the spread operator, destructuring objects, and higher-order components. Nevertheless, there are some further patterns that you should know about.

We will go over the most commonly used patterns that React offers, as follows:

- Controlled components
- Stateless functions
- Conditional rendering
- Rendering children

Many (but not all) of the examples here only represent illustrations of what each method looks like. Some of them will not be taken over to our real application code, so, if you are not interested in learning the essential aspects of patterns, or if you already know most of them, you can skip the examples.

Beyond the short explanation that I will provide, there is more extensive documentation on this topic. The official React documentation is always a good starting point, but you can find all React patterns, including those that we have already used, at `https://reactpatterns.com/`.

# Controlled components

When we wrote our post form to submit new posts or the message inputs inside chat in the previous chapters, we used controlled input by incident. To provide a better understanding, I am going to quickly explain the difference between controlled and uncontrolled components, and when to use each of them.

Let's start with uncontrolled input.

By definition, a component is uncontrolled whenever the value is not set by a property through React, but only saved and taken from the real browser DOM. The value of an input is then retrieved from a reference to the DOM Node, and is not managed and taken from React's component state.

The following code shows the post form where the user will be able to submit new posts. I have excluded the rendering logic for the complete feed, as it is not a part of the pattern that I want to show you:

```
import React, { Component } from 'react';
import gql from 'graphql-tag';
import { Mutation } from 'react-apollo';

const ADD_POST = gql`
  mutation addPost($post : PostInput!) {
    addPost(post : $post) {
    id
```

```
      text
      user {
        username
        avatar
      }
    }
  }`;

export default class Feed extends Component {
  constructor(props) {
    super(props);
    this.textArea = React.createRef();
  }
  render() {
    const self = this;
    return (
      <div className="container">
        <div className="postForm">
          <Mutation mutation={ADD_POST}>
            {addPost => (
              <form onSubmit={e => {
                e.preventDefault();
                addPost({ variables: { post: { text:
                  self.textArea.current.value } } });
              }}>
                <textarea ref={this.textArea} placeholder="Write your
                  custom post!"/>
                <input type="submit" value="Submit" />
              </form>
            )}
          </Mutation>
        </div>
      </div>
    )
  }
}
```

In this example, you can see that we no longer have a state initializer, since the `textarea` value is stored within the real DOM Node, and not the application state.

Now, we need a component constructor. As we stated in `Chapter 1`, *Preparing Your Development Environment*, you always need to run the `super` method inside of a constructor first.

Next, we run the `createRef` function provided by React. It prepares the variable to accept the DOM Node as a property. In earlier versions of React, you were required to use a callback to handle this on your own. From version 16.3 of React, the `createRef` function automates this process for you.

In the `render` method, the `ref` property fills in the reference that we just created with the DOM element.

Accessing the value of the DOM Node works by using the normal JavaScript DOM API. You can see this behavior when sending the `submit` event of our form. The value is extracted from the `self.textArea.current.value` field.

Everything that an uncontrolled component needs is already shown here; there is no more to it. You can compare this approach to our current implementation of the post form. In our implementation, we set up the state, listen for change events, and save and read the value directly from the component state, not from the DOM element.

When using uncontrolled components and working directly with DOM elements, the problem is that you leave the normal React workflow. You are no longer able to handle conditions and, therefore, trigger other events inside of React.

Nevertheless, the DOM reference can make it easier to use third-party plugins that were not written for the React ecosystem. There are thousands of great jQuery plugins, for example. I always recommend using the default approach of a controlled component. For 99% of cases, this works without leaving the React workflow.

If you need a deeper understanding of which approach is a better solution for your specific case, take a look at `https://goshakkk.name/controlled-vs-uncontrolled-inputs-react/`.

# Stateless functions

One fundamental and efficient solution for writing well-structured and reusable React components is the use of stateless functions.

As you might expect, stateless functions are functions, not React components. They are not able to store any states; only properties can be used to pass and render data. Property updates are directly rerendered inside of the stateless functions, and cannot be handled by the `componentWillReceiveProps` method, as in React components.

We have written a lot of code where stateless functions can be used very easily; while doing so, we have also structured and improved the readability of our React application.

Beginning with the file structure, we will create a new folder for our new components (or stateless functions), as follows:

```
mkdir src/client/components
```

Many parts of our application need to be reworked. Create a new file for our first stateless function, as follows:

```
touch src/client/components/loading.js
```

Currently, we display a dull and boring **Loading...** message when our GraphQL requests are running. Let's change this by inserting the following code into the `loading.js` file:

```
import React from 'react';

export default ({color, size}) => {
  var style = {
    backgroundColor: '#6ca6fd',
    width: 40,
    height: 40,
  };

  if(typeof color !== typeof undefined) {
    style.color = color;
  }
  if(typeof size !== typeof undefined) {
    style.width = size;
    style.height = size;
  }

  return <div className="bouncer" style={style}></div>
}
```

In the preceding code, we are using a simple function in ES6 arrow notation. It is an easy and more concise syntax for defining functions. In the code, you can see that we are extracting the `color` and `size` fields from the properties that our function receives.

We are building a default `style` object that represents the basic styling for a loading spinner. You can pass the `color` and `size` separately, in order to adjust those settings.

Lastly, we are returning a simple `div` tag with the CSS style and the `bouncer` class.

What's missing here is the CSS styling. The code should look as follows; just add it to our `style.css` file:

```
.bouncer {
  margin: 20px auto;
  border-radius: 100%;
  -webkit-animation: bounce 1.0s infinite ease-in-out;
  animation: bounce 1.0s infinite ease-in-out;
}

@-webkit-keyframes bounce {
  0% {
    -webkit-transform: scale(0)
  }
  100% {
    -webkit-transform: scale(1.0);
    opacity: 0;
  }
}

@keyframes bounce {
  0% {
    -webkit-transform: scale(0);
    transform: scale(0);
  }
  100% {
    -webkit-transform: scale(1.0);
    transform: scale(1.0);
    opacity: 0;
  }
}
```

Like in the previous examples, we use CSS animations to display our loading spinner correctly, and to let it animate as pulsating.

We have now finished the stateless function. You should place it into the existing code, wherever a loading state exists.

First, import the new loading spinner to the top of your files, as follows:

```
import Loading from './components/loading';
```

You can then render the stateless function like any normal component, as follows:

```
if (loading) return <Loading />;
```

Start the server with `npm run server` and the front end with `npm run client`. You should now see a pulsating blue bubble where you inserted it. I have tested this inside of my posts feed, and it looks pretty good.

The advantage of stateless functions is that they are minimal and efficient functions, rendering smaller parts of our application. The approach perfectly integrates with React, and we can improve the code that we have written.

# Conditional rendering

One important ability of React is rendering components or data conditionally. We will use this intensively in the next main features that we are going to implement.

Generally, you can accomplish conditional rendering by using the curly brace syntax. An example of an if statement is as follows:

```
render() {
  const { shouldRender } = this.state;

  return (
    <div className="conditional">
      {(shouldRender === true) && (
        <p>Successful conditional rendering!</p>
      )}
    </div>
  )
}
```

This code is the simplest example of conditional rendering. We have the `shouldRender` variable from the component state, and we use this as our condition. When the condition is true, the second part—which is our `Successful conditional rendering!` text—will also render. That is because we are using the `&&` characters. The text does not render if the condition is false.

You can replace the preceding condition with everything that you have in mind. It can be a complex condition, such as a function returning a Boolean value, or, just like in the preceding code, it can be a state variable.

You will see further examples in later steps and chapters in this book.

# Rendering child components

In all of the code that we have written so far, we have directly written the markup like it is rendered to real HTML.

A great feature that React offers is the ability to pass children to other components. The parent component decides what is done with its children.

Something that we are still missing now is a good error message for our users. So, we will use this pattern to solve the issue.

Create an `error.js` file next to the `loading.js` file in the `components` folder, as follows:

```
import React, { Component } from 'react';

export default class Error extends Component {
  render() {
    const { children } = this.props;
    return (
      <div className="error message">
        {children}
      </div>
    );
  }
}
```

When passing children to another component, a new property, called `children`, is added to the properties of the component. You specify `children` by writing normal React markup.

If you wanted to, you could perform actions, such as looping through each child. In our example, we render the children as usual, by using the curly braces and putting the `children` variable inside.

To start using the new `Error` component, you can simply import it. The markup for the new component is as follows:

```
if (error) return <Error><p>{error.message}</p></Error>;
```

Add some CSS, and everything should be finished, as shown in the following code snippet:

```
.message {
  margin: 20px auto;
  padding: 5px;
  max-width: 400px;
}
```

```
.error.message {
  border-radius: 5px;
  background-color: #FFF7F5;
  border: 1px solid #FF9566;
  width: 100%;
}
```

A working result might look as follows:

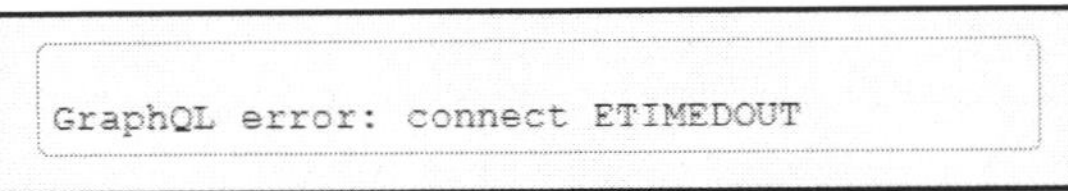


You can apply the stateless function pattern and the children pattern to many other use cases. Which one you use will depend on your specific scenario. In this case, you could also use a stateless function, rather than a React component.

# Structuring our React application

We have already improved some things by using React patterns. You should do some homework and introduce those patterns wherever possible.

When writing applications, one key objective is to keep them modular and readable, but also as understandable as possible. It is always hard to tell when splitting code up is useful, and when it overcomplicates things. This is something that you will learn more and more about by writing as many applications and as much code as possible.

Let's begin to structure our application further.

# The React file structure

We have already saved our `Loading` and `Error` components in the `components` folder. Still, there are many parts of our components that we did not save in separate files, to improve the readability of this book.

I will explain the most important solution for unreadable React code in one example. You can implement this on your own later, for all other parts of our application, as you should not read duplicate code.

Currently, we render the posts in our feed by mapping through all posts from the GraphQL response. There, we directly render the corresponding markup for all post items. Therefore, it is one big render function that does everything at once.

To make this a bit more intuitive, we should create a new `Post` component. Separating the components hugely improves the readability of our posts feed. Then, we can replace the return value from the loop with a new component, instead of real markup.

Instead of creating a `post.js` file in our `components` folder, we should first create another `post` folder, as follows:

```
mkdir src/client/components/post
```

The `Post` component consists of multiple tiny, nested components. A post is also a standalone GraphQL entity, making it logical to have a separate folder. We will store all related components in this folder.

Let's create those components. We will start with the post header, where the top part of a post item is defined. Create a new `header.js` file in the `components/post` folder, as follows:

```
import React from 'react';

export default ({post}) =>
  <div className="header">
    <img src={post.user.avatar} />
    <div>
      <h2>{post.user.username}</h2>
    </div>
  </div>
```

The `header` component is just a stateless function. As you can see, we are using a React pattern from the earlier pages of this chapter. We are only rendering the data that we already have, and we are not storing any state here, so we are free to use a stateless function.

Up next is the post content, which represents the body of a post item. Add the following code inside of a new file, called `content.js`:

```
import React from 'react';

export default ({post}) =>
  <p className="content">
    {post.text}
  </p>
```

The code is pretty much the same as that of the post header. At later points, you will be free to introduce real React components or extended markup to those two files. It is entirely open to your implementation.

The main file is a new `index.js` file in the new `post` folder. It should look as follows:

```
import React, { Component } from 'react';
import PostHeader from './header';
import PostContent from './content';

export default class Post extends Component {
  render() {
    const { post } = this.props;

    return (
      <div className={"post " + (post.id < 0 ? "optimistic": "")}>
        <PostHeader post={post}/>
        <PostContent post={post}/>
      </div>
    )
  }
}
```

The preceding code represents a very basic component, but instead of directly using markup to render a complete post item (like before), we are using two further components for this, with `PostHeader` and `PostContent`. Both of the components receive the `post` as a property.

You can now use the new `Post` component in the feed list with ease. Just replace the old code inside the loop, as follows:

```
<Post key={post.id} post={post} />
```

The improvement is that all three of the components give you a clear overview at first glance. Inside of the loop, we return a post item. A post item consists of a header and body content.

Still, there is room for enhancement, because the posts feed list is cluttered.

# Efficient Apollo React components

We have successfully replaced the post items in our feed with a React component, instead of raw markup.

A major part, which I dislike very much, is the Apollo `Query` component and `Mutation` component, and how we are using these at the moment directly inside the `render` method of our components. I will show you a quick workaround to make these components more readable.

Furthermore, the current solution does not allow us to reuse the query or mutation anywhere else. We would need to add duplicate code, just to send the same request again. A better way to structure the code would be to have separate files for the data layer and view layer of our client-side code.

As an example, we will fix those issues for `Feed.js` in the next section.

## The Apollo Query component

We will start by implementing the `Query` component. You should be able to easily follow the instructions here, as all of the patterns and React basics should be clear by now:

1. Create a new `queries` folder inside of the `components` folder, as follows:

   ```
   mkdir src/client/components/queries
   ```

2. The query that we want to remove from our view layer is the `postsFeed` query. You can define the naming conventions for this, but I would recommend using the `RootQuery` name as the filename, as long as it works. So, we should create a `postsFeed.js` file in the `queries` folder, and insert the following code:

   ```
   export default class PostsFeedQuery extends Component {
     getVariables() {
       const { variables } = this.props;
       var query_variables = {
         page: 0,
         limit: 10
       };

       if (typeof variables !== typeof undefined) {
         if (typeof variables.page !== typeof undefined) {
           query_variables.page = variables.page;
         }
         if (typeof variables.limit !== typeof undefined) {
   ```

```
            query_variables.limit = variables.limit;
          }
        }

        return query_variables;
      }
      render() {
        const { children } = this.props;
        const variables = this.getVariables();

        return(
          <Query query={GET_POSTS} variables={variables}>
            {({ loading, error, data, fetchMore }) => {
              if (loading) return <Loading />;
              if (error) return <Error><p>{error.message}</p></Error>;

              const { postsFeed } = data;
              const { posts } = postsFeed;

              return React.Children.map(children, function(child) {
                return React.cloneElement(child, { posts, fetchMore });
              })
            }}
          </Query>
        )
      }
    }
```

Do not forget to import all of the dependencies, such as the Apollo React client, the `Loading` and `Error` components, and parsing the `postsFeed` GraphQL query to the `GET_POSTS` variable with `graphql-tag`. If you do not remember how to do this, look inside of the implementation that we have in our `Feed` class at the moment.

For customization reasons, the component should be able to accept other variables, in case we want to adjust the number of parameters of our query. The `getVariables` function overwrites the default `query_variables` field with any parameter given to the component.

What's new in the preceding code is that we are using the **children pass-through** pattern of React. This pattern allows us to wrap the `PostsFeedQuery` component around many different custom components, and it allows us to use the query response inside of these children. That way, we keep a readable `render` method for our user-facing components and the data layer of our React application in a separate file.

We are using the `React.Children.map` function to loop through all of the provided children. By running the `React.cloneElement` method, we copy each element to a new rendered component. This enables us to pass further properties from the result of the GraphQL request initiated by the `Query` component. Each child receives the `posts` and the `fetchMore` function as a property.

3. Preparing our next component, we split the infinite scroll area into a second file. Place a `feedlist.js` into the `components/posts` folder, as follows:

```
import React, { Component } from 'react';
import InfiniteScroll from 'react-infinite-scroller';
import Post from './';

export default class FeedList extends Component {
  state = {
    page: 0,
    hasMore: true
  }
  loadMore = (fetchMore) => {
    const self = this;
    const { page } = this.state;
    fetchMore({
      variables: {
        page: page+1,
      },
      updateQuery(previousResult, { fetchMoreResult }) {
        if(!fetchMoreResult.postsFeed.posts.length) {
          self.setState({ hasMore: false });
          return previousResult;
        }
        self.setState({ page: page + 1 });
        const newData = {
          postsFeed: {
            __typename: 'PostFeed',
            posts: [
              ...previousResult.postsFeed.posts,
              ...fetchMoreResult.postsFeed.posts
            ]
          }
        };
        return newData;
      }
    });
  }
  render() {
    const self = this;
    const { posts, fetchMore } = this.props;
```

```
        const { hasMore } = this.state;
        return (
          <div className="feed">
            <InfiniteScroll
              loadMore={() => self.loadMore(fetchMore)}
              hasMore={hasMore}
              loader={<div className="loader" key={"loader"}>Loading
               ...</div>}
            >
              {posts.map((post, i) =>
                <Post key={post.id} post={post} />
              )}
            </InfiniteScroll>
          </div>
        );
      }
    }
```

We only handle the infinite scroller of our feed here, which is also the only part where the result of the `PostsFeedQuery` is needed. The preceding code is much tidier than before (at least, inside of the `render` method).

We extract the `posts` and the `fetchMore` function passed from the `PostsFeedQuery` component. Like before, we render the `posts` as they are passed from the parent component inside of the infinite scroller. While scrolling, the infinite scroller executes the `loadMore` function, which runs the `fetchMore` function that is also received by the `PostsFeedQuery` component, in order to get the next posts in our pagination. The data-fetching and the rendering logic are separated from each other.

4. To use the `PostsFeedQuery` component, we can restructure our `Feed.js` a bit. Remove the `Query` tag from the markup, as well as the `page` and `hasMore` state variables.
5. Import the new components in the `Feed.js`, as follows:

```
import FeedList from './components/post/feedlist';
import PostsFeedQuery from './components/queries/postsFeed';
```

6. Replace the `div` tag with the `feed` class name and our two new components, as follows:

```
<PostsFeedQuery>
  <FeedList />
</PostsFeedQuery>
```

This code allows the `Query` component to pass all of the required properties to the `FeedList` class.

The improvement that we implemented is that the post form is now rendered directly before the response of the query has arrived. Only the scroll component is rendered when the GraphQL request is finished. Although it is more of a coincidence, it is important to note that the form was previously not rendered until the response arrived.

If we wanted to, we could add multiple other components inside of the `PostsFeedQuery` tag. All children receive the response properties, as specified in our custom `Query` component. You can make changes to the `Query` class and add further fields at any time, and all of the corresponding files will receive the update.

Do the same for the chats to improve your skills in writing reusable React code. How deeply you separate the components into multiple, smaller parts will always be a design decision.

Next, we will look at the `Mutation` component, in order to submit new posts.

# The Apollo Mutation component

A big part of our main `Feed.js` file still consists of rendering the real form markup and using the Apollo Mutation component to pass and execute the mutation within the form. We will now separate those parts:

1. Create a new folder for all your mutations, as follows:

```
mkdir src/client/components/mutations
```

2. Next, we want to outsource the mutation into a special file. To do so, create the `addPost.js` file, named after the GraphQL mutation itself. Insert the following code:

```
export default class AddPostMutation extends Component {
  state = {
    postContent: ''
  }
  changePostContent = (value) => {
    this.setState({postContent: value})
  }
  render() {
    const self = this;
    const { children, variables } = this.props;
    const { postContent } = this.state;
```

```
      return (
        <Mutation
          update = {(store, { data: { addPost } }) => {
            var query = {
              query: GET_POSTS,
            };
            if(typeof variables !== typeof undefined) {
              query.variables = variables;
            }
            const data = store.readQuery(query);
            data.postsFeed.posts.unshift(addPost);
            store.writeQuery({ ...query, data });
          }}
          optimisticResponse= {{
            __typename: "mutation",
            addPost: {
              __typename: "Post",
              text: postContent,
              id: -1,
              user: {
                __typename: "User",
                username: "Loading...",
                avatar: "/public/loading.gif"
              }
            }
          }}
          mutation={ADD_POST}>
            {addPost =>
              React.Children.map(children, function(child){
                return React.cloneElement(child, { addPost,
                postContent, changePostContent:
                  self.changePostContent
                });
              })
            }
        </Mutation>
      )
    }
  }
```

Please import all of the dependencies at the top, and parse both the GraphQL requests `ADD_POST` and the `GET_POSTS` query. The `postsFeed` query is required, because we read all posts from the cache by specifying the query in our `update` function which we introduced in the previous chapter.

The solution is the same as it was for the `Query` component in the previous section. However, two things have changed, which will be explained next.

Our `AddPostMutation` class holds the real state of the form. To accomplish this, we hand over the `changePostContent` method to all child components. They execute this method by giving the text area value and setting the new state in the parent component, which is our custom `Mutation` component.

We do this because the `optimisticResponse` requires us to pass the current value, in order to simulate a positive response from our server. If we kept the state within our form, the `Mutation` component would not have access to it, and could not render the text in the optimistic response.

Instead of giving the result of the mutation to our underlying child components, we hand over the mutation method. The form runs this function upon submission.

It is important to mention that the component can take a `variables` property, which is then used to read the cached data. It must receive the same `variables` as the `Query` component to successfully read the data from the client's cache.

3. Going on, we should build a post form component that only handles the creation of new posts. Just call it `form.js`, and place it inside of the post's `components` folder. The code must look like the following snippet:

```
import React, { Component } from 'react';

export default class PostForm extends Component {
  handlePostContentChange = (event) => {
    this.props.changePostContent(event.target.value);
  }
  render() {
    const self = this;
    const { addPost, postContent } = this.props;

    return (
      <div className="postForm">
        <form onSubmit={e => {
          e.preventDefault();
          addPost({ variables: { post: { text: postContent } }
            }).then(() => {
            self.props.changePostContent('');
          });
        }}>
          <textarea value={postContent} onChange=
           {self.handlePostContentChange} placeholder="Write your
            custom post!"/>
          <input type="submit" value="Submit" />
```

```
            </form>
          </div>
        )
      }
    }
```

As you can see, again, we just copied the post form over to our new file. The `handlePostContentChange` does not directly call `setState`, but executes the `changePostContent` received from the custom `Mutation` component that we just wrote. The same goes for the `addPost` method that we execute in the `onSubmit` event handler of the form.

4. Lastly, we finalize the `Feed.js` main file. It should look as follows:

```
import React, { Component } from 'react';
import PostsQuery from './components/queries/postsFeed';
import AddPostMutation from './components/mutations/addPost';
import FeedList from './components/post/feedlist';
import PostForm from './components/post/form';

export default class Feed extends Component {
  render() {
    const query_variables = { page: 0, limit: 10};

    return (
      <div className="container">
        <AddPostMutation variables={query_variables}>
          <PostForm />
        </AddPostMutation>
        <PostsQuery variables={query_variables}>
          <FeedList/>
        </PostsQuery>
      </div>
    )
  }
}
```

We have introduced the `variables` property to our custom query and `Mutation` components. We hardcode the `query_variables` and pass it to both components. The `variables` are used to read and update the data in the client's cache.

This is a vast improvement, in comparison to our old implementation. It was impossible to understand what was going to be rendered when we had the `Query` and `Mutation` component, and all of the markup, in just one big file. Now, you can immediately see that a mutation is given to a form, a query is run, and the result is handed over to a list, which renders the post items.

Every part is saved in a separate file, so you can edit each of them without affecting the other components. You can test all changes by starting the back end with `npm run server` and the front end with `npm run client`.

The application is more stable and readable, and the new features are more comfortable to implement. However, there are still some areas for improvement. For example, we have the `postsFeed` GraphQL query defined in multiple files, and we parse it at multiple locations. A good alternative would be to store the queries together in one big file, or to store each of them in a separate file. Both solutions would allow us to edit the query at only one location, instead of editing multiple locations when just one query has changed. You can implement this on your own, as it is not very complicated.

Always keep an eye open for possible improvements to your application.

I recommend that you also make the equivalent changes to the chat entity, making the code more understandable. The following is a list of things that you should do:

- Split the mutations and queries from the `Chat.js` into separate files.
- Create a component for the chat panel.
- Create a component for the chat items in the chat panel.
- Create a component for the window bar at the bottom of the browser window.
- Create a component for the chat windows. A chat window consists of three very basic components:
    - A top bar component, handling the title, the closing function, and later bar actions.
    - A message feed, much like the one that we have for our posts. There are features that we have to implement first, such as reverse ordering and pagination.
    - An input component, making it possible to save the state to a `Mutation` component and send new messages. You can also handle other input formats, such as smileys, here. There are great packages that allow for the easy customization of input.
- Cut down the main `Chats.js` file to a minimum, loading only the wrapping subcomponents panel and the chat windows bar.

When you have finished all of these tasks, you can compare your results with the code provided in this book. While doing so, you may notice some parts where you can improve your code. There is nothing wrong with recommending ways to improve the code, so feel free to notify me if I could improve my code, too.

# Extending Graphbook

Our social network is still a bit rough. Aside from the fact that we are still missing authentication, all of the features are pretty basic; writing and reading the posts and messages is nothing exceptional.

If you compare it to Facebook, there are many things that we need to do. Of course, we cannot rebuild Facebook in its totality, but the usual features should be there. From my point of view, we should cover the following features:

- Adding a drop-down menu to the posts, in order to allow for deleting or updating the content.
- Creating a global user object with the React Context API.
- Using Apollo Consumer as an alternative to the React Context API.
- Implementing a top bar as the first component rendered above all of the views. We can search for users in our database from a search bar, and we can show the logged-in user from the global user object.

We will begin by looking at the first feature.

# The React context menu

You should be able to write the React context menu pretty much on your own. All of the required React patterns have been explained, and implementing the mutations should be clear by now.

Before we begin, we will lay out the plan that we want to follow:

- Rendering a simple icon with `FontAwesome`
- Building React helper components
- Handling the `onClick` event and setting the correct component state
- Using the conditional rendering pattern to show the drop-down menu, if the component state is set correctly
- Adding buttons to the menu and binding mutations to them

Continue reading to find out how to get the job done.

The following is a preview screenshot, showing how the final implemented feature should look:

source: https://www.vecteezy.com/

We will now start with the first task of setting up `FontAwesome` for our project.

## FontAwesome in React

As you may have noticed, we have not installed FontAwesome yet. Let's fix this with `npm`:

```
npm i --save @fortawesome/fontawesome-svg-core @fortawesome/free-solid-svg-icons @fortawesome/free-brands-svg-icons @fortawesome/react-fontawesome
```

Graphbook relies on the preceding four packages to import the FontAwesome icons into our front end code.

FontAwesome provides multiple configurations for use with React. The best, most production-ready approach is to import only the icons that we are explicitly going to use. For your next project or prototype, it might make sense to get started with the simplest approach. You can find all of the information on the official GitHub page, at `https://github.com/FortAwesome/react-fontawesome#get-started`.

Creating a separate file for FontAwesome will help us to have a clean import. Save the following code under the `fontawesome.js` file, inside of the `components` folder:

```
import { library } from '@fortawesome/fontawesome-svg-core';
import { faAngleDown } from '@fortawesome/free-solid-svg-icons';

library.add(faAngleDown);
```

First, we import the `library` object from the FontAwesome core package. For our specific use case, we only need one arrow image, called `angle-down`. Using the `library.add` function, we register this icon for later use.

There are many versions of FontAwesome. In this book, we are using FontAwesome 5, with the free icons only. More premium icons can be bought on the official FontAwesome web page. You can find an overview of all of the icons, and a detailed description of each, in the icon gallery at `https://fontawesome.com/icons?d=gallery`.

The only place where we need this file is within our root `App.js` file. It ensures that all of our custom React components can display the imported icons. Add the following import statement to the top:

```
import './components/fontawesome';
```

No variable is required to save the exported methods, since there won't be any. We want to execute this file in our application only once.

When you reach the point when your application needs a complete set of icons, you can get all of the icons grouped directly from the `@fortawesome/free-brands-svg-icons` package, which we also installed.

Nevertheless, you could also import a `close` icon from FontAwesome and replace the simple `x` that we used for our chat window. This is not a part of this chapter, but you should be able to handle it on your own.

Next, we are going to create a `Dropdown` helper component.

# React helper components

Production-ready applications need to be polished as much as possible. Implementing reusable React components is one of the most important things to do.

You should notice that drop-down menus are a common topic when building client-side applications. They are global parts of the front end and appear everywhere throughout our components.

It would be best to separate the actual menu markup that we want to display from the code, which handles the event-binding and showing the menu.

I always call this kind of code in React **helper components**. They are not implementing any business logic, but give us the opportunity to reuse drop-down menus or other features wherever we want.

Logically, the first step is to create a new folder to store all of the helper components, as follows:

```
mkdir src/client/components/helpers
```

Create a new file, called `dropdown.js`, as the helper component:

```
import React, { Component } from 'react';

export default class Dropdown extends Component {
  state = {
    show: false
  }
  handleClick = () => {
    const { show } = this.state;
    this.setState({show: !show});}
  render() {
    const { trigger, children } = this.props;
    const { show } = this.state;

    return(
      <div className="dropdown">
        <div>
          <div className="trigger" onClick={this.handleClick}>
            {trigger}
          </div>
          { show &&
            <div className="content">
              {children}
            </div>
          }
        </div>
      </div>
    )
  }
}
```

We do not require much code to write a drop-down component. It is also pretty efficient, since this works with nearly every scenario that you can think of.

We use basic event-handling in the preceding code. When the trigger `div` tag is clicked, we update the `show state` variable. Inside of the `div` trigger, we also render a property called `trigger`. A `trigger` can be anything from a regular text or HTML tag to a React component. It can be passed through the parent components, in order to customize the look of the drop-down component.

In addition to the `trigger` property, we are using two well-known React patterns:

- Conditional rendering, when the `show` variable is true
- Rendering children given by the parent component

This solution allows us to fill in the menu items that we want to render directly as children of the `Dropdown` component, which, as mentioned previously, is displayed after clicking on the trigger. In this case, the `show state` variable is true.

However, one thing is still not completely correct here. If you test the drop-down component by providing a simple text or icon as a trigger and another text as the content, you should see that the `Dropdown` only closes when clicking on the trigger again; it does not close when clicking anywhere else in our browser, outside of the drop-down menu.

This is one scenario where the React approach encounters problems. There is no DOM Node event, like `onClickOutside`, so we cannot directly listen to the outside click events of any DOM Node, such as our drop-down menu. The conventional approach is to bind an event listener to the complete document. Clicking anywhere in our browser closes the drop-down menu.

There are many cases when it might make sense to leave the React approach and use the DOM directly, through the standard JavaScript interface.

Read this article on *Medium* to get a better understanding: `https://medium.com/@garrettmac/reactjs-how-to-safely-manipulate-the-dom-when-reactjs-cant-the-right-way-8a20928e8a6`

Replace the `handleClick` method and add the `componentWillUnmount` React method, as follows:

```
componentWillUnmount() {
  document.removeEventListener('click', this.handleClick, true);
}
handleClick = () => {
  const { show } = this.state;

  this.setState({show: !show}, () => {
    if(!show) {
      document.addEventListener('click', this.handleClick);
    } else {
      document.removeEventListener('click', this.handleClick);
    }
  });
}
```

When clicking on the trigger button, we add the click event listener to the whole document with the `addEventListener` function of JavaScript. This way, the `handleClick` function is re-executed when clicking anywhere.

When clicking on the drop-down trigger, or anywhere in the DOM, the event listener is removed again, by using the `removeEventListener` function.

Do not forget to remove all of the manually created event listeners whenever a component is unmounted and removed from the DOM. Forgetting this can lead to many errors, since the `handleClick` method will no longer be available from the event listener that it tries to call.

As mentioned previously, this is the part where React fails at least a little bit, although it is not the fault of React. The DOM and JavaScript do not have the right abilities.

We can finally use our helper component and display the context menus for posts, but first, we need to prepare all of the menu items and components that we want to render.

# The GraphQL updatePost mutation

A mutation is always located at two points in our code. One part is written inside of our GraphQL API in the back end, and the other one is written in our front end code.

We should start with the implementation on the back end side, as follows:

1. There is a new mutation that we need to insert into our schema, as follows:

```
updatePost (
  post: PostInput!
  postId: Int!
): Post
```

2. Once it is inside of our schema, the implementation to execute the mutation will follow. Copy the following code over to the `resolvers.js` file, in the `RootMutation` field:

```
updatePost(root, { post, postId }, context) {
  return Post.update({
    ...post,
  },
  {
    where: {
      id: postId
    }
  }).then((rows) => {
```

```
        if(rows[0] === 1) {
          logger.log({
            level: 'info',
            message: 'Post ' + postId + ' was updated',
          });
          return Post.findById(postId);
        }
      });
    },
```

The only special thing here is that we need to specify which posts we want to update. This is done by having the `where` property inside of the function call. The first parameter of the `update` function receives the post that should be updated. Because we currently do not have authentication implemented yet, we cannot verify the user updating the post, but for our example, this is no problem.

When updating a post, we are required to fetch the post from our database again, in order to return the row. This is a limitation of Sequelize when working with MySQL server. If you are running Postgres, for example, you can remove this part and directly return the post, without a special, separate query.

We can now focus on the front end again.

Recall how we implemented the previous mutations; we always created reusable React components for them. We should do the same for the `update` mutation.

Create a new file, called `updatePost.js`, inside of the `mutations` folder:

1. As always, you have to import all of the dependencies. They should be the same as in the other mutations. This includes the `GET_POSTS` query, because we are going to read and update the cached data stored behind this query.
2. Add the new `updatePost` mutation to the new file, as follows:

```
const UPDATE_POST = gql`
  mutation updatePost($post : PostInput!, $postId : Int!) {
    updatePost(post : $post, postId : $postId) {
      id
      text
    }
  }
`;
```

3. Create an `UpdatePostMutation` class, as follows:

```
export default class UpdatePostMutation extends Component {
  state = {
    postContent: this.props.post.text
  }
  changePostContent = (value) => {
    this.setState({postContent: value})
  }
}
```

As you can see, the `postContent` is not just an empty string, but is taken from the properties, because updating a post requires that the post already exists and so does the text of it.

4. A React component always needs a `render` method. This one is going to be a bit bigger:

```
render() {
  const self = this;
  const { children } = this.props;
  const { postContent } = this.state;
  const postId = this.props.post.id;
  const variables = { page: 0, limit: 10};

  return (
    <Mutation
      update = {(store, { data: { updatePost } }) => {
        var query = {
          query: GET_POSTS,
        };
        if(typeof variables !== typeof undefined) {
          query.variables = variables;
        }
        const data = store.readQuery(query);
        for(var i = 0; i < data.postsFeed.posts.length; i++) {
          if(data.postsFeed.posts[i].id === postId) {
            data.postsFeed.posts[i].text = updatePost.text;
            break;
          }
        }
        store.writeQuery({ ...query, data });
      }}
      optimisticResponse= {{
        __typename: "mutation",
        updatePost: {
          __typename: "Post",
```

```
                    text: postContent,
                  }
                }}
                mutation={UPDATE_POST}>
                  {updatePost =>
                    React.Children.map(children, function(child){
                      return React.cloneElement(child, { updatePost,
                      postContent, postId, changePostContent:
                      self.changePostContent });
                    })
                  }
              </Mutation>
            )
          }
```

There are some differences from the other mutations that we have implemented before. The changes are as follows:

- We read the children and post id from the component's properties. Furthermore, we extract the `postContent` state variable.
- We have hardcoded the variables. This is not a good approach, however. It would be better to receive this from the parent component, too, but for this example, it is fine.
- The `update` method now searches through the cache and reads and updates the post's text when a post with a matching id is found.
- All underlying children accept the `updatePost` method and the `postId`.

This chapter is all about reusable React components. To make use of our mutation, we need to have a form allowing us to edit a post. We will handle this within the `Post` component itself, because we want to edit the post in place, and do not want to open a modal or a specific **Edit** page. Go to your post's `index.js` file and exchange it with the new one, as follows:

```
import React, { Component } from 'react';
import PostHeader from './header';
import PostContent from './content';
import PostForm from './form';
import UpdatePostMutation from '../mutations/updatePost';

export default class Post extends Component {
  state = {
    editing: false
  }
  changeState = () => {
    const { editing } = this.state;
```

```
      this.setState({ editing: !editing });
    }
    render() {
      const { post } = this.props;
      const { editing } = this.state;
      return (
        <div className={"post " + (post.id < 0 ? "optimistic": "")}>
          <PostHeader post={post} changeState={this.changeState}/>
          {!editing && <PostContent post={post}/>}
          {editing &&
            <UpdatePostMutation post={post}>
              <PostForm changeState={this.changeState}/>
            </UpdatePostMutation>
          }
        </div>
      )
    }
  }
```

We should quickly go over the changes, one by one, as follows:

- We are importing the `update` mutation that we just wrote at the top.
- We added an `editing` state variable. Based on this variable, we decide whether we show the normal `PostContent` component or our `PostForm`.
- We are using conditional rendering based on the `editing` variable, in order to switch between the standard and update form.
- The `changeState` function lets us switch between both states.
- Our `PostHeader` and the `PostForm` receive the new function, allowing them to control its parent state.
- Our `PostForm` is wrapped inside of our mutation. The form then receives the mutation's `updatePost` function.

We already have a post form that we can reuse with some adjustments, as you can see in the following code snippet. To use our standard post submission form as an update form, we must make some small adjustments. Open and edit the `form.js` file, as follows:

```
import React, { Component } from 'react';

export default class PostForm extends Component {
  handlePostContentChange = (event) => {
    this.props.changePostContent(event.target.value);
  }
  render() {
    const self = this;
    const { addPost, updatePost, postContent, postId } = this.props;
```

```
        return (
          <div className="postForm">
            <form onSubmit={e => {
              e.preventDefault();
              if(typeof updatePost !== typeof undefined) {
                updatePost({ variables: { post: { text: postContent },
                postId } }).then(() => {
                  self.props.changeState();
                });
              } else {
                addPost({ variables: { post: { text: postContent } }
                }).then(() => {
                  self.props.changePostContent('');
                });
              }
            }}>
              <textarea value={postContent} onChange=
              {self.handlePostContentChange} placeholder="Write your custom
                post!"/>
              <input type="submit" value="Submit" />
            </form>
          </div>
        )
      }
    }
```

We are reading the `updatePost` mutation from the component properties. If it is defined, we can assume that the parent component is our `UpdatePostMutation` component, so we can run the `updatePost` mutation with the `postContent` and `postId` variables. If not, we will just run the `addPost` mutation, like before.

The critical thing to note is that, upon finishing the request, we are running the `changeState` function, which switches our `Post` component back to the normal text mode, and also hides the form.

Where did it all begin? We wanted to have a context menu that allowed us to update the post.

Go to your post `header` file. The header is a great place to insert the drop-down component, as follows:

```
import React from 'react';
import Dropdown from '../helpers/dropdown';
import { FontAwesomeIcon } from '@fortawesome/react-fontawesome';

export default ({post, changeState}) =>
  <div className="header">
```

```
        <img src={post.user.avatar} />
        <div>
          <h2>{post.user.username}</h2>
        </div>
        <Dropdown trigger={<FontAwesomeIcon icon="angle-down" />}>
          <button onClick={changeState}>Edit</button>
        </Dropdown>
      </div>
```

FontAwesome is useful now. The drop-down trigger is displayed in the same row as the username.

Our drop-down component receives a `trigger` component, which is just a FontAwesome icon. Furthermore, the only child that our drop-down component has, for now, is a simple button. When it is clicked, it changes the parent `Post` component's editing state and makes the update post form visible, instead of the normal post content.

Nothing works without the magic of CSS. All of the CSS takes up a lot of space, so you should look it up in the official Git repository of this book. If you have added the new CSS, you should be able to see a small icon on the right-hand border of each post. Clicking on it makes a small drop-down menu visible, including the 'Edit' button, as shown at the beginning of this section. The user is now able to make in-place edits of posts with the post update form.

Something that we have not spoken about is user rights. At the moment, the user can edit everybody's posts, even if the user is not the author of the post. That is a problem that we will look into in the next chapter, when we have implemented authentication.

# The Apollo deletePost mutation

A basic drop-down menu, with one item, is there. We should add a second menu item to complete the drop-down menu.

This task is something that you can do as homework, in your own time. All of the techniques to get a `delete` mutation running have been explained.

For historical reasons, I want to cover the full CRUD workflow. After this chapter, you will be able to handle pretty advanced CRUD operations with Apollo, GraphQL, and React.

Just follow my instructions to get the `delete` action working:

1. Edit the GraphQL schema. The `deletePost` mutation needs to go inside of the `RootMutation` object. The new `Response` type serves as a return value, as deleted posts cannot be returned because they do not exist. Note that we only need the `postId` parameter, and do not send the complete post:

```
type Response {
  success: Boolean
}

deletePost (
  postId: Int!
): Response
```

2. Add the missing GraphQL resolver function. The code is pretty much the same as from the update resolver, except that only a number is returned by the `destroy` method of Sequelize, not an array. It represents the number of deleted rows. We return an object with the `success` field. This field indicates whether our front end should throw an error:

```
deletePost(root, { postId }, context) {
  return Post.destroy({
    where: {
      id: postId
    }
  }).then(function(rows){
    if(rows === 1){
      logger.log({
        level: 'info',
        message: 'Post ' + postId + 'was deleted',
      });
      return {
        success: true
      };
    }
    return {
      success: false
    };
  }, function(err){
    logger.log({
      level: 'error',
      message: err.message,
    });
  });
},
```

In short, our GraphQL API is now able to accept the `deletePost` mutation. We do not verify which user sends this mutation so for our example posts be deleted by anyone.

The next step is to create the `DeletePostMutation` component. Always ensure that you name your components uniquely, and in a self-explanatory manner. Let's start by implementing the `deletePost` mutation for the client, as follows:

1. Create the `deletePost.js` file within the `mutations` folder.
2. Just like with the `update` mutation, require all dependencies.
3. Add the new `deletePost` mutation, as follows:

```
const DELETE_POST = gql`
  mutation deletePost($postId : Int!) {
    deletePost(postId : $postId) {
      success
    }
  }
`;
```

4. Lastly, insert the new component's code:

```
export default class DeletePostMutation extends Component {
  render() {
    const { children } = this.props;
    const postId = this.props.post.id;
    const variables = { page: 0, limit: 10};

    return (
     <Mutation
      update = {(store, { data: { deletePost: { success } } }) => {
          if(success) {
            var query = {
              query: GET_POSTS,
            };
            if(typeof variables !== typeof undefined) {
              query.variables = variables;
            }
            const data = store.readQuery(query);
            for(var i = 0; i < data.postsFeed.posts.length; i++) {
              if(data.postsFeed.posts[i].id === postId) {
                break;
              }
            }
            data.postsFeed.posts.splice(i, 1);
            store.writeQuery({ ...query, data });
          }
```

```
            }}
            mutation={DELETE_POST}>
              {deletePost =>
                React.Children.map(children, function(child){
                  return React.cloneElement(child, { deletePost, postId
                  });
                })
              }
            </Mutation>
          )
        }
      }
```

We are saving a lot of code. There is no state that we are saving inside of the component, and no `optimisticReponse`. I have removed the optimistic update for the UI, since it is not intuitive if the requests fail. This would make your post disappear and reappear again.

The `update` routine searches for the post from the cache and removes it by splicing the array and saving the edited array again. We should add the new item to the drop-down menu now.

Again, our drop-down menu needs a new item. Follow these instructions to add it:

1. Open the `header.js` file and import the following mutation:

```
import DeletePostMutation from '../mutations/deletePost';
```

2. Instead of directly adding the new button to our header, we will create another stateless function, as follows:

```
const DeleteButton = ({deletePost, postId}) =>
  <button onClick={() => {
    deletePost({ variables: { postId } })
  }}>
    Delete
  </button>
```

Comparing the preceding code to our post form, the button needs to trigger the delete mutation. The form component did this via its props, so we are doing it here, too. There is no real difference, but now you can see how to handle such issues with stateless functions.

3. Insert both the mutation and the delete button into the `header` function, below the 'Edit' button, as follows:

```
<DeletePostMutation post={post}>
  <DeleteButton />
</DeletePostMutation>
```

You have now seen two approaches to sending mutations, as follows:

- Our form initiates the `update` mutation. The form is made visible from a drop-down component, which is a child component of the header of our leading `Post` component.
- The `delete` mutation is sent directly upon clicking the button within the drop-down menu.

I expect that you are now prepared for advanced scenarios, where communication between multiple components on different layers is required. Consequently, when starting the server and client you should be presented with the preview image that I gave you when starting this section.

To get some more practice, we will repeat this for another use case in the next section.

# The React application bar

In contrast with Facebook, we do not have an outstanding application bar. It is fixed to always stay at the top of the browser window, above all parts of the Graphbook. You will be able to search for other users, see notifications, and see the logged-in user inside of the application bar, after going through this section.

The first thing that we will implement is the simple search for users and the information about the logged-in user. We will begin with the search component, because it is really complex.

The following screenshot shows a preview of what we are going to build:

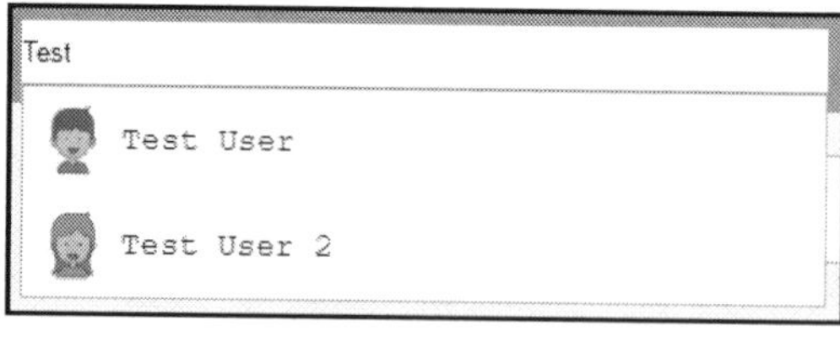


source: https://www.vecteezy.com/

It looks pretty basic, but what we are doing here is binding the `onChange` event of an input and re-fetching the query every time the value changes. Logically, this rerenders the search list in accordance with the responses from our GraphQL API.

Starting with the API, we need to introduce a new entity.

Just like with our `postsFeed` query, we will set up pagination from the beginning, because later, we might want to offer more advanced functionalities, such as loading more items while scrolling through the search list.

Edit the GraphQL schema and fill in the new `RootQuery` and type, as follows:

```
type UsersSearch {
  users: [User]
}

usersSearch(page: Int, limit: Int, text: String!): UsersSearch
```

The `UsersSearch` type expects one special parameter, which is the search text. Without the text parameter, the request would not make much sense. You should remember the `page` and `limit` parameters from the `postsFeed` pagination.

Furthermore, the `resolver` function looks pretty much the same as the `postsFeed` resolver function. You can add the following code straight into the `resolvers.js` file, as follows:

```
usersSearch(root, { page, limit, text }, context) {
  if(text.length < 3) {
    return {
      users: []
    };
  }
  var skip = 0;
  if(page && limit) {
    skip = page * limit;
  }
  var query = {
    order: [['createdAt', 'DESC']],
    offset: skip,
  };
  if(limit) {
    query.limit = limit;
  }
  query.where = {
    username: {
      [Op.like]: '%' + text + '%'
```

```
      }
    };
    return {
      users: User.findAll(query)
    };
  },
```

You should note that the first condition asks whether the provided text is larger than three characters. We do this to avoid sending too many unnecessary queries to our database. Searching for every user where the username consists of just one or two characters would result in providing us with nearly every user. Of course, this could have been done on the front end, too, but various clients could use our API, so we need to make sure that the back end makes this small improvement as well.

We send the `query` object to our database through Sequelize. The code works pretty much like the `postsFeed` resolver function from before, except that we are using a Sequelize operator. We want to find every user where the username includes the entered text, without specifying whether it is at the start, middle, or end of the name. Consequently, we will use the `Op.like` operator, which Sequelize parses into a pure SQL `LIKE` query, giving us the results we want. The `%` is used in MySQL to represent an unspecified number of characters. To enable this operator, we must import the `sequelize` package and extract the `Op` object from it, as follows:

```
import Sequelize from 'sequelize';
const Op = Sequelize.Op;
```

Going further, we can implement the client-side code as follows:

1. Create a file called `searchQuery.js` within the `queries` folder. We are creating a separate query component file for reusability reasons.

2. Import all of the dependencies, and parse the new GraphQL query with the `graphql-tag` package. Note that we have three parameters. The `text` field is a required property for the `variables` that we send with our GraphQL request:

```
import React, { Component } from 'react';
import { Query } from 'react-apollo';
import Loading from '../loading';
import Error from '../error';
import gql from 'graphql-tag';

const GET_USERS = gql`
  query usersSearch($page: Int, $limit: Int, $text: String!) {
    usersSearch(page: $page, limit: $limit, text: $text) {
```

```
      users {
        id
        avatar
        username
      }
    }
  }
`;
```

3. Paste in the `UsersSearchQuery` class, as shown in the following code. In comparison to the `PostsFeedQuery` class, I have added the text property to the variables and handed over the `refetch` method to all subsequent children:

```
export default class UsersSearchQuery extends Component {
  getVariables() {
    const { variables } = this.props;
    var query_variables = {
      page: 0,
      limit: 5,
      text: ''
    };
    if (typeof variables !== typeof undefined) {
      if (typeof variables.page !== typeof undefined) {
        query_variables.page = variables.page;
      }
      if (typeof variables.limit !== typeof undefined) {
        query_variables.limit = variables.limit;
      }
      if (typeof variables.text !== typeof undefined) {
        query_variables.text = variables.text;
      }
    }
    return query_variables;
  }
  render() {
    const { children } = this.props;
    const variables = this.getVariables();
    const skip = (variables.text.length < 3);
    return(
      <Query query={GET_USERS} variables={variables} skip={skip}>
        {({ loading, error, data, fetchMore, refetch }) => {
          if (loading || error || typeof data === typeof undefined)
          return null;

          const { usersSearch } = data;
          const { users } = usersSearch;
          return React.Children.map(children, function(child){
            return React.cloneElement(child, { users, fetchMore,
```

```
                variables, refetch });
              });
            }}
          </Query>
        )
      }
    }
```

As mentioned previously, we only want to send the query when the entered text is equal to or longer than three characters. Here, we use the `skip` property of the Apollo query component. If the `skip` parameter is set to true, the execution of the GraphQL request is skipped.

4. Continuing with our plan, we will create the application bar in a separate file. Create a new folder, called `bar`, below the `components` folder and the `index.js` file. Fill it in with the following code:

```
import React, { Component } from 'react';
import SearchBar from './search';

export default class Bar extends Component {
  render() {
    return (
      <div className="topbar">
        <div className="inner">
          <SearchBar/>
        </div>
      </div>
    );
  }
}
```

This file works as a wrapper for all of the components we want to render in the application bar; it does not implement any custom logic. We have already imported the `SearchBar` component which we must create.

5. The `SearchBar` class lives inside of a separate file. Just create a `search.js` file in the `bar` folder, as follows:

```
import React, { Component } from 'react';
import UsersSearchQuery from '../queries/searchQuery';
import SearchList from './searchList';

export default class SearchBar extends Component {
  state = {
    text: ''
  }
```

```
  changeText = (event) => {
    this.setState({text: event.target.value});
  }
  render() {
    const { text } = this.state;
    return (
      <div className="search">
        <input type="text" onChange={this.changeText} value={text}
        />
        <UsersSearchQuery variables={{text}}>
          <SearchList />
        </UsersSearchQuery>
      </div>
    );
  }
}
```

We are storing the current input value inside of a state variable, called `text`. Every time the text is changed, the `UsersSearchQuery` component is rerendered with the new `text` property. Inside of the query component, the value is merged into the variables and sent with a GraphQL request. The result is then handed over to the `SearchList` component, which is a child of the `UsersSearchQuery` class.

6. Next, we will implement the `SearchList`. This behaves like the posts feed, but only renders something if a response is given with at least one user. The list is displayed as a drop-down menu and is hidden whenever the browser window is clicked on. Create a file called `searchList.js` inside of the `bar` folder, with the following code:

```
import React, { Component } from 'react';
export default class SearchList extends Component {
  closeList = () => {
    this.setState({showList: false});
  }
  state = {
    showList: this.checkLength(this.props.users),
  }
  componentWillReceiveProps(props) {
    this.showList(props.users);
  }
  checkLength(users) {
    if(users.length > 0) {
      document.addEventListener('click', this.closeList);
      return true;
    } else {
```

```
        return false;
      }
    }
    showList(users) {
      if(this.checkLength(users)) {
        this.setState({showList: true});
      } else {
        this.closeList();
      }
    }
    componentWillUnmount() {
      document.removeEventListener('click', this.closeList);
    }
    render() {
      const { users } = this.props;
      const { showList } = this.state;
      return (
        showList &&
          <div className="result">
            {users.map((user, i) =>
              <div key={user.id} className="user">
                <img src={user.avatar} />
                <span>{user.username}</span>
              </div>
            )}
          </div>
      )
    }
  }
```

We are using the `componentWillReceiveProps` function here, which is executed whenever the parent component sets new properties on the current one. In this case, we check whether the properties include at least one user, and then set the state accordingly, in order to make the drop-down menu visible. The drop-down menu is hidden when clicked on, or when an empty result is given. The users come directly from the `UsersSearchQuery` component.

There are just two things to do now, as follows:

1. You should copy the CSS from the official GitHub repository of this chapter in order to get the correct styling; or, you can do it on your own
2. You need to import the bar wrapper component inside of the `App` class and render it between React Helmet and the news feed

The first feature of our application bar is now complete.

Let's continue and take a look at React's Context API, the Apollo Consumer feature, and how to store data globally in our React front end.

# The React Context API versus Apollo Consumer

There are two ways to handle global variables in the stack that we are using at the moment. These are the new React Context API and the Apollo Consumer functionality.

From version 16.3 of React, there is a new Context API that allows you to define global providers offering data through deeply nested components. These components do not require your application to hand over the data through many components, from the top to the bottom of the React tree. Instead, it uses so-called consumers and providers. These are useful when you set up the user object at a global point of your application, and you can access it from anywhere. In earlier versions of React, you needed to pass the property down from component to component to get it to the correct component at the bottom of the React component tree.

An alternative approach to the React Context API is the Apollo Consumer. It is a specific implementation for Apollo. The React Context API is a general way of doing things, for Apollo or anything else that you can imagine.

The great thing about the Apollo Consumer is that it enables you to access the Apollo cache and use it as data storage. Using the Apollo Consumer saves you from handling all of the data, but you are also not required to implement the provider itself; you can consume the data wherever you want.

Both of the approaches will result in the following output:

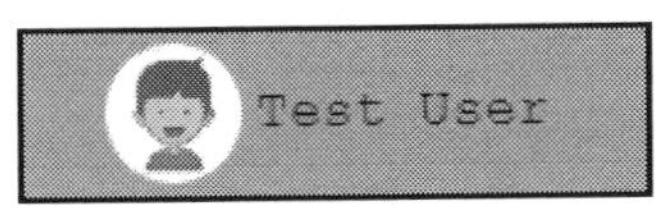


source: https://www.vecteezy.com/

The best option is to show you the two alternatives right away, so that you can identify your preferred method.

## The React Context API

We will start with the React method for storing and accessing global data in your front end.

The following is a short explanation of this method:

- **Context**: This is a React approach for sharing data between components, without having to pass it through the complete tree.
- **Provider**: This is a global component, mostly used at just one point in your code. It enables you to access the specific context data.
- **Consumer**: This is a component that can be used at many different points in your application, reading the data behind the context that you are referring to.

To get started, create a folder called `context` below the `components` folder. In that folder, create a `user.js` file, where we can set up the Context API.

We will go over every step, one by one, as follows:

- As always, we need to import all of the dependencies. Furthermore, we will set up a new empty context. The `createContext` function will return one provider and consumer to use throughout the application, as follows:

```
import React, { Component, createContext } from 'react';
const { Provider, Consumer } = createContext();
```

- Now, we want to use the provider. The best option here is to create a special `UserProvider` component. Later, when we have authentication, we can adjust it to do the GraphQL query, and then share the resultant data in our front end. For now, we will stick with fake data. Insert the following code:

```
export class UserProvider extends Component {
  render() {
    const { children } = this.props;
    const user = {
      username: "Test User",
      avatar: "/uploads/avatar1.png"
    };
    return (
      <Provider value={user}>
        {children}
      </Provider>
    );
  }
}
```

- In the preceding code, we render the `Provider` component from Apollo and wrap all of the children in it. There is a `Consumer` component that reads from the `Provider`. We will set up a special `UserConsumer` component that takes care of passing the data to the underlying components by cloning them with React's `cloneElement` function:

```
export class UserConsumer extends Component {
  render() {
    const { children } = this.props;
    return (
      <Consumer>
        {user => React.Children.map(children, function(child){
          return React.cloneElement(child, { user });
        })}
      </Consumer>
    )
  }
}
```

We will export both classes directly under their names.

We need to introduce the provider at an early point in our code base. The best approach is to import the `UserProvider` in the `App.js` file, as follows:

```
import { UserProvider } from './components/context/user';
```

Use the provider as follows, and wrap it around all essential components:

```
<UserProvider>
  <Bar />
  <Feed />
  <Chats />
</UserProvider>
```

Everywhere in the `Bar`, `Feed`, and `Chats` components, we can now read from the provider.

As stated previously, we want to show the logged-in user, with their name, inside the application.

The component using the data is the `UserBar`. We need to create a `user.js` file inside of the `bar` folder. We could also have written the `UserBar` class as a stateless function, but we might need to extend this component in a later chapter. Insert the following code:

```
import React, { Component } from 'react';
export default class UserBar extends Component {
  render() {
    const { user } = this.props;
```

```
        if(!user) return null;
        return (
          <div className="user">
            <img src={user.avatar} />
            <span>{user.username}</span>
          </div>
        );
      }
    }
```

For the moment, we render a simple user container inside of the application bar, from the data of the `user` object.

To get the user data into the `UserBar` component, we need to use the `UserConsumer` component, of course.

Open the `index.js` file for the top bar and add the following code to the `render` method, next to the `SearchBar` component:

```
<UserConsumer>
  <UserBar />
</UserConsumer>
```

Obviously, you need to import both of the components at the top of the file, as follows:

```
import UserBar from './user';
import { UserConsumer } from '../context/user';
```

You have now successfully configured and used the React Context API to save and read data globally.

The solution that we have is a general approach that will work for all scenarios that you can think of, including Apollo. Nevertheless, we should cover the solution offered by Apollo itself.

## Apollo Consumer

Nearly all of the code that we have written can stay as it was in the previous section. We just need to remove the `UserProvider` from the `App` class, because it is not needed anymore for the Apollo Consumer.

Open up the `user.js` in the `context` folder and replace the contents with the following code:

```
import React, { Component } from 'react';
import { ApolloConsumer } from 'react-apollo';

export class UserConsumer extends Component {
  render() {
    const { children } = this.props;
    return (
      <ApolloConsumer>
        {client => {
          // Use client.readQuery to get the current logged in user.
          const user = {
            username: "Test User",
            avatar: "/uploads/avatar1.png"
          };
          return React.Children.map(children, function(child){
            return React.cloneElement(child, { user });
          });
        }}
      </ApolloConsumer>
    )
  }
}
```

As you can see, we import the `ApolloConsumer` from the `react-apollo` package. This package enables us to get access to the Apollo Client that we set up in `Chapter 4`, *Integrating React into the Back end with Apollo.*

The problem we have here is that we do not have a `CurrentUser` query, which would respond with the logged-in user from the GraphQL; so, we are not able to run the `readQuery` function. You would typically run the query against the internal cache of Apollo, and be able to get the user object easily. Once we have implemented authentication, we will fix this problem.

For now, we will return the same fake object as we did with the React Context API. The Apollo Client replaces the `Provider` that we used with the React Context API.

I hope that you can understand the difference between these two solutions. In the next chapter, you will see the `ApolloConsumer` in full action, when the user query is established and can be read through the client of its cache.

# Documenting React applications

We have put a lot of work and code into our React application. To be honest, we can improve upon our code base by documenting it. We did not comment on our code, we did not add React component property type definitions, and we have no automated documentation tool. Of course, we did not write any comments because you learned all of the techniques and libraries from the book, so no comments were needed. However, be sure to always comment your code outside of this book.

In the JavaScript ecosystem, many different approaches and tools exist to document your application. For this book, we will use a tool called React Styleguidist. It was made especially for React. You cannot document other frameworks or code with it.

Generally speaking, this is an area that you can put months of work into without coming to a real end. If you are searching for a general approach for any framework or back end and front end, I can recommend JSDoc, but there are many more.

Let's get started with the configuration for React Styleguidist.

## Setting up React Styleguidist

React Styleguidist and our application rely on webpack. Just follow these instructions to get a working copy of it:

1. Install React Styleguidist using `npm`, as follows:

   ```
   npm install --save-dev react-styleguidist
   ```

2. Usually, the folder structure is expected to be `src/components`, but we have a `client` folder between the `src` and `components` folder. So, we must configure React Styleguidist to let it understand our folder structure. Create a `styleguide.config.js` in the root folder of the project to configure it, as follows:

   ```
   const path = require('path')
   module.exports = {
     components: 'src/client/components/**/*.js',
     require: [
       path.join(__dirname, 'assets/css/style.css')
     ]
     webpackConfig: require('./webpack.client.config')
   }
   ```

We export an object containing all of the information needed for React Styleguidist. In addition to specifying the `components` path, we also require our main CSS style file. You will see why this can be useful later in this chapter. We must define the `webpackConfig` option, because our `config` file has a custom name that is not found automatically.

Styleguidist provides two ways to view the documentation. One is to build the documentation statically, in production mode, with this command:

```
npx styleguidist build
```

This command creates a `styleguide` folder inside of the HTML files for our documentation. It is an excellent method when releasing new versions of your application, so that you can save and back up those files with each version.

The second method, for development cases, lets Styleguidist run and create the documentation on the fly, using webpack:

```
npx styleguidist server
```

You can view the results under `http://localhost:6060`. The documentation should look like the following screenshot:

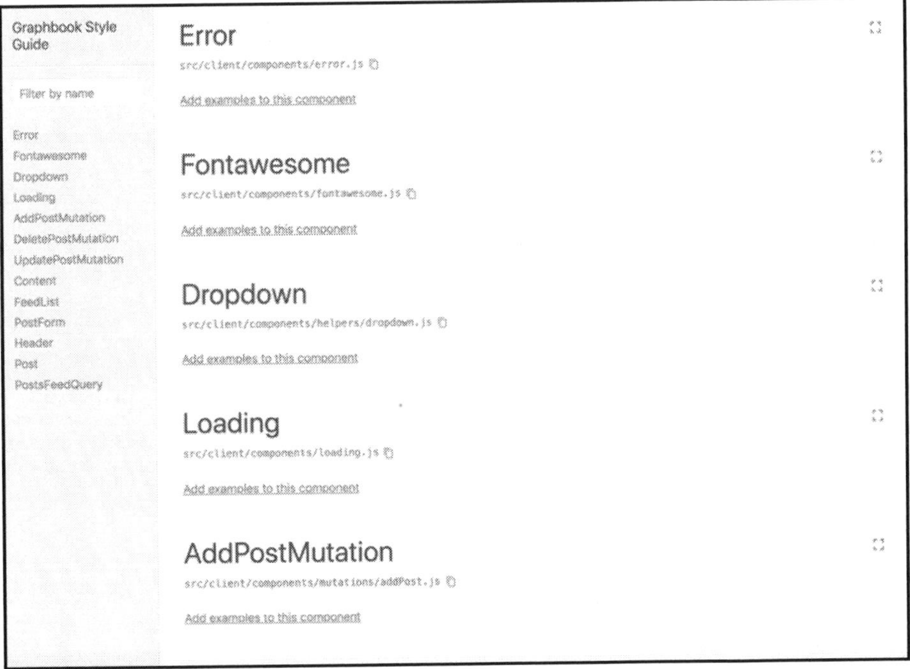

In the left-hand panel, all of the components are listed in the order of our folder structure. You will always have an excellent overview of the existing components this way.

In the main panel, each component is explained in detail. You may have noticed that the components are missing further information. We will change that next.

# React PropTypes

An essential feature of React is passing the properties to the child components. These can be anything from basic strings to numbers, but also complete components. We have already seen all of the scenarios in our application.

Developers that are new to your code base need to read through all of the components and identify which properties they can accept.

React offers a way to describe properties from within each component. Documenting the properties of your components makes it easier for other developers to understand your React components.

We will take a look at how to do this with an example in our `Post` component.

There are two React features that we did have covered yet, as follows:

- If your components have optional parameters, it can make sense to have default properties in the first place. To do this, you can specify `defaultProps` as a static property, in the same way as with the state initializers.
- The important part is the `propTypes` field, which you can fill for all of your components with the custom properties that they accept.

A new package is required to define the property types, as follows:

```
npm install --save prop-types
```

This package includes everything that we need to set up our property definitions.

Now, open your `Post` component's `index.js` file. We need to import the new package at the top of the `Post` component's `index.js` file:

```
import PropTypes from 'prop-types';
```

Next, we will add the new field to our component, above the state initializers:

```
static propTypes = {
  /** Object containing the complete post. */
  post: PropTypes.object.isRequired,
}
```

The preceding code should help everyone to understand your component a bit better. Every developer should know that a `post` object is required for this component to work.

The `PropTypes` package offers various types that we can use. You can access each type with `PropTypes.X`. If it is a required property, you can append the word `isRequired` in the same way as in the preceding code.

Not only does React now throw an error inside of our console when the property does not exist, but React Styleguidist is also able to show which properties are needed, as you can see in the following screenshot:

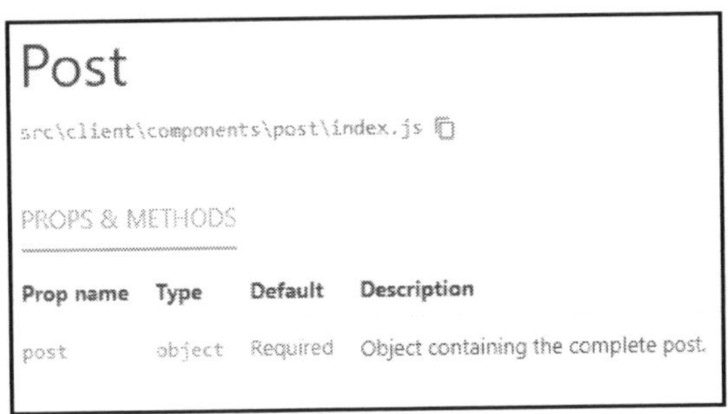


However, what is a `post` object? What kind of fields does it include?

The best way to document a `post` object is to define which properties a post should include, at least for this specific component. Replace the property definition, as follows:

```
static propTypes = {
  /** Object containing the complete post. */
  post: PropTypes.shape({
    id: PropTypes.number.isRequired,
    text: PropTypes.string.isRequired,
    user: PropTypes.shape({
      avatar: PropTypes.string.isRequired,
      username: PropTypes.string.isRequired,
    }).isRequired
  }).isRequired,
}
```

Here, we use the `shape` function. It allows you to hand over a list of fields that the object contains. Each of those is given a type from the `PropTypes` package.

The output from React Styleguidist now looks like the following screenshot:

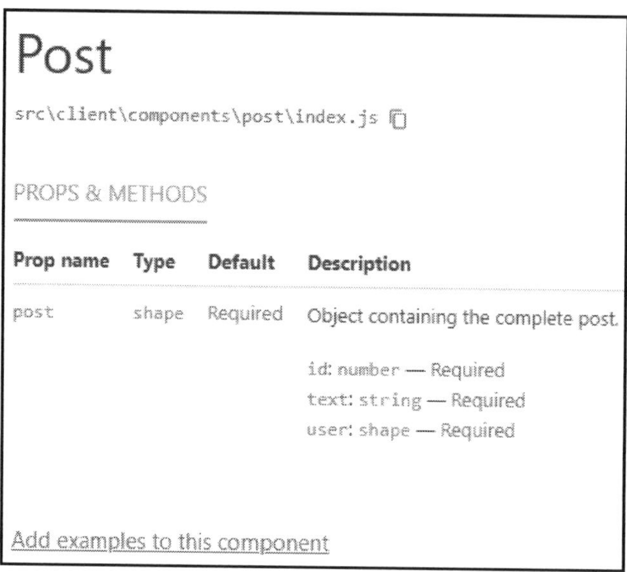


All of the fields that we specified are listed separately. At the time of writing this book, React Styleguidist does not offer a recursive view of all properties. As you can see, the user object inside of the `post` object is not listed with its properties, but it is only listed as a second shape. If you need this feature, you can, of course, implement it yourself, and send a `pull` request on the official GitHub repo, or switch to another tool.

React offers way more prop types and functions that you can use to document all of the components and their properties. To learn a bit more about this, visit the official documentation at `https://reactjs.org/docs/typechecking-with-proptypes.html`.

One last great feature of React Styleguidist is that you can enter examples for every component. You can also use markdown to add some more descriptions.

For our `Post` component, we need to create an `index.md` file, next to the `index.js` file in the `post` folder. React Styleguidist proposes creating either a `Readme.md` or `Post.md` file, but those did not work for me. The `index.md` file should look as follows:

````
Post example:

```js
  const post = {
    id: 3,
    text: "This is a test post!",
    user: {
      avatar: "/uploads/avatar1.png",
      username: "Test User"
    }
  };

  <Post key={post.id} post={post} />
```
````

React Styleguidist automatically rerenders the documentation and generates the following output:

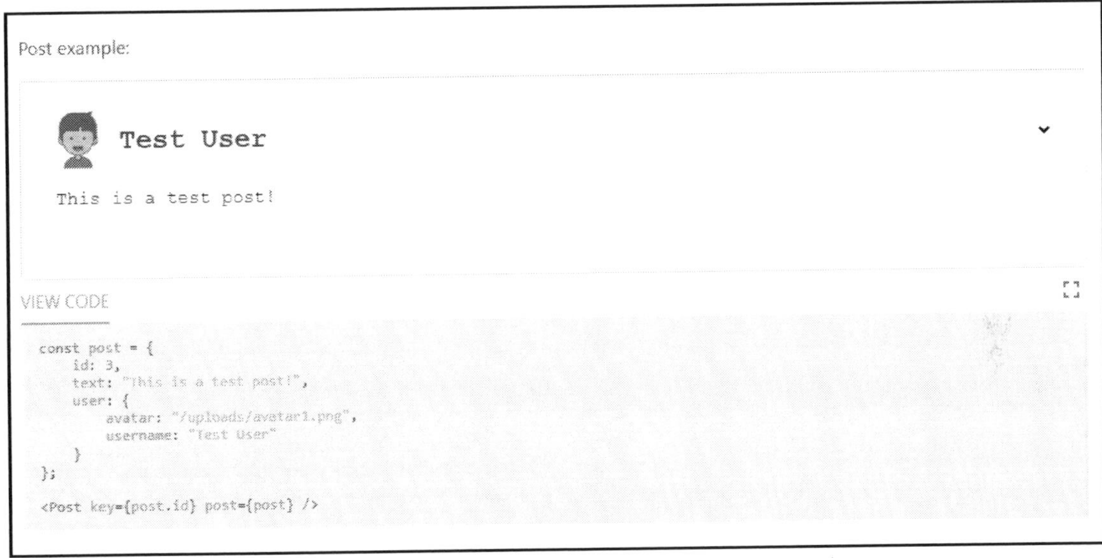


source: https://www.vecteezy.com/

Now, you can see why it was useful to use the CSS style. Not only can React Styleguidist document the code, but it can also execute it within the documentation. Like in the preceding code, providing the correct properties inside of the `post` object enables us to see how the component should look, including the correct styling.

This example shows how reusable our `Post` component is, since it is usable without having to run the Apollo query. The drop-down component is not working, though, because the whole application setup is incorrect, including the required Apollo Client.

The basics should be clear by now. Continue to read up on this topic, because there are more things to learn.

# Summary

Through this chapter, you have gained a lot of experience in writing a React application. You have applied multiple React patterns to different use cases, such as children passing through a pattern and conditional rendering. Furthermore, you now know how to document your code correctly.

You also learned how to use the React Context API, in comparison with the Apollo Consumer feature, to retrieve the currently logged-in user in our application.

In the next chapter, you will learn how to implement authentication in your back end and use it in the front end.

# 6 Authentication with Apollo and React

We have come a long way over the past few chapters. We have now finally reached the point at which we are going to implement authentication for our React and GraphQL web applications. In this chapter, you are going to learn some essential concepts for building an application with authentication using GraphQL.

This chapter covers the following topics:

- What is a JWT?
- Cookies versus localStorage
- Implementing authentication in Node.js and Apollo
- Signing up and logging in users
- Authenticating GraphQL queries and mutations
- Accessing the user from the request context

## JSON Web Tokens

**JSON Web Tokens (JWTs)** are still a pretty new standard for carrying out authentication; not everyone knows about them, and even fewer people use them. This section does not provide a theoretical excursion through the mathematical or cryptographic basics of JWTs.

In traditional web applications written in PHP, for example, you commonly have a session cookie. This cookie identifies the user session on the server. The session must be stored on the server to retrieve the initial user. The problem here is that the overhead of saving and querying all sessions for all users can be high. When using JWTs, however, there is no need for the server to preserve any kind of session id.

Generally speaking, a JWT consists of everything you need to identify a user. The most common approach is to store the creation time of the token, the username, the user id, and maybe the role, such as an admin or a normal user. You should not include any personal or critical data for security reasons.

The reason a JWT exists is not to encrypt or secure data in any way. Instead, to authorize yourself at a resource like a server, you send a signed JWT that your server can verify. It can only verify the JWT if it was created by a service stated as authentic by your server. In most cases, your server will have used its public key to sign the token. Any person or service that can read the communication between you and the server can access the token and can extract the payload without further ado. They are not able to edit the content though, because the token is signed with a signature.

The token needs to be transported and stored securely in the browser of the client. If the token gets into the wrong hands, that person is able to access the affected application with your identity, initiate actions in your name, or read personal data. It is also hard to invalidate a JWT. With a session cookie, you can delete the session on the server, and the user will no longer be authenticated through the cookie. With a JWT, however, we do not have any information on the server. It can only validate the signature of the token and find the user in your database. One common approach is to have a blacklist of all the disallowed tokens. Alternatively, you can keep the lifetime of a JWT low by specifying the expiration date. This solution, however, requires the user to frequently repeat the login process, which makes the experience less comfortable.

JWTs do not require any server-side storage. The great thing about server-side sessions is that you can store specific application states for your user and, for example, remember the last actions a user made. Without a server-side store, you either need to implement these features in `localStorage` or implement a session store, which is not required for using JWT authentication at all.

JSON Web Tokens are an important topic in developer communities. There is some excellent documentation available related to what JWTs are, how they can be used, and their technological background. Visit the following web page to learn more and to see a demonstration of the generation of a JWT: `https://jwt.io/`.

In our example, we are going to use JWTs, since they are a modern and decentralized method of authentication. Still, you can choose to opt out of this at any point and instead use regular sessions, which can be quickly realized in Express.js and GraphQL.

# localStorage versus cookie

Let's take a look at another critical question. It is crucial to understand at least the basics of how authentication works and how it is secured. You are responsible for any faulty implementation that allows data breaches, so always keep this in mind. Where do we store the token we receive from the server?

In whichever direction you send a token, you should always be sure that your communication is secure. For web applications like ours, be sure that HTTPS is enabled and used for all requests. After the user has successfully authenticated the use, it receives the JWT, according to the JWT authentication workflow. A JWT is not tied to any particular storage medium, so you are free to choose whichever you prefer. If we do not store the token when it is received, it will be only available in the memory. While the user is browsing our site, this is fine, but the moment they refresh the page, they will need to log in again because we haven't stored the token anywhere.

There are two standard options: to store the JWT inside the `localStorage` or to store it inside a cookie. Let's start by discussing the first option. `localStorage` is the option often suggested in tutorials. It is fine, assuming you are writing a single-page web application in which the content changes dynamically, depending on the actions of the user and client-side routing. We do not follow any links and load new sites to see new content; instead, the old one is just replaced with the new page that you want to show.

Storing the token in `localStorage` has the following disadvantages:

- `localStorage` is not transmitted on every request. When the page is loaded initially, you are not able to send the token within your request, and so resources needing authentication cannot be given back to you. When your application has finished loading, you have to make a second request to your server, including the token to access the secured content. This behavior has the consequence that it is not possible to build server-rendered applications.
- The client needs to implement the mechanics to attach the token on every request to the server.
- From the nature of `localStorage`, there is no built-in expiry date on the client. If at some point the token reaches its expiration date, it still exists on the client inside `localStorage`.
- The `localStorage` is accessed through pure JavaScript and is therefore open to XSS attacks. If someone manages to integrate custom JavaScript in your code or site through unsanitized inputs, they are able to read the token from `localStorage`.

There are, however, many advantages of using `localStorage`:

- As `localStorage` is not sent automatically with every request, it is secure against any **Cross-Site-Request-Forgery (CSRF)** attacks attempting to run actions from external sites by making random requests
- The `localStorage` is easy to read in JavaScript since it is stored as a key value pair
- It supports a bigger data size, which is great for storing an application state or data

The main problem with storing such critical tokens inside web storage is that you cannot guarantee that there is no unwanted access. Unless you can be sure that every single input is sanitized and you are not relying on any third-party tools that gets bundled into your JavaScript code, there is always a potential risk. Just one package you did not build yourself could share your users' web storage with its creator, without you or the user ever noticing. Furthermore, when you are using a public **Content Delivery Network (CDN)** the attack base and consequently the risk for your application is multiplied.

Now, let's take a look at cookies. These are great, despite their bad press due to the cookie compliance law initiated by the EU. Putting aside the more negative things that cookies can enable companies to do, such as tracking users, there are many good things about them. One significant difference compared to `localStorage` is that cookies are sent with every request, including the initial request for the site your application is hosted on.

Cookies come with the following advantages:

- Server-side rendering is no problem at all since cookies are sent with every request
- No further logic needs to be implemented in the front end to send the JWT.
- Cookies can be declared as `httpOnly`, which means JavaScript can't access them. It secures our token from XSS attacks
- Cookies have a built-in expiration date, which can be set to invalidate the cookie in the client browser
- Cookies can be configured to be readable only from specific domains or paths.
- All browsers support cookies

These advantages sound good so far, but let's consider the downsides:

- Cookies are generally open to CSRF attacks, which are situations in which an external website makes requests to your API. They expect that you are authenticated and hope that they can execute actions on your behalf. We can't stop the cookie from being sent with each request to your domain. A common prevention tactic is to implement an CSRF token. This special token is also transmitted by your server and saved as a cookie. The external website cannot access the cookie with JavaScript since it is stored under a different domain. Your server does not read a token from the cookies that are transmitted with each request, but only from an HTTP header. This behavior guarantees that the token was sent by the JavaScript that was hosted on your application, because only this can have access to the token. Setting up the XSRF token for verification, however, introduces a lot of work.
- Accessing and parsing cookies is not intuitive, because they are just stored as a big comma-separated string.
- They can only store a small amount of data.

We can see that both approaches have their advantages and disadvantages.

The most common method is to use `localStorage`, as this is the easiest method. In this book, we start by using `localStorage`, but later switch over to cookies when using server-side rendering to give you experience in both. You may not need server-side rendering at all. If this is the case, you can skip this part and the cookie implementation too.

# Authentication with GraphQL

The basics of authentication should now be clear to you. Our task is now to implement a secure way for users to authenticate. If we have a look at our current database, we are missing the required fields. Let's prepare and add a `password` and an `email` field. As we learned in `Chapter 3`, *Connecting to the Database*, we create a migration to edit our user table. You can look up the commands in the third chapter if you have forgotten them:

```
sequelize migration:create --migrations-path src/server/migrations --name
add-email-password-to-post
```

The preceding command generates the new file for us. You can replace the content of it and try writing the migration on your own, or check for the right commands in the following code snippet:

```
'use strict';

module.exports = {
  up: (queryInterface, Sequelize) => {
    return Promise.all([
      queryInterface.addColumn('Users',
        'email',
        {
          type: Sequelize.STRING,
          unique : true,
        }
      ),
      queryInterface.addColumn('Users',
        'password',
        {
          type: Sequelize.STRING,
        }
      ),
    ]);
  },

  down: (queryInterface, Sequelize) => {
    return Promise.all([
      queryInterface.removeColumn('Users', 'email'),
      queryInterface.removeColumn('Users', 'password'),
    ]);
  }
};
```

All fields are simple strings. You can execute the migration, as stated in the `Chapter 3`, *Connecting to The Database*. The email address needs to be unique. Our old seed file for the users needs to be updated now to represent the new fields that we have just added. Copy the following fields:

```
password: '$2a$10$bE3ovf9/Tiy/d68bwNUQ0.zCjwtNFq9ukg9h4rhKiHCb6x5ncKife',
email: 'test1@example.com',
```

Do this for all three users and change the email address for each of them. Otherwise, it will not work. The password is in hashed format and represents the plain password 123456789. As we have added new fields in a separate migration, we have to add these to the model.

Open and add the new lines as fields to the `user.js` file in the `model` folder:

```
email: DataTypes.STRING,
password: DataTypes.STRING,
```

The first thing to do now is get the login running. At the moment, we are just faking being logged in as the first user in our database.

# Apollo login mutation

We are now going to edit our GraphQL schema and implement the matching resolver function. Let's start with the schema and a new mutation to the `RootMutation` object of our `schema.js` file:

```
login (
  email: String!
  password: String!
): Auth
```

The preceding schema gives us a login mutation that accepts an email address and a password. Both are required to identify and authenticate the user. We then need to respond with something to the client. For now, the `Auth` type returns a token, which is a JWT in our case. You might want to add a different option according to your requirements:

```
type Auth {
  token: String
}
```

The schema is now ready. Head over to the `resolvers` file and add the login function inside the mutation object. Before doing this, we have to install and import two new packages:

```
npm install --save jsonwebtoken bcrypt
```

The `jsonwebtoken` package handles everything required to sign, verify, and decode JWTs.

The important part is that all passwords for our users are not saved as plain text but are first encrypted using hashing, including a random salt. This generated hash cannot be decoded or decrypted to a plain password, but the package can verify if the password that was sent with the login attempt matches with the password hash saved on the user. Import these packages at the top of the resolvers file:

```
import bcrypt from 'bcrypt';
import JWT from 'jsonwebtoken';
```

The `login` function receives `email` and `password` as parameters. It should look like the following code:

```
login(root, { email, password }, context) {
  return User.findAll({
    where: {
      email
    },
    raw: true
  }).then(async (users) => {
    if(users.length = 1) {
      const user = users[0];
      const passwordValid = await bcrypt.compare(password,
      user.password);
      if (!passwordValid) {
        throw new Error('Password does not match');
      }
      const token = JWT.sign({ email, id: user.id }, JWT_SECRET, {
        expiresIn: '1d'
      });

      return {
        token
      };
    } else {
      throw new Error("User not found");
    }
  });
},
```

The preceding code goes through the following steps:

1. We query all users where the email address matches.
2. If a user is found, we can go on. It is not possible to have multiple users with the same address, as the MySQL unique constraint forbids this.
3. Next, we use the user password and compare it with the submitted password, using the `bcrypt` package, as explained previously.
4. If the password was correct, we generate a JWT token to the `jwt` variable using the `jwt.sign` function. It takes three arguments: the payload, which is the user id and their email address; the key with which we sign the JWT; and the amount of time in which the JWT is going to expire.
5. In the end, we return an object containing our JWT.

Something that you might need to rethink is how much detail you give in an error message. For example, we might not want to distinguish between an incorrect password and a non-existent user. It gives possible attackers or data collectors the opportunity to know which email address is in use.

The `login` function is not working yet, because we are missing `JWT_SECRET`, which is used to sign the JWT. In production, we use the environment variables to pass the JWT secret key into our back end code so that we use this approach in development too.

For Linux or Mac, you can use the following command directly in the Terminal:

```
export
JWT_SECRET=awv4BcIzsRysXkhoSAb8t8lNENgXSqBruVlLwd45kGdYjeJHLap9LUJ1t9DTdw36
DvLcWs3qEkPyCY6vOyNljlh2Er952h2gDzYwG82rs1qfTzdVIg89KTaQ4SWI1YGY
```

The `export` function sets the `JWT_SECRET` environment variable for you. Replace the JWT provided with a random one. You can use any password generator by setting the character count to 128 and excluding any special characters. Setting the environment variable allows us to read the secret in our application. You have to replace it when going to production.

Insert the following code at the top of the file:

```
const { JWT_SECRET } = process.env;
```

This code reads the environment variable from the global Node.js `process` object. Be sure to replace the JWT once you publish your application, and be sure to always store the secret securely. After letting the server reload, we can send the first login request. We are going to take a look how to do this in React later, but the following code shows an example using Postman:

```
{
  "operationName":null,
  "query": "mutation login($email : String!, $password : String!) {
   login(email: $email, password : $password) { token }}",
  "variables":{
    "email": "test1@example.com",
    "password": "123456789"
  }
}
```

This request should return a token:

```
{
  "data": {
    "login": {
      "token":
"eyJhbGciOiJIUzI1NiIsInR5cCI6IkpXVCJ9.eyJlbWFpbCI6InRlc3QxQGV4YW1wbGUuY29tI
iwiaWQiOjEsImlhdCI6MTUzNzIwNjI0MywiZXhwIjoxNTM3MjkyNjQzfQ.HV4dPIBzvU1yn6REM
v42N0DS0ZdgebFDX-Uj0MPHvlY"
    }
  }
}
```

As you can see, we have generated a signed JWT and returned it within the mutation's response. We can go on and send the token with every request inside the HTTP authorization header. We can then get the authentication running for all the other GraphQL queries or mutations that we have implemented so far.

Let's continue and learn how to set up React to work with our authentication on the back end.

# The React login form

We need to handle the different authentication states of our application:

- The first scenario is that the user is not logged in and cannot see any posts or chats. In this case, we need to show a login form to allow the user to authenticate themselves.
- The second scenario is that an email and password are sent through the login form. The response needs to be interpreted, and if the result is correct, we need to save the JWT inside the `localStorage` of the browser for now.
- When changing the `localStorage`, we also need to rerender our React application to show the logged-in state.
- Furthermore, the user should be able to log out again.
- We must also handle if the JWT expires and the user is unable to access any functionalities.

The result for our form looks as follows:

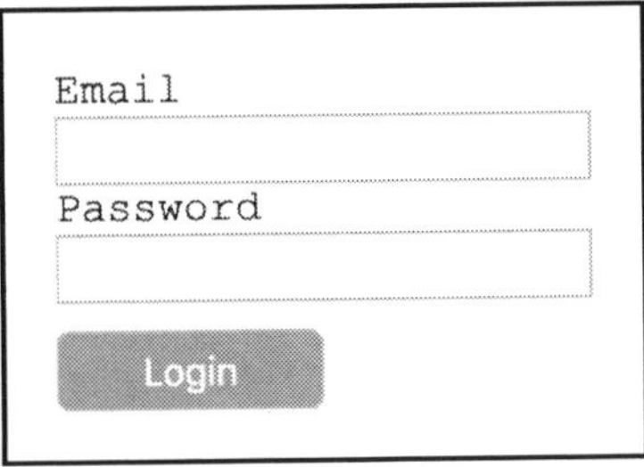


To get started with the login form, observe the following steps:

1. Set up the login `Mutation` component. It is likely that we only need this component at one place in our code, but it is a good idea to save Apollo requests in separate files.
2. Build the login form component, which uses the login mutation to send the form data.
3. Create the `CurrentUser` query to retrieve the logged-in user object.
4. Conditionally render the login form if the user is not authenticated or the real application like the news feed if the user is logged in.

Begin by creating a new `login.js` file inside the `mutations` folder for the client components:

```
import React, { Component } from 'react';
import { Mutation } from 'react-apollo';
import gql from 'graphql-tag';

const LOGIN = gql`
  mutation login($email : String!, $password : String!) {
    login(email : $email, password : $password) {
      token
    }
  }`;

export default class LoginMutation extends Component {
  render() {
    const { children } = this.props;
    return (
      <Mutation
        update = {(store, { data: { login } }) => {
          if(login.token) {
            localStorage.setItem('jwt', login.token);
```

```
            }
          }}
          mutation={LOGIN}>
            {(login, { loading, error}) =>
              React.Children.map(children, function(child){
                return React.cloneElement(child, { login, loading, error });
              })
            }
        </Mutation>
      )
    }
  }
```

Like in the previous mutations, we parse the query string and hand the resulting `login` function over to all the children of the component. We now give the `loading` and `error` states to those children, in case we want to show an error or loading message. The `update` function is a bit different than before. We don't write the return value in the Apollo cache, but we do need to store the JWT inside the `localStorage`. The syntax is pretty simple. You can directly use `localStorage.get` and `localStorage.set` to interact with the web storage.

Now, we implement the underlying children, which makes up the login form. To do this, we create a `loginregister.js` file directly in the `components` folder. As you may expect, we handle the login and registration of users in one component. Import the dependencies:

```
import React, { Component } from 'react';
import Error from './error';
import LoginMutation from './mutations/login';
```

The `LoginForm` class will store the form state, display an error message if something goes wrong, and send the login mutation including the form data:

```
class LoginForm extends Component {
  state = {
    email: '',
    password: '',
  }
  login = (event) => {
    event.preventDefault();
    this.props.login({ variables: { email: this.state.email, password:
    this.state.password }});
  }
  render() {
    const { error } = this.props;
    return (
      <div className="login">
```

```
        <form onSubmit={this.login}>
          <label>Email</label>
          <input type="text" onChange={(event) => this.setState({email:
           event.target.value})} />
          <label>Password</label>
          <input type="password" onChange={(event) =>
           this.setState({password: event.target.value})} />
          <input type="submit" value="Login" />
        </form>
        {error && (
          <Error><p>There was an error logging in!</p></Error>
        )}
      </div>
    )
  }
}
```

We render the login form inside the wrapping component, which is called `LoginRegisterForm`. It is important to surround the form with the login mutation so that we can send the Apollo request:

```
export default class LoginRegisterForm extends Component {
  render() {
    return (
      <div className="authModal">
        <LoginMutation><LoginForm/></LoginMutation>
      </div>
    )
  }
}
```

All the basics for authenticating the user are now ready, but they have not been imported yet or displayed anywhere. Open the `App.js` file. There, we directly display the feed, chats, and the top bar. The user should not be allowed to see everything if he is not logged in. Continue reading to change this.

Import the new form that we have just created:

```
import LoginRegisterForm from './components/loginregister';
```

We then have to store whether the user is logged in or not. We save it in the component state, as follows:

```
state = {
  loggedIn: false
}
```

When loading our page, this variable needs to be set to `true` if we have a token in our `localStorage`. We handle this inside the `componentWillMount` function provided by React:

```
componentWillMount() {
  const token = localStorage.getItem('jwt');
  if(token) {
      this.setState({loggedIn: true});
  }
}
```

Then, in the `render` method, we can use conditional rendering to show the login form when the `loggedIn` state variable is set to `false`, which means that there is no JWT inside our `localStorage`:

```
{this.state.loggedIn ?
  <div>
    <Bar />
    <Feed />
    <Chats />
  </div>
  : <LoginRegisterForm/>
}
```

If you try the login page, you will see that nothing happens, even though no error message is shown. That happens because we save the JWT, but we do not tell React to rerender our `App` class. We only check for the JWT when the page loads initially. To test your implementation, you can reload the window, and you should be logged in.

We have to pass a function down the React tree to the components, who are then able to trigger a logged-in state so that React can rerender and show the logged in area. We call this function `changeLoginState` and implement it inside the `App.js` file as follows:

```
changeLoginState = (loggedIn) => {
  this.setState({ loggedIn });
}
```

The function can change the current application state as specified through the `loggedIn` parameter. We then integrate this method into the `LoginMutation` component. To do this, we edit the `render` method of the `App` class to pass the right property:

```
<LoginRegisterForm changeLoginState={this.changeLoginState}/>
```

Then, inside the `LoginRegisterForm` class, we replace the `render` method with the following code:

```
render() {
  const { changeLoginState } = this.props;
  return (
    <div className="authModal">
      <LoginMutation
changeLoginState={changeLoginState}><LoginForm/></LoginMutation>
    </div>
  )
}
```

Edit the `LoginMutation` component and extract the new function from the properties:

```
const { children, changeLoginState } = this.props;
```

We can then execute the `changeLoginState` function within the `update` method:

```
if(login.token) {
  localStorage.setItem('jwt', login.token);
  changeLoginState(true);
}
```

When logging in, our application presents us with the common posts feed as before. The authentication flow is now working, but there is one more open task. In the next step, we allow new users to register at Graphbook.

# Apollo sign up mutation

You should now be familiar with creating new mutations. First, edit the schema to accept the new mutation:

```
signup (
  username: String!
  email: String!
  password: String!
): Auth
```

We only need the `username`, `email`, and `password` properties that were mentioned in the preceding code to accept new users. If your application requires a gender or something else, you can add it here. When trying to sign up, we need to ensure that neither the email address nor the username is already taken. You can copy over the code to implement the resolver for signing up new users:

```
signup(root, { email, password, username }, context) {
  return User.findAll({
    where: {
      [Op.or]: [{email}, {username}]
    },
    raw: true,
  }).then(async (users) => {
    if(users.length) {
      throw new Error('User already exists');
    } else {
      return bcrypt.hash(password, 10).then((hash) => {
        return User.create({
          email,
          password: hash,
          username,
          activated: 1,
        }).then((newUser) => {
          const token = JWT.sign({ email, id: newUser.id }, JWT_SECRET,
          {
            expiresIn: '1d'
          });
          return {
            token
          };
        });
      });
    }
  });
},
```

Let's go through the code step by step:

1. As mentioned previously, we first check if a user with the same email or username exists. If this is the case, we throw an error. We use the `Op.or` Sequelize operator to implement the MySQL OR condition.

2. If the user does not exist, we can hash the password using `bcrypt`. You cannot save the plain password for security reasons. When running the `bcrypt.hash` function, a random salt is used to make sure nobody ever gets access to the original password. This command takes quite some computing time, so the `bcrypt.hash` function is asynchronous, and the promise must be resolved before continuing.
3. The encrypted password, including the other data the user has sent, is then inserted in our database as a new user.
4. After creating the user, we generate a JWT and return it to the client. The JWT allows us to log in the user directly after signing up. If you do not want this behavior, you can of course just return a message to indicate that the user has signed up successfully.

You can now test the `signup` mutation again with Postman if you want while starting the back end using `npm run server`. We have now finished the back end implementation, so we start working on the front end.

# React sign up form

The registration form is nothing special. We follow the same steps as we took with the login form. You can clone the `LoginMutation` component, replace the request at the top with the `signup` mutation, and hand over the `signup` method to the underlying children. At the top, import all the dependencies and then parse the new query:

```
import React, { Component } from 'react';
import { Mutation } from 'react-apollo';
import gql from 'graphql-tag';

const SIGNUP = gql`
  mutation signup($email : String!, $password : String!, $username :
   String!) {
    signup(email : $email, password : $password, username : $username) {
    token
  }
}`;
```

As you can see, the `username` field is new here, which we send with every `signup` request. The component itself has not changed, so we have to extract the JWT from the `signup` field when logging the user in after a successful request.

We use the `changeLoginState` method to do so. We also changed the name of the mutation function we pass from `login` to `signup`, of course:

```
export default class SignupMutation extends Component {
  render() {
    const { children, changeLoginState } = this.props;
    return (
      <Mutation
        update = {(store, { data: { signup } }) => {
          if(signup.token) {
            localStorage.setItem('jwt', signup.token);
            changeLoginState(true);
          }
        }}
        mutation={SIGNUP}>
          {(signup, { loading, error}) =>
            React.Children.map(children, function(child){
              return React.cloneElement(child, { signup, loading, error
              });
            })
          }
      </Mutation>
    )
  }
}
```

It is a good thing for the developer to see, that the `login` and `signup` mutations are quite similar. The biggest change is that we conditionally render the login form or the registration form. In the `loginregister.js` file, you first import the new mutation. Then, you replace the complete `LoginRegisterForm` class with the following new one:

```
export default class LoginRegisterForm extends Component {
  state = {
    showLogin: true
  }
  render() {
    const { changeLoginState } = this.props;
    const { showLogin } = this.state;
    return (
      <div className="authModal">
        {showLogin && (
          <div>
            <LoginMutation changeLoginState=
              {changeLoginState}><LoginForm/></LoginMutation>
            <a onClick={() => this.setState({ showLogin: false })}>Want
             to sign up? Click here</a>
          </div>
```

```
        )}
        {!showLogin && (
          <div>
            <RegisterMutation changeLoginState=
              {changeLoginState}><RegisterForm/></RegisterMutation>
            <a onClick={() => this.setState({ showLogin: true })}>Want to
             login? Click here</a>
          </div>
        )}
      </div>
    )
  }
}
```

You should notice that we are storing a `showLogin` variable in the component state, which decides if the login or register form is shown. The matching mutation wraps each form, and they handle everything from there. The last thing to do is insert the new register form in the `login.js` file:

```
class RegisterForm extends Component {
  state = {
    email: '',
    password: '',
    username: '',
  }
  login = (event) => {
    event.preventDefault();
    this.props.signup({ variables: { email: this.state.email, password:
    this.state.password, username: this.state.username }});
  }
  render() {
    const { error } = this.props;
    return (
      <div className="login">
        <form onSubmit={this.login}>
          <label>Email</label>
          <input type="text" onChange={(event) => this.setState({email:
           event.target.value})} />
          <label>Username</label>
          <input type="text" onChange={(event) =>
           this.setState({username: event.target.value})} />
          <label>Password</label>
          <input type="password" onChange={(event) =>
           this.setState({password: event.target.value})} />
          <input type="submit" value="Sign up" />
        </form>
        {error && (
          <Error><p>There was an error logging in!</p></Error>
```

```
          )}
        </div>
      )
    }
  }
```

In the preceding code, I have added the `username` field, which has to be given to the mutation. Everything is now set to invite new users to join our social network and log in as often as they want.

In the next section, we will see how to use authentication with our existing GraphQL requests.

# Authenticating GraphQL requests

The problem is that we are not using the authentication everywhere at the moment. We verify that the user is who they say they are, but we do not recheck this when the requests for chats or messages come in. To accomplish this, we have to send the JWT token, which we generated specifically for this case, with every Apollo request. On the back end, we have to specify which request requires authentication, read the JWT from the HTTP authorization header, and verify it.

Open the `index.js` file from the `apollo` folder for the client-side code.
Our `ApolloClient` is currently configured as explained in `Chapter 4`, *Integrating React into the Back end with Apollo*. Before sending any request, we have to read the JWT from the `localStorage` and add it as an HTTP authorization header. Inside the `link` property, we have specified the links for our `ApolloClient` processes. Before the configuration of the HTTP link, we insert a third preprocessing hook as follows:

```
const AuthLink = (operation, next) => {
  const token = localStorage.getItem('jwt');
  if(token) {
    operation.setContext(context => ({
      ...context,
      headers: {
        ...context.headers,
        Authorization: `Bearer ${token}`,
      },
    }));
  }
  return next(operation);
};
```

Here, we have called the new link `AuthLink`, because it allows us to authenticate the client on the server. You can copy the `AuthLink` approach to other situations in which you need to customize the header of your Apollo requests. Here, we just read the JWT from the `localStorage` and, if it is found, we construct the header using the spread operator and adding our token to the Authorization field as a Bearer token. It is everything that needs to be done on the client-side.

To clarify things, take a look at the following `link` property to see how to use this new preprocessor. There is no initialization required; it is merely a function that is called every time a request is made. Copy the `link` configuration to our Apollo Client setup:

```
link: ApolloLink.from([
  onError(({ graphQLErrors, networkError }) => {
    if (graphQLErrors) {
      graphQLErrors.map(({ message, locations, path }) =>
      console.log(`[GraphQL error]: Message: ${message}, Location:
      ${locations}, Path: ${path}`));
      if (networkError) {
        console.log(`[Network error]: ${networkError}`);
      }
    }
  }),
  AuthLink,
  new HttpLink({
    uri: 'http://localhost:8000/graphql',
    credentials: 'same-origin',
  }),
]),
```

For our back end, we need a pretty complex solution. Create a new file called `auth.js` inside the `graphql services` folder. We want to be able to mark specific GraphQL requests in our schema with a so-called directive. If we add this directive to our GraphQL schema, we execute a function whenever the marked GraphQL action is requested. In this function, we can verify whether the user is logged in or not. Have a look at the following function and save it right to the `auth.js` file:

```
import { SchemaDirectiveVisitor, AuthenticationError } from 'apollo-server-
express';

class AuthDirective extends SchemaDirectiveVisitor {
  visitFieldDefinition(field) {
    const { resolve = defaultFieldResolver } = field;
    field.resolve = async function(...args) {
      const ctx = args[2];
      if (ctx.user) {
        return await resolve.apply(this, args);
```

```
      } else {
        throw new AuthenticationError("You need to be logged in.");
      }
    };
  }
}

export default AuthDirective;
```

Starting from the top, we import the `SchemaDirectiveVisitor` class from the `apollo-server-express` package. This class allows us to handle all requests that have the `AuthDirective` attached. We extend the `SchemaDirectiveVisitor` class and override the `visitFieldDefinition` method. Within the method, we resolve the current context of the request with the `field.resolve` function. If the context has a user attached, we can be sure that the authorization header has been checked before and the identified user has been added to the request context. If not, we throw an error. The `AuthError` we are throwing gives us the opportunity to implement certain behaviors when an `UNAUTHENTICATED` error is sent to the client.

We have to load the new `AuthDirective` class in the `graphql index.js` file, which sets up the whole Apollo Server:

```
import auth from './auth';
```

While using the `makeExecutableSchema` function to combine the schema and the resolvers, we can add a further property to handle all schema directives, as follows:

```
const executableSchema = makeExecutableSchema({
  typeDefs: Schema,
  resolvers: Resolvers.call(utils),
  schemaDirectives: {
    auth: auth
  },
});
```

Here, we combine the schema, the resolvers, and the directives into one big object. It is important to note that the `auth` index inside the `schemaDirectives` object is the mark that we have to set at every GraphQL request in our schema that requires authentication. To verify what we have just done, go to the GraphQL schema and edit `postsFeed RootQuery` by adding `@auth` at the end of the line like this:

```
postsFeed(page: Int, limit: Int): PostFeed @auth
```

Because we are using a new directive, we also must define it in our GraphQL schema so that our server knows about it. Copy the following code directly to the top of the schema:

```
directive @auth on QUERY | FIELD_DEFINITION | FIELD
```

This tiny snippet tells the Apollo Server that the `@auth` directive is usable with queries, fields, and field definitions so that we can use it everywhere.

If you reload the page and manually set the `loggedIn` state variable to true via the React Developer Tools, you will see the following error message:

```
GraphQL error: You need to be logged in.
```

As we have implemented the error component earlier, we are now correctly receiving an unauthenticated error for the `postsFeed` query if the user is not logged in. How can we use the JWT to identify the user and add it into the request context?

Schema directives are a complex topic as there are many important things to bear in mind to do with Apollo and GraphQL. I recommend that you read up on directives in detail in the official Apollo documentation: `https://www.apollographql.com/docs/graphql-tools/schema-directives.html`.

In `Chapter 2`, *Setting Up GraphQL with Express.js*, we set up the Apollo Server by providing the executable schema and the context, which has been the request object until now. We have to check if the JWT is inside the request. If this is the case, we need to verify it and query the user to see if the token is valid. Let's start by verifying the authorization header. Before doing so, import the new dependencies in the Graphql `index.js` file:

```
import JWT from 'jsonwebtoken';
const { JWT_SECRET } = process.env;
```

The `context` field of the `ApolloServer` initialization has to look as follows:

```
const server = new ApolloServer({
  schema: executableSchema,
  context: async ({ req }) => {
    const authorization = req.headers.authorization;
    if(typeof authorization !== typeof undefined) {
      var search = "Bearer";
      var regEx = new RegExp(search, "ig");
      const token = authorization.replace(regEx, '').trim();
      return jwt.verify(token, JWT_SECRET, function(err, result) {
        return req;
```

```
        });
      } else {
        return req;
      }
    },
  });
```

We have extended the `context` property of the `ApolloServer` class to a full-featured function. We read the `auth` token from the headers of the requests. If the `auth` token exists, we need to strip out the bearer string, because it is not part of the original token that was created by our back end. The bearer token is the best method of JWT authentication.

There are other authentication methods like basic authentication, but the bearer method is the best to follow. You can find a detailed explanation under RFC6750 by the IETF at this link: `https://tools.ietf.org/html/rfc6750`.

Afterwards, we use the `jwt.verify` function to check if the token matches the signature generated by the secret from the environment variables. The next step is to retrieve the user after successful verification. Replace the content of the `verify` callback with the following code:

```
if(err) {
  return req;
} else {
  return utils.db.models.User.findById(result.id).then((user) => {
    return Object.assign({}, req, { user });
  });
}
```

If the `err` object in the previous code has been filled, we can only return the ordinary request object, which triggers an error when it reaches the `AuthDirective` class, since there is no user attached. If there are no errors, we can use the `utils` object we are already passing to the Apollo Server setup to access the database. If you need a reminder, take a look at `Chapter 2`, *Setting Up GraphQL with Express.js*. After querying the user, we add them to the request object and return the merged user and request object as the context. This leads to a successful response from our authorizing directive.

You can now test this behavior. Start the front end with `npm run client` and the back end using `npm run server`. Don't forget that all Postman requests now have to include a valid JWT if the `auth` directive is used in the GraphQL query. You can run the login mutation and copy it over to the authorization header to run any query. We are now able to mark any query or mutation with the authorization flag and, as a result, require the user to be logged in.

# Accessing the user context from resolver functions

At the moment, all the API functions of our GraphQL server allow us to simulate the user by selecting the first available one from the database. As we have just introduced a full-fledged authentication, we can now access the user from the request context. This section quickly explains how to do this for the chat and message entities. We also implement a new query called `currentUser`, where we retrieve the logged-in user in our client.

## Chats and messages

First of all, you have to add the `@auth` directive to the chats inside GraphQL's `RootQuery` to ensure that users need to be logged in to access any chats or messages.

Take a look at the resolver function for the chats. Currently, we use the `findAll` method to get all users, take the first one, and query for all chats of that user. Replace the code with the new resolver function:

```
chats(root, args, context) {
  return Chat.findAll({
    include: [{
      model: User,
      required: true,
      through: { where: { userId: context.user.id } },
    },
    {
      model: Message,
    }],
  });
},
```

We skip the retrieval of the user and directly insert the user ID from the context, as you can see in the preceding code. That's all we have to do: all chats and messages belonging to the logged-in user are queried directly from the chats table.

## CurrentUser GraphQL query

The JWT gives us the opportunity to query for the currently logged-in user. Then, we can display the correct authenticated user in the top bar. To request the logged-in user, we require a new query called `currentUser` on our back end. In the schema, you simply have to add the following line to the `RootQuery` queries:

```
currentUser: User @auth
```

Like the `postsFeed` and `chats` queries, we also need the `@auth` directive to extract the user from the request context.

Similarly, in the resolver functions, you only need to insert the following three lines:

```
currentUser(root, args, context) {
  return context.user;
},
```

We return the user from the context right away, because it is already a user model instance with all the appropriate data returned by Sequelize. On the client side, we create this query in a separate component and file. Bear in mind that you don't need to pass the result on to all the children because this is done automatically by `ApolloConsumer` later on. You can follow the previous query component examples. Just use the following query, and you are good to continue:

```
const GET_CURRENT_USER = gql`
  query currentUser {
    currentUser {
      id
      username
      avatar
    }
  }
`;
```

If you had problems setting up the query component on your own, you could have a look at the official repository of this book.

You can now import the new query component inside the `App.js` file. Replace the old `div` tag within the logged-in state with the following code:

```
<CurrentUserQuery>
  <Bar />
  <Feed />
  <Chats />
</CurrentUserQuery>
```

Now, every time the `loggedIn` state variable is true, the `CurrentUserQuery` component is mounted and the query is executed. To get access to the response, we use the `ApolloConsumer` in the bar component that we implemented in the previous chapter. I have surrounded the feed and the chats with the `currentUser` query to be sure that the user already exists in the local cache of the Apollo Client before the other components are rendered, including the bar component.

We have to adjust the `user.js` context file. First, we parse the `currentUser` query. The query is only needed to extract the user from the cache. It is not used to trigger a separate request. Insert the following code at the top of the `user.js` file:

```
import gql from 'graphql-tag';
const GET_CURRENT_USER = gql`
  query currentUser {
    currentUser {
      id
      username
      avatar
    }
  }
`;
```

Instead of having a hardcoded fake user inside `ApolloConsumer`, we use the `client.readQuery` function to extract the data stored in the `ApolloClient` cache to give it to the underlying child component:

```
{client => {
  const {currentUser} = client.readQuery({ query: GET_CURRENT_USER});
  return React.Children.map(children, function(child){
    return React.cloneElement(child, { user: currentUser });
  });
}}
```

We pass the extracted `currentUser` result from the `client.readQuery` method directly to all the wrapped children of the current component.

The chats that are created from now on and the user in the top bar are no longer faked but instead are filled with the user who is currently logged in.

The mutations to create new posts or messages still use a static user id. We can switch over to the real logged-in user in the same way as we did previously in this section by using the user id from the `context.user` object. You should now be able to do this on your own.

# Logging out using React

To complete the circle, we still have to implement the functionality to log out. There are two cases when the user can be logged out:

- The user wants to log out and hits the logout button
- The JWT has expired after one day as specified; the user is no longer authenticated, and we have to set the state to logged out

We will begin by adding a new logout button to the top bar of our application's front end. To do this, we need to create a new `logout.js` component inside the `bar` folder. It should appear as follows:

```
import React, { Component } from 'react';
import { withApollo } from 'react-apollo';

class Logout extends Component {
  logout = () => {
    localStorage.removeItem('jwt');
    this.props.changeLoginState(false);
    this.props.client.resetStore();
  }
  render() {
    return (
      <button className="logout" onClick={this.logout}>Logout</button>
    );
  }
}

export default withApollo(Logout);
```

As you can see from the preceding code, the logout button triggers the component's logout method when it is clicked. Inside the `logout` method, we remove the JWT from `localStorage` and execute the `changeLoginState` function that we receive from the parent component. Be aware that we do not send a request to our server to log out, but instead we remove the token from the client. That is because there is no black or white list that we are using to disallow or allow a certain JWT to authenticate on our server. The easiest way to log out a user is to remove the token on the client side so that neither the server nor the client has it.

We also reset the client cache. When a user logs out, we must remove all data. Otherwise, other users of the same browser will be able to extract all the data, which we have to prevent. To get access to the underlying Apollo Client, we import the `withApollo` HoC and export the `Logout` component wrapped inside it. When logging out, we execute the `client.resetStore` function and all data is deleted. To use our new `Logout` component, open the `index.js` file from the `bar` folder and import it at the top. We can render it within the `div` top bar, below the other inner `div` tag:

```
<Logout changeLoginState={this.props.changeLoginState}/>
```

We pass the `changeLoginState` function to the `Logout` component. In the `App.js` main file, you have to ensure that you hand over this function not only to the `LoginRegisterForm` but also to the bar component, as follows:

```
<Bar changeLoginState={this.changeLoginState}/>
```

If you copy the complete CSS from the official GitHub repository, you should see a new button at the top-right corner of the screen when you are logged in. Hitting it logs you out and requires you to sign in again since the JWT has been deleted.

The other situation in which we implement a logout functionality is when the JWT we are using expires. In this case, we log the user out automatically and require them to log in again. Go to the `App` class and add the following lines:

```
constructor(props) {
  super(props);
  this.unsubscribe = props.client.onResetStore(
    () => this.changeLoginState(false)
  );
}
componentWillUnmount() {
  this.unsubscribe();
}
```

We need a `constructor` because we are using the `client.onResetStore` event, which is caught through the `client.onResetStore` function.

To get the preceding code working, we have to access the Apollo Client in our `App` component. The easiest way is to use the `withApollo` HoC. Just import it from the `react-apollo` package in the `App.js` file:

```
import { withApollo } from 'react-apollo';
```

Then, export the `App` class—not directly, but through the HoC. The following code must go directly beneath the `App` class:

```
export default withApollo(App);
```

Now, the component can access the client through its properties. The `resetStore` event is thrown whenever the client restore is reset, as the name suggests. You are going to see why we need this shortly. When listening to events in React, we have to stop listening when the component is unmounted. We handle this inside the `componentWillUnmount` function in the preceding code. Now, we have to reset the client store to initiate the logout state. When the event is caught, we execute the `changeLoginState` function automatically. Consequently, we could remove the section in which we passed the `changeLoginState` to the logout button initially because it is no longer needed, but this not what we want to do here.

Instead, go to the `index.js` file in the `apollo` folder. There, we already catch and loop over all errors returned from our GraphQL API. What we do now is loop over all errors but check each of them for an `UNAUTHENTICATED` error. Then, we execute the `client.resetStore` function. Insert the following code into the Apollo Client setup:

```
onError(({ graphQLErrors, networkError }) => {
  if (graphQLErrors) {
    graphQLErrors.map(({ message, locations, path, extensions }) => {
      if(extensions.code === 'UNAUTHENTICATED') {
        localStorage.removeItem('jwt');
        client.resetStore()
      }
      console.log(`[GraphQL error]: Message: ${message}, Location:
      ${locations}, Path: ${path}`);
    });
    if (networkError) {
      console.log(`[Network error]: ${networkError}`);
    }
  }
}),
```

As you can see, we access the `extensions` property of the error. The `extensions.code` field holds the specific error type that's returned. If we are not logged in, we remove the JWT and then reset the store. By doing this, we trigger the event in our `App` class, which sends the user back to the login form.

A further extension would be to offer a refresh token API function. The feature could be run every time we successfully use the API. The problem with this is that the user would stay logged in forever, as long as they are using the application. Usually, this is no problem, but if someone else is accessing the same computer, they will be authenticated as the original user. There are different ways to implement these kinds of functionalities to make the user experience more comfortable, but I am not a big fan of these for security reasons.

# Summary

Until now, one of the main issues we had with our application is that we didn't have any authentication. We can now tell who is logged in every time a user accesses our application. This allows us to secure the GraphQL API and insert new posts or messages in the name of the correct user. In this chapter, we discussed the fundamental aspects of JSON Web Tokens, `localStorage`, and cookies. We also looked at how the verification of hashed passwords or signed tokens works. This chapter then covered how to implement JWTs inside React and how to trigger the correct events to log in and log out.

In the next chapter, we are going to implement image uploads with a reusable component that allows the user to upload new avatar images.

# 7
# Handling Image Uploads

All social networks have one thing in common: each of them allows their users to upload custom and personal pictures, videos, or any other kind of document. This feature can take place inside chats, posts, groups, or profiles. To offer the same functionality, we are going to implement an image upload feature in Graphbook.

This chapter will cover the following topics:

- Setting up Amazon Web Services
- Configuring an AWS S3 bucket
- Accepting file uploads on the server
- Uploading images with React through Apollo
- Cropping images

## Setting up Amazon Web Services

First, I have to mention that Amazon (or, to be specific, **Amazon Web Services** (**AWS**)) is not the only provider of hosting, storage, or computing systems. There are many such providers, including the following:

- Heroku
- Digital Ocean
- Google Cloud
- Microsoft Azure

Many specialize in specific services, or try to provide a general solution for all use cases.

AWS, however, offers everything that you need to run a full-fledged web application. Their services span from databases, to object storage, to security services, and so much more. Furthermore, AWS is the go-to solution that you will find in most other books and tutorials, and many big companies use it in production.

This book only uses AWS for serving static files, such as images, and for providing the production database for our application in the last chapter of this book.

Before continuing with this chapter, you will be required to have an account for Amazon Web Services. You can create one on the official web page at `https://aws.amazon.com/`. For this, you will need a valid credit card; you can also run nearly all of the services on the free tier while working through this book without facing any problems.

Once you have successfully registered for AWS, you will see the following dashboard. This screen is called the Amazon Web Services Console:

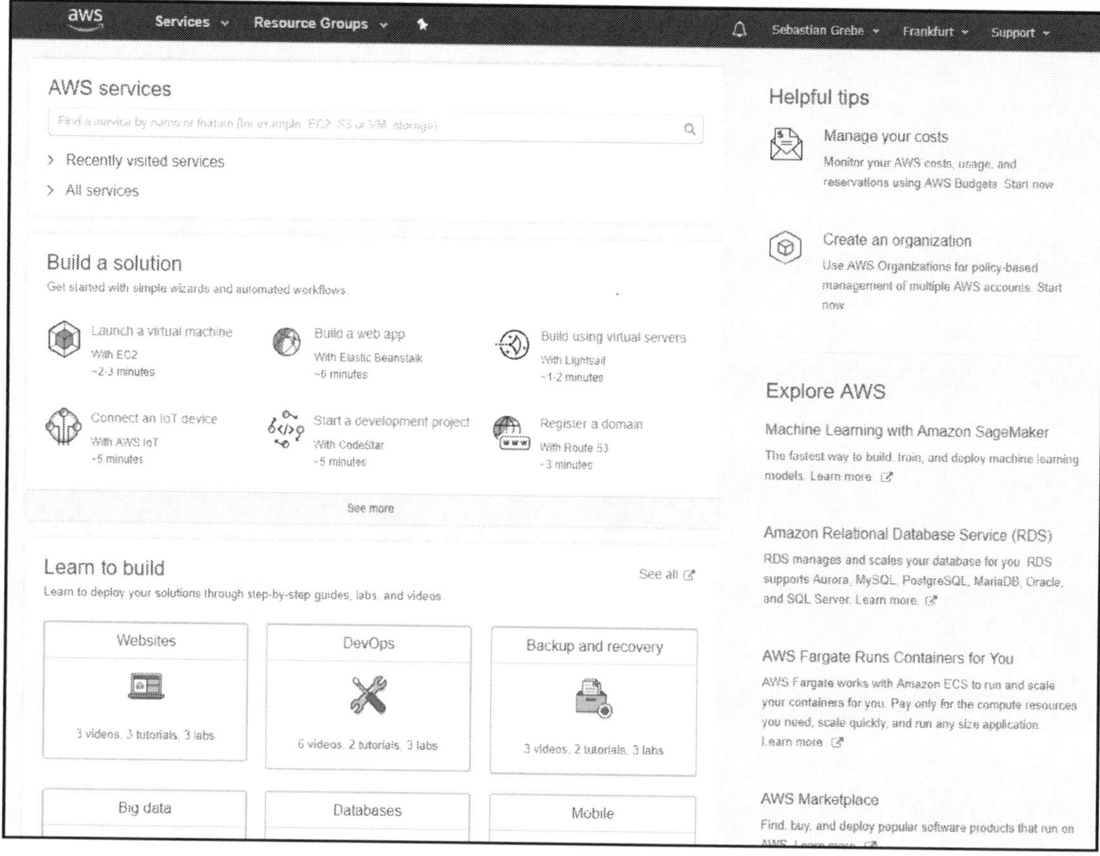


The next section will cover the options for storing files with AWS.

# Creating an AWS S3 bucket

For this chapter, we will require a storage service to save all uploaded images. AWS provides different storage types, for various use cases. In our scenario of a social network, we will have dozens of people accessing many images at once. **AWS Simple Storage Service** (**AWS S3**) is the best option for our scenario.

You can visit the S3 screen by clicking on the **Services** drop-down menu at the top of the page, and then looking under the **Storage** category in the drop-down menu. There, you will find the link to S3. Having clicked on it, the screen will look as follows:

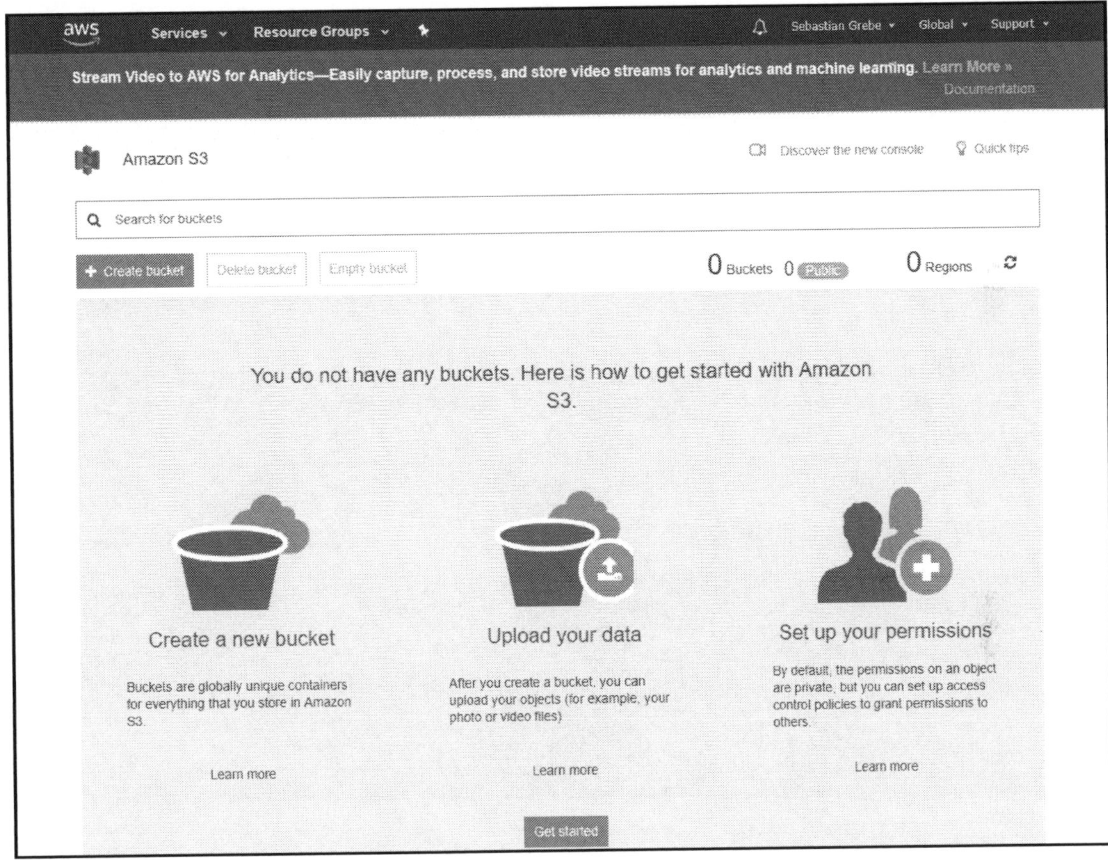


In S3, you create a bucket inside of a specific AWS region, where you can store files.

The preceding screen provides many features for interacting with your S3 bucket. You can browse all of the files, upload your files via the management interface, and configure more settings.

We will now create a new bucket for our project by clicking on **Create Bucket** in the upper-left corner, as shown in the preceding screenshot. You will be presented with a formula, as shown in the following screenshot. To create the bucket, you must fill it out:

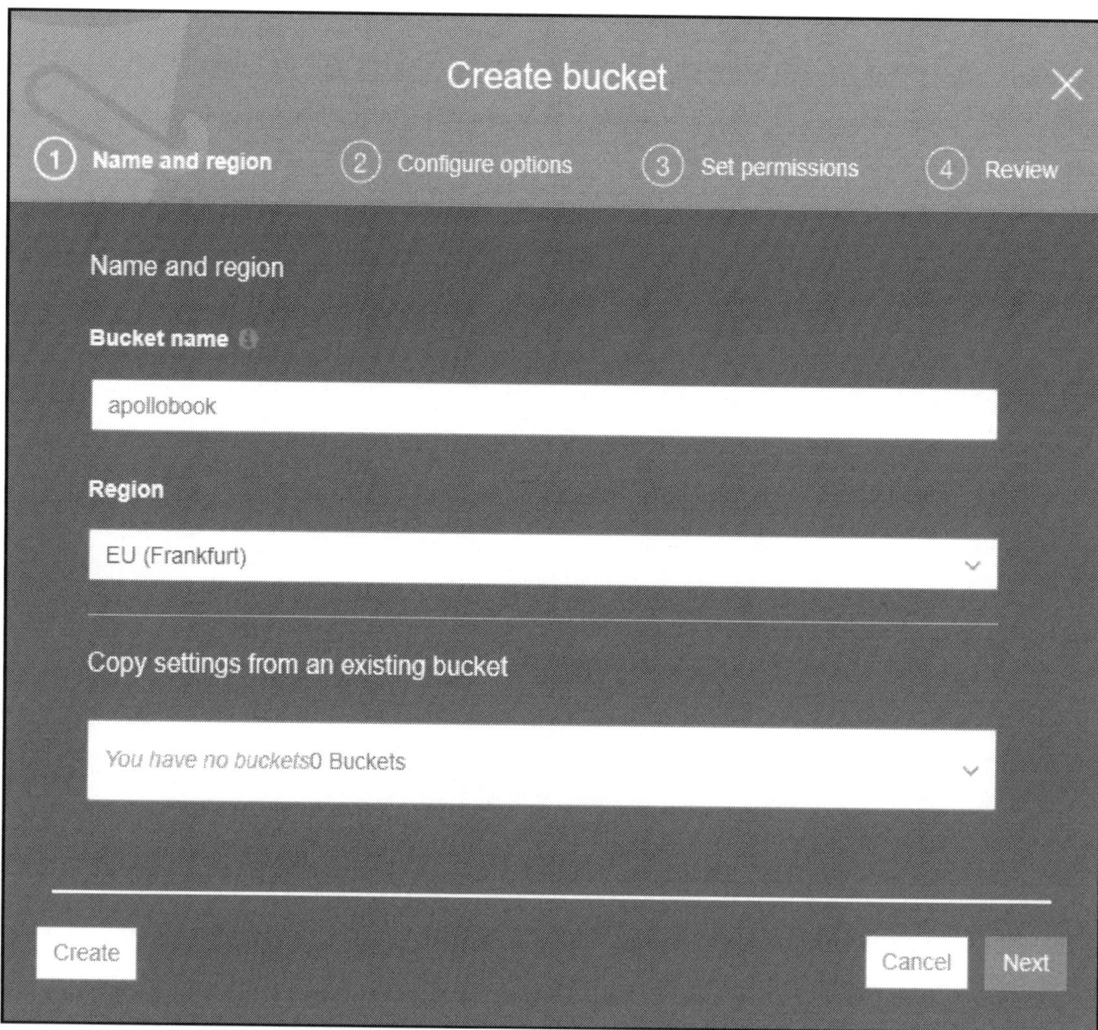


The bucket has to have a unique name across all buckets in S3. Then, we need to pick a region. For me, **EU (Frankfurt)** is the best choice, as it is the nearest origin point. Choose the best option for you, since the performance of a bucket corresponds to the distance between the region of the bucket and its accessor.

Once you have picked a region, continue by clicking on **Next**. You will be confronted with a lot of new options:

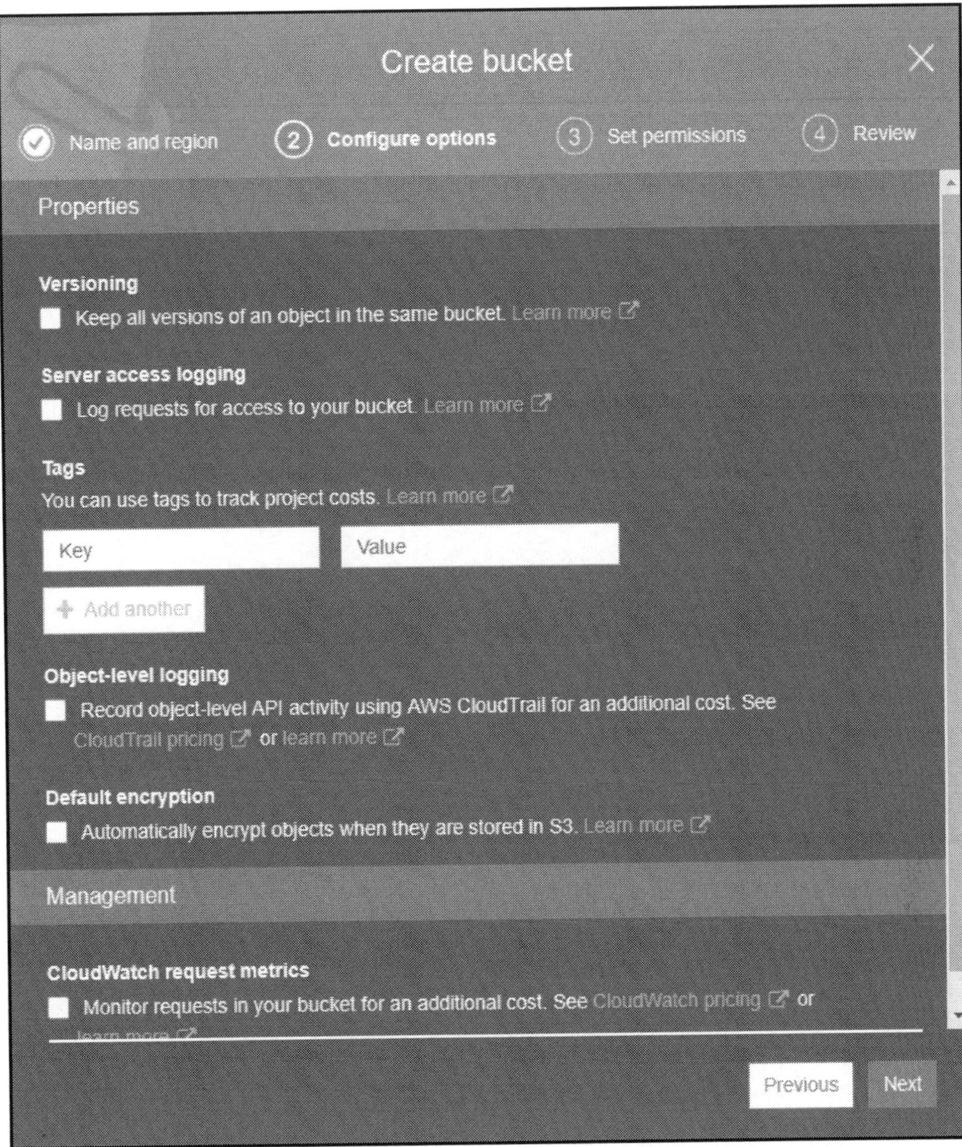


For our use case, we will not select any of these options, but they can be helpful in more advanced scenarios. AWS offers many features, such as a complete access log and versioning, which you can configure in this menu.

Many bigger companies have users across the globe, which requires a highly available application. When you reach this point, you can create many more S3 buckets in other regions, and you can set up the replication of one bucket to others living in various regions around the world. The correct bucket can then be distributed with AWS CloudFront and a router specific for each user. This approach gives every user the best possible experience.

Move on with the creation of the bucket by clicking on **Next**.

This step defines the permissions for other AWS users, or the public. Under **Manage public permissions**, you have to select **Grant public read access to this bucket** to enable public access to all files saved in your S3 bucket. Take a look at the following screenshot to ensure that everything is correct:

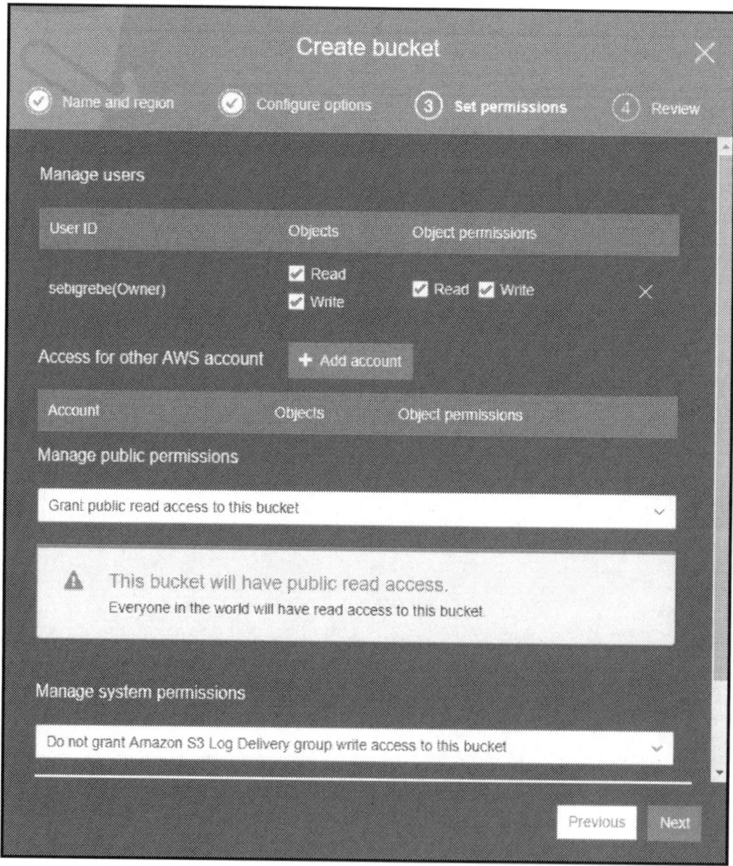

Finish the setup process by clicking on **Next**, and then **Create bucket**. You should be redirected to your empty bucket.

## Generating AWS access keys

Before implementing the upload feature, we must create an AWS API key to authorize our back end at AWS, in order to upload new files to the S3 bucket.

Click on your username in the top bar of AWS. There, you find a tab called **My Security Credentials**, which navigates to a screen offering various options to secure access to your AWS account.

You will probably be confronted with a dialog box like the following:

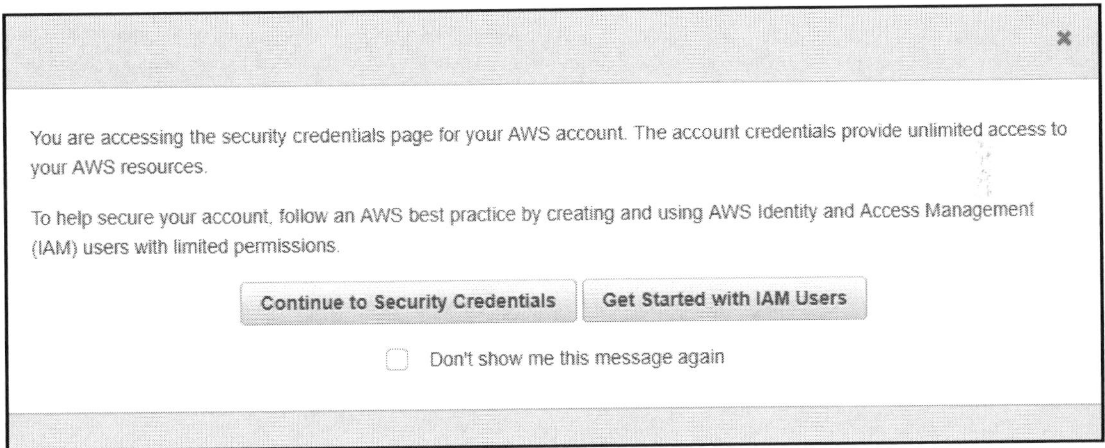


You can click on **Continue to Security Credentials** to continue. It is generally recommended to use **AWS Identity and Access Management (IAM)**. It allows you to efficiently manage secure access to AWS resources with separate IAM users. Throughout this book, we are going to use the root user in the same way that we are now, but I recommend looking at AWS IAM when writing your next application.

You should now see the credentials page, with a big list of different methods for storing credentials. This should look like the following screenshot:

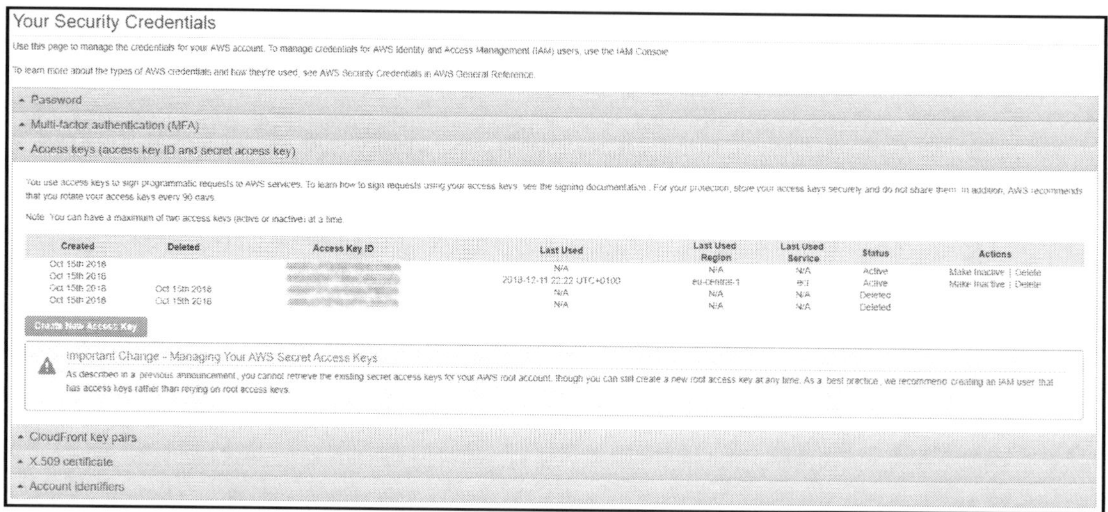


In the list, expand the tab titled **Access keys** shown in the preceding screenshot. In this tab, you will find all access tokens for your AWS account.

To generate a new access token, click on **Create New Access Key**. The output should look as follows:

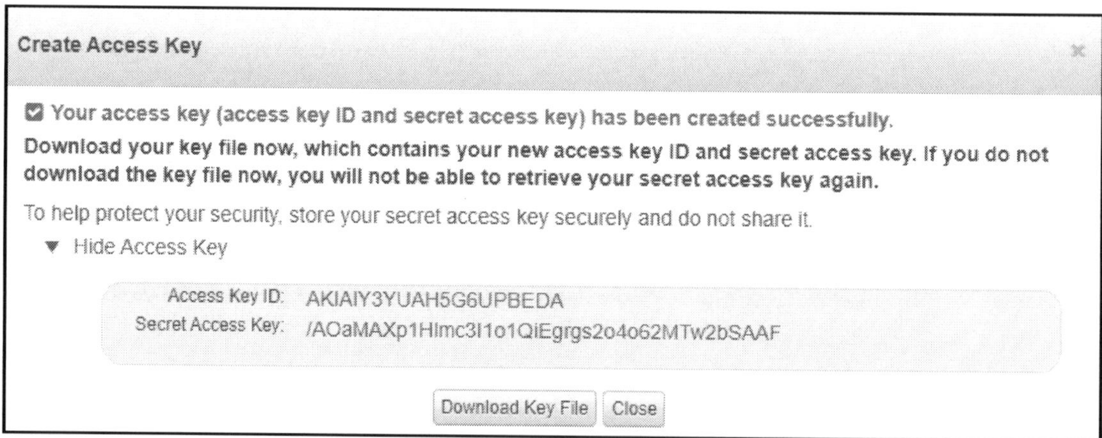

The best practice is to download the key file as prompted, and save it somewhere securely, just in case you lose the key at any time. You cannot retrieve access keys again after closing the window; so, if you lose them, you will have to delete the old key and generate a new one.

This approach is acceptable for explaining the basics of AWS. With such a huge platform, there are further steps that you have to take to secure your application even more. For example, it is recommended to renew API keys every 90 days. You can read more about all of the best practices at `https://docs.aws.amazon.com/de_de/general/latest/gr/aws-access-keys-best-practices.html`.

As you can see in the preceding screenshot, AWS gives us two tokens. Both are required to gain access to our S3 bucket.

Now, we can start to program the uploading mechanism.

# Uploading images to Amazon S3

Implementing file uploads and storing files is always a huge task, especially for image uploads in which the user may want to edit his files again.

For our front end, the user should be able to drag and drop his image into a dropzone, crop the image, and then submit it when he is finished. The back end needs to accept file uploads in general, which is not easy at all. The files must be processed and then stored efficiently, so that all users can access them quickly.

As this is a vast topic, the chapter only covers the basic upload of images from React, using a multipart HTTP `post` request to our GraphQL API, and then transferring the image to our S3 bucket. When it comes to compressing, converting, and cropping, you should check out further tutorials or books on this topic, including techniques for implementing them in the front end and back end, since there is a lot to think about. For example, in many applications, it makes sense to store images in various resolutions, which will be shown to the users in different situations, in order to save bandwidth.

Let's start by implementing the upload process on the back end.

# GraphQL image upload mutation

When uploading images to S3, it is required to use an API key, which we have already generated. Because of this, we cannot directly upload the files from the client to S3 with the API key. Anyone accessing our application could read out the API key from the JavaScript code and access our bucket without us knowing.

Uploading images directly from the client into the bucket is generally possible, however. To do this, you would need to send the name and type of the file to the server, which would then generate a URL and signature. The client can then use the signature to upload the image. This technique results in many round-trips for the client, and does not allow us to post-process the image, such as by converting or compressing, if needed.

The better solution is to upload the images to our server, have the GraphQL API accept the file, and then make another request to S3—including the API key—to store the file in our bucket.

We have to prepare our back end to communicate with AWS and accept file uploads. The preparation steps are as follows:

1. Interact with AWS to install the official `npm` package. It provides everything that's needed to use any AWS feature, not just S3:

   ```
   npm install --save aws-sdk
   ```

2. The next thing to do is edit the GraphQL schema and add a `scalar Upload` to the top of it. The `scalar` is used to resolve details such as the MIME type and encoding when uploading files:

   ```
   scalar Upload
   ```

3. Add the `File` type to the schema. This type returns the filename and the resulting URL under which the image can be accessed in the browser:

   ```
   type File {
     filename: String!
     url: String!
   }
   ```

4. Create the new `uploadAvatar` mutation. It is required that the user is logged in to upload avatar images, so append the `@auth` directive to the mutation. The mutation takes the previously mentioned `Upload` scalar as input:

```
uploadAvatar (
  file: Upload!
): File @auth
```

5. Next, we will implement the mutation's resolver function in the `resolvers.js` file. For this, we will import and set up our dependencies at the top of the `resolvers.js` file, as follows:

```
import aws from 'aws-sdk';
const s3 = new aws.S3({
  signatureVersion: 'v4',
  region: 'eu-central-1',
});
```

We will initialize the `s3` object that we will use to upload images in the next step. It is required to pass a `region`, like the instance in which we created the bucket. We set the `signatureVersion` to version `'v4'`, as this is recommended.

You can find details about the signature process of AWS requests at `https://docs.aws.amazon.com/general/latest/gr/signature-version-4.html`.

6. Inside the `mutation` property, insert the `uploadAvatar` function, as follows:

```
async uploadAvatar(root, { file }, context) {
  const { stream, filename, mimetype, encoding } = await file;
  const bucket = 'apollobook';
  const params = {
    Bucket: bucket,
    Key: context.user.id + '/' + filename,
    ACL: 'public-read',
    Body: stream
  };
  const response = await s3.upload(params).promise();

  return User.update({
    avatar: response.Location
  },
  {
    where: {
      id: context.user.id
```

```
      }
    }).then(() => {
      return {
        filename: filename,
        url: response.Location
      }
    });
  },
```

In the preceding code, we start by specifying the function as `async`, so that we can use the `await` method to resolve the file and its details. The result of the resolved `await file` method consists of the properties `stream`, `filename`, `mimetype`, and `encoding`.

Then, we collect the following parameters in the `params` variable, in order to upload our avatar image:

- The `Bucket` field holds the name of the bucket where we save the image. I took the name `'apollobook'`, but you will need to enter the name that you entered during the creation of the bucket. You could have specified this directly inside of the `s3` object, but this approach is a bit more flexible, since you can have multiple buckets for different file types, without the need for multiple `s3` objects.
- The `Key` property is the path and name under which the file is saved. Notice that we store the file under a new folder, which is just the user id taken from the `context` variable. In your future application, you can introduce some kind of hash for every file. That would be good, since the filename should not include characters that are not allowed. Furthermore, the files cannot be guessed programmatically when using a hash.
- The `ACL` field sets the permission for who can access the file. Since uploaded images on a social network are publicly viewable by anyone on the internet, we set the property to `'public-read'`.
- The `Body` field receives the `stream` variable, which we initially got by resolving the file. The `stream` is nothing more than the image itself as a stream, which we can directly upload into the bucket.

The `params` variable is given to the `s3.upload` function, which saves the file to our bucket. We directly chain the `promise` function onto the `upload` method. In the preceding code, we use the `await` statement to resolve the promise returned by the upload function. Therefore, we specified the function as `async`. The `response` object of the AWS S3 upload includes the public URL under which the image is accessible for everyone.

The last step is to set the new avatar picture on the user in our database. We execute the `User.update` model function from Sequelize by setting the new URL from `response.Location`, which S3 gave us after we resolved the promise.

An example link to an S3 image is as follows:

```
https://apollobook.s3.eu-central-1.amazonaws.com/1/test.png
```

As you can see, the URL is prefixed with the name of the bucket and then the region. The suffix is, of course, the folder, which is the user id and the filename. The preceding URL will differ from the one that your back end generates, because your bucket name and region will vary.

After updating the user, we can return the AWS response to update the UI accordingly, without refreshing the browser window.

In the previous section, we generated the access tokens, in order to authorize our back end at AWS. By default, the AWS SDK expects both tokens to be available in our environment variables. Like we did before with the `JWT_SECRET`, we will set the tokens as follows:

```
export AWS_ACCESS_KEY_ID=YOUR_AWS_KEY_ID
export AWS_SECRET_ACCESS_KEY=YOUR_AWS_SECRET_KEY
```

Insert your AWS tokens into the preceding code. The AWS SDK will detect both environment variables automatically. We do not need to read and configure them anywhere in our code.

We will now continue and implement all of the image upload features in the front end.

# React image cropping and uploading

In social networks such as Facebook, there are multiple locations where you can select and upload files. You can send images in chats, attach them to posts, create galleries in your profile, and much more. For now, we will only look at how to change our user's avatar image. This is a great example for easily showing all of the techniques.

The result that we are targeting looks like the following screenshot:

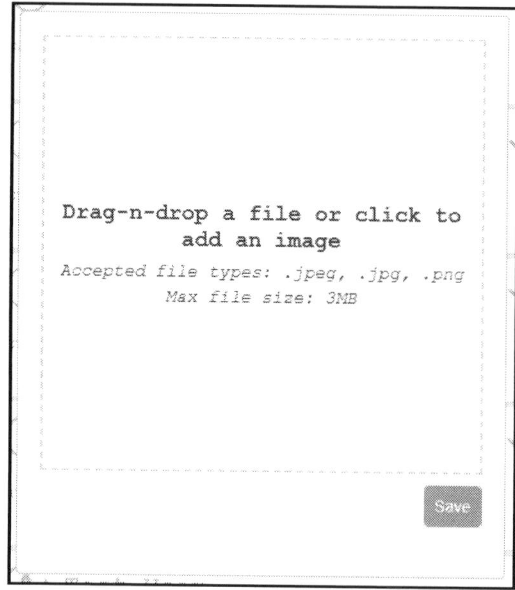


The user can select a file, crop it directly in the modal, and save it to AWS with the preceding dialog.

I am not a big fan of using too many `npm` packages, as this often makes your application unnecessarily big. As of writing this book, we cannot write custom React components for everything, such as displaying dialog or cropping, no matter how easy it might be.

To get the image upload working, we will install two new packages. To do this, you can follow these instructions:

1. Install the packages with `npm`:

   ```
   npm install --save react-modal @synapsestudios/react-drop-n-crop
   ```

   The `react-modal` package offers various dialog options that you can use in many different situations. The `react-drop-n-crop` package is a wrapper package around `Cropper.js` and `react-dropzone`. Personally, I dislike wrapper packages, since they are often poorly maintained or leave features unimplemented. Against all prejudice, this package does a really excellent job of allowing users to drop images with `react-dropzone`, and then cropping them with the well-known `Cropper.js` library.

2. When using the `react-drop-n-crop` package, we can rely on its included CSS package. In your main `App.js`, import it straight from the package itself, as follows:

```
import '@synapsestudios/react-drop-n-crop/lib/react-drop-n-
crop.min.css';
```

webpack takes care of bundling all assets, like we are already doing with our custom CSS.

3. The next package that we will install is an extension for the Apollo Client, which will enable us to upload files, as follows:

```
npm install --save apollo-upload-client
```

4. To get the `apollo-upload-client` package running, we have to edit the `index.js` from the `apollo` folder where we initialize the Apollo Client and all of its links. Import the `createUploadLink` function at the top of the `index.js` file, as follows:

```
import { createUploadLink } from 'apollo-upload-client';
```

5. You must replace the old `HttpLink` at the bottom of the link array with the new upload link. Instead of having a new `HttpLink`, we will now pass the `createUploadLink`, but with the same parameters. When executing it, a regular link is returned. The link should look like the following code:

```
createUploadLink({
  uri: 'http://localhost:8000/graphql',
  credentials: 'same-origin',
}),
```

It is important to note that when we make use of the new upload link and send a file with a GraphQL request, we do not send the standard `application/json` `Content-Type` request, but instead send a `multi-part` `FormData` request. This allows us to upload files with GraphQL. Standard JSON HTTP bodies, like we use with our GraphQL requests, cannot hold any file objects.

Alternatively, it is possible to send a `base64` instead of a file object when transferring images. This procedure would save you from the work that we are doing right now, as sending and receiving strings is no problem with GraphQL. You have to convert the `base64` string to a file if you want to save it in AWS S3. This approach only works for images, however, and web applications should be able to accept any file type.

6. Now that the packages are prepared, we can start to implement our `uploadAvatar` mutation component for the client. Create a new file, called `uploadAvatar.js`, in the `mutations` folder.
7. At the top of the file, import all dependencies and parse all GraphQL requests with `graphql-tag` in the conventional way, as follows:

```
import React, { Component } from 'react';
import { Mutation } from 'react-apollo';
import gql from 'graphql-tag';

const GET_CURRENT_USER = gql`
  query currentUser {
    currentUser {
      id
      username
      avatar
    }
  }
`;

const UPLOAD_AVATAR = gql`
  mutation uploadAvatar($file: Upload!) {
    uploadAvatar(file : $file) {
      filename
      url
    }
  }
`;
```

As you can see, we have the `uploadAvatar` mutation, which takes the `file` as a parameter of the `Upload` type. Furthermore, we have the `currentUser` GraphQL query, which we are going to use in the next step to update the avatar image without re-fetching all queries, but only by updating the cache.

8. Next, you can copy the `UploadAvatarMutation` class. It passes the `uploadAvatar` mutation function to the underlying children, and sets the newly uploaded avatar image inside of the cache for the `currentUser` query. It shows the new user avatar directly in the top bar when the request is successful:

```
export default class UploadAvatarMutation extends Component {
  render() {
    const { children } = this.props;
    return (
      <Mutation
        update = {(store, { data: { uploadAvatar } }) => {
          var query = {
            query: GET_CURRENT_USER,
          };
          const data = store.readQuery(query);
          data.currentUser.avatar = uploadAvatar.url;
          store.writeQuery({ ...query, data });
        }}
        mutation={UPLOAD_AVATAR}>
          {uploadAvatar =>
            React.Children.map(children, function(child){
              return React.cloneElement(child, { uploadAvatar });
            })
          }
      </Mutation>
    )
  }
}
```

The preceding code is nothing utterly new, as we used the same approach for the other mutations that we implemented.

The preparation is now complete. We have installed all of the required packages, configured them, and implemented the new mutation component. We can begin to program the user-facing dialog to change the avatar image.

For the purposes of this book, we are not relying on separate pages or anything like that. Instead, we are giving the user the opportunity to change his avatar when he clicks on his image in the top bar. To do so, we are going to listen for the click event on the avatar, opening up a dialog that includes a file dropzone and a button to submit the new image.

Execute the following steps to get this logic running:

1. It is always good to make your components as reusable as possible, so create an `avatarModal.js` file inside of the `components` folder.
2. As always, you will have to import the two new `react-modal` and `react-drop-n-crop` packages first, as follows:

```
import React, { Component } from 'react';
import Modal from 'react-modal';
import DropNCrop from '@synapsestudios/react-drop-n-crop';

Modal.setAppElement('#root');

const modalStyle = {
  content: {
    width: '400px',
    height: '450px',
    top: '50%',
    left: '50%',
    right: 'auto',
    bottom: 'auto',
    marginRight: '-50%',
    transform: 'translate(-50%, -50%)'
  }
};
```

As you can see in the preceding code snippet, we tell the modal package at which point in the browser's DOM we want to render the dialog, using the `setAppElement` method. For our use case, it is okay to take the `root` DOMNode, as this is the starting point of our application. The modal is instantiated in this DOMNode.

The modal component accepts a special `style` parameter for the different parts of the dropzone. We can style all parts of the modal by specifying the `modalStyle` object with the correct properties.

3. The `react-drop-n-crop` package enables the user to select or drop the file. Beyond this feature, it gives the user the opportunity to crop the image. The result is not a `file` or `blob` object, but a `data URI`, formatted as `base64`. Generally, this is not a problem, but our GraphQL API expects that we sent a real file, not just a string, as we explained previously. Consequently, we have to convert the `data URI` to a blob that we can send with our GraphQL request. Add the following function to take care of the conversion:

```
function dataURItoBlob(dataURI) {
  var byteString = atob(dataURI.split(',')[1]);
  var mimeString = dataURI.split(',')[0].split(':')[1].split(';')
  [0];
  var ia = new Uint8Array(byteString.length);

  for (var i = 0; i < byteString.length; i++) {
    ia[i] = byteString.charCodeAt(i);
  }

  const file = new Blob([ia], {type:mimeString});
  return file;
}
```

   Let's not get too deep into the logic behind the preceding function. The only thing that you need to know it is that it converts all readable ASCII characters into 8-bit binary data, and at the end, it returns a blob object to the calling function. It converts data URIs to blobs.

4. The new component that we are implementing at the moment is called `AvatarUpload`. It receives the `isOpen` property, which sets the modal to visible or invisible. By default, the modal is invisible. Furthermore, when the modal is shown, the dropzone is rendered inside. The `Modal` component takes an `onRequestClose` method, which executes the `showModal` function when the user tries to close the modal (by clicking outside of it, for example). We receive the `showModal` function from the parent component, which we are going to cover in the next step.

   The `DropNCrop` component does not need any properties except for the `onChange` event and the state variable as a default value. The `value` of the `DropNCrop` component is filled with the `AvatarUpload` component's state. The state only holds a default set of fields that the `DropNCrop` component understands.

It tells the package to start with an empty dropzone. Switching between file selection and cropping is handled by the package on its own:

```
export default class AvatarUpload extends Component {
  state = {
    result: null,
    filename: null,
    filetype: null,
    src: null,
    error: null,
  }
  onChange = value => {
    this.setState(value);
  }
  uploadAvatar = () => {
    const self = this;
    var file = dataURItoBlob(this.state.result);
    file.name = this.state.filename;
    this.props.uploadAvatar({variables: { file }}).then(() => {
      self.props.showModal();
    });
  }
  changeImage = () => {
    this.setState({ src: null });
  }
  render() {
    return (
      <Modal
        isOpen={this.props.isOpen}
        onRequestClose={this.props.showModal}
        contentLabel="Change avatar"
        style={modalStyle}
      >
        <DropNCrop onChange={this.onChange} value={this.state} />
        {this.state.src !== null && (
          <button className="cancelUpload" onClick=
          {this.changeImage}>Change image</button>
        )}
        <button className="uploadAvatar" onClick=
        {this.uploadAvatar}>Save</button>
      </Modal>
    )
  }
}
```

The `AvatarUpload` class receives an `isOpen` property from its parent component. We directly pass it to the `DropNCrop` component. Whenever the parent component changes the passed property's value, the modal is either shown or not, based on the value.

When a file is selected or cropped, the component state is updated with the new image. The response of the cropper package is saved in the `result` state variable.

We are using the conditional rendering pattern to show a `Change image` button when the `src` state variable is filled, which happens when a file is selected. The `changeImage` function sets the `src` of the `DropNCrop` component back to `null`, which lets it switch back to the file selection mode.

When the user has finished editing his picture, he can hit the **Save** button. The `uploadAvatar` method will be executed. It converts the `base64` string returned from the cropper component to a `blob` object, using the `dataURItoBlob` function. We send the result with the GraphQL request inside of the mutation's `variables` parameter. When the request has finished, the modal is hidden again by running the `showModal` functions from the properties.

5. Now, switch over to the `user.js` file in the `bar` folder, where all of the other application bar-related files are stored. Import the mutation and the new `AvatarUpload` component that we wrote before, as follows:

```
import UploadAvatarMutation from '../mutations/uploadAvatar';
import AvatarUpload from '../avatarModal';
```

6. The `UserBar` component is the parent of `AvatarUploadModal`. Open the `user.js` file from the `bar` folder. That is why we handle the `isOpen` state variable of the dialog in the `UserBar` class. We introduce an `isOpen` state variable and catch the `onClick` event on the avatar of the user. Copy the following code to the `UserBar` class:

```
state = {
  isOpen: false,
}
showModal = () => {
  this.setState({ isOpen: !this.state.isOpen });
}
```

7. Replace the return value of the `render` method with the following code:

```
return (
  <div className="user">
    <img src={user.avatar} onClick={this.showModal}/>
    <UploadAvatarMutation>
      <AvatarUpload isOpen={this.state.isOpen}
showModal={this.showModal}/>
    </UploadAvatarMutation>
    <span>{user.username}</span>
  </div>
);
```

The `UploadAvatarMutation` surrounds the modal component to pass the mutation function over.

Furthermore, the modal component directly receives the `isOpen` property, as we explained earlier. The `showModal` method is executed when the avatar image is clicked. This function updates the property of the `AvatarUpload` class, and either shows or hides the modal.

Start the server and client with the matching `npm run` commands. Reload your browser and try out the new feature. When an image is selected, the cropping tool is displayed. You can drag and resize the image area that should be uploaded. You can see an example of this in the following screenshot:

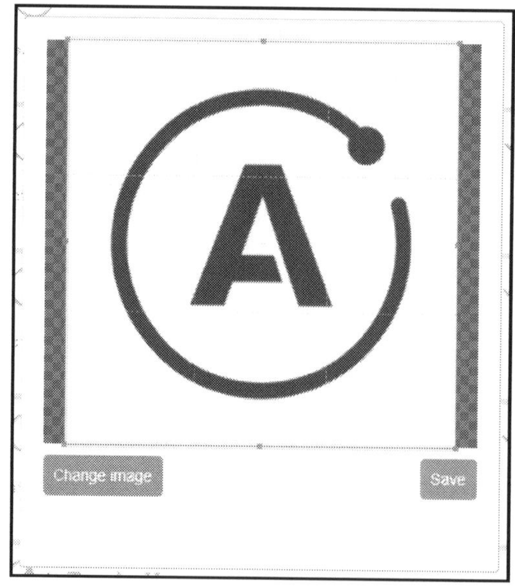

Hitting **Save** uploads the image under the `user` folder in the S3 bucket. Thanks to the Mutation component that we wrote, the avatar image in the top bar is updated with the new URL to the S3 bucket location of the image.

The great thing that we have accomplished is that we send the images to our server. Our server transfers all of the images to S3. AWS responds with the public URL, which is then placed directly into the avatar field in the browser. The way that we query the avatar image from the back end, using our GraphQL API, does not change. We return the URL to the S3 file, and everything works.

# Summary

In this chapter, we started by creating an AWS account and an S3 bucket for uploading static images from our back end. Modern social networks consist of many images, videos, and other types of files. We introduced the Apollo Client, which allows us to upload any type of file. In this chapter, we managed to upload an image to our server, and we covered how to crop images and save them through a server in AWS S3. Your application should now be able to serve your users with images at any time.

The next chapter will cover the basics of client-side routing, with the use of React Router.

# 8
# Routing in React

Currently, we have one screen and one path that our users can visit. When users visit Graphbook, they can log in and see their news feed and chats. Another requirement for a social network is that users have their own profile pages. We will implement this feature in this chapter.

We will introduce client-side routing for our React application.

This chapter will cover the following topics:

- Installing React Router
- Implementing routes
- Securing routes
- Manual navigation

## Setting up React Router

Routing is essential to most web applications. You cannot cover all of the features of your application in just one page. It would be overloaded, and your user would find it difficult to understand. Sharing links to pictures, profiles, or posts is also very important for a social network such as Graphbook. One advantageous feature, for example, is being able to send links to specific profiles. This requires each profile to have its own URL and page. Otherwise, it will not be possible to share a direct link to a single item of your application. It is also crucial to split content into different pages, due to **search engine optimization (SEO)**.

At the moment, we render our complete application to HTML in the browser, based on the authentication status. Only the server implements a simple routing functionality. Carrying out client-side routing can save a lot of work and time for the user, if the router merely swaps out the correct parts in React, instead of reloading the page completely when following a link. It is vital that the application makes use of the HTML5 history implementation, so that it handles the history of the browser. Importantly, this should also work for navigation in different directions. We should be able to go forward and backward with the arrow navigation buttons in the browser, without the need to rerender the application. No unnecessary page reloads should happen with this solution.

Common routing libraries that you may know about, such as Angular, Ember, or Ruby on Rails, use static routing. That is also the case for Express.js, which we covered in `Chapter 2`, *Setting up GraphQL with Express.js*, of this book. **Static routing** means that you configure your routing flow and the components to render upfront. Your application then processes the routing table in a separate step, renders the required components, and presents the results to the user.

With version 4 of React Router, which we are going to use, **dynamic routing** was introduced. The unique thing about it is that the routing takes place while the rendering of your application is running. It doesn't require the application to first process a configuration, in order to show the correct components. This approach fits with React's workflow well. The routing happens directly in your application, not in a preprocessed configuration.

# Installing React Router

In the past, there were a lot of of React Router, with various implementations and features. As we mentioned previously, we are going to install and configure version 4 for this book. If you search for other tutorials on this topic, make sure that you follow the instructions for this version. Otherwise, you might miss some of the changes that React Router has gone through.

To install React Router, simply run `npm` again, as follows:

```
npm install --save react-router-dom
```

From the package name, you might assume that this is not the main package for React. The reason for this is that React Router is a multi-package library. That comes in handy when using the same tool for multiple platforms. The core package is called `react-router`.

There are two further packages. The first one is the `react-router-dom` package, which we installed in the preceding code, and the second one is the `react-router-native` package. If, at some point, you plan to build a React Native app, you can use the same routing, instead of using the browser's DOM for a real mobile app.

The first step that we will take introduces a simple router to get our current application working, including different paths for all of the screens. The routes that we are going to add are as follows:

- Our posts feed, chats, and the top bar, including the search box, should be accessible under the `/app` route of our application. The path is self-explanatory, but you could also use the / root as the main path.
- The login and signup forms should have a separate path, which will be accessible under the root / path.
- As we do not have any further screens, we also have to handle a situation in which none of the preceding routes match. In that case, we could display a so-called 404 page, but instead, we are going to redirect to the root path directly.

There is one thing that we have to prepare before continuing. For development, we are using the webpack development server, as this is what we configured in the `Chapter 1`, *Preparing Your Development Environment*. To get the routing working out of the box, we will add two parameters to the `webpack.client.config.js` file. The `devServer` field should look as follows:

```
devServer: {
  port: 3000,
  open: true,
  historyApiFallback: true,
},
```

The `historyApiFallback` field tells the `devServer` to serve the `index.html` file, not only for the root path, `http://localhost:3000/`, but also when it would typically receive a 404 error (such as for paths like `http://localhost:3000/app`). That happens when the path does not match a file or folder that is normal when implementing routing.

The `output` field at the top of the `config` file must have a `publicPath` property, as follows:

```
output: {
  path: path.join(__dirname, buildDirectory),
  filename: 'bundle.js',
  publicPath: '/',
},
```

The `publicPath` property tells webpack to prefix the bundle URL to an absolute path, instead of a relative path. When this property is not included, the browser cannot download the bundle when visiting the sub-directories of our application, as we are implementing client-side routing. Let's begin with the first path, and bind the central part of our application, including the news feed, to the `/app` path.

## Implementing your first route

Before implementing the routing, we will clean up the `App.js` file. Create a `Main.js` file next to the `App.js` file in the `client` folder. Insert the following code:

```
import React, { Component } from 'react';
import Feed from './Feed';
import Chats from './Chats';
import Bar from './components/bar';
import CurrentUserQuery from './components/queries/currentUser';

export default class Main extends Component {
  render() {
    return (
      <CurrentUserQuery>
        <Bar changeLoginState={this.props.changeLoginState}/>
        <Feed />
        <Chats />
      </CurrentUserQuery>
    );
  }
}
```

As you might have noticed, the preceding code is pretty much the same as the logged in condition inside the `App.js` file. The only change is that the `changeLoginState` function is taken from the properties, and is not directly a method of the component itself. That is because we split this part out of the `App.js` and put it into a separate file. This improves reusability for other components that we are going to implement.

Now, open and replace the `render` method of the `App` component to reflect those changes, as follows:

```
render() {
  return (
    <div>
      <Helmet>
        <title>Graphbook - Feed</title>
        <meta name="description" content="Newsfeed of all your friends
```

```
          on Graphbook" />
        </Helmet>
        <Router loggedIn={this.state.loggedIn} changeLoginState=
         {this.changeLoginState}/>
      </div>
    )
  }
```

If you compare the preceding method with the old one, you can see that we have inserted a `Router` component, instead of directly rendering either the posts feed or the login form. The original components of the `App.js` file are now in the previously created `Main.js` file. Here, we pass the `loggedIn` state variable and the `changeLoginState` function to the `Router` component. Remove the dependencies at the top, such as the `Chats` and `Feed` components, because we won't use them anymore thanks to the new `Main` component. Add the following line to the dependencies of our `App.js` file:

```
import Router from './router';
```

To get this code working, we have to implement our custom `Router` component first. Generally, it is easy to get the routing running with React Router, and you are not required to separate the routing functionality into a separate file, but, that makes it more readable. To do this, create a new `router.js` file in the `client` folder, next to the `App.js` file, with the following content:

```
import React, { Component } from 'react';
import LoginRegisterForm from './components/loginregister';
import Main from './Main';
import { BrowserRouter as Router, Route, Redirect, Switch } from 'react-
router-dom';

export default class Routing extends Component {
  render() {
    return (
      <Router>
        <Switch>
          <Route path="/app" component={() => <Main changeLoginState=
          {this.props.changeLoginState}/>}/>
        </Switch>
      </Router>
    )
  }
}
```

At the top, we import all of the dependencies. They include the new `Main` component and the `react-router` package. The following is a quick explanation of all of the components that we are importing from the React Router package:

- `BrowserRouter` (or `Router`, for short, as we called it here) is the component that keeps the URL in the address bar in sync with the UI; it handles all of the routing logic.
- The `Switch` component forces the first matching `Route` or `Redirect` to be rendered. We need it to stop rerendering the UI if the user is already in the location to which a redirect is trying to navigate. I generally recommend that you use the `Switch` component, as it catches unforeseeable routing errors.
- `Route` is the component that tries to match the given path to the URL of the browser. If this is the case, the `component` property is rendered. You can see in the preceding code snippet that we are not setting the `Main` component directly as a parameter; instead, we return it from a stateless function. That is required because the `component` property of a `Route` only accepts functions, and not a component object. This solution allows us to pass the `changeLoginState` function to the `Main` component.
- `Redirect` navigates the browser to a given location. The component receives a property called `to`, filled by a path starting with a `/`. We are going to use this component in the next section.

The problem with the preceding code is that we are only listening for one route, which is `/app`. If you are not logged in, there will be many errors that are not covered. The best thing to do would be to redirect the user to the root path, where they can log in.

# Secured routes

**Secured routes** represent a to specific paths that are only the is authenticated, or has the correct authorization.

The recommended solution to implement secure routes in React Router version 4 is to write a small, stateless function that conditionally renders either a `Redirect` component or the component specified on the route that requires an authenticated user. We extract the `component` property of the route into the `Component` variable, which is a renderable React object. Insert the following code into the `router.js` file:

```
const PrivateRoute = ({ component: Component, ...rest }) => (
  <Route {...rest} render={(props) => (
    rest.loggedIn === true
```

```
        ? <Component {...props} />
        : <Redirect to={{
            pathname: '/',
          }} />
    )} />
  )
```

We call the stateless function `PrivateRoute`. It returns a standard `Route` component, which receives all of the properties initially given to the `PrivateRoute` function. To pass all properties, we use a destructuring assignment with the `...rest` syntax. Using the syntax inside of curly braces on a React component passes all fields of the `rest` object as properties to the component. The `Route` component is only rendered if the given path is matched.

Furthermore, the rendered component is dependent on the user's `loggedIn` state variable, which we have to pass. If the user is logged in, we render the `Component` without any problems. Otherwise, we redirect the user to the root path of our application using the `Redirect` component.

Use the new `PrivateRoute` component in the `render` method of the `Router` and replace the old `Route`, as follows:

```
<PrivateRoute path="/app" component={() => <Main changeLoginState=
 {this.props.changeLoginState}/>} loggedIn={this.props.loggedIn}/>
```

Notice that we pass the `loggedIn` property by taking the value from the properties of the `Router` itself. It initially receives the `loggedIn` property from the `App` component that we edited previously. The great thing is that the `loggedIn` variable can be updated from the parent `App` component at any time. That means that the `Redirect` component is rendered and the user is automatically navigated to the login form (if the user logs out, for example). We do not have to write separate logic to implement this functionality.

However, we have now created a new problem. We redirect from `/app` to `/` if the user is not logged in, but we do not have any routes set up for the initial `'/'` path. It makes sense for this path to either show the login form or to redirect the user to `/app` if the user is logged in. The pattern for the new component is the same as the preceding code for the `PrivateRoute` component, but in the opposite direction. Add the new `LoginRoute` component to the `router.js` file, as follows:

```
const LoginRoute = ({ component: Component, ...rest }) => (
  <Route {...rest} render={(props) => (
    rest.loggedIn === false
      ? <Component {...props} />
      : <Redirect to={{
```

```
            pathname: '/app',
          }} />
      )} />
    )
```

The preceding condition is inverted to render the original component. If the user is not logged in, the login form is rendered. Otherwise, they will be redirected to the posts feed.

Add the new path to the router, as follows:

```
<LoginRoute exact path="/" component={() => <LoginRegisterForm
changeLoginState={this.props.changeLoginState}/>}
loggedIn={this.props.loggedIn}/>
```

The code looks the same as that of the `PrivateRoute` component, except that we now have a new property, called `exact`. If we pass this property to a route, the browser's location has to match one hundred percent. The following table shows a quick example, taken from the official React Router documentation:

| **Router path** | **Browser path** | **exact** | **matches** |
|---|---|---|---|
| /one | /one/two | true | no |
| /one | /one/two | false | yes |

For the root path, we set `exact` to true, because otherwise the path matches with any browser's location where a `/` is included, as you can see in the preceding table.

There are many more configuration options that React Router offers, such as enforcing trailing slashes, case sensitivity, and much more. You can find all of the options and examples in the official documentation at `https://reacttraining.com/react-router/web/api/`.

# Catch-all routes in React Router

Currently, we have two paths set up, which are `/app` and `/`. If a user visits a non-existent path, such as `/test`, they will see an empty screen. The solution is to implement a route that matches any path. For simplicity, we redirect the user to the root of our application, but you could easily replace the redirection with a typical 404 page.

Add the following code to the `router.js` file:

```
class NotFound extends Component {
  render() {
    return (
      <Redirect to="/"/> );
  }
}
```

The `NotFound` component is minimal. It just redirects the user to the root path. Add the next `Route` component to the `Switch` in the `Router`. Ensure that it is the last one on the list:

```
<Route component={NotFound} />
```

As you can see, we are rendering a simple `Route` in the preceding code. What makes the route special is that we are not passing a `path` property with it. By default, the `path` is completely ignored and the component is rendered every time, except if there is a match with a previous component. That is why we added the route to the bottom of the `Router`. When no route matches, we redirect the user to the login screen in the root path, or, if the user is already logged in, we redirect them to a different screen using the routing logic of the root path. Our `LoginRoute` component handles this last case.

You can test all changes when starting the front end with `npm run client` and the back end with `npm run server`. We have now moved the current state of our application from a standard, single-route application to an application that differentiates the login form and the news feed based on the location of the browser.

# Advanced routing with React Router

The primary goal of this chapter is to build a profile page for your users. We need a separate page to show all of the content that a single user has entered or created. The content would not fit next to the posts feed. When looking at Facebook, we can see that every user has their own address, under which we can find the profile page of a specific user. We are going to create our profile page in the same way, and use the username as the custom path.

We have to implement the following features:

1. We add a new parameterized route for the user profile. The path starts with `/user/` and follows a username.
2. We change the user profile page to send all GraphQL queries, including the `username` route parameter, inside of the `variables` field of the GraphQL request.
3. We edit the `postsFeed` query to filter all posts by the `username` parameter provided.
4. We implement a new GraphQL query on the back end to request a user by their username, in order to show information about the user.
5. When all of the queries are finished, we render a new user profile header component and the posts feed.
6. Finally, we enable navigation between each page without reloading the complete page, but only the changed parts.

Let's start by implementing routing for the profile page in the next section.

# Parameters in routes

We have prepared most of the work required to add a new user route. Open up the `router.js` file again. Add the new route, as follows:

```
<PrivateRoute path="/user/:username" component={props => <User {...props}
changeLoginState={this.props.changeLoginState}/>}
loggedIn={this.props.loggedIn}/>
```

The code contains two new elements, as follows:

- The path that we entered is `/user/:username`. As you can see, the username is prefixed with a colon, telling React Router to pass the value of it to the underlying component being rendered.
- The component that we rendered previously was a stateless function that returned either the `LoginRegisterForm` or the `Main` component. Neither of these received any parameters or properties from React Router. Now, however, it is required that all properties of React Router are transferred to the child component. That includes the username parameter that we just introduced. We use the same destructuring assignment with the `props` object to pass all properties to the `User` component.

Those are all of the changes that we need to accept parameterized paths in React Router. We read out the value inside of the new user page component. Before implementing it, we import the dependency at the top of `router.js` to get the preceding route working:

```
import User from './User';
```

Create the preceding `User.js` file next to the `Main.js` file. Like the `Main` component, we are collecting all of the components that we render on this page. You should stay with this layout, as you can directly see which main parts each page consists of. The `User.js` file should look as follows:

```
import React, { Component } from 'react';
import UserProfile from './components/user';
import Chats from './Chats';
import Bar from './components/bar';
import CurrentUserQuery from './components/queries/currentUser';

export default class User extends Component {
  render() {
    return (
      <CurrentUserQuery>
        <Bar changeLoginState={this.props.changeLoginState}/>
        <UserProfile username={this.props.match.params.username}/>
        <Chats />
      </CurrentUserQuery>
    );
  }
}
```

Like before, we use the `CurrentUserQuery` component as a wrapper for the `Bar` component and the `Chats` component. If a user visits the profile of a friend, they see the common application bar at the top. They can access their chats on the right-hand side, like in Facebook. It is one of the many situations in which React and the reusability of components come in handy.

We removed the `Feed` component and replaced it with a new `UserProfile` component. Importantly, the `UserProfile` receives the `username` property. Its value is taken from the properties of the `User` component. These properties were passed over by React Router. If you have a parameter, such as a `username`, in the routing path, the value is stored in the `match.params.username` property of the child component. The `match` object generally contains all matching information of React Router.

From this point on, you can implement any custom logic that you want with this value. We will now continue with implementing the profile page.

Follow these steps to build the user's profile page:

1. Create a new folder, called `user`, inside the `components` folder.
2. Create a new file, called `index.js`, inside the `user` folder.
3. Import the dependencies at the top of the file, as follows:

```
import React, { Component } from 'react';
import PostsQuery from '../queries/postsFeed';
import FeedList from '../post/feedlist';
import UserHeader from './header';
import UserQuery from '../queries/userQuery';
```

   The first three lines should look familiar. The last two imported files, however, do not exist at the moment, but we are going to change that shortly. The first new file is `UserHeader`, which takes care of rendering the avatar image, the name, and information about the user. Logically, we request the data that we will display in this header through a new Apollo query, called `UserQuery`.

4. Insert the code for the `UserProfile` component that we are building at the moment beneath the dependencies, as follows:

```
export default class UserProfile extends Component {
  render() {
    const query_variables = { page: 0, limit: 10, username:
    this.props.username };
    return (
      <div className="user">
        <div className="inner">
          <UserQuery variables={{username: this.props.username}}>
            <UserHeader/>
          </UserQuery>
        </div>
        <div className="container">
          <PostsQuery variables={query_variables}>
            <FeedList/>
          </PostsQuery>
        </div>
      </div>
    )
  }
}
```

The `UserProfile` class is not complex. We are running two Apollo queries simultaneously. Both have the `variables` property set. The `PostQuery` receives the regular pagination fields, `page` and `limit`, but also the username, which initially came from React Router. This property is also handed over to the `UserQuery`, inside of a `variables` object.

5. We should now edit and create the Apollo queries, before programming the profile header component. Open the `postsFeed.js` file from the `queries` folder.

To use the username as input to the GraphQL query we first have to change the query string from the `GET_POSTS` variable. Change the first two lines to match the following code:

```
query postsFeed($page: Int, $limit: Int, $username: String) {
  postsFeed(page: $page, limit: $limit, username: $username) {
```

Add a new line to the `getVariables` method, above the `return` statement:

```
if(typeof variables.username !== typeof undefined) {
  query_variables.username = variables.username;
}
```

If the custom query component receives a `username` property, it is included in the GraphQL request. It is used to filter posts by the specific user that we are viewing.

6. Create a new `userQuery.js` file in the `queries` folder to create the missing query class.
7. Import all of the dependencies and parse the new query schema with `graphl-tag`, as follows:

```
import React, { Component } from 'react';
import { Query } from 'react-apollo';
import Loading from '../loading';
import Error from '../error';
import gql from 'graphql-tag';

const GET_USER = gql`
  query user($username: String!) {
    user(username: $username) {
      id
      email
      username
      avatar
```

```
        }
      }
    `;
```

The preceding query is nearly the same as the `currentUser` query. We are going to implement the corresponding `user` query later, in our GraphQL API.

8. The component itself is as simple as the ones that we created before. Insert the following code:

```
export default class UserQuery extends Component {
  getVariables() {
    const { variables } = this.props;
    var query_variables = {};
    if(typeof variables.username !== typeof undefined) {
      query_variables.username = variables.username;
    }
    return query_variables;
  }
  render() {
    const { children } = this.props;
    const variables = this.getVariables();
    return(
      <Query query={GET_USER} variables={variables}>
        {({ loading, error, data }) => {
          if (loading) return <Loading />;
          if (error) return <Error><p>{error.message}</p></Error>;
          const { user } = data;
          return React.Children.map(children, function(child){
            return React.cloneElement(child, { user });
          })
        }}
      </Query>
    )
  }
}
```

We set the `query` property and the parameters that are collected by the `getVariables` method to the GraphQL `Query` component. The rest is the same as any other query component that we have written. All child components receive a new property, called `user`, which holds all the information about the user, such as their name, their email, and their avatar image. You can extend that later on, but always remember to not publish data that should be private.

9. The last step is to implement the `UserProfileHeader` component. This component renders the `user` property, with all its values. It is just simple HTML markup. Copy the following code into the `header.js` file, in the `user` folder:

```
import React, { Component } from 'react';

export default class UserProfileHeader extends Component {
  render() {
    const { avatar, email, username } = this.props.user;
    return (
      <div className="profileHeader">
        <div className="avatar">
          <img src={avatar}/>
        </div>
        <div className="information">
          <p>
            {username}
          </p>
          <p>
            {email}
          </p>
          <p>You can provide further information here and build
          your really personal header component for your users.</p>
        </div>
      </div>
    )
  }
}
```

If you need help getting the CSS styling right, take a look at the official repository for this book. The preceding code only renders the user's data; you could also implement features such as a chat button, which would give the user the option to start messaging with other people. Currently, we have not implemented this feature anywhere, but it is not necessary to explain the principles of React and GraphQL.

We have finished the new front end components, but the `UserProfile` component is still not working. The queries that we are using here either do not accept the username parameter or have not yet been implemented.

The next section will cover which parts of the back end have to be adjusted.

# Querying the user profile

With the new profile page, we have to update our back end accordingly. Let's take a look at what needs to be done, as follows:

1. We have to add the `username` parameter to the schema of the `postsFeed` query and adjust the resolver function.
2. We have to create the schema and the resolver function for the new `UserQuery` component.

We will begin with the `postsFeed` query.

Edit the `postsFeed` query in the `RootQuery` type of the `schema.js` file to match the following code:

```
postsFeed(page: Int, limit: Int, username: String): PostFeed @auth
```

Here, I have added the `username` as an optional parameter.

Now, head over to the `resolvers.js` file, and take a look at the corresponding resolver function. Replace the signature of the function to extract the username from the variables, as follows:

```
postsFeed(root, { page, limit, username }, context) {
```

To make use of the new parameter, add the following lines of code above the return statement:

```
if(typeof username !== typeof undefined) {
  query.include = [{model: User}];
  query.where = { '$User.username$': username };
}
```

We have already covered the basic Sequelize API and how to query associated models by using the `include` parameter in `Chapter 3`, *Connecting to the Database*. An important point is how we filter posts associated with a user by their username:

1. In the preceding code, we fill the `include` field of the `query` object with the Sequelize model that we want to join. This allows us to filter the associated `Chats` model in the next step.

2. Then, we create a normal `where` object, in which we write the filter condition. If you want to filter the posts by an associated table of users, you can wrap the model and field names that you want to filter by with dollar signs. In our case, we wrap `User.username` with dollar signs, which tells Sequelize to query the `User` model's table and filter by the value of the `username` column.

No adjustments are required for the pagination part. The GraphQL query is now ready. The great thing about the small changes that we have made is that we have just one API function that accepts several parameters, either to display posts on a single user profile, or to display a list of posts like a news feed.

Let's move on and implement the new `user` query. Add the following line to the `RootQuery` in your GraphQL schema:

```
user(username: String!): User @auth
```

This query only accepts a `username`, but this time it is a required parameter in the new query. Otherwise, the query would make no sense, since we only use it when visiting a user's profile through their username. In the `resolvers.js` file, we will now implement the resolver function using Sequelize:

```
user(root, { username }, context) {
  return User.findOne({
    where: {
      username: username
    }
  });
},
```

In the preceding code, we use the `findOne` method of the `User` model by Sequelize, and search for exactly one user with the username that we provided in the parameter.

We also want to display the email of the user on the user's profile page. Add the email as a valid field on the `User` type in your GraphQL schema with the following line of code:

```
email: String
```

Now that the back end code and the user page are ready, we have to allow the user to navigate to this new page. The next section will cover user navigation using React Router.

## Programmatic navigation in React Router

We created a new site with the user profile, but now we have to offer the user a link to get there. The transition between the news feed and the login and registration forms is automated by React Router, but not the transition from the news feed to a profile page. The user decides whether they want to view the profile of the user. React Router has multiple ways to handle navigation. We are going to extend the news feed to handle clicks on the username or the avatar image, in order to navigate to the user's profile page. Open the `header.js` file in the `post` components folder. Import the `Link` component provided by React Router, as follows:

```
import { Link } from 'react-router-dom';
```

The `Link` component is a tiny wrapper around a regular HTML `a` tag. Apparently, in standard PHP applications or websites, there is no complex logic behind hyperlinks; you click on them, and a new page is loaded from scratch. With React Router or most single-page application JS frameworks, you can add more logic behind hyperlinks. Importantly, instead of completely reloading the pages when navigating between different routes, this now gets handled by React Router. There won't be complete page reloads when navigating; instead, only the required parts are exchanged, and the GraphQL queries are run. This method saves the user expensive bandwidth, because it means that we can avoid downloading all of the HTML, CSS, and image files again.

To test this, wrap the username and the avatar image in the `Link` component, as follows:

```
<Link to={'/user/'+post.user.username}>
  <img src={post.user.avatar} />
  <div>
    <h2>{post.user.username}</h2>
  </div>
</Link>
```

In the rendered HTML, the `img` and `div` tags are surrounded by a common `a` tag, but are handled inside React Router. The `Link` component receives a `to` property, which is the destination of the navigation. You have to copy one new CSS rule, because the `Link` component has changed the markup:

```
.post .header a > * {
  display: inline-block;
  vertical-align: middle;
}
```

If you test the changes now, clicking on the username or avatar image, you should notice that the content of the page dynamically changes, but does not entirely reload. A further task would be to copy this approach to the user search list in the application bar and the chats. Currently, the users are displayed, but there is no option to visit their profile pages by clicking on them.

Now, let's take a look at another way to navigate with React Router. If the user has reached a profile page, we want them to navigate back by clicking on a button in the application bar. First of all, we will create a new `home.js` file in the `bar` folder, and we will enter the following code:

```
import React, { Component } from 'react';
import { withRouter } from 'react-router';

class Home extends Component {
  goHome = () => {
    this.props.history.push('/app');
  }
  render() {
    return (
      <button className="goHome" onClick={this.goHome}>Home</button>
    );
  }
}

export default withRouter(Home);
```

We are using multiple React Router techniques here. We export the `Home` component through a HoC, which we covered in `Chapter 4`, *Integrating React into the Back end with Apollo*. The `withRouter` HoC gives the `Home` component access to the `history` object of React Router. That is great, because it means that we do not need to pass this object from the top of our React tree down to the `Home` component.

Furthermore, we use the `history` object to navigate the user to the news feed. In the `render` method, we return a button, which, when clicked, runs the `history.push` function. This function adds the new path to the history of the browser and navigates the user to the `'/app'` main page. The good thing is that it works in the same way as the `Link` component, and does not reload the entire website.

There are a few things to do in order to get the button working, as follows:

1. Import the component into the `index.js` file of the `bar` folder, as follows:

```
import Home from './home';
```

2. Then, replace the `Logout` button with the following lines of code:

```
<div className="buttons">
  <Home/>
  <Logout changeLoginState={this.props.changeLoginState}/>
</div>
```

3. I have wrapped the two buttons in a separate `div` tag, so that it is easier to align them correctly. You can replace the old CSS for the logout button and add the following:

```
.topbar .buttons {
  position: absolute;
  right: 5px;
  top: 5px;
  height: calc(100% - 10px);
}

.topbar .buttons > * {
  height: 100%;
  margin-right: 5px;
  border: none;
  border-radius: 5px;
}
```

Now that we have everything together, the user can visit the profile page and navigate back again. Our final result looks as follows:

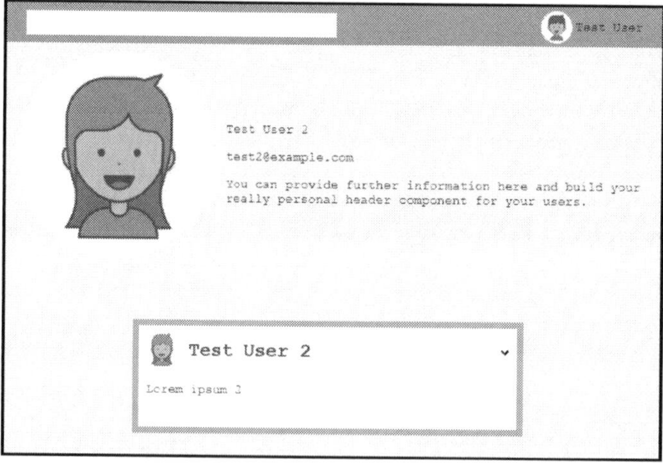


source: https://www.vecteezy.com/

We have a big profile header for the user and their posts at the bottom of the window. At the top, you can see the top bar with the currently logged in user.

# Remembering the redirect location

When a visitor comes to your page, they have probably followed a link that was posted elsewhere. This link is likely to be a direct address for a user, a post, or anything else that you offer direct access to. For those that are not logged in, we configured the application to redirect that person to the login or signup forms. This behavior makes sense. However, once that person has either logged in or signed up with a new account, they are then navigated to the news feed. A better way of doing this would be to remember the initial destination that the person wanted to visit. To do this, we will make a few changes to the router. Open the `router.js` file. With all of the routing components provided by React Router, we always get access to the properties inside of them. We will make use of this and save the last location that we were redirected from.

In the `PrivateRoute` component, swap out the `Redirect` with the following code:

```
<Redirect to={{
  pathname: '/',
  state: { from: props.location }
}} />
```

Here, I have added the `state` field. The value that it receives comes from the parent `Route` component, which holds the last matched path in the `props.location` field generated by React Router. The path can be a user's profile page or the news feed, since both rely on the `PrivateRoute` component where authentication is required. When the preceding redirect is triggered, you receive the `from` field inside of the router's state.

We want to use this variable when the user is logging in. Replace the `Redirect` component in the `LoginRoute` component with the following lines:

```
<Redirect to={{
  pathname: (typeof props.location.state !== typeof undefined) ?
  props.location.state.from.pathname : '/app',
}} />
```

Here, I have introduced a small condition for the `pathname`. If the `location.state` property is defined, we can rely on the `from` field. Previously, we stored the redirect path in the `PrivateRoute` component. If the `location.state` property does not exist, the user was not visiting a direct hyperlink, but just wanted to log in normally. They will be navigated to the news feed with the `/app` path.

Your application should now be able to handle all routing scenarios, and this should allow your users to view your site comfortably.

# Summary

In this chapter, we transitioned from our one-screen application to a multi-page setup. React Router, our main library for routing purposes, now has three paths, under which we display different parts of Graphbook. Furthermore, we now have a catch-all route, in which we can redirect the user to a valid page.

We will continue with this progression by implementing server-side rendering, which needs many adjustments on both the front end and the back end.

# 9
# Implementing Server-Side Rendering

With our progress from the last chapter, we are now serving multiple pages under different paths with our React application. All of the routing happens directly on the client. In this chapter, we will look at the advantages and disadvantages of server-side rendering. By the end of the chapter, you will have configured Graphbook to serve all pages as pre-rendered HTML from the server instead of the client.

This chapter covers the following topics:

- An introduction to server-side rendering
- Setting up Express.js to render React on the server
- Enabling JWT authentication in connection with server-side rendering
- Running all GraphQL queries in the React tree

## Introduction to server-side rendering

First, you have to understand the differences between using a server-side rendered and a client-side rendered application. There are numerous things to bear in mind when transforming a pure client rendered application to support server-side rendering. The current user flow begins with requesting a standard `index.html`. The file includes very few things, such as a small `body` with one `div`, a `head` tag with some very basic `meta` tags, and a vital `script` tag that downloads the bundled JavaScript file created by webpack. The server merely serves the `index.html` and the `bundle.js`. Then, the client's browser begins processing the React markup that we wrote. When React has finished evaluating the code, we see the HTML of the application that we wanted to see. All CSS files or images are also downloaded from our server, but only when React has inserted the HTML into the browser's DOM. During the rendering by React, the Apollo components are executed, and all queries are sent. These are, of course, handled by our back end and database.

In comparison with server-side rendering, the client-side approach is straightforward. Before the development of Angular, Ember, React, or other JS frameworks (as we have them nowadays), the conventional approach was to have a back end that implemented all of the business logic, and also a high number of templates or functions that returned valid HTML. The back end queried the database, processed the data, and inserted it into the HTML. The HTML was directly served at the request of the client. The browser then downloaded the JavaScript, CSS, and image files, according to the HTML. Most of the time, the JavaScript was only responsible for allowing for dynamic content or layout changes, rather than rendering the entire application. This could include drop-down menus, accordions, or just pulling new data from the back end via Ajax. The main HTML of the application, however, was directly returned from the back end. A significant benefit of this solution is that the client does not process all of the business logic, since it has been done on the server.

However, when speaking of server-side rendering for React applications, we are referring to something different. Our current situation is that we have written a React application that renders on the client. We do not want to re-implement the rendering for the back end in a slightly different way. We also don't want to lose the ability to change data, pages, or the layout dynamically in the browser, since we already have an excellent working application with many interaction possibilities for the user.

An approach that allows us to make use of the pre-rendered HTML, and also the dynamic features provided by React, is called **universal rendering**. With universal rendering, the first request of the client includes a pre-rendered HTML page. The HTML should be the exact HTML that the client generates when processing it on its own. If this is the case, React can reuse the HTML provided by the server. Since server-side rendering not only involves reusing HTML, but also saving requests made by Apollo, the client also needs a starting cache that React can rely on. The server makes all of the requests before sending the rendered HTML, and inserts a state variable for Apollo and React into the HTML. The result is that on the first request of the client, our front end should not need to rerender or refresh any HTML or data that is returned by the server. For all following actions, such as navigating to other pages or sending messages, the same client-side React code from before is used. **Server-side rendering (SSR)** is only used on the first page load. Afterwards, these features do not require SSR, because the client-side code continues to work as dynamically as before.

Let's get started with writing some code.

# SSR in Express.js

The first step is to implement basic server-side rendering on the back end. We are going to extend this functionality later to validate the authentication of the user. An authenticated user allows us to execute Apollo or GraphQL requests, and not only to render the pure React markup. First, we need some new packages. Because we are going to use universal rendered React code, we require an advanced webpack configuration; hence, we will install the following packages:

```
npm install --save-dev webpack-dev-middleware webpack-hot-middleware
@babel/cli
```

Let's quickly go through the packages that we are installing here. We only need these packages for development:

- The first webpack module, called `webpack-dev-middleware`, allows the back end to serve bundles generated by webpack, without creating files, but from memory. It is convenient for cases in which we need to run JavaScript directly, and do not want to use separate files.
- The second package, called `webpack-hot-middleware`, only handles client-side updates. If a new version of a bundle was created, the client is notified, and the bundle is exchanged.
- The last package, called `@babel/cli`, allows us to introduce the great features that Babel provides to our back end. We are going to use React code that has to be transpiled.

In a production environment, it is not recommended to use these packages. Instead, the bundle is built once, before deploying the application. The client downloads the bundle when the application has gone live.

For development with SSR enabled, the back end uses these packages to distribute the bundled React code to the client, after the server-side rendering has finished. The server itself relies on the plain `src` files, and not on the webpack bundle that the client receives.

We also depend on one further essential package, as follows:

```
npm install --save node-fetch
```

To set up the Apollo Client on the back end, we require a replacement of the standard `window.fetch` method. The Apollo Client uses it to send GraphQL requests, which is why we install `node-fetch` as a polyfill. We are going to set up the Apollo Client for the back end later in this chapter.

Before starting with the primary work, ensure that your `NODE_ENV` environment variable is set to `development`.

Head over to the server's `index.js` file, where all of the Express magic happens. We didn't cover this file in the previous chapter, because we are going to adjust it now to support server-side including the routing directly.

First, we will set up the development environment for server-side rendering, as it is essential for the next tasks. Follow these steps to get your development environment ready for SSR:

1. The first step is to import the two new webpack modules: `webpack-dev-middleware` and `webpack-hot-middleware`. These should only be used in a development environment, so we should require them conditionally, by checking the environment variables. In a production environment, we generate the webpack bundles in advance. Put the following code underneath the setup for the Express.js helmet, in order to only use the new packages in development:

   ```
   if(process.env.NODE_ENV === 'development') {
     const devMiddleware = require('webpack-dev-middleware');
     const hotMiddleware = require('webpack-hot-middleware');
     const webpack = require('webpack');
     const config = require('../../webpack.server.config');
     const compiler = webpack(config);
     app.use(devMiddleware(compiler));
     app.use(hotMiddleware(compiler));
   }
   ```

2. After loading those packages, we will also require webpack, because we will parse a new webpack configuration file. The new configuration file is only used for the server-side rendering.
3. After both the webpack and the configuration file have been loaded, we will use the `webpack(config)` command to parse the configuration and create a new webpack instance.
4. We are going to create the webpack configuration file next. We pass the created webpack instance to our two new modules. When a request reaches the server, the two packages take action according to the configuration file.

The new configuration file has only a few small differences, as compared to the original configuration file, but these have a big impact. Create the new `webpack.server.config.js` file, and enter the following configuration:

```
const path = require('path');
const webpack = require('webpack');
```

```
const buildDirectory = 'dist';
module.exports = {
  mode: 'development',
  entry: [
    'webpack-hot-middleware/client',
    './src/client/index.js'
  ],
  output: {
    path: path.join(__dirname, buildDirectory),
    filename: 'bundle.js',
    publicPath: '/'
  },
  module: {
    rules: [
      {
        test: /\.js$/,
        exclude: /node_modules/,
        use: {
          loader: 'babel-loader',
        },
      },
      {
        test: /\.css$/,
        use: ['style-loader', 'css-loader'],
      },
      {
        test: /\.(png|woff|woff2|eot|ttf|svg)$/,
        loader: 'url-loader?limit=100000',
      },
    ],
  },
  plugins: [
    new webpack.HotModuleReplacementPlugin(),
    new webpack.NamedModulesPlugin(),
  ],
};
```

We have made three changes in the preceding configuration, in comparison to the original `webpack.client.config.js`, as follows:

- In the `entry` property, we now have multiple entry points. The `index` file for the front end code, like before, is one entry point. The second one is the new `webpack-hot-middleware` module, which initiates the connection between the client and the server. The connection is used to send the client notifications to update the bundle to a newer version.

- I removed the `devServer` field, as this configuration does not require webpack to start its own server. Express.js is the web server, which we are already using when loading the configuration.
- The plugins are entirely different from those of the client's webpack configuration. We do not need the `CleanWebpackPlugin` plugin, as this cleans the `dist` folder, nor the `HtmlWebpackPlugin`, which inserts the webpack bundles into the `index.html` file; this is handled by the server differently. These plugins are only useful for client-side development. Now, we have the `HotModuleReplacementPlugin` plugin, which enables **Hot Module Replace** (**HMR**). It allows for JS and CSS to be exchanged on the fly. `NamedModulesPlugin` displays the relative paths for modules injected by HMR. Both plugins are only recommended for developmental use.

The webpack preparation is now finished.

Now, we have to focus on how to render React code, and how to serve the generated HTML. However, we cannot use the complete React code that we have written. There are specific adjustments that we have to make to the main files: `index.js`, `App.js`, `router.js`, and `apollo/index.js`. Many packages that we use, such as React Router or Apollo Client, have default settings or modules that we have to configure differently when executed on the server.

We will begin with the root of our React application, which is the `index.js` file. We are going to implement an individual SSR `index` file, as there are server-specific adjustments to do.

Create a new folder, called `ssr`, inside the `server` folder. Insert the following code into an `index.js` file inside the `ssr` folder:

```
import React from 'react';
import { ApolloProvider } from 'react-apollo';
import App from './app';

export default class ServerClient extends React.Component {
  render() {
    const { client, location, context } = this.props;
    return(
      <ApolloProvider client={client}>
        <App location={location} context={context}/>
      </ApolloProvider>
    );
  }
}
```

The preceding code is a modified version of our client `index.js` root file. The changes that the file has gone through are listed as follows:

- Instead of using the `ReactDOM.render` function to insert the HTML into the DOMNode with the id `root`, we are now exporting a React component. The returned component is called `ServerClient`. There is no DOM that we can access to let ReactDOM render anything, so we skip this step when rendering on the server.
- Also, the `ApolloProvider` component now receives the Apollo Client directly from the `ServerClient` properties, whereas we previously set up the Apollo Client directly inside this file by importing the `index.js` file from the `apollo` folder and passing it to the provider. You will soon see why we are doing this.
- The last change that we made was to extract a `location` and a `context` property. We pass these properties to the `App` component. In the original version, there were no properties passed to the `App` component. Both properties are required in order to configure React Router to work with SSR. We are going to implement the properties later in the chapter.

Before looking at why we made these changes in more detail, let's create the new `App` component for the back end. Create an `app.js` file next to the `index.js` file in the `ssr` folder, and insert the following code:

```
import React, { Component } from 'react';
import { Helmet } from 'react-helmet';
import { withApollo } from 'react-apollo';
import '../../client/components/fontawesome';
import Router from '../../client/router';

class App extends Component {
  state = {
    loggedIn: false
  }
  changeLoginState = (loggedIn) => {
    this.setState({ loggedIn });
  }
  render() {
    return (
      <div>
        <Helmet>
          <title>Graphbook - Feed</title>
          <meta name="description" content="Newsfeed of all your
           friends on Graphbook" />
        </Helmet>
        <Router loggedIn={this.state.loggedIn} changeLoginState=
```

```
            {this.changeLoginState} location={this.props.location}
            context={this.props.context}/>
        </div>
      )
    }
  }

  export default withApollo(App)
```

The following are a few changes that we made:

- The first change, in comparison to the original client-side `App` class, was to adjust the `import` statements to load the router and the `fontawesome` component from the `client` folder, as they do not exist in the `server` folder.
- The second change was to remove the `constructor`, the `componentWillMount`, and the `componentWillUnmount` methods. We did this because the authentication that we built uses the `localStorage`. It is fine for client-side authentication. Neither Node.js nor the server support such storage, in general. That is the reason why we remove the authentication when moving our application to server-side rendering. We are going to replace the `localStorage` implementation with cookies in a later step. For the moment, the user stays logged out of the server.
- The last change involves passing the two new properties, `context` and `location`, to the `Router` in the preceding code.

React Router provides instant support for SSR. Nevertheless, we need to make some adjustments. The best is that we use the same router for the back end and front end, so that we do not need to define routes twice, which is inefficient and can lead to problems. Open the `router.js` inside the `client` folder and follow these steps:

1. Delete the `import` statement for the `react-router-dom` package.
2. Insert the following code to import the package properly:

```
const ReactRouter = require("react-router-dom");
let Router;
if(typeof window !== typeof undefined) {
  const { BrowserRouter } = ReactRouter;
  Router = BrowserRouter;
}
else {
  const { StaticRouter } = ReactRouter;
  Router = StaticRouter;
}
const { Route, Redirect, Switch } = ReactRouter;
```

We use the `require` statement in the preceding code. The reason is that `import` statements are statically analyzed and do not allow for conditional extracting of the package's modules. Notice that after requiring the React Router package, we check whether the file is executed on the server or the client by looking for the `window` object. Since there is no `window` object in Node.js, this is a sufficient check. An alternative approach would be to set up the `Switch` component, including the routes, in a separate file. This approach would allow us to import the routes directly into the correct router, if we create two separate router files for client-side and server-side rendering.

If we are on the client-side, we use the `BrowserRouter`, and if not, we use the `StaticRouter`. The logic is that with the `StaticRouter`, we are in a stateless environment, where we render all routes with a fixed location. The `StaticRouter` does not allow for the location to be changed by redirects, since no user interaction can happen when using server-side rendering. The other components, `Route`, `Redirect`, and `Switch`, can be used as before.

No matter which of the routers is extracted, we save them in the `Router` variable. We then use them in the `render` method of the `Routing` class.

3. We prepared the properties `context` and `location`, which are passed from the top `ServerClient` component to the `Router`. If we are on the server, these properties should be filled, because the `StaticRouter` requires them. You can replace the `Router` tag in the bottom `Routing` component, as follows:

   ```
   <Router context={this.props.context}
   location={this.props.location}>
   ```

   The `location` holds the path that the router should render. The `context` variable stores all of the information the `Router` processes, such as redirects. We can inspect this variable after rendering the `Router` to trigger the redirects manually. This behavior is the big difference between the `BrowserRouter` and the `StaticRouter`. The `BrowserRouter` redirects the user automatically, but the `StaticRouter` does not.

The crucial components to render our React code successfully have now been prepared. However, there are still some modules that we have to initialize before rendering anything with React. Open the `index.js` server file again. At the moment, we are serving the `dist` path statically on the root / path for client-side rendering, which can be found at `http://localhost:8000`. When moving to SSR, we have to serve the HTML generated by our React application at the / path instead.

Furthermore, any other path, such as `/app`, should also use SSR to render those paths on the server. Remove the current `app.get` method at the bottom of the file, right before the `app.listen` method. Insert the following code as a replacement:

```
app.get('*', (req, res) => {
  res.status(200);
  res.send(`<!doctype html>`);
  res.end();
});
```

The asterisk that we are using in the preceding code can overwrite any path that is defined later in the Express routing. Always remember that the `services` routine that we use in Express can implement new paths, such as `/graphql`, that we do not want to overwrite. To avoid this, put the code at the bottom of the file, below the `services` setup. The route catches any requests sent to the back end.

You can try out this route by running the `npm run server` command. Just visit `http://localhost:8000`.

Currently, the preceding catch-all route only returns an empty site, with a status of **200**. Let's change this. The logical step would be to load and render the `ServerClient` class from the `index.js` file of the `ssr` folder, since it is the starting point of the React SSR code. The `ServerClient` component, however, requires an initialized Apollo Client, as we explained before. We are going to create a special Apollo Client for SSR next.

Create a `ssr/apollo.js` file, as it does not exist yet. We will set up the Apollo Client in this file. The content is nearly the same as the original setup for the client:

```
import { ApolloClient } from 'apollo-client';
import { InMemoryCache } from 'apollo-cache-inmemory';
import { onError } from 'apollo-link-error';
import { ApolloLink } from 'apollo-link';
import { HttpLink } from 'apollo-link-http';
import fetch from 'node-fetch';

export default (req) => {
  const AuthLink = (operation, next) => {
```

```
      return next(operation);
    };
    const client = new ApolloClient({
      ssrMode: true,
      link: ApolloLink.from([
        onError(({ graphQLErrors, networkError }) => {
          if (graphQLErrors) {
            graphQLErrors.map(({ message, locations, path, extensions })
            => {
              console.log(`[GraphQL error]: Message: ${message},
              Location: ${locations}, Path: ${path}`);
            });
            if (networkError) {
              console.log(`[Network error]: ${networkError}`);
            }
          }
        }),
        AuthLink,
        new HttpLink({
          uri: 'http://localhost:8000/graphql',
          credentials: 'same-origin',
          fetch
        })
      ]),
      cache: new InMemoryCache(),
    });
    return client;
};
```

There are a few changes that we made to get the client working on the server. These changes were pretty big, so we created a separate file for the server-side Apollo Client setup. Take a look at the changes, as follows, to understand the differences between the front end and the SSR setup for the Apollo Client:

- Instead of using the `createUploadLink` function that we introduced to allow the user to upload images or other files, we are now using the standard `HttpLink` again. You could have used the `UploadClient`, but the functionalities that it provides won't be used on the server, as the server won't upload files (of course).
- The `AuthLink` skips to the next link, as we have not implemented server-side authentication yet.
- The `HttpLink` receives the `fetch` property, which is filled by the `node-fetch` package that we installed at the beginning of the chapter. It is used instead of the `window.fetch` method, which is not available in Node.js.

- Rather than exporting the `client` directly, we export a wrapping function that accepts a `request` object. We pass it as a parameter in the Express route. As you can see in the preceding code, we haven't used the object yet, but that will change soon.

Import the `ApolloClient` class at the top of the server `index.js`, as follows:

```
import ApolloClient from './ssr/apollo';
```

The imported `ApolloClient` function accepts the `request` object of our Express server.

Add the following line to the top of the new Express catch-all route:

```
const client = ApolloClient(req);
```

This way, we set up a new `client` instance that we can hand over to our `ServerClient` component.

We can continue and implement the rendering of our `ServerClient` component. To make the future code work, we have to load React and, of course, the `ServerClient` itself:

```
import React from 'react';
import Graphbook from './ssr/';
```

The `ServerClient` class is imported under the `Graphbook` name. We import React because we use the standard JSX syntax while rendering our React code.

Now that we have access to the Apollo Client and the `ServerClient` component, insert the following two lines below the `ApolloClient` setup in the Express route:

```
const context= {};
const App = (<Graphbook client={client} location={req.url} context=
 {context}/>);
```

We pass the initialized `client` variable to the `Graphbook` component. We use the regular React syntax to pass all properties. Furthermore, we set the `location` property to the request object's `url`, to tell the router which path to render. The `context` property is passed as an empty object.

However, why do we pass an empty object as `context` to the Router at the end?

The reason is that after rendering the `Graphbook` component to HTML, we can access the `context` object and see whether a redirect, or something else, would have been triggered regularly. As we mentioned before, redirects have to be implemented by the back end code. The `StaticRouter` component of React Router does not make assumptions about the Node.js web server that you are using. That is why the `StaticRouter` does not execute them automatically. Tracking and post-processing these events is possible with the `context` variable.

The resulting React object is saved to a new variable, called `App`. Now, there should be no errors if you start the server with `npm run server` and visit `http://localhost:8000`. Still, we see an empty page. That happens because we only return an empty HTML page; we haven't rendered the React `App` object to HTML. To render the object to HTML, import the following package at the top of the server `index.js` file:

```
import ReactDOM from 'react-dom/server';
```

The `react-dom` package not only provides bindings for the browser, but also provides a special module for the server, which is why we use the suffix `/server` while importing it. The returned module provides a number of server-only functions.

To learn some more advanced features of server-side rendering and the dynamics behind it, you should read up on the official documentation of the server package of `react-dom` at `https://reactjs.org/docs/react-dom-server.html`.

We can translate the React `App` object into HTML by using the `ReactDOM.rendertoString` function. Insert the following line of code beneath the `App` object:

```
const content = ReactDOM.renderToString(App);
```

This function generates HTML and stores it inside the `content` variable. It can be returned to the client now. If you return pre-rendered HTML from the server, the client goes through it and checks whether its current state would match the returned HTML. The comparison is made by identifying certain points in the HTML, such as the `data-reactroot` property.

If, at any point, the markup between the server-rendered HTML and the one that the client would generate does not match, an error is thrown. The application will still work, but the client will not be able to make use of server-side rendering; the client will replace the complete markup returned from the server by rerendering everything again. The server's HTML response is thrown away in this case. This is, of course, very inefficient and not what we are aiming for.

We have to return the rendered HTML to the client. The HTML that we have rendered begins with the root `div` tag, and not the `html` tag. We must wrap the `content` variable inside a template, which includes the surrounding HTML tags. Create a `template.js` file, inside the `ssr` folder. Enter the following code to implement the template for our rendered HTML:

```
import React from 'react';
import ReactDOM from 'react-dom/server';

export default function htmlTemplate(content) {
  return `
    <html lang="en">
      <head>
        <meta charSet="UTF-8"/>
        <meta name="viewport" content="width=device-width, initial-
         scale=1.0"/>
        <meta httpEquiv="X-UA-Compatible" content="ie=edge"/>
        <link rel="shortcut icon" href="data:image/x-icon;," type="image/x-
         icon">
        ${(process.env.NODE_ENV === 'development')? "":"<link
           rel='stylesheet' href='/bundle.css'/>"}
      </head>
      <body>
        ${ReactDOM.renderToStaticMarkup(<div id="root"
          dangerouslySetInnerHTML={{ __html: content }}></div>)}
        <script src="/bundle.js"></script>
      </body>
    </html>
  `;
};
```

The preceding code is pretty much the same HTML markup as that in the `index.html` that we usually serve to the client. The difference is that we use React and `ReactDOM` here.

First, we export a function, which accepts the `content` variable with the rendered HTML.

Secondly, we render a `link` tag inside the `head` tag, which downloads the CSS bundle if we are in a production environment. For our current development scenario, there is no bundled CSS.

The important part is that we use a new `ReactDOM` function called `rendertoStaticMarkup` inside the `body` tag. This function inserts the React root tag into the body of our HTML template. Before, we used the `renderToString` method, which included special React tags, such as the `data-reactroot` property. We use the `rendertoStaticMarkup` function to generate standard HTML, without special React tags. The only parameter that we pass to the function is the `div` tag with the id `root` and a new property, `dangerouslySetInnerHTML`. This attribute is a replacement for the regular `innerHTML` attribute, but for use in React. It lets React insert the HTML inside the root `div` tag. As the name suggests, it is dangerous to do this, but only if it is done on the client, as there is no possibility for XSS attacks on the server. We use the `ReactDOM.renderToStaticMarkup` function to make use of the attribute. The inserted HTML was initially rendered with the `renderToString` function, so that it would include all critical React HTML attributes and the wrapping `div` tag with the id `root`. It can then be reused in the browser by the front end code without any problems.

Require this `template.js` file in the server `index` file, at the top of the file:

```
import template from './ssr/template';
```

The template function can now be used directly in the `res.send` method, as follows:

```
res.send(`<!doctype html>\n${template(content)}`);
```

We do not only return a `doctype` anymore; we also respond with the return value of the `template` function. As you should see, the `template` function accepts the rendered `content` variable as a parameter, and composes it to a valid HTML document.

At this point, we have managed to get our first version of a server-side rendered React application working. You can prove this by right-clicking in your browser window and choosing to view the source code. The window shows you the original HTML that is returned by the server. The output equals the HTML from the `template` function, including the login and signup forms.

Nevertheless, there are two problems that we face, as follows:

- There is no description meta `head` tag included in the server response. Something must have gone wrong with React Helmet.
- When logged in on the client side and, for example, viewing the news feed under the `/app` path, the server responds without having rendered the news feed, nor the login form. Normally, React Router would have redirected us to the login form, since we are not logged in on the server side. Since we use the `StaticRouter`, however, we have to initiate the redirect separately, as we explained before. We are going to implement the authentication in a separate step.

We will start with the first issue. To fix the problem with React `Helmet`, import it at the top of the server `index.js` file, as follows:

```
import { Helmet } from 'react-helmet';
```

Now, before setting the response status with `res.status`, you can extract the React `Helmet` status, as follows:

```
const head = Helmet.renderStatic();
```

The `renderStatic` method is specially made for server-side rendering. We can use it after having rendered the React application with the `renderToString` function. It gives us all `head` tags that would have been inserted throughout our code. Pass this `head` variable to the `template` function as a second parameter, as follows:

```
res.send(`<!doctype html>\n${template(content, head)}`);
```

Go back to the `template.js` from the `ssr` folder. Add the `head` parameter to the exported function's signature. Add the following two new lines of code to the HTML's `head` tag:

```
${head.title.toString()}
${head.meta.toString()}
```

The `head` variable extracted from React Helmet holds a property for each `meta` tag. They provide a `toString` function that returns a valid HTML tag, which you can directly enter into the document's `head`. The first problem should be fixed: all `head` tags are now inside the server's HTML response.

Let's focus on the second problem. The server response returns an empty React `root` tag when visiting a `PrivateRoute`. As we explained previously, the reason is that the naturally initiated redirect does not get through to us, since we are using the `StaticRouter`. We are redirected away from the `PrivateRoute`, because the authentication is not implemented for the server-rendered code. The first thing to fix is to handle the redirect, and at least respond with the login form, instead of an empty React `root` tag. Later, we need to fix the authentication problem.

You would not notice the problem without viewing the source code of the server's response. The front end downloads the `bundle.js` and triggers the rendering on its own, as it knows about the authentication status of the user. The user would not notice that. Still, it is more efficient if the server sends the correct HTML directly. The HTML will be wrong if the user is logged in, but in the case of an unauthenticated user, the login form is pre-rendered by the server as it initiates the redirects.

To fix this issue, we can access the `context` object that has been filled by React Router after it has used the `renderToString` function. The final Express route should look as follows:

```
app.get('*', (req, res) => {
  const client = ApolloClient(req);
  const context= {};
  const App = (<Graphbook client={client} location={req.url} context=
  {context}/>);
  const content = ReactDOM.renderToString(App);
  if (context.url) {
    res.redirect(301, context.url);
  } else {
    const head = Helmet.renderStatic();
    res.status(200);
    res.send(`<!doctype html>\n${template(content, head)}`);
    res.end();
  }
});
```

The condition for rendering the correct route on the server is that we inspect the `context.url` property. If it is filled, we can initiate a redirect with Express.js. That will navigate the browser to the correct path. If the property is not filled, we can return the HTML generated by React.

This route renders the React code correctly, up to the point at which authentication is required. The SSR route correctly renders all public routes, but none of the secure routes. That means that we only respond with the login form at the moment, since it is the only route that doesn't require authentication.

The next step is to implement authentication in connection with SSR, in order to fix this huge issue.

# Authentication with SSR

You should have noticed that we have removed most of the authentication logic from the server-side React code. The reason is that the `localStorage` cannot be transmitted to the server on the initial loading of a page, which is the only case where SSR can be used at all. This leads to the problem that we cannot render the correct route, because we cannot verify whether a user is logged in. The authentication has to be transitioned to cookies, which are sent with every request.

It is important to understand that cookies also introduce some security issues. We will continue to use the regular HTTP authorization header for the GraphQL API that we have written. If we use cookies for the GraphQL API, we will expose our application to potential CSRF attacks. The front end code continues to send all GraphQL requests with the HTTP authorization header.

We will only use the cookies to verify the authentication status of a user, and to initiate requests to our GraphQL API for server-side rendering of the React code. The SSR GraphQL requests will include the authorization cookie's value in the HTTP authorization header. Our GraphQL API only reads and verifies this header, and does not accept cookies. As long as you do not mutate data when loading a page and only query for data to render, there will be no security issues.

As the whole topic of CSRF and XSS is big, I recommend that you read up on it, in order to fully understand how to protect yourself and your users. You can find a great article at `https://www.owasp.org/index.php/Cross-Site_Request_Forgery_(CSRF)`.

The first thing to do is install a new package with `npm`, as follows:

```
npm install --save cookies
```

The `cookies` package allows us to easily interact through the Express request object with the cookies sent by the browser. Instead of parsing and reading through the cookie string (which is just a comma-separated list) manually, you can access the cookies with simple `get` and `set` methods. To get this package working, you have to initialize it inside Express.

Import the `cookies` and `jwt` packages, and also extract the `JWT_SECRET` from the environment variables at the top of the server `index.js` file:

```
import Cookies from 'cookies';
import JWT from 'jsonwebtoken';
const { JWT_SECRET } = process.env;
```

To use the `cookies` package, we are going to set up a new middleware route. Insert the following code before initializing the webpack modules and the services routine:

```
app.use(
  (req, res, next) => {
    const options = { keys: ['Some random keys'] };
    req.cookies = new Cookies(req, res, options);
    next();
  }
);
```

This new Express middleware initializes the `cookies` package under the `req.cookies` property for every request that it processes. The first parameter of the `Cookies` constructor is the request, the second is the response object, and the last one is an `options` parameter. It takes an array of `keys`, with which the cookies are signed. The `keys` are required if you want to sign your cookies for security reasons. You should take care of this in a production environment. You can specify a `secure` property, which ensures that the cookies are only transmitted on secure HTTPS connections.

We can now extract the `authorization` cookie and verify the authentication of the user. To do this, replace the beginning of the SSR route with the following code in the server's `index.js` file:

```
app.get('*', async (req, res) => {
  const token = req.cookies.get('authorization', { signed: true });
  var loggedIn;
  try {
    await JWT.verify(token, JWT_SECRET);
    loggedIn = true;
  } catch(e) {
    loggedIn = false;
  }
```

Here, I have added the `async` declaration to the callback function, because we use the `await` statement inside it. The second step is to extract the `authorization` cookie from the request object with `req.cookies.get`. Importantly, we specify the `signed` field in the `options` parameter, because only then will it successfully return the signed cookies.

The extracted value represents the JWT that we generate when a user logs in. We can verify this with the typical approach that we implemented in `Chapter 6`, *Authentication with Apollo and React*. We use the `await` statement while verifying the JWT. If an error is thrown, the user is not logged in. The state is saved in the `loggedIn` variable. Pass the `loggedIn` variable to the `Graphbook` component, as follows:

```
const App = (<Graphbook client={client} loggedIn={loggedIn}
location={req.url} context={context}/>);
```

Now, we can access the `loggedIn` property inside `index.js` from the `ssr` folder. Extract the `loggedIn` sate from the properties, and pass it to the `App` component in the `ssr` `index.js` file, as follows:

```
<App location={location} context={context} loggedIn={loggedIn}/>
```

Inside the `App` component, we do not need to set the `loggedIn` state directly to false, but we can take the property's value, because it is determined before the `App` class is rendered. This flow is different from the client procedure, where the `loggedIn` state is determined inside the `App` class. Change the `App` class in the `app.js` file in order to match the following code:

```
class App extends Component {
  state = {
    loggedIn: this.props.loggedIn
  }
```

The result is that we pass down the `loggedIn` value from our Express.js route, over the `Graphbook` and `App` components, to our `Router`. It already accepts the `loggedIn` property, in order to render the correct path for the user. At the moment, we still do not set the cookie on the back end when a user successfully logs in.

Open the `resolvers.js` file of our GraphQL server to fix that. We will change a few lines for the `login` and `signup` functions. Both resolver functions need the same changes, as both set the authentication token after login or signup. Insert the following code directly above the return statement:

```
context.cookies.set(
  'authorization',
  token, { signed: true, expires: expirationDate, httpOnly: true,
  secure: false, sameSite: 'strict' }
);
```

The preceding function sets the cookies for the user's browser. The context object is only the Express.js request object where we have initialized the cookies package. The properties of the `cookies.set` function are pretty self-explanatory, as follows:

- The `signed` field specifies whether the keys entered during the initialization of the `cookies` object should be used to sign the cookie's value.
- The `expires` property takes a `date` object. It represents the time until which the cookie is valid. You can set the property to whatever date you want, but I would recommend a short period, such as one day. Insert the following code above the `context.cookies.set` statement, in order to initialize the `expirationDate` variable correctly:

```
const cookieExpiration = 1;
var expirationDate = new Date();
expirationDate.setDate(
  expirationDate.getDate() + cookieExpiration
);
```

- The `httpOnly` field secures the cookie so that it is not accessible by client-side JavaScript.
- The `secure` property has the same meaning as it did when initializing the `Cookie` package. It restricts cookies to SSL connections only. This is a must when going to production, but it cannot be used while developing, since most developers develop locally, without an SSL certificate.
- The `sameSite` field takes either `strict` or `lax` as a value. I recommend setting it to `strict`, since you only want your GraphQL API or server to receive the cookie with every request, but to exclude all cross-site requests, as this could be dangerous.

Now, we should clean up our code. Since we are using cookies, we can remove the `localStorage` authentication flow in the front end code. Open the `App.js` of the `client` folder. Remove the `componentWillMount` method, as we are reading from the `localStorage` there.

The cookies are automatically sent with any request, and they do not need a separate binding, like the `localStorage`. That also means that we need a special `logout` mutation that removes the cookie from the browser. JavaScript is not able to access or remove the cookie, because we specified it as `httpOnly`. Only the server can delete it from the client.

Create a new `logout.js` inside the `mutations` folder, in order to create the new `LogoutMutation` class. The content should look as follows:

```
import React, { Component } from 'react';
import { Mutation } from 'react-apollo';
import gql from 'graphql-tag';

const LOGOUT = gql`
  mutation logout {
    logout {
      success
    }
  }
`;

export default class LogoutMutation extends Component {
  render() {
    const { children } = this.props;
    return (
      <Mutation
        mutation={LOGOUT}>
        {(logout, { loading, error}) =>
          React.Children.map(children, function(child){
            return React.cloneElement(child, { logout, loading, error });
          })
        }
      </Mutation>
    )
  }
}
```

The preceding mutation component only sends a simple `logout` mutation, without any parameters or further logic. We should use the `LogoutMutation` component inside the `index.js` file of the `bar` folder in order to send the GraphQL request. Import the component at the top of the file, as follows:

```
import LogoutMutation from '../mutations/logout';
```

The `Logout` component renders our current **Log out** button in the application bar. It removes the token and cache from the client upon clicking it. Use the `LogoutMutation` class as a wrapper for the `Logout` component, to pass the mutation function:

```
<LogoutMutation><Logout changeLoginState=
 {this.props.changeLoginState}/></LogoutMutation>
```

Inside the `bar` folder, we have to edit the `logout.js` file, because we should make use of the `logout` mutation that this component receives from its parent `LogoutMutation` component. Replace the `logout` method with the following code, in order to send the mutation upon clicking the `logout` button:

```
logout = () => {
  this.props.logout().then(() => {
    localStorage.removeItem('jwt');
    this.props.client.resetStore();
  });
}
```

We have wrapped the original two functions inside the call to the parent `logout` mutation function. It sends the GraphQL request to our server.

To implement the mutation on the back end, add one line to the GraphQL `RootMutation` type, inside `schema.js`:

```
logout: Response @auth
```

It's required that the user that's trying to log out is authorized, so we use the `@auth` directive. The corresponding resolver function looks as follows. Add it to the `resolvers.js` file, in the `RootMutation` property:

```
logout(root, params, context) {
  context.cookies.set(
    'authorization',
    '', { signed: true, expires: new Date(), httpOnly: true, secure:
    false, sameSite: 'strict' }
  );
  return {
    message: true
  };
},
```

The resolver function is minimal. It removes the cookie by setting the expiration date to the current time. This removes the cookie on the client when the browser receives the response, because it is expired then. This behavior is an advantage, in comparison to the `localStorage`.

We have completed everything to make the authorization work with SSR. It is a very complex task, since authorization, server-side rendering, and client-side rendering have effects on the whole application. Every framework out there has its own approach to implementing this feature, so please take a look at them too.

If you look at the source code returned from our server after the rendering, you should see that the login form is returned correctly, like before. Furthermore, the server now recognizes whether the user is logged in. However, the server does not return the rendered news feed, the application bar, or the chats yet. Only a loading message is included in the returned HTML. The client-side code also does not recognize that the user is logged in. We will take a look at these problems in the next section.

# Running Apollo queries with SSR

By nature, GraphQL queries via `HttpLink` are asynchronous. We have implemented a `loading` component to show the user a loading message while the data is being fetched.

This is the same thing that is happening while rendering our React code on the server. All of the routing is evaluated, including whether we are logged in. If the correct route is found, all GraphQL requests are sent. The problem is that the first rendering of React returns the loading state, which is sent to the client by our server. The server does not wait until the GraphQL queries are finished and it has received all of the responses to render our React code.

We will fix this problem now. The following is a list of things that we have to do:

- We need to implement authentication for the SSR Apollo Client. We already did this for the routing, but now we need to pass the cookie to the server-side GraphQL request too.
- We need to use a React Apollo specific method to render the React code asynchronously, to wait for all responses of the GraphQL requests.
- Importantly, we need to return the Apollo cache state to the client. Otherwise, the client will re-fetch everything, as its state is empty upon the first load of the page.

Let's get started, as follows:

1. The first step is to pass the `loggedIn` variable from the Express.js SSR route to the `ApolloClient` function, as a second parameter. Change the `ApolloClient` call inside the server's `index.js` file to the following line of code:

   ```
   const client = ApolloClient(req, loggedIn);
   ```

   Change the signature of the exported function from the `apollo.js` file to also include this second parameter.

2. Replace the `AuthLink` function inside the Apollo Client's setup for SSR with the following code:

   ```
   const AuthLink = (operation, next) => {
     if(loggedIn) {
       operation.setContext(context => ({
         ...context,
         headers: {
           ...context.headers,
           Authorization: req.cookies.get('authorization')
         },
       }));
     }
     return next(operation)
   };
   ```

   This `AuthLink` adds the cookies to the GraphQL requests by using the `request` object given by Express. The request object already holds the initialized cookies package, which we use to extract the authorization cookie. This only needs to be done if the user has been verified as logged in previously.

3. Import a new function from the `react-apollo` package inside the server's `index.js` file. Replace the import of the ReactDOM package with the following line of code:

   ```
   import { renderToStringWithData }  from 'react-apollo';
   ```

4. Originally, we used the ReactDOM server methods to render the React code to HTML. These functions are synchronous; that is why the GraphQL request did not finish. To wait for all GraphQL requests, replace all of the lines, beginning from the `rendertoString` function until the end of the SSR route inside the server's `index.js` file. The result should look as follows:

   ```
   renderToStringWithData(App).then((content) => {
     if (context.url) {
       res.redirect(301, context.url);
     } else {
       const head = Helmet.renderStatic();
       res.status(200);
       res.send(`<!doctype html>\n${template(content, head)}`);
       res.end();
     }
   });
   ```

The `renderToStringWithData` function renders the React code, including the data received by the Apollo requests. Since the method is asynchronous, we wrap the rest of our code inside a callback function.

Now, if you take a look at the HTML returned by your server, you should see the correct markup, including chats, images, and everything else. The problem is that the client does not know that all of the HTML is already there, and can be reused. The client would rerender everything.

5. To let the client reuse the HTML that our server sends, we have to include the Apollo Client's state with our response. Inside the preceding callback, access the Apollo Client's state by inserting the following code:

```
const initialState = client.extract();
```

The `client.extract` method returns a big object, holding all cache information that the client has stored after using the `renderToStringWithData` function.

6. The state must be passed to the `template` function as a third parameter. Change the `res.send` call to the following:

```
res.send(`<!doctype html>\n${template(content, head,
initialState)}`);
```

7. Inside the `template.js` file, extend the function declaration and append the `state` variable as a third parameter, after the `head` variable.
8. Insert the `state` variable, with the following line of code, inside the HTML body and above the `bundle.js` file. If you add it below the `bundle.js` file, it won't work correctly:

```
${ReactDOM.renderToStaticMarkup(<script dangerouslySetInnerHTML=
{{__html: `window.__APOLLO_STATE__=${JSON.stringify(state).replace
(/</g, '\\u003c')}`}}/>)}
```

We use the `renderToStaticMarkup` function to insert another `script` tag. It sets a large, stringified JSON object as Apollo Client's starting cache value. The JSON object holds all results of the GraphQL requests returned while rendering our server-side React application. We directly store the JSON object as a string, in a new field inside the `window` object. The `window` object is helpful, since you can directly access the field globally.

9. Apollo has to know about the state variable. It can be used by the Apollo Client, in order to initialize its cache with the specified data, instead of sending all GraphQL requests again. Open the `index.js` from the client's `apollo` folder. The last property of the initialization process is the cache. We need to set our `__APOLLO_STATE__` as the starting value of the cache. Replace the `cache` property with the following code:

   ```
   cache: new InMemoryCache().restore(window.__APOLLO_STATE__)
   ```

   We create the `InMemoryCache` instance and run its `restore` method, where we insert the value from the window object. The Apollo Client should recreate its cache from this variable.

10. We have now set up the cache for Apollo. It will no longer run unnecessary requests, for which the results already exist. Now, we can finally reuse the HTML, with one last change. We have to change `ReactDOM.render` to `ReactDOM.hydrate` in the client's `index.js` file. The difference between these functions is that React reuses the HTML if it was correctly rendered by our server. In this case, React only attaches some necessary event listeners. If you use the `ReactDOM.render` method, it dramatically slows down the initial rendering process, because it compares the initial DOM with the current DOM and may change it accordingly.

The last problem that we have is that the client-side code does not show the logged in state of our application after refreshing a page. The server returns the correct markup with all the data, but the front end redirects us to the login form. The reason for this is that we statically set the `loggedIn` state variable to false in the `App.js` file of the client-side code.

The best way to check whether the user is authenticated is to verify whether the `__APOLLO_STATE__` field on the window object is filled and has a `currentUser` object attached. If that is the case, we can assume that the user was able to fetch their own data record, so they must be `loggedIn`. To change our `App.js` file accordingly, add the following condition to the `loggedIn` state variable:

```
(typeof window.__APOLLO_STATE__ !== typeof undefined && typeof
window.__APOLLO_STATE__.ROOT_QUERY !== typeof undefined && typeof
window.__APOLLO_STATE__.ROOT_QUERY.currentUser !== typeof undefined)
```

As you can see in the preceding code, we verify whether the Apollo starting cache variable includes a `ROOT_QUERY` property with the subfield `currentUser`. The `ROOT_QUERY` property is filled if any query can be fetched successfully. The `currentUser` field is only filled if the authenticated was successfully requested.

If you execute `npm run server`, you will see that now everything works perfectly. Take a look at the markup that's returned; you will see either the login form or, when logged in, all of the content of the page that you are visiting. You can log in on the client, the news feed is fetched dynamically, you can refresh the page, and all of the posts are directly there, without the need for a single GraphQL request, because the server returned the data side by side with the HTML. This works not only for the `/app` path, but for any path that you implement.

We are now finished with the SSR setup.

So far, we have only looked at the developmental part of server-side rendering. When we get to the point at which we want to make a production build and publicize our application, there are a few other things that we will have to consider, which we will look at in a later chapter.

# Summary

In this chapter, we changed a lot of the code that we have programmed so far. You learned the advantages and disadvantages of offering server-side rendering. The main principles behind React Router, Apollo, and authentication with cookies while using SSR should be clear by now. There is much work required to get SSR running, and it needs to be managed with every change made to your application. Nevertheless, it has excellent performance and experience benefits for your users.

In the next chapter, we will look at how to offer real-time updates through Apollo Subscriptions, instead of using the old and inefficient polling.

# 10
# Real-Time Subscriptions

The GraphQL API we have built is very advanced, as is the front end. In the previous chapter, we introduced server-side rendering to our application. We provided the user with a lot of information through the news feed, chats, and profile pages. The problem we are facing now, however, is that the user currently has to either refresh the browser or we have set a `pollInterval` to all `Query` components to keep the display up to date. A better solution is to implement Apollo Subscriptions through WebSockets. This allows us to refresh the UI of the user with the newest user information in real time without manual user interaction or polling.

This chapter covers the following topics:

- Using GraphQL with WebSockets
- Implementing Apollo Subscriptions
- JWT authentication with Subscriptions

## GraphQL and WebSockets

In `Chapter 1`, *Preparing Your Development Environment*, I explained all the main features that make GraphQL so useful. We mentioned that HTTP is the standard network protocol when using GraphQL. The problem with regular HTTP connections, however, is that they are one-time requests. They can only respond with the data that exists at the time of the request. If the database receives a change concerning the posts or the chats, the user won't know about this until they execute another request. The user interface shows outdated data in this case.

To solve this issue, you can refetch all requests in a specific interval, but this is a bad solution because there's no time range that makes polling efficient. Every user would make unnecessary HTTP requests, which neither you nor the user wants.

The best solution relies on WebSockets instead of HTTP requests. Like HTTP, WebSockets are also based on TCP. One of the main features of WebSockets is that they allow bidirectional communication between the client and the server. Arguably, you could say that HTTP does the same, since you send a request and get a response, but WebSockets work very differently. One requirement is that the web server supports WebSockets in general. If that's the case, the client can open a WebSocket connection to the server. The initial request to establish a WebSocket connection is a standard HTTP request. The server should then respond with a 101 status code. It tells the browser that it agrees to change the protocols from HTTP to WebSockets. If the connection is successful, the server can send updates through this connection to the client. These updates are also called messages or frames. There are no further requests needed by the client to let the server speak with the browser, unlike HTTP, where you always need a request first so that the server can respond to it.

Using WebSockets or Apollo Subscriptions would fix the issue we encounter when using polling, which is the process where a computer waits for an external device to check whether or not it is ready. We have one connection that stays open all the time. The server can send messages to the client whenever data is added or updated. WebSocket URLs start with `ws` or `wss` instead of the ordinary `http` or `https`. With WebSockets, you can also save valuable bandwidth for the users, but these are not included for WebSocket messages.

One disadvantage is that WebSockets are not a standard approach for implementing APIs. If you make your API public to third parties at some point, it's likely that a standard HTTP API would fit better. Also, HTTP is much more optimized. HTTP requests can be cached and proxied easily with common web servers, such as Nginx or Apache, but also by the browser itself, which is hard for WebSockets to do. The most significant impact on performance is that WebSocket connections are kept open as long as the user stays on your site. It's not a problem for one or a few hundred users, but scaling this to more people is likely to present you with some problems. However, it's still a very efficient solution to real-time web communication in contrast to polling, for example.

Most GraphQL client libraries are specialized and optimized for the standard HTTP protocol. It's the most common approach, so that's understandable. The people behind Apollo have got you covered; they've built packages to support WebSockets and the implementation of GraphQL subscriptions. You can use those packages not only with Apollo but also with many other libraries. Let's get started with implementing Apollo Subscriptions.

# Apollo Subscriptions

When we started implementing Apollo in our stack, I explained how to set it up manually. As an alternative, there is the `apollo-boost` package, which does this for you automatically. We have now reached a point where this package cannot be used anymore since subscriptions are an advanced feature that isn't supported. If you rely on the `apollo-boost` package, take a look at `Chapter 4`, *Integrating React into the Back end with Apollo*, to see how to switch to a manual setup.

You can find an excellent overview and more details about Apollo Subscriptions in the official documentation at `https://www.apollographql.com/docs/react/advanced/subscriptions.html`.

The first step is to install all the required packages to get GraphQL subscriptions working. Install them using npm:

```
npm install --save graphql-subscriptions subscriptions-transport-ws apollo-link-ws
```

The following three packages provide necessary modules for a subscription system:

- The `graphql-subscriptions` package provides the ability to connect our GraphQL back end with a PubSub system. It gives the client the option to subscribe to specific channels, and lets the back end publish new data to the client.
- The `subscriptions-transport-ws` package gives our Apollo Server or other GraphQL libraries the option to accept WebSocket connections and accept queries, mutations, and subscriptions over WebSockets.
- The `apollo-link-ws` package is similar to the `HttpLink` or `UploadLink` that we're currently using, but, as the name suggests, it relies on WebSockets, not HTTP, to send requests and allows us to use subscriptions.

Let's take a look at how we can implement subscriptions.

First, we are going to create a new subscription type next to the `RootQuery` and `RootMutation` types inside the GraphQL schema. You can set up events or entities that a client can subscribe to and receive updates inside the new subscription type. It only works by adding the matching `resolver` functions as well. Instead of returning real data for this new subscription type, you return a special object that allows the client to subscribe to events for the specific entity. These entities can be things such as notifications, new chat messages, or comments on a post. Each of them has got their own subscription channel.

The client can subscribe to these channels. It receives updates any time the back end sends a new WebSocket message – because data has been updated, for example. The back end calls a `publish` method that sends the new data through the subscription to all clients. You should be aware that not every user should receive all WebSocket messages since the content may include private data such as chat messages. There should be a filter before the update is sent to target only specific users. We'll see this feature later in the *Authentication with Apollo Subscriptions* section.

# Subscriptions on the Apollo Server

We have now installed all the essential packages. Let's start with the implementation for the back end. As mentioned previously, we are going to rely on WebSockets, as they allow real-time communication between the front end and the back end. We are first going to set up the new transport protocol for the back end.

Open the `index.js` file of the server. Import a new Node.js interface at the top of the file:

```
import { createServer } from 'http';
```

The `http` interface is included in Node.js by default. It handles the traditional HTTP protocol, making the use of many HTTP features easy for the developer.

We are going to use the interface to create a standardized Node.js HTTP server object because the Apollo `SubscriptionServer` module expects such an object. We'll cover the Apollo `SubscriptionServer` module soon in this section. Add the following line of code beneath the initialization of Express.js inside the `app` variable:

```
const server = createServer(app);
```

The `createServer` function creates a new HTTP `server` object, based on the original Express.js instance. We pass the Express instance, which we saved inside the `app` variable. As you can see in the preceding code, you only pass the `app` object as a parameter to the `createServer` function. We're going to use the new `server` object instead of the `app` variable to let our back end start listening for incoming requests. Remove the old `app.listen` function call from the bottom of the file because we'll be replacing it in a second. To get our server listening again, edit the initialization routine of the services. The `for` loop should now look as follows:

```
for (let i = 0; i < serviceNames.length; i += 1) {
  const name = serviceNames[i];
  switch (name) {
    case 'graphql':
```

```
        services[name].applyMiddleware({ app });
        break;
      case 'subscriptions':
        server.listen(8000, () => {
          console.log('Listening on port 8000!');
          services[name](server);
        });
      break;
      default:
        app.use(`/${name}`, services[name]);
        break;
    }
  }
```

Here, we have changed the old `if` statement to a `switch`. Furthermore, we have added a second service beyond `graphql`, called `subscriptions`. We are going to create a new `subscriptions` service next to the `graphql` services folder.

The `subscriptions` service requires the `server` object as a parameter to start listening for WebSocket connections. Before initializing `SubscriptionServer`, we need to have started listening for incoming requests. That is why we use the `server.listen` method in the preceding code before initializing the new `subscriptions` service that creates the Apollo `SubscriptionServer`. We pass the `server` object to the service after it started listening. The service has to accept this parameter, of course, so keep this in mind.

To add the new service into the preceding `serviceNames` object, edit the `index.js` services file with the following content:

```
import graphql from './graphql';
import subscriptions from './subscriptions';

export default utils => ({
  graphql: graphql(utils),
  subscriptions: subscriptions(utils),
});
```

The `subscriptions` service also receives the `utils` object, like the `graphql` service.

Now, create a `subscriptions` folder next to the `graphql` folder. To fulfil the import of the preceding `subscriptions` service, insert the service's `index.js` file into this folder. There, we can implement the `subscriptions` service. As a reminder, we pass the `utils` object and also the `server` object from before. The `subscriptions` service must accept two parameters in separate function calls.

If you have created the new subscriptions `index.js` file, import all the dependencies at the top of the file:

```
import { makeExecutableSchema } from 'graphql-tools';
import Resolvers from'../graphql/resolvers';
import Schema from'../graphql/schema';
import auth from '../graphql/auth';
import jwt from 'jsonwebtoken';
const { JWT_SECRET } = process.env;
import { SubscriptionServer } from 'subscriptions-transport-ws';
import { execute, subscribe } from 'graphql';
```

The preceding dependencies are almost the same as those that we are using for the `graphql` service, but we've added the `subscriptions-transport-ws` package. Furthermore, we've removed the `apollo-server-express` package. `SubscriptionServer` is the equivalent of `ApolloServer`, but used for WebSocket connections rather than HTTP. It usually makes sense to set up the Apollo Server for HTTP and `SubscriptionServer` for WebSockets in the same file, as this saves us from processing `Schema` and `Resolvers` twice. It's easier to explain the implementation of subscriptions without the `ApolloServer` code in the same file, though. The last two things that are new in the preceding code are the `execute` and `subscribe` functions that we import from the `graphql` package. You will see why we need these in the following section.

We begin the implementation of the new service by exporting a function with the `export default` statement and creating the `executableSchema` (as you saw in `Chapter 2`, *Setting up GraphQL with Express.js*):

```
export default (utils) => (server) => {
  const executableSchema = makeExecutableSchema({
    typeDefs: Schema,
    resolvers: Resolvers.call(utils),
    schemaDirectives: {
      auth: auth
    },
  });
}
```

As you can see, we use the ES6 arrow notation to return two functions at the same time. The first one accepts the `utils` object and the second one accepts the `server` object that we create with the `createServer` function inside the `index.js` file of the server. This approach fixes the problem of passing two parameters in separate function calls. The schema is only created when both functions are called.

The second step is to start `SubscriptionServer` to accept WebSocket connections and, as a result, be able to use the GraphQL subscriptions. Insert the following code under `executableSchema`:

```
new SubscriptionServer({
  execute,
  subscribe,
  schema: executableSchema,
},
{
  server,
  path: '/subscriptions',
});
```

We initialized a new `SubscriptionServer` instance in the preceding code. The first parameter we pass is a general options object for GraphQL and corresponds to the options of the `ApolloServer` class. The options are as following:

- The `execute` property should receive a function that handles all the processing and execution of incoming GraphQL requests. The standard is to pass the `execute` function that we imported from the `graphql` package previously.
- The `subscribe` property also accepts a function. This function has to take care of resolving a subscription to **AsyncIterator**, which is no more than an asynchronous `for` loop. It allows the client to listen for execution results and reflect them to the user.
- The last option we pass is the GraphQL schema. We do this in the same way as for `ApolloServer`.

The second parameter our new instance accepts is the `socketOptions` object. This holds settings to describe the way in which the WebSockets work:

- The `server` field receives our `server` object, which we pass from the `index.js` file of the server as a result of the `createServer` function. `SubscriptionServer` then relies on the existing server.
- The `path` field represents the endpoint under which the subscriptions are accessible. All subscriptions use the `/subscriptions` path.

The official documentation for the `subscriptions-transport-ws` package offers a more advanced explanation of `SubscriptionServer`. Take a look to get an overview of all its functionalities: `https://github.com/apollographql/subscriptions-transport-ws#subscriptionserver`.

The client would be able to connect to the WebSocket endpoint at this point. There are currently no subscriptions and the corresponding resolvers are set up in our GraphQL API.

Open the `schema.js` file to define our first subscription. Add a new type called `RootSubscription` next to the `RootQuery` and `RootMutation` types, including the new subscription, called `messageAdded`:

```
type RootSubscription {
  messageAdded: Message
}
```

Currently, if a user sends a new message to another user, this isn't shown to the recipient right away.

The first option I showed you was to set an interval to request new messages. Our back end is now able to cover this scenario with subscriptions. The event or channel that the client can subscribe to is called `messageAdded`. We can also add further parameters, such as a chat ID, to filter the WebSocket messages if necessary. When creating a new chat message, it is publicized through this channel.

We have added `RootSubscription`, but we need to extend the schema root tag too. Otherwise, the new `RootSubscription` won't be used. Change the schema as follows:

```
schema {
  query: RootQuery
  mutation: RootMutation
  subscription: RootSubscription
}
```

We have successfully configured the tree GraphQL main types. Next, we have to implement the corresponding resolver functions. Open the `resolvers.js` file and perform the following steps:

1. Import all dependencies that allow us to set up our GraphQL API with a `PubSub` system:

   ```
   import { PubSub, withFilter } from 'graphql-subscriptions';
   const pubsub = new PubSub();
   ```

   The `PubSub` system offered by the `graphql-subscriptions` package is a simple implementation based on the standard Node.js `EventEmitter`. When going to production, it's recommended to use an external store, such as Redis, with this package.

2. We've already added the third `RootSubscription` type to the schema, but not the matching property on the `resolvers` object. The following code includes the `messageAdded` subscription. Add it to the resolvers:

```
RootSubscription: {
  messageAdded: {
    subscribe: () => pubsub.asyncIterator(['messageAdded']),
  }
},
```

   The `messageAdded` property isn't a function but just a simple object. It contains a `subscribe` function that returns **AsyncIterable**. It allows our application to subscribe to the `messageAdded` channel by returning a promise that's only resolved when a new message is added. The next item that's returned is a promise, which is also only resolved when a message has been added. This method makes **AsyncIterators** great for implementing subscriptions.

   You can learn more about how AsyncIterators work by reading through the proposal at `https://github.com/tc39/proposal-async-iteration`.

3. When subscribing to the `messageAdded` subscription, there needs to be another method that publicizes the newly created message to all clients. The best location is the `addMessage` mutation where the new message is created. Replace the `addMessage` resolver function with the following code:

```
addMessage(root, { message }, context) {
  logger.log({
      level: 'info',
      message: 'Message was created',
    });
  return Message.create({
      ...message,
  }).then((newMessage) => {
      return Promise.all([
          newMessage.setUser(context.user.id),
          newMessage.setChat(message.chatId),
      ]).then(() => {
          pubsub.publish('messageAdded', {messageAdded:
          newMessage});
          return newMessage;
      });
    );
},
```

I have edited the `addMessage` mutation so that the correct user from the context is chosen. All of the new messages that you send are now saved with the correct user id. This allows us to filter WebSocket messages for the correct users later in *Authentication with Apollo Subscriptions* section.

We use the `pubsub.publish` function to send a new WebSocket frame to all clients that are connected and that have subscribed to the `messageAdded` channel. The first parameter of the `pubsub.publish` function is the subscription, which in this case is `messageAdded`. The second parameter is the new message that we save to the database. All clients that have subscribed to the `messageAdded` subscription through **AsyncIterator** now receive this message.

We've finished preparing the back end. The part that required the most work was to get the Express.js and WebSocket transport working together. The GraphQL implementation only involves the new schema entities, correctly implementing the resolvers functions for the subscription, and then publishing the data to the client via the `PubSub` system.

We have to implement the subscription feature in the front end to connect to our WebSocket endpoint.

# Subscriptions on the Apollo Client

As with the back end code, we also need to make adjustments to the Apollo Client configuration before using subscriptions. In `Chapter 4`, *Integrating React into the Back end with Apollo*, we set up the Apollo Client with the normal `HttpLink`. Later, we exchanged it with the `createUploadLink` function, which enables the user to upload files through GraphQL.

We are going to extend our Apollo Client by using `WebSocketLink` as well. This allows us to use subscriptions through GraphQL. Both links work side by side. We use the standard HTTP protocol to query data, such as the chat list or the news feed; all of these are real-time updates to keep the UI up to date rely on WebSockets.

To configure the Apollo Client correctly, follow these steps:

1. Open the `index.js` file from the `apollo` folder. Import the following dependencies:

```
import { WebSocketLink } from 'apollo-link-ws';
import { SubscriptionClient } from 'subscriptions-transport-ws';
import { getMainDefinition } from 'apollo-utilities';
import { ApolloLink, split } from 'apollo-link';
```

   To get the subscriptions working, we need `SubscriptionClient`, which uses `WebSocketLink` to subscribe to our GraphQL API using WebSockets.

   We import the `getMainDefinition` function from the `apollo-utilities` package. It's installed by default when using the Apollo Client. The purpose of this function is to give you the operation type, which can be `query`, `mutation`, or `subscription`.

   The `split` function from the `apollo-link` package allows us to conditionally control the flow of requests through different Apollo links based on the operation type or other information. It accepts one condition and one (or a pair of) link from which it composes a single valid link that the Apollo Client can use.

2. We are going to create both links for the `split` function. Detect the protocol and port where we send all GraphQL subscriptions and requests. Add the following code beneath the imports:

```
const protocol = (location.protocol != 'https:') ? 'ws://':
'wss://';
const port = location.port ? ':'+location.port: '';
```

   The `protocol` variable saves the WebSocket protocol by detecting whether the client uses `http` or `https`. The `port` variable is either an empty string if we use port `80` to server our front end, or any other port, such as `8000`, which we currently use. Previously, we had to statically save `http://localhost:8000` in this file. With the new variables, we can dynamically build the URL where all requests should be sent.

3. The `split` function expects two links to combine them to one. The first link is the normal `httpLink`, which we must set up before passing the resulting link to the initialization of the Apollo Client. Remove the `createUploadLink` function call from the `ApolloLink.from` function and add it before the `ApolloClient` class:

```
const httpLink = createUploadLink({
  uri: location.protocol + '//' + location.hostname + port +
   '/graphql',
  credentials: 'same-origin',
});
```

   We concatenate the `protocol` of the server, which is either `http:` or `https:`, with two slashes. The `hostname` is, for example, the domain of your application or, if in development, `localhost`. The result of the concatenation is `http://localhost:8000/graphql`.

4. Add the WebSocket link that's used for the subscriptions next to `httpLink`. It's the second one we pass to the `split` function:

```
const SUBSCRIPTIONS_ENDPOINT = protocol + location.hostname + port
 + '/subscriptions';
const subClient = new SubscriptionClient(SUBSCRIPTIONS_ENDPOINT, {
  reconnect: true,
  connectionParams: () => {
    var token = localStorage.getItem('jwt');
    if(token) {
      return { authToken: token };
    }
    return { };
  }
});
const wsLink = new WebSocketLink(subClient);
```

   We define the URI that's stored inside the `SUBSCRIPTIONS_ENDPOINT` variable. It's built with the `protocol` and `port` variables, which we detected earlier, and the application's `hostname`. The URI ends with the specified endpoint of the back end with the same port as the GraphQL API. The URI is the first parameter of `SubscriptionsClient`. The second parameter allows us to pass options, such as the `reconnect` property. It tells the client to automatically reconnect to the back end's WebSocket endpoint when it has lost the connection. This usually happens if the client has temporarily lost their internet connection or the server has gone down.

Furthermore, we use the `connectionParams` field to specify the JWT as an authorization token. We define this property as a function so that the JWT is read from `localStorage` whenever the user logs in. It's sent when the WebSocket is created.

We initialize `SubscriptionClient` to the `subClient` variable. We pass it to the `WebSocketLink` constructor under the `wsLink` variable with the given settings.

5. Combine both links into one. This allows us to insert the composed result into our `ApolloClient` at the bottom. To do this, we have imported the `split` function. The syntax to combine the two links should look as follows:

```
const link = split(
  ({ query }) => {
    const { kind, operation } = getMainDefinition(query);
    return kind === 'OperationDefinition' && operation ===
     'subscription';
  },
  wsLink,
  httpLink,
);
```

The `split` function accepts three parameters. The first parameter must be a function with a Boolean return value. If the return value is `true`, the request is sent over the first link, which is the second required parameter. If the return value is `false`, the operation is sent over the second link, which we pass via the optional third parameter. In our case, the function that's passed as the first parameter determines the operation type. If the operation is a subscription, the function returns `true` and sends the operation over the WebSocket link. All other requests are sent via the HTTP Apollo Link. We save the result of the `split` function in the `link` variable.

6. Insert the preceding `link` variable directly before the `onError` link. The `createUploadLink` function shouldn't be inside the `Apollo.from` function.

We've now got the basic Apollo Client setup to support subscriptions via WebSockets.

In `Chapter 5`, *Reusable React Components*, I gave the reader some homework to split the complete chat feature into multiple subcomponents. This way, the chat feature would follow the same pattern as we used for the post feed. We split it into multiple components so that it's a clean code base. We're going to use this and have a look at how to implement subscriptions for the chats.

If you haven't implemented the chat's functionality in multiple subcomponents, you can get the working code from the official GitHub repository. I personally recommend you use the code from the repository if it's unclear what the following examples refer to.

Using the chats as an example makes sense because they are, by nature, real-time: they require the application to handle new messages and display them to the recipient. We take care of this in the following steps.

We begin with the main file of our chats feature, which is the `Chats.js` file in the client folder. I've reworked the `render` method so that all the markup that initially came directly from this file is now entirely rendered by other child components. You can see all the changes in the following code:

```
render() {
  const { user } = this.props;
  const { openChats } = this.state;
  return (
    <div className="wrapper">
      <ChatsQuery><ChatsList openChat={this.openChat} user={user}/>
      </ChatsQuery>
      <div className="openChats">
        {openChats.map((chatId, i) =>
          <ChatQuery key={"chatWindow" + chatId} variables={{ chatId
           }}>
            <ChatWindow closeChat={this.closeChat} user={user}/>
          </ChatQuery>
        )}
      </div>
    </div>
  )
}
```

All the changes are listed here:

- We extract the `user` from the properties of the `Chats` component. Consequently, we have to wrap the `Chats` component with the `UserConsumer` component to let it pass the user. You have to apply this change to the `Main.js` file.
- I have split the GraphQL queries we originally sent inside this file into separate query components. One is called `ChatsQuery` and gives us all the chats that the current user is attached to. The other one is called `ChatQuery` and is executed when a chat is opened to request all the messages inside that chat.

- All the inner markup that was previously the GraphQL queries is now also in separate files to improve reusability. Each component that's exported from these files is wrapped in the corresponding query components. The `ChatsList` class renders a list of chats if `ChatsQuery` is successful. The other one is the `ChatWindow` component, which receives a chat property by `ChatQuery` to render all messages. Both receive a user property to show the correct user.
- The `openChat` and `closeChat` functions are executed either by `ChatsList` or the `ChatWindow` component. All other functions from the `Chats` class have been moved to one or both components: `ChatsList` and `ChatWindow`.

The changes I have made here had nothing to do with the subscriptions directly, but it's much easier to understand what I'm trying to explain when the code is readable. If you need help implementing these changes by yourself, I recommend you check out the official GitHub repository. All the following examples are based on these changes, but they should be understandable without having the full source code.

More important, however, is `ChatsQuery`, which has a special feature. We want to subscribe to the `messageAdded` subscription to listen for new messages. That's possible by using a new function of the Apollo `Query` component.

To continue, first create a separate `ChatsQuery` component. We send the request for all chats like before. The `render` method of the `ChatsQuery` component should look as follows:

```
render() {
  const { children } = this.props;
  return(
    <Query query={GET_CHATS}>
      {({ loading, error, data, subscribeToMore }) => {
        if (loading) return <Loading/>;
        if (error) return <Error><p>{error.message}</p></Error>;
        const { chats } = data;
        return React.Children.map(children, function(child){
          return React.cloneElement(child, { chats, subscribeToMore });
        })
      }}
    </Query>
  )
}
```

The preceding code looks much like all the render methods of the other query components we've written so far. The `GET_CHATS` query requests all chats the current user is related to. The one thing that's different is that we extract a `subscribeToMore` function and pass it as a property to every child.

The `subscribeToMore` function is provided by default with every result of an Apollo Query component. It lets you run an update function whenever a message is created. It works in the same way as the `fetchMore` function. It's best to use the `subscribeToMore` function inside the `ChatsList` component. It already receives the chats property from the preceding `ChatsQuery` component to render the chats panel.

Let's have a look how we can use this function to implement subscriptions on the front end.

Because we pass the `subscribeToMore` function to the `ChatsList` class, we're going to implement this class now. Just follow these steps:

1. We have three necessary dependencies that you should import at the top of the `list.js` file where the `ChatsList` class is saved:

   ```
   import React, { Component } from 'react';
   import gql from 'graphql-tag';
   import { withApollo } from 'react-apollo';
   ```

   The `withApollo` HoC gives you access to the Apollo Client directly in your component's properties. We only have to export the `ChatsList` class through this HoC. We need access to the client to read and write to the Apollo Client's cache.

2. Parse the GraphQL subscription string. The chats query was executed previously, and `ChatsList` receives the response. The new `messageAdded` subscription has to look as follows:

   ```
   const MESSAGES_SUBSCRIPTION = gql`
     subscription onMessageAdded {
       messageAdded {
         id
         text
         chat {
           id
         }
         user {
           id
           __typename
         }
         __typename
       }
     }
   `;
   ```

The subscription looks exactly like all the other queries or mutations we are using. The only difference is that we request the `__typename` field, as it isn't included in the response of our GraphQL API when using subscriptions. From my point of view, this seems like a bug in the current version of `SubscriptionServer`. You should check whether you still need to do this at the time of reading this book.

We specify the operation type, `subscription`, of the request, as you can see in the preceding code. Otherwise, it attempts to execute the default query operation, which leads to an error because there's no `messageAdded` query, only a subscription. The subscription events the client receives when a new message is added holds all fields, as stated in the preceding code.

3. Create the new `ChatsList` class like a standard React component. You can copy the `shorten` function from `Chats.js` and remove it from there. It should look like this:

```
class ChatsList extends Component {
  shorten(text) {
    if(!text.length) {
      return "";
    }
    if (text.length > 12) {
      return text.substring(0, text.length - 9) + '...';
    }
    return text;
  }
}
```

We have to move all the standard functions we were already using for the chats list to this new class.

4. The `usernamesToString` function changes a bit, and I have also added a new `getAvatar` function. When we first created the chats functionality, there was no authentication system. We are now going to rewrite this and use the information we have at our disposal to display the correct data. Copy these functions into our new class:

```
usernamesToString = (userList) => {
  const { user } = this.props;
  var usernamesString = '';
  for(var i = 0; i < userList.length; i++) {
    if(userList[i].username !== user.username) {
      usernamesString += userList[i].username;
    }
```

```
        if(i - 1 === userList.length) {
          usernamesString += ', ';
        }
      }
      return usernamesString;
    }
    getAvatar = (userList) => {
      const { user } = this.props;
      if(userList.length > 2 ) {
        return '/public/group.png';
      } else {
        if(userList[0].id !== user.id) {
          return userList[0].avatar;
        } else {
          return userList[1].avatar;
        }
      }
    }
```

The `usernamesToString` function can access the `user` property that the `ChatsList` component receives from its parent through `UserConsumer`. It concatenates the usernames of all users except the logged-in user to display the names in the chats panel. The `getAvatar` function returns the correct image for a chat. It either shows the group image, if there are more than two people involved in a chat, or the avatar image of the second user if exactly two users are involved. This is possible because the getAvatar function can filter by the logged in user

5. The `render` method returns the same markup we had in the `Chats` component. It's now way more readable as it's in a separate file. The code should look as follows:

```
render() {
  const { chats } = this.props;
  return (
    <div className="chats">
      {chats.map((chat, i) =>
        <div key={"chat" + chat.id} className="chat" onClick={() =>
         this.props.openChat(chat.id)}>
          <div className="header">
            <img src={this.getAvatar(chat.users)} />
            <div>
              <h2>{this.shorten(this.usernamesToString(chat.users))
                }
              </h2>
              <span>{chat.lastMessage &&
```

```
                        this.shorten(chat.lastMessage.text)}</span>
                    </div>
                </div>
            </div>
        )}
    </div>
  )
}
```

6. To export your `ChatsList` class correctly, use the `withApollo` HoC:

   ```
   export default withApollo(ChatsList)
   ```

7. Here's the crucial part. At the moment, the `ChatsList` component is mounted, so we subscribe to the `messageAdded` channel. Only then is the `messageAdded` subscription used to receive new data or, to be exact, new chat messages. To start subscribing to the GraphQL subscription, we have to add a new method to the `componentDidMount` method:

   ```
   componentDidMount() {
     this.subscribeToNewMessages();
   }
   ```

In the preceding code, we execute a new `subscribeToNewMessages` method inside the `componentDidMount` function of our React component.

It's common to start async operations, such as fetching or listening for a subscription, in the `componentDidMount` method of a React component. You can also use the `componentWillMount` function, but this isn't recommended, as the `componentWillMount` method is executed twice if you support SSR. Furthermore, the `componentWillMount` function first returns after an initial render. There's no way to let the rendering wait until the data has been fetched.

With the `componentDidMount` method, it's clear that the component has rendered at least once without data. The method only executes on the client-side code as the SSR implementation doesn't throw this event because there's no DOM.

We have to add the corresponding `subscribeToNewMessages` method as well. We're going to explain every bit of this function in a moment. Insert the following code into the `ChatsList` class:

```
subscribeToNewMessages = () => {
  const self = this;
  const { user } = this.props;
  this.props.subscribeToMore({
```

```
        document: MESSAGES_SUBSCRIPTION,
        updateQuery: (prev, { subscriptionData }) => {
          if (!subscriptionData.data || !prev.chats.length) return prev;

          var index = -1;
          for(var i = 0; i < prev.chats.length; i++) {
            if(prev.chats[i].id ==
            subscriptionData.data.messageAdded.chat.id) {
              index = i;
              break;
            }
          }

          if (index === -1) return prev;

          const newValue = Object.assign({},prev.chats[i], {
            lastMessage: {
              text: subscriptionData.data.messageAdded.text,
              __typename: subscriptionData.data.messageAdded.__typename
            }
          });
          var newList = {chats:[...prev.chats]};
          newList.chats[i] = newValue;
          return newList;
        }
      });
    }
```

The preceding `subscribeToNewMessages` method looks very complex, but once we understand its purpose, it's straightforward. We primarily rely on the `subscribeToMore` function here, which was passed from `ChatsQuery` to `ChatsList`. The purpose of this function is to start subscribing to our `addedMessage` channel, and to accept the new data from the subscription and merge it with the current state and cache so that it's reflected directly to the user.

The `document` parameter accepts the parsed GraphQL subscription.

The second parameter is called `updateQuery`. It allows us to insert a function that implements the logic to update the Apollo Client cache with the new data. This function needs to accept a new parameter, which is the previous data from where the `subscribeToMore` function has been passed. In our case, this object contains an array of chats that already exist in the client's cache.

The second parameter holds the new message inside the `subscriptionData` index. The `subscriptionData` object has a `data` property that has a further `messageAdded` field under which the real message that's been created is saved.

We'll quickly go through the logic of the `updateQuery` function so that you can understand how we merge data from a subscription to the application state.

If `subscriptionData.data` is empty or there are no previous chats in the `prev` object, there's nothing to update. In this case, we return the previous data because a message was sent in a chat that the client doesn't have in their cache. Otherwise, we loop through all the previous chats of the `prev` object and find the index of the chat for which the subscription has returned a new message by comparing the chat ids. The found chat's index inside the `prev.chats` array is saved in the `index` variable. If the chat cannot be found, we can check this with the index variable and return the previous data. If we find the chat, we need to update it with the new message. To do this, we compose the chat from the previous data and set `lastMessage` to the new message's text. We do this by using the `Object.assign` function, where the chat and the new message are merged. We save the result in the `newValue` variable. It's important that we also set the returned `__typename` property, because otherwise the Apollo Client throws an error.

Now that we have an object that contains the updated chat in the `newValue` variable, we write it to the client's cache. To write the updated chat to the cache, we return an array of all chats at the end of the `updateQuery` function. Because the `prev` variable is read-only, we can't save the updated chat inside it. We have to create a new array to write it to the cache. We set the `newValue` chat object to the `newList` array at the index where we found the original chat. At the end, we return the `newList` variable. We update the cache that's given to us inside the `prev` object with the new array. Importantly, the new cache has to have the same fields as before. The schema of the return value of the `updateQuery` function must match the initial `ChatsQuery` schema.

You can now test the subscription directly in your browser by starting the application with `npm run server`. If you send a new chat message, it's shown directly in the chat panel on the right-hand side.

We have, however, got one major problem. If you test this with a second user, you'll notice that the `lastMessage` field is updated for both users. That is correct, but the new message isn't visible inside the chat window for the recipient. We've updated the client store for the `ChatsQuery` request, but we haven't added the message to the single `ChatQuery` that's executed when we open a chat window.

We're going to solve this problem by making use of the `withApollo` HoC. The `ChatsList` component has no access to the `ChatQuery` cache directly like with the `ChatsQuery` above. The `withApollo` HoC gives the exported component a `client` property, which allows us to interact directly with the Apollo Client. We can use it to read and write to the whole Apollo Client cache and it isn't limited to only one GraphQL request. Before returning the updated chats array from the `updateQuery` function, we have to read the state of the `ChatQuery` and insert the new data if possible. Insert the following code right before the final return statement inside the `updateQuery` function:

```
try {
  const data = self.props.client.store.cache.readQuery({ query:
  GET_CHAT, variables: { chatId:
  subscriptionData.data.messageAdded.chat.id } });
  if(user.id !== subscriptionData.data.messageAdded.user.id) {
    data.chat.messages.push(subscriptionData.data.messageAdded);
    self.props.client.store.cache.writeQuery({ query: GET_CHAT,
    variables: { chatId: subscriptionData.data.messageAdded.chat.id },
    data });
  }
} catch(e) {}
```

In the preceding code, we use the `client.store.cache.readQuery` method to read the cache. This accepts the `GET_CHAT` query as one parameter and the chat id of the newly sent message to get a single chat in return. The `GET_CHAT` query is the same request we sent in the `Chats.js` file before, and which the `ChatQuery` component is sending when opening a chat window. We wrap the `readQuery` function in a `try-catch` block because it throws an unhandled error if nothing is found for the specified `query` and `variables`. This can happen if the user hasn't opened a chat window yet and so no data has been requested with the `GET_CHAT` query for this specific chat.

You can test these new changes by viewing the chat window and sending a message from another user account. The new message should appear almost directly for you without the need to refresh the browser.

In this section, we learned how to subscribe to events sent from a back end through Apollo Subscriptions. Currently, we use this feature to update the UI on the fly with the new data. Later in *Notifications with Apollo subscriptions* section, we'll see another scenario where subscriptions can be useful. Nevertheless, there's one thing left to do: we haven't authorized the user for the `messageAdded` subscription through a JWT, such as our GraphQL API, and still, the user received the new message without verifying its identity. We're going to change this in the next section.

# Authentication with Apollo Subscriptions

In `Chapter 6`, *Authentication with Apollo and React*, of this book, we implemented authentication through the localStorage of your browser. The back end generates a signed JWT that the client sends with every request inside the HTTP headers. In `Chapter 9`, *Implementing Server-side Rendering*, we extended this logic to support cookies to allow server-side rendering. Now that we've introduced WebSockets, we need to take care of them separately, as we did with the server-side rendering and our GraphQL API.

How is it possible for the user to receive new messages when they aren't authenticated on the back end for the WebSocket transport protocol?

The best way to figure this out is to have a look at your browser's developer tools. Let's assume that we have one browser window where we log in with user A. This user chats with another user, B. Both send messages to each other and receive the new updates directly in their chat window. Another user, C, shouldn't be able to receive any of the WebSocket updates. We should play through this scenario in reality.

If you use Chrome as your default browser, go to the **Network** tab. There, you can filter all network requests by type. Since the data is transported via a WebSocket, you can filter by the **WS** option. You should see one connection, which is the `subscriptions` endpoint of our back end.

Try this scenario with the Developer Tools open. You should see the same WebSocket frames for all browsers. It should look like the following screenshot:

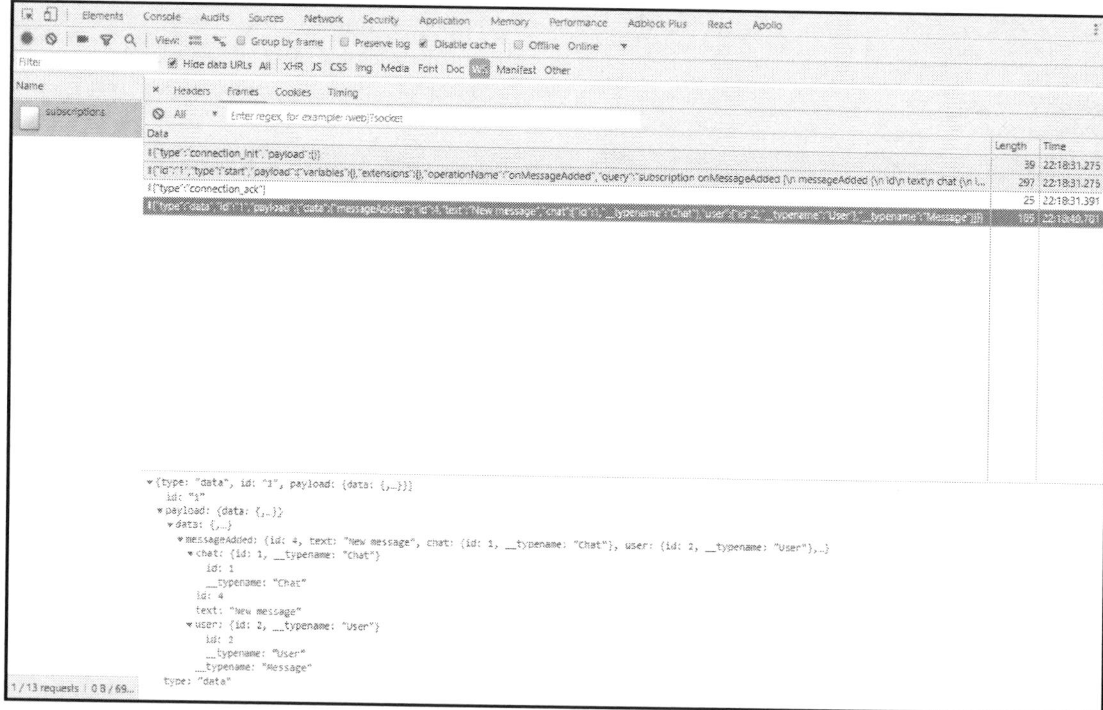

In the left panel, you can see all WebSocket connections. In our case, this is only the `subscriptions` connection. If you click on the connection, you will find all the frames that are sent over this connection. The first frame in the preceding list is the initial connection frame. The second frame is the subscription request to the `messageAdded` channel, which is initiated by the client. Both frames are marked green because the client sends them.

The last two are marked in red as the server sent them. The first of the red-marked frames is the server's acknowledgement of the established connection. The last frame was sent by our back end to publish a new message to the client. While the frame might look alright at first glance, it represents a vital problem. The last frame was sent to all clients, not just those who are members of the specific chat in which the message was sent. Average users are not likely to notice it since our `updateQuery` function only updates the UI if the chat was found in the client store. Still, an experienced user or developer is able to spy on all users of our social network as it's readable in the **Network** tab.

We need to take a look at the back end code that we have written and compare the initialization of ApolloServer and SubscriptionServer. We have a context function for ApolloServer that extracts the user from the JWT. It can then be used inside the resolver functions to filter the results by the currently logged in user. For SubscriptionServer, there's no such context function at the moment. We have to know the currently logged in user to filter the subscription messages for the correct users. We can use the standard WebSockets events, such as onConnect or onOperation, to implement the authorization of the user.

The onOperation function is executed for every WebSocket frame that is sent. The best approach is to implement the authorization in the onConnect event in the same way as the context function that's taken from ApolloServer so that the WebSocket connection is authenticated only once when it's established and not for every frame that's sent.

In index.js, from the subscriptions folder of the server, add the following code to the first parameter of the SubscriptionServer initialization. It accepts an onConnect parameter as a function, which is executed whenever a client tries to connect to the subscriptions endpoint. Add the code just before the schema parameter:

```
onConnect: async (params,socket) => {
  const authorization = params.authToken;
  if(typeof authorization !== typeof undefined) {
    var search = "Bearer";
    var regEx = new RegExp(search, "ig");
    const token = authorization.replace(regEx, '').trim();
    return jwt.verify(token, JWT_SECRET, function(err, result) {
      if(err) {
        throw new Error('Missing auth token!');
      } else {
        return utils.db.models.User.findById(result.id).then((user) =>
        {
          return Object.assign({}, socket.upgradeReq, { user });
        });
      }
    });
  } else {
    throw new Error('Missing auth token!');
  }
},
```

This code is very similar to the `context` function. We rely on the normal JWT authentication but via the connection parameters of the WebSocket. We implement the WebSocket authentication inside the `onConnect` event. In the original `context` function of `ApolloServer`, we extract the JWT from the HTTP headers of the request, but here we are using the `params` variable, which is passed in the first parameter.

Before the client finally connects to the WebSocket endpoint, an `onConnect` event is triggered where you can implement special logic for the initial connection. With the first request, we send the JWT because we have configured the Apollo Client to read the JWT to the `authToken` parameter of the `connectionParams` object when `SubscriptionClient` is initialized. That's why we can access the JWT-not from a `request` object, directly but from `params.authToken` in the preceding code. `socket` is also given to us inside the `onConnect` function; there, you can access the initial upgrade request inside the `socket` object. After extracting the JWT from the connection parameters, we can verify it and authenticate the user by that.

At the end of this `onConnect` function, we return the `upgradeReq` variable and the user, just like we do with a normal `context` function for the Apollo Server. Instead of returning the `req` object to the `context` if the user isn't logged in, we are now throwing an error. This is because we only implement subscriptions for entities that require you to be logged in, such as chats or posts. It lets the client try to reconnect until it's authenticated. You can change this behavior to match your needs and let the user connect to the WebSocket. Don't forget, however, that every open connection costs you performance and a user who isn't logged in doesn't need an open connection at least for the use case of **Graphbook**.

We have now identified the user that has connected to our back end with the preceding code, but we're still sending every frame to all users. This is a problem with the resolver functions because they don't use the context yet. Replace the `messageAdded` subscription with the following code in the `resolvers.js` file:

```
messageAdded: {
  subscribe: withFilter(() => pubsub.asyncIterator('messageAdded'),
  (payload, variables, context) => {
    if (payload.messageAdded.UserId !== context.user.id) {
      return Chat.findOne({
        where: {
          id: payload.messageAdded.ChatId
        },
        include: [{
          model: User,
          required: true,
          through: { where: { userId: context.user.id } },
        }],
```

```
          }).then((chat) => {
            if(chat !== null) {
              return true;
            }
            return false;
          })
        }
        return false;
      }),
    }
```

Earlier in this chapter, we imported the `withFilter` function from the `graphql-subscriptions` package. It allows us to wrap `AsyncIterator` with a filter. The purpose of this filter is to conditionally send publications through connections to users who should see the new information. If one user shouldn't receive a publication, the return value of the condition for the `withFilter` function should be false. For all users who should receive a new message, the return value should be true.

`withFilter` accepts the `AsyncIterator` in its first parameter. The second parameter is the function that decides whether a user receives a subscription update. We extract the following properties from the function call:

- The `payload` parameter is the new message that has been sent in the `addMessage` mutation.
- The `variables` field holds all GraphQL parameters that could be sent with the `messageAdded` subscription, not with the mutation. For our scenario, we are not sending any variables with the subscription.
- The `context` variable holds all the information that we implemented in the `onConnect` hook. It includes the regular `context` object with the user as a separate property.

The filter function is executed for every user that has subscribed to the `messageAdded` channel. First, we check whether the user for which the function is executed is the author of the new message by comparing the user ids. In this case, they don't need to get a subscription notification, because they already have the data.

If this isn't the case, we query the database for the chat where the new message was added. To find out whether a user needs to receive the new message, we select only chats where the logged in user's Id, and the chat Id, is included. If a chat is found in the database, the user should see the new message. Otherwise, they aren't allowed to get the new message, and we return "false".

Remember that the `withFilter` function is run for each connection. If there are thousands of users, we would have to run the database query very frequently. It's better to keep such filter functions as small and efficient as possible. For example, we could query the chat once to get the attached users and loop through them manually for all the connections. This solution would save us expensive database operations.

This is all you need to know about authentication with subscriptions. We now have a working setup, which includes server-side rendering with cookies and real-time subscriptions with JWT authentication. The server-side rendering doesn't implement subscriptions because it doesn't make sense to offer real-time updates for the initial rendering of our application. Next, you will see another scenario where Apollo Subscriptions can be useful.

# Notifications with Apollo Subscriptions

In this section, I'll quickly guide you through the second use case for subscriptions. Showing notifications to a user are traditional events that a user should see as you know from Facebook. Instead of relying on the `subscribeToMore` function, we use the `Subscription` component that's provided by Apollo. This component works like the `Query` and `Mutation` components, but for subscriptions.

Follow these steps to get your first `Subscription` component running:

1. Create a `subscriptions` folder inside the client's `components` folder. You can save all subscriptions that you implement using Apollo's `Subscription` component inside this folder.
2. Insert a `messageAdded.js` file into the folder and paste in the following code:

```
import React, { Component } from 'react';
import { Subscription } from 'react-apollo';
import gql from 'graphql-tag';
const MESSAGES_SUBSCRIPTION = gql`
  subscription onMessageAdded {
    messageAdded {
        id
        text
        chat {
          id
        }
        user {
            id
            __typename
```

```
            }
            __typename
        }
    }
`;
export default class MessageAddedSubscription extends Component {
  render() {
    const { children } = this.props;
    return(
        <Subscription subscription={MESSAGES_SUBSCRIPTION}>
            {({ data }) => {
                return React.Children.map(children,
                  function(child){
                    return React.cloneElement(child, { data });
                })
            }}
        </Subscription>
    )
  }
}
```

The general workflow for the `Subscription` component is the same as for the `Mutation` and `Query` components. First, we parse the subscription with the `graphql-tag` package. The `render` method of the `MessageAddedSubscription` class returns the `Subscription` component. The only difference is that we don't use a loading or error state. You could get access to both, but as we're using WebSockets, the loading state only becomes true when a new message arrives, which isn't useful. Furthermore, the error property could be used to display alerts to the user, but this isn't required. In the `render` method, we pass the data field to all underlying children. By default, it's an empty object. It's filled with `data` when a new message arrives through the subscription.

3. Because we want to show notifications to the user when a new message is received, we install a package that takes care of showing pop-up notifications. Install it using npm:

```
npm install --save react-toastify
```

4. To set up `react-toastify`, add a `ToastContainer` component to a global point of the application where all notifications are rendered. This container isn't only used for the notifications for new messages but for all notifications, so choose wisely. I decided to attach `ToastContainer` to the `Chats.js` file. Import the dependency at the top of it:

```
import { ToastContainer } from 'react-toastify';
```

Inside the `render` method, the first thing to render should be `ToastContainer`. Add it like in the following code:

```
<div className="wrapper">
  <ToastContainer/>
```

5. To handle the subscription data, we need a child component that gets the data as a property. To do this, create a `notification.js` file inside the `chats component` folder. The file should look as follows:

```
import React, { Component } from 'react';
import { toast } from 'react-toastify';

export default class ChatNotification extends Component {
  componentWillReceiveProps(props) {
      if(typeof props.data !== typeof undefined && typeof
      props.data.messageAdded !== typeof undefined && props.data
      && props.data.messageAdded)
      toast(props.data.messageAdded.text, { position:
      toast.POSITION.TOP_LEFT });
  }
  render() {
      return (null);
  }
}
```

We only import React and the `react-toastify` package. The `render` method of the `ChatNotification` class returns `null` because we don't render anything directly through this component. Instead, we listen for the `componentWillReceiveProps` method for new data from the subscription. If the properties passed to this class were a filled with `data` property, we can use the `react-toastify` package.

To display a new notification, we execute the `toast` function from the `react-toastify` package with the text to show as the first parameter. The second parameter takes optional settings to indicate how the notification should display. I've given the top-left corner as the position for all notifications because the right part of the screen is already pretty full.

6. Import `ChatNotification` and the `MessageAddedSubscription` component inside the `Chats.js` file:

```
import MessageAddedSubscription from './components/subscriptions
/messageAdded';
import ChatNotification from './components/chat/notification';
```

7. Include both components in the `render` method of the `Chats` class from the `Chats.js` file. The final method looks like this:

```
return (
  <div className="wrapper">
      <ToastContainer/>
      <MessageAddedSubscription><ChatNotification/>
      </MessageAddedSubscription>
      <ChatsQuery><ChatsList openChat={this.openChat} user=
      {user}/></ChatsQuery>
      <div className="openChats">
          {openChats.map((chatId, i) =>
              <ChatQuery key={"chatWindow" + chatId} variables={{
               chatId }}>
                  <ChatWindow closeChat={this.closeChat} user=
                  {user}/>
              </ChatQuery>
          )}
      </div>
  </div>
)
```

I've wrapped the `ChatNotification` component inside the `MessageAddedSubscription` component. The subscription component triggers a new notification every time it receives new data over the WebSocket and updates the properties of the `ChatNotification` component.

8. Add a small CSS rule and import the CSS rules of the `react-toastify` package. Import the CSS in the `App.js` file:

```
import 'react-toastify/dist/ReactToastify.css';
```

Then, add these few lines to the custom `style.css` file:

```
.Toastify__toast-container--top-left {
  top: 4em !important;
}
```

You can see an example of a notification in the following screenshot:

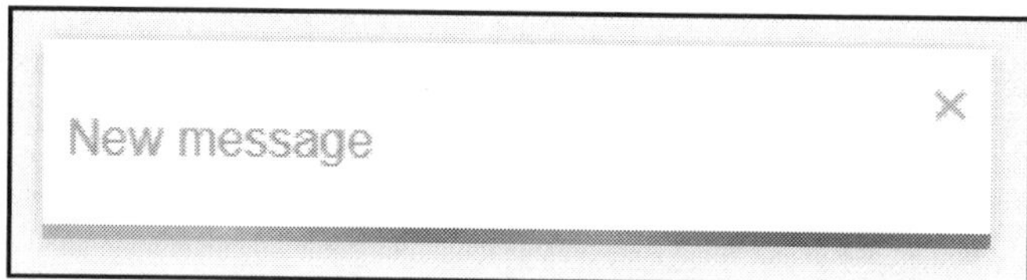


The entire subscriptions topic is complex, but we managed to implement it for two use cases and thus provided the user with significant improvements to our application.

# Summary

This chapter aimed to offer the user a real-time user interface that allows them to chat comfortably with other users. We also looked at how to make this UI extendable. You learned how to set up subscriptions with any Apollo or GraphQL back end for all entities. We also implemented WebSocket-specific authentication to filter publications so that they only arrive to the correct user.

In the next chapter, you'll learn how to verify and test the correct functionality of your application by implementing automated testing for your code.

# 11
# Writing Tests

So far, we've written a lot of code and come across a variety of problems. We haven't implemented automated testing for our software. However, it's a common approach to make sure everything works after making changes to your application. Automated testing drastically improves the quality of your software and reduces errors in production.

This chapter covers the following topics:

- How to use Mocha for testing
- Testing a GraphQL API with Mocha and Chai
- Testing React with Enzyme and JSDOM

## Testing with Mocha

The problem we're facing is that we have to ensure the quality of our software without increasing the amount of manual testing. It isn't possible to recheck every feature of our software when new updates are released. To solve this problem, we're going to use Mocha, which is a JavaScript testing framework. It gives you the opportunity to run a series of asynchronous tests. If all the tests pass successfully, your application is ready for the next release.

Many developers follow the **test-driven development** (**TDD**) approach. Often, when you implement tests for the first time, they fail because the business logic that's being tested is missing. After implementing all the tests, we have to write the actual application code to meet the requirements of the tests. In this book, we haven't followed this approach, but it isn't a problem as we can implement tests afterward too. Typically, I tend to write tests in parallel with the application code.

To get started, we have to install all the dependencies to test our application with npm:

```
npm install --save-dev mocha chai @babel/polyfill request
```

The `mocha` package includes almost everything to run tests. Along with Mocha, we also install `chai`, which is an assertion library. It offers excellent ways to chain tests with many variables and types for use inside a Mocha test. We also install the `@babel/polyfill` package, which allows our test to support ES2015+ syntax. This package is crucial because we use this syntax everywhere throughout our React code. Finally, we install the `request` package as a library to send all the queries or mutations within our test. I recommend you set the `NODE_ENV` environment variable to `production` to test every functionality, as in a live environment. Be sure that you set the environment variable correctly so that all production features are used.

# Our first Mocha test

First, let's add a new command to the `scripts` field of our `package.json` file:

```
"test": "mocha --exit test/ --require babel-hook --require @babel/polyfill
--recursive"
```

If you now execute `npm run test`, we'll run the `mocha` package in the `test` folder, which we'll create in a second. The preceding `--require` option loads the specified file or package. We'll also load a `babel-hook.js` file, which we'll create as well. The `--recursive` parameter tells Mocha to run through the complete file tree of the `test` folder, not just the first layer. This behavior is useful because it allows us to structure our tests in multiple files and folders.

Let's begin with the `babel-hook.js` file by adding it to the root of our project, next to the `package.json` file. Insert the following code:

```
require("@babel/register")({
  "plugins": [
    "require-context-hook"
  ],
  "presets": ["@babel/env","@babel/react"]
});
```

The purpose of this file is to give us an alternative Babel configuration file to our standard `.babelrc` file. If you compare both files, you should see that we use the `require-context-hook` plugin. We already use this plugin when starting the back end with `npm run server`. It allows us to import our Sequelize models using a regular expression.

If we start our test with `npm run test`, we require this file at the beginning. Inside the `babel-hook.js` file, we load `@babel/register`, which compiles all the files that are imported afterward in our test according to the preceding configuration.

Notice that when running a production build or environment, the production database is also used. All changes are made to this database. Verify that you have configured the database credentials correctly in the server's `configuration` folder. You have only to set the `host`, `username`, `password`, and `database` environment variables correctly.

This gives us the option to start our back end server from within our test file and render our application on the server. The preparation for our test is now finished. Create a folder named `test` inside the root of our project to hold all runnable tests. Mocha will scan all files or folders, and all tests will be executed. To get a basic test running, create `app.test.js`. This is the main file, which makes sure that our back end is running and in which we can subsequently define further tests. The first version of our test looks as follows:

```
const assert = require('assert');
const request = require('request');
const expect = require('chai').expect;
const should = require('chai').should();

describe('Graphbook application test', function() {

  it('renders and serves the index page', function(done) {
    request('http://localhost:8000', function(err, res, body) {
      should.not.exist(err);
      should.exist(res);
      expect(res.statusCode).to.be.equal(200);
      assert.ok(body.indexOf('<html') !== -1);
      done(err);
    });
  });

});
```

Let's take a closer look at what's happening here:

1. We import the Node.js `assert` function. It gives us the ability to verify the value or the type of a variable.
2. We import the `request` package, which we use to send queries against our back end.

3. We import two Chai functions, `expect` and `should`, from the `chai` package. Neither of these is included in Mocha, but they both improve the test's functionality significantly.
4. The beginning of the test starts with the `describe` function. Because Mocha executes the `app.test.js` file, we're in the correct scope and can use all Mocha functions. The `describe` function is used to structure your test and its output.
5. We use the `it` function, which initiates the first test.

The `it` function can be understood as a feature of our application that we want to test inside the callback function. As the first parameter, you should enter a sentence, such as `'it does this and that'`, that's easily readable. The function itself waits for the complete execution of the `callback` function in the second parameter. The result of the callback will either be that all assertions were successful, or that, for some reason, a test failed or the callback didn't complete in a reasonable amount of time.

The `describe` function is the header of our test's output. Then, we have a new row for each `it` function we execute. Each row represents a single test step. The `it` function passes a `done` function to the callback. The `done` function has to be executed once all assertions are finished and there's nothing left to do. If it isn't executed in a certain amount of time, the current test is marked as failed. In the preceding code, the first thing we did was send an HTTP `GET` request to `http://localhost:8000`, which is accepted by our back end server. The expected answer will be in the form of server-side rendered HTML created through React.

To prove that the response holds this information, we make some assertions in our preceding test:

1. We use the `should` function from Chai. The great thing is that it's chainable and represents a sentence that directly explains the meaning of what we're doing. The `should.not.exist` function chain makes sure that the given value is empty. The result is true if the value is `undefined` or `null`, for example. The consequence is that when the `err` variable is filled, the assertion fails and so our test, `'renders and serves the index page'`, fails too.
2. The same goes for the `should.exist` line. It makes sure that the `res` variable, which is the response given by the back end, is filled. Otherwise, there's a problem with the back end.
3. The `expect` function can also represent a sentence, like both functions before. We expect `res.statusCode` to have a value of `200`. This assertion can be written as `expect(res.statusCode).to.be.equal(200)`. We can be sure that everything has gone well if the HTTP status is `200`.

4. If nothing has failed so far, we check whether the returned `body`, which is the third callback parameter of the `request` function, is valid. For our test scenario, we only need to check whether it contains an `html` tag.
5. We execute the `done` function. We pass the `err` object as a parameter. The result of this function is much like the `should.not.exist` function. If you pass a filled error object to the `done` function, the test fails. The tests become more readable when using the Chai syntax.

If you execute `npm run test` now, you'll receive the following error:

```
Graphbook application test
  1) renders and serves the index page


0 passing (1s)
1 failing

1) Graphbook application test
     renders and serves the index page:
   Uncaught AssertionError: expected [Error: connect ECONNREFUSED 127.0.0.1:8000] to not exist
    at Object.should.not.exist (node_modules\chai\lib\chai\interface\should.js:207:38)
    at Request._callback (E:/Arbeit/Buch/chapter 11 - final/test/app.test.js:24:18)
    at self.callback (E:\node_modules\request\request.js:185:22)
    at Request.onRequestError (E:\node_modules\request\request.js:877:8)
    at Socket.socketErrorListener (_http_client.js:387:9)
    at emitErrorNT (internal/streams/destroy.js:64:8)
    at _combinedTickCallback (internal/process/next_tick.js:138:11)
    at process._tickCallback (internal/process/next_tick.js:180:9)
```

Our first `should.not.exist` assertion failed and threw an error. This is because we didn't start the back end when we ran the test. Start the back end in a second terminal with the correct environment variables using `npm run server` and rerun the test. Now, the test is successful:

```
Graphbook application test
  √ renders and serves the index page (52ms)


1 passing (238ms)
```

The output is good, but the process isn't very intuitive. The current workflow is hard to implement when running the tests automatically while deploying your application or pushing new commits to your version-control system. We'll change this behavior next.

# Starting the back end with Mocha

When we want to run a test, the server should start automatically. There are two options to implement this behavior:

- We add the `npm run server` command to the `test` script inside our `package.json` file.
- We import all the necessary files to launch the server within our `app.test.js`. This allows us to run further assertions or commands against the back end.

The best option is to start the server within our test and not rely on a second command, because we can run further tests on the back end. We to import a further package to allow the server to start within our test:

```
require('babel-plugin-require-context-hook/register')();
```

We use and execute this package because we load the Sequelize models using the `require.context` function. By loading the package, the `require.context` function is executable for the server-side code. Before we started the server within the test, the plugin hadn't been used, although it was loaded in the `babel-hooks.js` file.

Now we can load the server directly in the test. Add the following lines at the top of the `describe` function, just before the test we've just written:

```
var app;
this.timeout(50000);

before(function(done) {
  app = require('../src/server').default;
  app.on("listening", function() {
    done();
  });
});
```

The idea is to load the server's `index.js` file inside of our test, which starts the back end automatically. To do this, we define an empty variable called `app`. Then, we use `this.timeout` to set the timeout for all tests inside Mocha to `50000`, because starting our server, including Apollo Server, takes some time. Otherwise, the test will probably fail because the start time is too long for the standard Mocha timeout.

We must make sure that the server has been completely started before any of our tests are executed. This logic can be achieved with Mocha's `before` function. Using this function, you can set up and configure things such as starting a back end in our scenario. To continue and process all the tests, we need to execute the `done` function to complete the callback of the `before` function. To be sure that the server has started, we do not just run the `done` function after loading the `index.js` file. We bind the `listening` event of the server using the `app.on` function. If the server emits the `listening` event, we can securely run the `done` function, and all tests can send requests to the server. We could also require the server directly into the `app` variable at the top. The problem with this order, however, is that the server may start listening before we can bind the `listening` event. The way we are doing it now makes sure the server hasn't yet started.

The test, however, still isn't working. You'll see an error message that says `'TypeError: app.on is not a function'`. Take a closer look at the server's `index.js` file. At the end of the file, we aren't exporting the server object because we only used it to start the back end. This means that the `app` variable in our test is empty and we can't run the `app.on` function. The solution is to export the `server` object at the end of the server's `index.js` file:

```
export default server;
```

You can now execute the test again. Everything should look fine, and all tests should pass.

There is, however, one last problem. If you compare the behavior from the test before importing the server directly in our test or starting it in a second terminal, you might notice that the test isn't finished, or at least the process isn't stopped. Previously, all steps were executed, we returned to the normal shell, and we could execute the next command. The reason for this is that the server is still running in our `app.test.js` file. Therefore, we must stop the back end after all tests have been executed. Insert the following code after the `before` function:

```
after(function(done) {
  app.close(done);
});
```

The `after` function is run when all tests are finished. Our `app` object offers the `close` function, which terminates the server. As a callback, we hand over the `done` function, which is executed once the server has stopped. It means that our test has also finished.

# Verifying the correct routing

We now want to check whether all the features of our application are working as expected. One major feature of our application is that React Router redirects the user in two cases:

- The user visits a route that cannot be matched.
- The user visits a route that can be matched, but they aren't allowed to view the page.

In both cases, the user should be redirected to the login form. In the first case, we can follow the same approach as for our first test. We send a request to a path that isn't inside our router. Add the code to the bottom of the `describe` function:

```
describe('404', function() {
  it('redirects the user when not matching path is found', function(done) {
    request({
      url: 'http://localhost:8000/path/to/404',
    }, function(err, res, body) {
      should.not.exist(err);
      should.exist(res);
      expect(res.statusCode).to.be.equal(200);
      assert.ok(res.req.path === '/');
      assert.ok(body.indexOf('<html') !== -1);
      assert.ok(body.indexOf('class="authModal"') !== -1);
      done(err);
    });
  });
});
```

Let's quickly go through all steps of the preceding test:

1. We add a new `describe` function to structure our test's output.
2. We send a request inside another `it` function to an unmatched path.
3. The checks are the same as the ones we used when starting the server.
4. We verify that the response's path is the / root. That happens when the redirect is executed. Therefore, we use the `res.req.path === '/'` condition.
5. We check whether the returned `body` includes an HTML tag with the `authModal` class. This should happen when the user isn't logged in, and the login or register form is rendered.

If the assertions are successful, we know that the React Router works correctly in the first scenario. The second scenario relates to the private routes that can only be accessed by authenticated users. We can copy the preceding check and replace the request. The assertions we are doing stay the same, but the URL of the request is different. Add the following test under the previous one:

```
describe('authentication', function() {
  it('redirects the user when not logged in', function(done) {
    request({
      url: 'http://localhost:8000/app',
    }, function(err, res, body) {
      should.not.exist(err);
      should.exist(res);
      expect(res.statusCode).to.be.equal(200);
      assert.ok(res.req.path === '/');
      assert.ok(body.indexOf('<html') !== -1);
      assert.ok(body.indexOf('class="authModal"') !== -1);
      done(err);
    });
  });
});
```

If an unauthenticated user requests the `/app` route, they're redirected to the / root path. The assertions verify whether the login form is displayed as before. To differentiate the tests, we add a new `describe` function so that it has a better structure.

Next, we want to test the GraphQL API that we built, not only the SSR functionality.

# Testing GraphQL with Mocha

We must verify that all the API functions we're offering work correctly. I'm going to show you how to do this with two examples:

- The user needs to sign up or log in. This is a critical feature where we should verify that the API works correctly.
- The user queries or mutates data via the GraphQL API. For our test case, we will request all chats the logged-in user is related to.

Those two examples should explain all the essential techniques to test every part of your API. You can add more functions that you want to test at any point.

# Testing the authentication

We extend the authentication tests of our test with the signup functionality. We're going to send a simple GraphQL request to our back end, including all the required data to sign up a new user. We've already sent requests, so there's nothing new here. In comparison to all the requests before, however, we have to send a `POST` request, not a `GET` request. Also, the endpoint for the signup is the `/graphql` path, where our Apollo Server listens for incoming mutations or queries. Normally, when a user signs up for Graphbook, the authentication token is returned directly, and the user is logged in. We must preserve this token to make future GraphQL requests. We don't use Apollo Client for our test as we don't need to test the GraphQL API.

Create a global variable next to the `app` variable, where we can store the JWT returned after signup:

```
var authToken;
```

Inside the test, we can set the returned JWT. Add the following code to the `authentication` function:

```
it('allows the user to sign up', function(done) {
  const json = {
    operationName: null,
    query: "mutation signup($username: String!, $email : String!,
    $password : String!) { signup(username: $username, email: $email,
    password : $password) { token }}",
    variables: {
      "email": "mocha@test.com",
      "username": "mochatest",
      "password": "123456789"
    }
  };

  request.post({
    url: 'http://localhost:8000/graphql',
    json: json,
  }, function(err, res, body) {
    should.not.exist(err);
    should.exist(res);
    expect(res.statusCode).to.be.equal(200);
    body.should.be.an('object');
    body.should.have.property('data');
    authToken = body.data.signup.token;
    done(err);
  });
});
```

We begin by creating a `json` variable. This object is sent as a JSON body to our GraphQL API. The content of it should be familiar to you. It's nearly the same format we used when testing the GraphQL API in Postman.

The JSON we send represents a manual way of sending GraphQL requests. There are libraries that you can easily use to save this and directly send the query without wrapping it inside an object, such as `graphql-request`: `https://github.com/prisma/graphql-request`.

The `json` object includes fake signup `variables` to create a user with the `mochatest` username. We'll send an HTTP `Post` with the `request.post` function. To use the `json` variable, we pass it into the `json` field. The `request.post` function automatically adds the body as a JSON string and the correct `Content-Type` header for you. When the response arrives, we run the standard checks, such as checking for an error or checking an HTTP status code. We also check the format of the returned `body`, because the response's `body` won't return HTML, but will return JSON instead. We make sure that it's an object with the `should.be.an('object')` function. The `should` assertion can directly be used and chained to the `body` variable. If `body` is an object, we check whether there's a `data` property inside. That's enough security to read the token from the `body.data.signup.token` property.

The user is now created in our database. We can use this token for further requests. Be aware that running this test a second time on your local machine is likely to result in a failure because the user already exists. In this case, you can delete it manually from your database. This problem won't occur when running this test while using Continuous Integration. We'll focus on this topic in the last chapter. Next, we'll make an authenticated query to our Apollo Server and test the result of it.

# Testing authenticated requests

We set the `authToken` variable after the signup request. You could also do this with a login request if a user already exists while testing. Only the query and the assertions we are using are going to change. Also insert the following code into the `before` authentication function:

```
it('allows the user to query all chats', function(done) {
  const json = {
    operationName: null,
    query: "query {chats {id users {id avatar username}}}",
    variables: {}
  };

  request.post({
```

```
        url: 'http://localhost:8000/graphql',
        headers: {
          'Authorization': authToken
        },
        json: json,
      }, function(err, res, body) {
        should.not.exist(err);
        should.exist(res);
        expect(res.statusCode).to.be.equal(200);
        body.should.be.an('object');
        body.should.have.property('data');
        body.data.should.have.property('chats').with.lengthOf(0);
        done(err);
      });
    });
```

As you can see in the preceding code, the `json` object doesn't include any variables because we only query the chats of the logged-in user. We changed the `query` string accordingly. Compared to the login or signup request, the chat query requires the user to be authenticated. The `authToken` we saved is sent inside the `Authorization` header. We now verify again whether the request was successful and check for a `data` property in the `body`. Notice that, before running the `done` function, we verify that the `data` object has a field called `chats`. We also check the length of the `chats` field, which proves that it's an array. The length can be statically set to `0` because the user who's sending the query just signed up and doesn't have any chats yet. The output from Mocha looks as follows:

```
Graphbook application test
  √ renders and serves the index page
  404
    √ redirects the user when not matching path is found
  authentication
    √ redirects the user when not logged in
    √ allows the user to sign up
    √ allows the user to query all chats


5 passing (3s)
```

This is all you need to know to test all the features of your API.

# Testing React with Enzyme

So far, we've managed to test our server and all GraphQL API functions. Currently, however, we're still missing the tests for our front end code. While we render the React code when requesting any server route, such as the `/app` path, we only have access to the final result and not to each component. We should change this to execute the functions of certain components that aren't testable through the back end. First, install some dependencies before using npm:

```
npm install --save-dev enzyme enzyme-adapter-react-16 ignore-styles jsdom
isomorphic-fetch
```

The various packages are as follows:

- The `enzyme` and `enzyme-adapter-react-16` packages provide React with specific features to render and interact with the React tree. This can either be through a real DOM or shallow rendering. We are going to use a real DOM in this chapter because it allows us to test all features, while shallow rendering is limited to just the first layer of components.
- The `ignore-styles` package strips out all `import` statements for CSS files. This is very helpful, since we don't need CSS for our tests.
- The `jsdom` package creates a DOM object for us, which is then used to render the React code into.
- The `isomorphic-fetch` package replaces the `fetch` function that all browsers provide by default. This isn't available in Node.js, so we need a polyfill.

We start by importing the new packages directly under the other `require` statements:

```
require('isomorphic-fetch');
import React from 'react';
import { configure, mount } from 'enzyme';
import Adapter from 'enzyme-adapter-react-16';
configure({ adapter: new Adapter() });
import register from 'ignore-styles';
register(['.css', '.sass', '.scss']);
```

To use Enzyme, we import React. Then, we create an adapter for Enzyme that supports React 16. We insert the adapter into Enzyme's `configure` statement. Before starting with the front end code, we import the `ignore-styles` package to ignore all CSS imports. I've also directly excluded SASS and SCSS files. The next step is to initialize our DOM object, where all the React code is rendered:

```
const { JSDOM } = require('jsdom');
const dom = new JSDOM('<!doctype html><html><body></body></html>', { url:
```

```
'http://graphbook.test' });
const { window } = dom;
global.window = window;
global.document = window.document;
```

We require the `jsdom` package and initialize it with a small HTML string. We don't take the template file that we're using for the server or client because we just want to render our application to any HTML, so how it looks isn't important. The second parameter is an options object. We specify a `url` field, which is the host URL, under which we render the React code. Otherwise, we might get an error when accessing `localStorage`. After initialization, we extract the `window` object and define two global variables that are required to mount a React component to our fake DOM. These two properties behave like the `document` and `window` objects in the browser, but instead of the browser they are global objects inside our Node.js server.

In general, it isn't a good idea to mix up the Node.js `global` object with the DOM of a browser and render a React application in it. Still, we're merely testing our application and not running it in production in this environment, so while it might not be recommended, it helps our test to be more readable. We'll begin the first front end test with our login form. The visitor to our page can either directly log in or switch to the signup form. Currently, we don't test this switch functionality in any way. This is a complex example, but you should be able to understand the techniques behind it quickly.

To render our complete React code, we're going to initialize an Apollo Client for our test. Import all the dependencies:

```
import { ApolloClient } from 'apollo-client';
import { InMemoryCache } from 'apollo-cache-inmemory';
import { ApolloLink } from 'apollo-link';
import { createUploadLink } from 'apollo-upload-client';
import App from '../src/server/ssr';
```

We also import the `index.js` component of the server-rendered React code. This component will receive our client, which we'll initialize shortly. Add a new `describe` function for all front end tests:

```
describe('frontend', function() {
  it('renders and switches to the login or register form',
  function(done) {
    const httpLink = createUploadLink({
      uri: 'http://localhost:8000/graphql',
      credentials: 'same-origin',
    });
    const client = new ApolloClient({
      link: ApolloLink.from([
```

```
        httpLink
      ]),
      cache: new InMemoryCache()
    });
  });
});
```

The preceding code creates a new Apollo Client. The client doesn't implement any logic, such as authentication or WebSockets, because we don't need this to test the switch from the login form to the signup form. It's merely a required property to render our application completely. If you want to test components that are only rendered when being authenticated, you can, of course, implement it easily. Enzyme requires us to pass a real React component, which will be rendered to the DOM. Add the following code directly beneath the `client` variable:

```
class Graphbook extends React.Component {
  render() {
    return(
      <App client={client} context={{}} loggedIn={false} location=
       {"/"}/>
    )
  }
}
```

The preceding code is a small wrapper around the `App` variable that we imported from the server's `ssr` folder. The `client` property is filled with the new Apollo Client. Follow the given instructions to render and test your React front end code. The following code goes directly under the `Graphbook` class:

1. We use the `mount` function of Enzyme to render the `Graphbook` class to the DOM:

   ```
   const wrapper = mount(<Graphbook />);
   ```

2. The `wrapper` variable provides many functions to access or interact with the DOM and the components inside it. We use it to prove that the first render displays the login form:

   ```
   expect(wrapper.html()).to.contain('<a>Want to sign up? Click
   here</a>');
   ```

   The `html` function of the `wrapper` variable returns the complete HTML string that has been rendered by the React code. We check this string with the `contain` function of Chai. If the check is successful, we can continue.

3. Typically, the user clicks on the **Want to sign up?** message and React rerenders the signup form. We need to handle this via the `wrapper` variable. Enzyme comes with that functionality innately:

```
wrapper.find('LoginRegisterForm').find('a').simulate('click');
```

The `find` function gives us access to the `LoginRegisterForm` component. Inside the markup of the component, we search for an `a` tag, of which there can only be one. If the `find` method returns multiple results, we can't trigger things such as a click, because the `simulate` function is fixed to only one possible target. After running both `find` functions, we execute Enzyme's `simulate` function. The only parameter needed is the event that we want to trigger. In our scenario, we trigger a click event on the `a` tag, which lets React handle all the rest.

4. We check whether the form was changed correctly:

```
expect(wrapper.html()).to.contain('<a>Want to login? Click
 here</a>');
done();
```

We use the `html` and `contain` functions to verify that everything was rendered correctly. The `done` method of Mocha is used to finish the test.

For a more detailed overview of the API and all the functions that Enzyme provides, have a look at the official documentation: `https://airbnb.io/enzyme/docs/api/`.

This was the easy part. How does this work when we want to verify whether the client can send queries or mutations with authentication? It's actually not that different. We already registered a new user and got a JWT in return. All we need to do is attach the JWT to our Apollo Client, and the Router needs to receive the correct `loggedIn` property. The final code for this test looks as follows:

```
it('renders the current user in the top bar', function(done) {
  const AuthLink = (operation, next) => {
    operation.setContext(context => ({
        ...context,
        headers: {
            ...context.headers,
            Authorization: authToken
        },
    }));
    return next(operation);
  };
```

```
    const httpLink = createUploadLink({
      uri: 'http://localhost:8000/graphql',
      credentials: 'same-origin',
    });

    const client = new ApolloClient({
      link: ApolloLink.from([
        AuthLink,
        httpLink
      ]),
      cache: new InMemoryCache()
    });

    class Graphbook extends React.Component {
      render() {
        return(
          <App client={client} context={{}} loggedIn={true} location=
           {"/app"}/>
        )
      }
    }

    const wrapper = mount(<Graphbook />);
    setTimeout(function() {
      expect(wrapper.html()).to.contain('<div class="user"><img>
       <span>mochatest</span></div>');
      done();
    },2000);
  });
```

Here, we are using the `AuthLink` that we used in the original front end code. We pass the `authToken` variable to every request that's made by the Apollo Client. In the `Apollo.from` method, we add it before `httpLink`. In the `Graphbook` class, we set `loggedIn` to `true` and the `location` to `/app` to render the newsfeed. Because the requests are asynchronous by default and the `mount` method doesn't wait for the Apollo Client to fetch all queries, we couldn't directly check the DOM for the correct content. Instead, we wrapped the assertions and the `done` function in a `setTimeout` function. A timeout of 2,000 milliseconds should be enough for all requests to finish and React to have rendered everything. If this isn't enough time, you can increase the number. When all assertions are successful, we can be sure that the `currentUser` query has been run and the top bar has been rendered to show the logged-in user. With these two examples, you should now be able to run any test you want with your application's front end code.

# Summary

In this chapter, we learned all the essential techniques to test your application automatically, including testing the server, the GraphQL API, and the user's front end. You can apply the Mocha and Chai patterns you learned to other projects to reach a high software quality at any time. Your personal testing time will be greatly reduced.

In the next chapter, we'll have a look at how to improve performance and error logging so we're always providing a good user experience.

# 12
# Optimizing GraphQL with Apollo Engine

In the last chapter, we introduced testing for our development process. We can now be sure that all of the features that are covered by our tests work as expected. There's still, however, the chance that we've overlooked some bugs or cases that could lead to an error. How is our GraphQL API performing, are there any errors, and how can we improve the GraphQL schema? We can answer these questions using Apollo Engine.

This chapter covers the following topics:

- Setting up Apollo Engine
- Schema analysis
- Performance analytics
- Error tracking

## Setting up Apollo Engine

Apollo Engine provides many great features, which we'll explore in this chapter. Before moving on, however, you need to sign up for an Apollo Engine account. Apollo Engine is a commercial product produced by **MDG**, the **Meteor Development Group**, the company behind Apollo.

At the time of writing, they offer three different plans, which you can find by going to `https://www.apollographql.com/plans/`. When signing up, you get a two-week trial of the Team plan, which is one of the paid plans. Afterward, you'll be downgraded to the free plan. You should compare all three plans to understand how they differ—they're all worth checking out.

To sign up, visit `https://engine.apollographql.com/login`. Currently, you can only sign up using a GitHub account. If you don't have one already, create a GitHub account at `https://https://github.com/join`.

The good thing is that you don't have to enter any payment information unless you subscribe to a paid plan. The trial phase doesn't ask you to enter credit card information or anything else.

After logging in, you will see a dashboard that looks as follows:

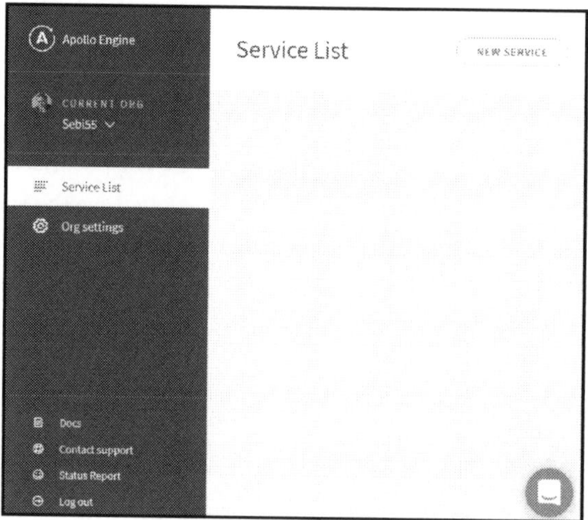


The next step is to add a service with the **NEW SERVICE** button in the top-right corner. The first thing you need to enter is a unique id for your service across all **Apollo Engine** services. This id will be auto generated through the organization you select, but can be customized. Secondly, you will be asked to publish your GraphQL schema to **Apollo Engine**. Publishing your GraphQL schema means that you upload your schema to Apollo Engine so that it can be processed. It won't get publicized to external users. You can do this using the command provided by Apollo Engine. Copy it directly from the website and execute it. For me, this command looked as follows:

```
npx apollo service:push --endpoint="http://localhost:8000/graphql" --
key="YOUR_KEY"
```

The preceding `endpoint` must match your GraphQL route. The `key` comes from Apollo Engine itself, so you don't generate it on your own. Before running the preceding command, you have to start the server, otherwise the GraphQL schema isn't accessible. Once you've uploaded the schema, Apollo Engine will redirect you to the service you just set up.

Notice that the GraphQL introspection feature needs to be enabled. Introspection means that you can ask your GraphQL API which operations it supports.

Introspection is only enabled when you run your Apollo Server in a development environment, or if you explicitly enable introspection in production. I highly discourage this because it involves giving away information about queries and mutations that are accepted by your back end. However, if you want to enable it, you can do this by setting the `introspection` field when initializing Apollo Server. It can be added inside the `index.js` file of the `graphql` folder:

```
const server = new ApolloServer({
  schema: executableSchema,
  introspection: true,
```

Ensure that you remove the `introspection` field when deploying your application.

If you aren't able to run the GraphQL server, you also have the ability to specify a schema file. Once you publish the GraphQL schema, the setup process for your Apollo Engine service should be done. We'll explore the features that we can now use in the following sections of this chapter. Before doing this, however, we have to change one thing on the back end to get Apollo Engine working with our back end. We already used our API Key to upload our GraphQL schema to Apollo Engine. Everything, such as error tracking and performance analysis, relies on this key. We also have to insert it in our GraphQL server. If you entered a valid API key, all requests will be collected in Apollo Engine.

Open `index.js` in the server's `graphql` folder and add the following object to the `ApolloServer` initialization:

```
engine: {
  apiKey: ENGINE_KEY
}
```

The `ENGINE_KEY` variable should be extracted from the environment variables at the top of the file. We also need to extract `JWT_SECRET` with the following line:

```
const { JWT_SECRET, ENGINE_KEY } = process.env;
```

Verify that everything is working by running some GraphQL requests. You can view all past requests by clicking on the **Clients** tab in Apollo Engine. You should see that a number of requests happened, under the **Activity in the last hour** panel. If this isn't the case, there must be a problem with the Apollo Server configuration.

There are many advanced options you can configure with Apollo Engine. You can find the appropriate documentation at `https://www.apollographql.com/docs/engine/`.

The basic setup is finished now. Apollo Engine doesn't support subscriptions at the time of writing; it can only track normal HTTP operations. Let's now take a closer look at the features of Apollo Engine.

# Analyzing schemas with Apollo Engine

The Community plan of Apollo Engine offers schema registry and explorer tools. You can find them by clicking on the **Explorer** tab in the left-hand panel. If your setup has gone well, the page should look as follows:

Let's take a closer look at this screenshot:

- On the page, you see the last GraphQL schema that you have published. Each schema you publish has a unique version, as long as the schema includes changes.

- Beneath the version number, you can see your entire GraphQL schema. You can inspect all operations and types. All relations between types and operations are directly linked to each other.
- You can directly see the number of clients and various usage statistics next to each operation, type, and field.
- You can search through your GraphQL schema in the top bar and filter the usage statistics in the panel on the right.

You can also switch to the **Deprecation** tab at the top. This page gives you a list of fields that are deprecated. We won't use this page because we are using the latest field definitions, but it's vital if you're running an application for a longer time.

As well as Apollo Engine, there are numerous tools that can give you an overview of your GraphQL schema. I'm a big fan of GraphQL Voyager, which generates a mindmap-like graph, using which you can identify all operations, including the relations of GraphQL types. It requires you to run an introspection query, whose result is rendered. You can find more information at `https://apis.guru/graphql-voyager/`.

Having an overview of our schema is beneficial. In production, every new release of our application is likely to also bring changes to the GraphQL schema. With Apollo Engine, you can track those changes easily. This feature is called schema-change validation and is only included in the paid Team plan of Apollo Engine. It's worth the extra money because it allows you to track schema changes and also to compare how those fields are used. It allows us to draw conclusions about which clients and versions are being used at the moment.

I have created an example for you in the following screenshot:

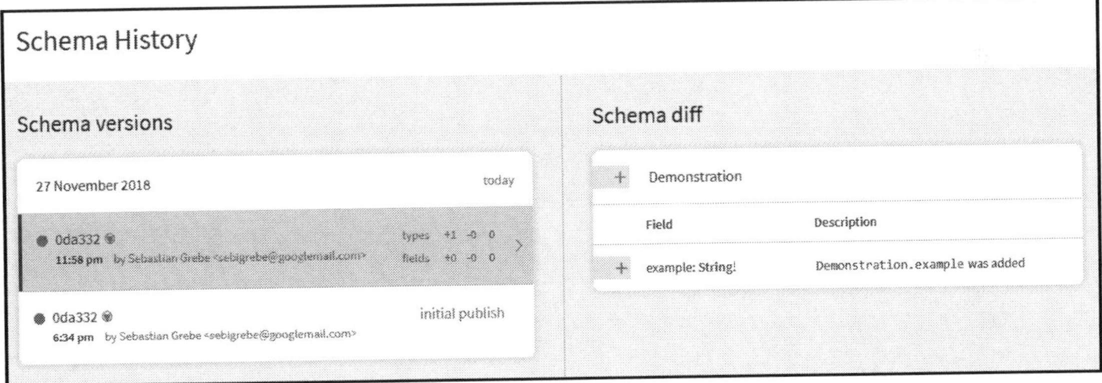

Here, I published an initial version of our current GraphQL schema. Afterward, I added a `demonstration` type with one field, called `example`. On the right-hand side, you can see the schema difference between the initial and second releases of the GraphQL schema.

Viewing your schema inside Apollo Engine, including the history of all previous schemas, is very useful. In the next section, we'll cover how Apollo Engine enables you to get detailed metrics about the performance of your GraphQL API.

# Performance metrics with Apollo Engine

When your application is live and heavily used, you can't check the status of every feature yourself; it would lead to an impossible amount of work. Apollo Engine can tell you how your GraphQL API is performing by collecting statistics with each request that's received. You always have an overview of the general usage of your application, the number of requests it receives, the request latency, the time taken to process each operation, the type, and also each field that is returned. Apollo Server can provide these precise analytics, since each field is represented in a `resolver` function. The time elapsed to resolve each field is then collected and stored inside Apollo Engine.

At the top of the **Metrics** page, you have four tabs. The first tab will look as follows:

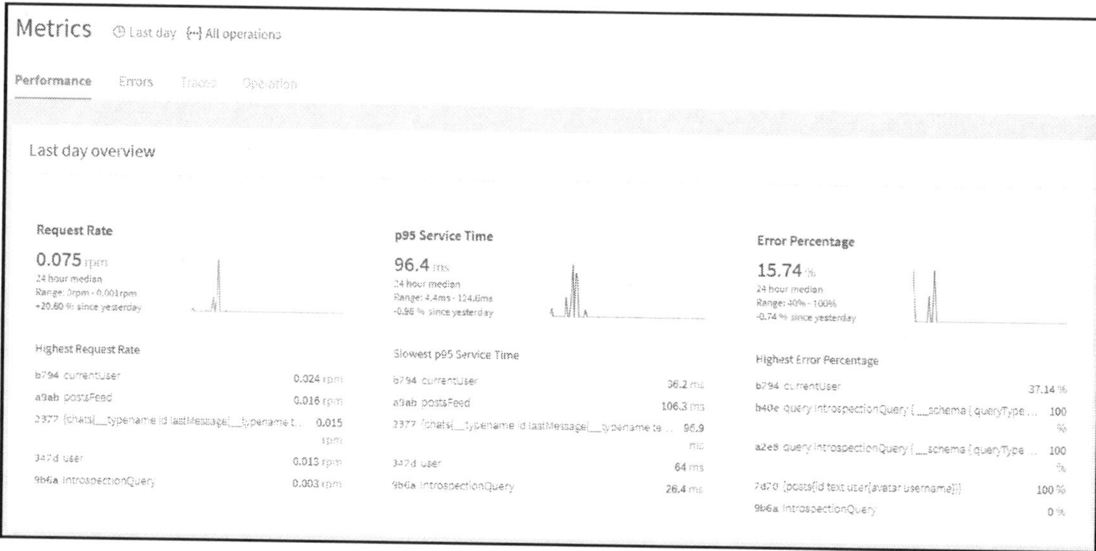

If your GraphQL API is running for more than a day, you'll receive an overview that looks like the one here. The left-hand graph shows you the request rate over the last day. The graph in the middle shows the service time, which sums up the processing time of all requests. The right-hand graph gives you the amount of errors, along with the queries that caused them.

Under the overview, you'll find details about the current day, including the requests per minute, the request latency over time, and the request latency distribution:

- **Requests Per Minute** (**rpm**) is useful when your API is used very often. It indicates which requests are sent more often than others.
- The latency over time is useful when the requests to your API take too long to process. You can use this information to look for a correlation between the number of requests and increasing latency.
- The request-latency distribution shows you the processing time and the amount of requests. You can compare the number of slow requests with the number of fast requests in this chart.

In the right-hand panel of Apollo Engine, under **Metrics**, you'll see all your GraphQL operations. If you select one of these, you can get even more detailed statistics.

Now, switch to the **Traces** tab at the top. The first chart on this page looks as follows:

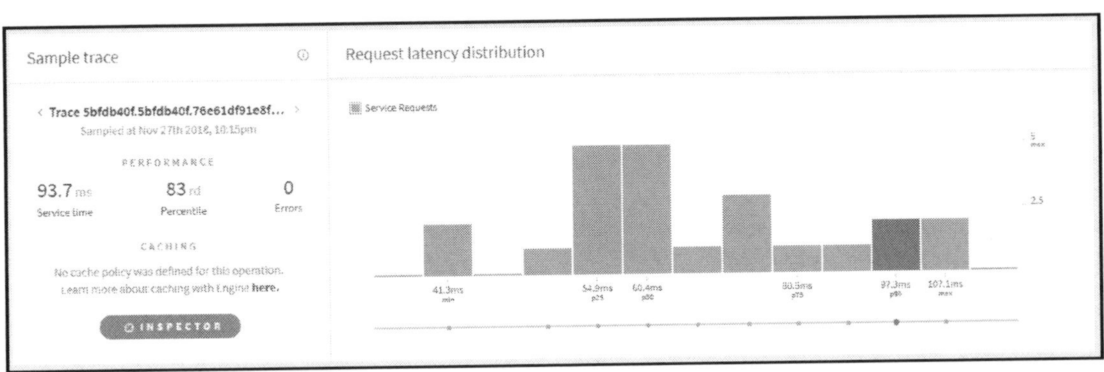


The latency distribution chart shows all the different latencies for the currently-selected operation, including the number of sent requests with that latency. In the preceding example, I used the `postsFeed` query.

Each request latency has its own execution timetable. You can see it by clicking on any column in the preceding chart. The table should look like the following screenshot:

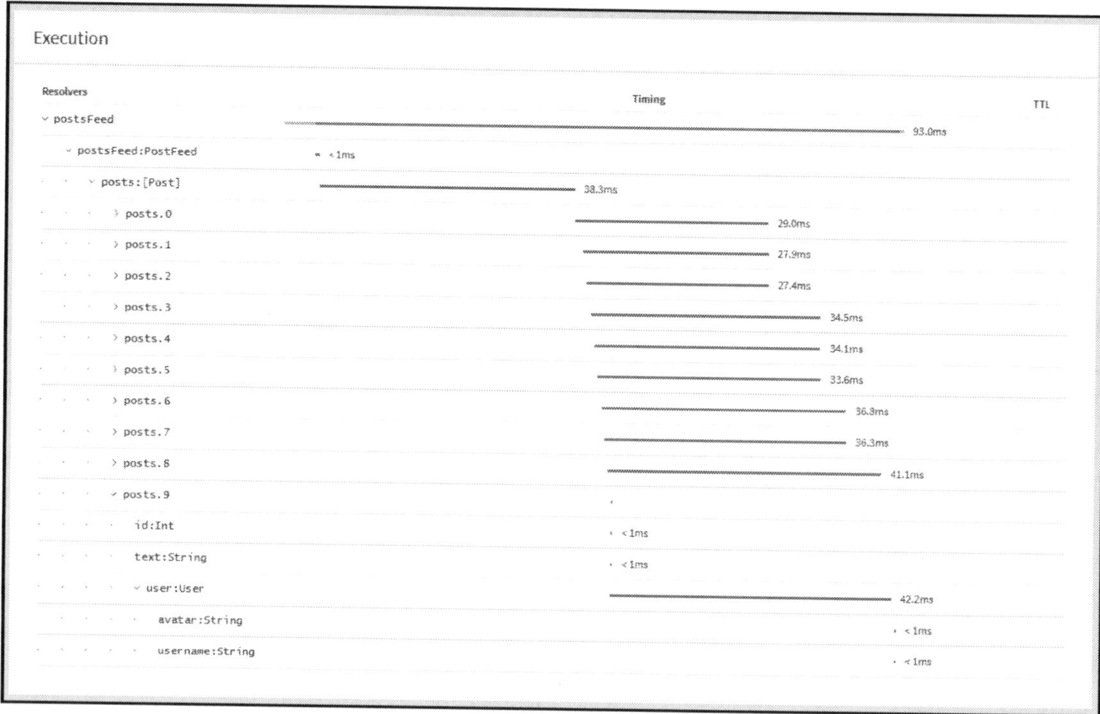


The execution timetable is a big foldable tree. It starts at the top with the root query, `postsFeed`, in this case. You can also see the overall time it took to process the operation. Each resolver function has got its own latency, which might include, for example, the time taken for each post and user to be queried from the database. All the times from within the tree are summed up and result in a total time of about 90 milliseconds.

It's obvious that you should always check all operations and their latencies to identify performance breakdowns. Your users should always have responsive access to your API. This can easily be monitored with Apollo Engine.

Next, we'll see how Apollo Engine implements error tracking.

# Error tracking with Apollo Engine

We've already looked at how to inspect single operations using Apollo Engine. Under the **Clients** tab, you will find a separate view that covers all client types and their requests:

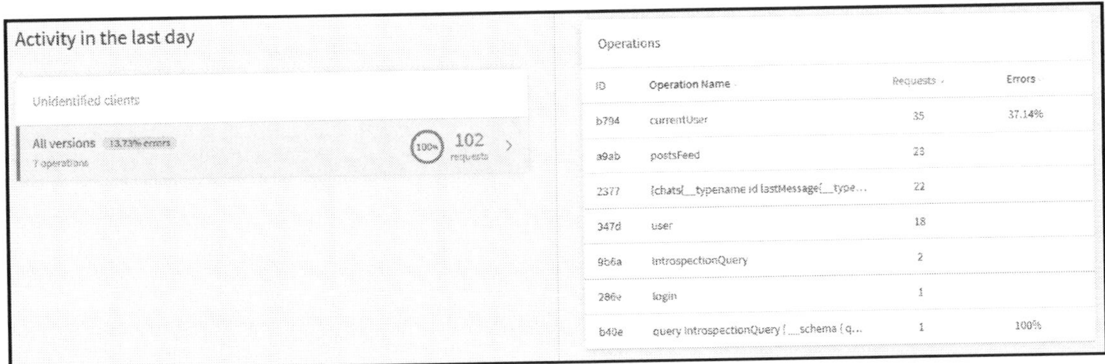


In this tab, you can directly see the percentage of errors that happened during each operation. In the `currentUser` query, there were **37.14%** errors out of the total `currentUser` requests.

If you take a closer look at the left-hand side of the image, you will see that it says **Unidentified clients**. Since version 2.2.3 of Apollo Server, client awareness is supported. It allows you to identify the client and track how consumers use your API. Apollo automatically extracts an `extensions` field inside each GraphQL operation, which can hold a name and version. Both fields—**Name** and **Version**—are then directly transferred to Apollo Engine. We can filter by these fields in Apollo Engine. We will have a look at how to implement this in our back end next.

In this example, we'll use HTTP header fields to track the client type. There will be two header fields: `apollo-client-name` and `apollo-client-version`. We'll use these to set custom values to filter requests later in the **Clients** page. Open the `index.js` file from the `graphql` folder. Add the following function to the `engine` property of the `ApolloServer` initialization:

```
engine: {
  apiKey: ENGINE_KEY,
  generateClientInfo: ({
    request
  }) => {
    const headers = request.http.headers;
    const clientName = headers.get('apollo-client-name');
    const clientVersion = headers.get('apollo-client-version');
```

```
        if(clientName && clientVersion) {
          return {
            clientName,
            clientVersion
          };
        } else {
          return {
            clientName: "Unknown Client",
            clientVersion: "Unversioned",
          };
        }
      },
    },
```

The `generateClientInfo` function is executed with every request. We extract the two fields from the header. If they exist, we return an object with the `clientName` and `clientVersion` properties that have the values from the headers. Otherwise, we return a static `Unkown Client` text.

To get both of our clients – the front end and back end – set up, we have to add these fields. Perform the following steps:

1. Open the `index.js` file of the client's `apollo` folder file.
2. Add a new `InfoLink` to the file to set the two new header fields:

   ```
   const InfoLink = (operation, next) => {
     operation.setContext(context => ({
       ...context,
       headers: {
         ...context.headers,
         'apollo-client-name': 'Apollo Frontend Client',
         'apollo-client-version': '1'
       },
     }));

     return next(operation);
   };
   ```

   Like `AuthLink`, this link will add the two new header fields next to the authorization header. It sets the version header to `'1'` and the name of the client to `'Apollo Frontend Client'`. We will see both in Apollo Engine soon.

3. Add `InfoLink` in front of `AuthLink` in the `ApolloLink.from` function.

4. On the back end, we need to edit the `apollo.js` file in the `ssr` folder:

```
const InfoLink = (operation, next) => {
  operation.setContext(context => ({
    ...context,
    headers: {
      ...context.headers,
      'apollo-client-name': 'Apollo Backend Client',
      'apollo-client-version': '1'
    },
  }));

return next(operation);
};
```

5. The link is almost the same as the one for the front end, except that we set another `apollo-client-name` header. Add it just before `AuthLink` in the `ApolloLink.from` function.

The client name differs between the front end and back end code so you can compare both clients inside Apollo Engine. If you execute some requests from the back end and front end, you can see the result of these changes directly in Apollo Engine. Here, you can see an example of how that result should look:

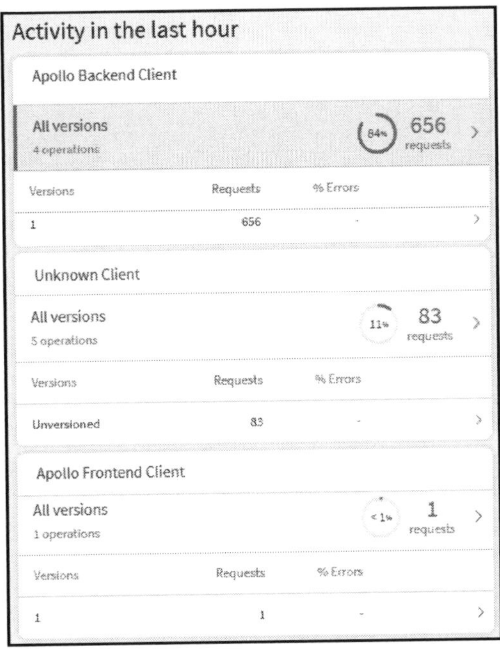

At the top of the screenshot, we see the number of requests the back end has made. In the middle, all the clients that we have no further information on are listed, while at the bottom, we can see all requests that have been made by the client-side code. Unknown clients might be external applications that are accessing your API.

When releasing a new version of your application, you can increase the version number of the client. The version number represents another comparable field.

We now know which clients have accessed our API from the information provided by Apollo Engine. Let's take a look at what Apollo Engine can tell us about errors.

When you visit the **Error** tab, you will be presented with a screen that looks like the following screenshot:

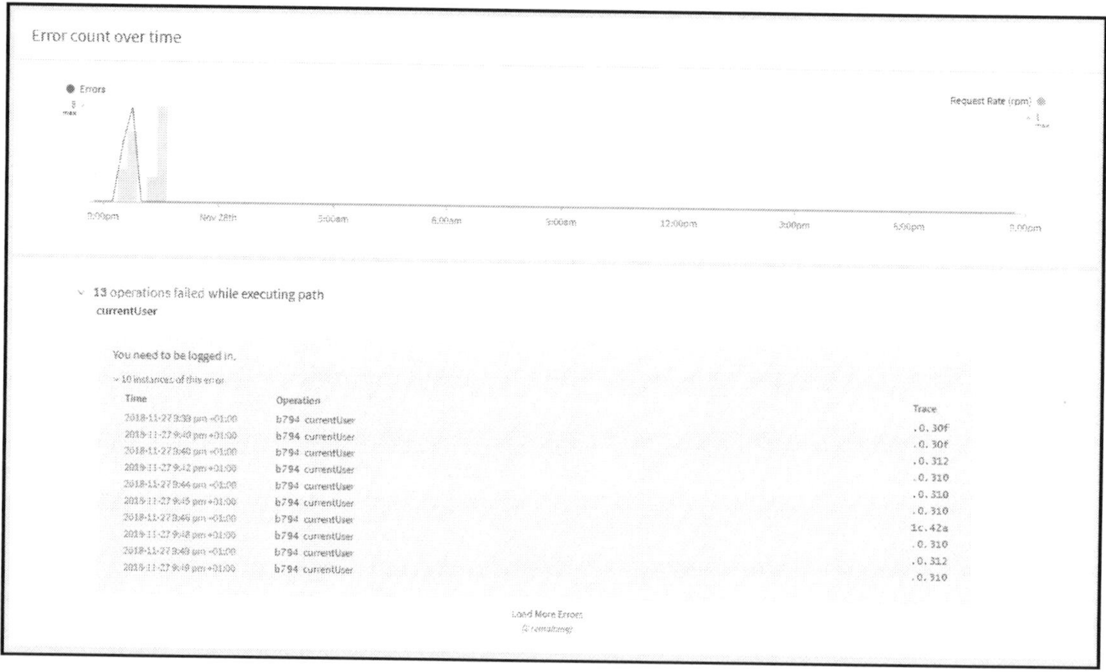

The first chart shows the number of errors over a timeline. Under the graph, you can see each error with a timestamp and the stack trace. You can follow the link to see the trace in detail, with the location of the error. If you paid for the Team plan, you can also set alerts when the number of errors increases or the latency time goes up. You can find these alerts under the **Integrations** tab.

Next, we'll see how to improve the performance of our GraphQL API.

## Caching with Apollo Server and the Client

Hopefully, when deploying your first application, you'll soon get a growing user base. You're required to improve the performance and efficiency of your application. One way this can be done is through standard improvements, such as code refactoring. Another crucial thing to do is caching. Not just files such as our CSS and JavaScript files should be cached, but also the requests that we send.

Apollo provides **Automatic Persisted Queries** (**APQ**), which is a technique that significantly reduces bandwidth usage and carries out caching through unique IDs per request. The workflow of this technique is as follows:

1. The client sends a hash instead of the full query string.
2. Apollo Server tries to find this hash inside its cache.
3. If the server finds the corresponding query string to the hash, it'll execute it and respond with its result.
4. If the server doesn't find the hash inside its cache, it'll ask the client to send the hash along with the actual query string. The back end will then save this hash with the query string for all future requests and respond to the client's request.

There are two server-side changes that we have to do. One is in the initialization of Apollo Server. Extend the graphql `index.js` by adding the following two parameters to the `ApolloServer` options:

```
cacheControl: {
  defaultMaxAge: 5,
  stripFormattedExtensions: false,
  calculateCacheControlHeaders: true,
},
```

The `cacheControl` object sets `cacheControl` properties for all our requests. The standard time inserted in this case is 5 seconds. Using cache control, you can also store public GraphQL requests inside a CDN to improve performance.

Setting up a CDN for your application is a vast topic that wouldn't be possible to cover in just one chapter. It requires a significant amount of work. If you want to use Apollo together with a CDN, read up on this in the official documentation: `https://www.apollographql.com/docs/apollo-server/v2/whats-new.html#CDN-integration`.

The second change is to enable cache control in the GraphQL schema. Just copy the following code into the `schema.js` file:

```
enum CacheControlScope {
  PUBLIC
  PRIVATE
}

directive @cacheControl (
  maxAge: Int
  scope: CacheControlScope
) on FIELD_DEFINITION | OBJECT | INTERFACE
```

We have to add the preceding lines of code because there seems to be a problem with the `makeExecutableSchema` function, which removes the `@cacheControl` directive. By adding it in our schema, we add our custom directive, which we can use.

If you now execute any query, the response will include an extensions object that looks like the following example:


```
▾ cacheControl: {version: 1, hints: [{path: ["postsFeed"], maxAge: 5}, {path: ["postsFeed", "posts"], maxAge: 5},…]}
  ▾ hints: [{path: ["postsFeed"], maxAge: 5}, {path: ["postsFeed", "posts"], maxAge: 5},…]
    ▸ 0: {path: ["postsFeed"], maxAge: 5}
    ▸ 1: {path: ["postsFeed", "posts"], maxAge: 5}
    ▸ 2: {path: ["postsFeed", "posts", 0, "user"], maxAge: 120}
    ▸ 3: {path: ["postsFeed", "posts", 1, "user"], maxAge: 120}
    ▸ 4: {path: ["postsFeed", "posts", 2, "user"], maxAge: 120}
    ▸ 5: {path: ["postsFeed", "posts", 3, "user"], maxAge: 120}
    ▸ 6: {path: ["postsFeed", "posts", 4, "user"], maxAge: 120}
    ▸ 7: {path: ["postsFeed", "posts", 5, "user"], maxAge: 120}
    ▸ 8: {path: ["postsFeed", "posts", 6, "user"], maxAge: 120}
    ▸ 9: {path: ["postsFeed", "posts", 7, "user"], maxAge: 120}
    ▸ 10: {path: ["postsFeed", "posts", 8, "user"], maxAge: 120}
    ▸ 11: {path: ["postsFeed", "posts", 9, "user"], maxAge: 120}
    ▸ 12: {path: ["postsFeed", "posts", 0, "user", "avatar"], maxAge: 240}
    ▸ 13: {path: ["postsFeed", "posts", 1, "user", "avatar"], maxAge: 240}
    ▸ 14: {path: ["postsFeed", "posts", 3, "user", "avatar"], maxAge: 240}
    ▸ 15: {path: ["postsFeed", "posts", 4, "user", "avatar"], maxAge: 240}
    ▸ 16: {path: ["postsFeed", "posts", 2, "user", "avatar"], maxAge: 240}
    ▸ 17: {path: ["postsFeed", "posts", 5, "user", "avatar"], maxAge: 240}
    ▸ 18: {path: ["postsFeed", "posts", 6, "user", "avatar"], maxAge: 240}
    ▸ 19: {path: ["postsFeed", "posts", 7, "user", "avatar"], maxAge: 240}
    ▸ 20: {path: ["postsFeed", "posts", 8, "user", "avatar"], maxAge: 240}
    ▸ 21: {path: ["postsFeed", "posts", 9, "user", "avatar"], maxAge: 240}
    version: 1
```

In this case, the **maxAge** field has been applied to each layer of our GraphQL request. As you can see, the users in the third layer and the avatar images all have different maximum ages when compared to the posts. You can define the **maxAge** per type and field specifically.

If you open your `schema.js` file, you can change your `User` type to reflect the preceding screenshot, as follows:

```
type User @cacheControl(maxAge: 120) {
  id: Int
  avatar: String @cacheControl(maxAge: 240)
  username: String
  email: String
}
```

The `@cacheControl` directive takes care of all of this internally in Apollo Server.

To persist our queries, we have to change some aspects of our SSR code. Before we do this, however, we need to install a package using npm:

```
npm install --save apollo-link-persisted-queries
```

This package provides a special Apollo Client link to use persisted queries. Import it at the top of both the `apollo.js` file in the `ssr` folder and the `index.js` in the `apollo` folder of the client:

```
import { createPersistedQueryLink } from 'apollo-link-persisted-queries';
```

We'll now create a new link with the `createPersistedQueryLink` function and then connect it with our existing `HttpLink`, which is initialized by the `createUploadLink` function. The following snippet shows how this can be implemented for the client-side code:

```
const httpLink = createPersistedQueryLink().concat(createUploadLink({
  uri: location.protocol + '//' + location.hostname + port +
  '/graphql',
  credentials: 'same-origin',
}));
```

We execute the `createPersistedQueryLink` function and then use the `concat` function for our `UploadLink`. The result is then normally inserted into the `split` function, which is used to decide between the WebSocket link and `UploadLink`.

The SSR-related code looks pretty similar, but the function is directly executed within the `Apollo.from` function instead. In the `apollo.js` file from the `apollo` folder, replace the initialization of `HttpLink` with the following code:

```
createPersistedQueryLink().concat(new HttpLink({
  uri: 'http://localhost:8000/graphql',
  credentials: 'same-origin',
  fetch
}));
```

As you know, we don't have `UploadLink` on the server side, so we're using the normal `HttpLink` instead. A GraphQL request will now include a hash instead of the regular query string on the first try. You can see an example in the following screenshot:


```
▾{operationName: "postsFeed", variables: {page: 0, limit: 10}, extensions: {,…}}
  ▾extensions: {,…}
    ▾persistedQuery: {version: 1, sha256Hash: "03ce590cb5e466a07ca4620a2d6067a8e66c94019fabd678c3e25ced41fa6ea6"}
       sha256Hash: "03ce590db5e466a07ca4620a2d6067a8e66c94019fabd678c3e25ced41fa6ea6"
       version: 1
   operationName: "postsFeed"
  ▸variables: {page: 0, limit: 10}
```


The `variables` are of course included, because they can change dynamically, but the query will always be the same. The server will try to find the hash or let the client resend the complete `query` string. This solution will save you and your users a significant amount of bandwidth and, as a result, speed up API requests.

# Summary

In this chapter, we learned how to sign up to and set up Apollo Engine. You should now understand all the features that Apollo Engine provides and how to make use of collected data. We also looked at how to set up `cacheControl` and Automatic Persisted Queries to improve the performance of your application.

In the next chapter, we'll finally deploy a production release of Graphbook, with the help of CircleCI and Heroku.

# 13 Continuous Deployment with CircleCI and Heroku

In the last two chapters, we prepared our application through tests with Mocha and added detailed reporting of our GraphQL API by introducing Apollo Engine. We have built an application that is ready for the production environment.

We will now generate a production build that's ready for deployment. We've arrived at the point where we can set up our Heroku app and implement the ability to build and deploy Docker images through a continuous deployment workflow.

This chapter covers the following topics:

- Production-ready bundling
- What is Docker?
- What is continuous integration/deployment?
- Configuring Docker
- Setting up continuous deployment with CircleCI
- Deploying our application to Heroku

## Preparing the final production build

We have come a long way to get here. Now is the time where we should take a look at how we currently run our application, and how we should prepare it for a production environment.

Currently, we use our application in a development environment while working on it. It is not highly optimized for performance or low bandwidth usage. We include developer functionalities with the code so that we can debug it properly. We also only generate one bundle, which is distributed at all times. No matter which page the user visits, the code for our entire application is sent to the user or browser.

For use in a real production environment, we should solve these issues. When setting the `NODE_ENV` variable to `production`, we remove most of the unnecessary development mechanics. Still, it would be great to send as little code to the user as possible to save bandwidth. We will take a look at this problem in the next section.

# Code-splitting with React Loadable and webpack

The best option to increase the efficiency of our application is to introduce code-splitting to our React code. It allows us to send the user only the parts of our code that are needed to view or render the current page. Everything else is excluded, and will be dynamically fetched from the server while the user navigates through our application. The aim of this section is to generate a bundle that's specific to every page or component that we use.

We will begin by installing a few packages that we need to implement this technique. Install them using npm, as follows:

```
npm install --save-dev @babel/plugin-syntax-dynamic-import babel-plugin-dynamic-import-node webpack-node-externals @babel/plugin-transform-runtime
npm install --save react-loadable
```

Let's go through them one by one, in order to understand the purpose of each package:

- The `@babel/plugin-syntax-dynamic-import` package allows you to transpile dynamic import syntax using Babel.
- The `babel-plugin-dynamic-import-node` package implements the same functionality as the previous package, but is specifically targeted at Node.js.
- The `webpack-node-externals` package gives you the option to exclude specific modules while bundling your application with webpack. It reduces the final bundle size.
- The `@babel/plugin-transform-runtime` package is a small plugin that enables us to reuse Babel's helper methods, which usually get inserted into every processed file. It reduces the final bundle size by that.
- The `react-loadable` package is the only package that we do not install in our `devDependencies`. The reason is that our front end (and also the back end) will rely on it to dynamically import our React components.

You will soon learn why we need all of these packages.

The first package that we are going to use is the `react-loadable` package, as it is the central point around which we will adjust our front end and back end.

To allow for the dynamic import of React components, it makes sense to take a look at our current React Router code. Open the `router.js` file in the `client` folder. At the top of the file, you'll see that we directly import all components of our application. However, React Router only renders one of them at a time, as specified by our routes. We will improve this procedure by introducing React Loadable here, in order to load the one component that is required.

Aside from React and React Router, you can replace all `import` statements at the top of the file with the following code:

```
import loadable from 'react-loadable';
import Loading from './components/loading';
const User = loadable({
  loader: () => import('./User'),
  loading: Loading,
});
const Main = loadable({
  loader: () => import('./Main'),
  loading: Loading,
});
const LoginRegisterForm = loadable({
  loader: () => import('./components/loginregister'),
  loading: Loading,
});
```

We import the `react-loadable` package in the preceding code. Using the `loadable` HoC, we can dynamically load a component before rendering it. This allows us to asynchronously import the components, whereas our earlier approach was to directly load all of the components synchronously, without the need for all of them.

We implement this solution for all of the main pages, which are the `User`, the `Main` (the news feed), and the `LoginRegisterForm` components. The `loadable` HoC receives the import statement as an executable function that returns a promise. Until the promise is resolved, the `loading` property is rendering, which is the `Loading` component that we already use when a request ongoing. Instead of using the standard `import ... from ...` syntax, we directly pass the filename to load as a parameter. The result of each `loadable` HoC is saved in a variable that matches the component names in the following `Routing` class.

Now that we have set up `react-loadable` properly, we can adjust the webpack configuration that generates the production build for the front end code. Open the `webpack.client.build.config.js` file. Our production build currently creates one big `bundle.js` file that includes all of our front end code at once. We will change this and split the bundle into multiple small chunks. These will be loaded by React Loadable at the time of rendering a specific component.

Edit the `output` property of the webpack configuration to include the `chunkFilename` field, as follows:

```
output: {
  path: path.join(__dirname, outputDirectory),
  filename: "bundle.js",
  publicPath: '/',
  chunkFilename: '[name].[chunkhash].js'
},
```

The `chunkFilename` field defines how the name of a non-entry chunk file is built. Those files implement specific features, and are not root files from which our application can be started. The preceding code specifies that all chunks are named after the module name of the chunk, following a hash of the chunk content.

To make use of React Loadable, we rely on the `ReactLoadablePlugin` that it provides. Import the following plugin at the top of the file:

```
const { ReactLoadablePlugin } = require('react-loadable/webpack');
```

Since we are using SSR with our application, we can remove the part where we insert our bundle and other files in the HTML template by using the `HtmlWebpackPlugin`. We are going to replace it with the preceding `ReactLoadablePlugin`. Insert the following code, instead of the `HtmlWebpackPlugin`:

```
new ReactLoadablePlugin({
  filename: './dist/react-loadable.json',
}),
```

The `ReactLoadablePlugin` stores all of the information about the bundles that we are going to generate in a JSON file. This file is based on the dynamically imported components that we use in our front end code. This includes information on what modules are found in each bundle. You will learn what we will use this JSON file for later on.

For an application that is not server-rendered, this setup would be almost everything that you have to do. Because we use SSR, we have to adjust our back end to fulfill all of the requirements when using code-splitting for our entire application.

# Code-splitting with SSR

When rendering our application on the server, we have to tell the client which bundles to download on the initial page load. Open the server's `index.js` file to implement this logic. Import the `react-loadable` dependencies at the top of the file, as follows:

```
import Loadable, { Capture } from 'react-loadable';
import { getBundles } from 'react-loadable/webpack';
```

We import the `Loadable` module itself, but also the `Capture` module. The last one is rendered along with your server-rendered application to collect all modules or components that were rendered for the current route that the user is visiting. It allows us to include those bundles along with the initial HTML that our server returns. To let our back end know which bundles exist, we load the previously generated JSON file with the following code. Insert it directly underneath the `import` statements:

```
if(process.env.NODE_ENV !== 'development') {
  var stats = require('../../dist/react-loadable.json');
}
```

The preceding code loads the `react-loadable.json` file if we are in a production environment. In this case, we can expect that it will be saved in the `dist` folder of our application. When using `react-loadable` for server-side rendering, we have to ensure that all dynamically loadable components are loaded before any of them are rendered. There is a `preloadAll` method that the `Loadable` module provides, which can load all of the modules before starting the server for us. Replace the `server.listen` method call in the services `for` loop with the following code:

```
Loadable.preloadAll().then(() => {
  server.listen(process.env.PORT? process.env.PORT:8000, () => {
    console.log('Listening on port '+(process.env.PORT?
    process.env.PORT:8000)+'!');
    services[name](server);
  });
});
```

As you should have noticed, we execute the `Loadable.preloadAll` method, which, when resolved, starts the server. Furthermore, we have replaced our standard port 8000 with an environment variable called `PORT`. If the `PORT` is set, we spawn the back end under this port; otherwise, the standard port 8000 is used. This behavior will be useful in the upcoming sections. When the server has started, we can expect that all components are loaded and ready for rendering.

To reuse the server-side rendered code and declare which modules are being used, we have to edit our `.babelrc` file. Add the following lines of code to the `plugins` section of the `.babelrc` file:

```
"@babel/plugin-syntax-dynamic-import",
"react-loadable/babel"
```

To allow for dynamic imports, we use Babel with the `@babel/plugin-syntax-dynamic-import` plugin. It transpiles our dynamic imports throughout our React code. Furthermore, we use the `react-loadable/babel` plugin to indicate which modules are being used to render the current page, so that we can use the same bundles for the client.

The preparation for the server-side rendering is complete. Now, we have to collect all of the components that are rendered so that we can acquire the correct bundles for the user upon the initial page load. In our `app.get` catch-all Express route, where all SSR requests are processed, we have to add the `Capture` component of React Loadable to our `App` component. Replace the current `App` variable with the following code lines:

```
const modules = [];
const App = (<Capture report={moduleName =>
modules.push(moduleName)}><Graphbook client={client} loggedIn={loggedIn}
location={req.url} context={context}/></Capture>);
```

We have wrapped the `Graphbook` component that we imported earlier with the `Capture` component. Furthermore, we have created a new variable, called `modules`. All `modules` that are used throughout the rendering of our application will be stored there. We pass a small function to the `report` property of the `Capture` component, which executes the regular `push` method to insert the module names to the `modules` array.

Consequently, we have to include those modules with the HTML that we send to the user. The problem is that we have to identify the bundles that include those modules. Consequently, we imported the `getBundles` function from the `react-loadable/webpack` package earlier. The final `renderToStringWithData` function call should look as follows:

```
renderToStringWithData(App).then((content) => {
  if (context.url) {
    res.redirect(301, context.url);
  } else {
    var bundles;
    if(process.env.NODE_ENV !== 'development') {
      bundles = getBundles(stats, Array.from(new Set(modules)));
    } else {
      bundles = [];
    }
```

```
        const initialState = client.extract();
        const head = Helmet.renderStatic();
        res.status(200);
        res.send(`<!doctype html>\n${template(content, head, initialState,
        bundles)}`);
        res.end();
    }
});
```

The first six lines of the `else` case, where we pass the rendered `content` variable to our `template` function, implement the logic to give us the bundle names. We have created a new `bundles` variable. If we are in a development environment, the `bundles` variable is initialized as an empty array.

If we are in a production environment, we use the `getBundles` function. The first parameter is the JSON file that was created by our webpack configuration, using the `ReactLoadablePlugin`. The second parameter of the `getBundles` function is the modules that have been transformed into a one-dimensional array. The result of the `getBundles` function is an array of `bundles` that we have to include with our HTML.

To do so, we pass the final `bundles` array to our `template` function. We have to adjust our `template.js` file from the server's `ssr` folder to accept and render the `bundles` variable. First, change the `template` function's signature to match the following line of code:

```
export default function htmlTemplate(content, head, state, bundles) {
```

We just added the `bundles` as the fourth parameter. Next, we have to include all of the bundles in the HTML. As it is a simple array of objects, we can use the JavaScript `map` function to process all bundles. Insert the following line of code above the `script` tag, with the `bundle.js` file as the `src` attribute:

```
${bundles.map(bundle => `<script
src="${bundle.publicPath}"></script>`).join('\n')}
```

The preceding line loops over all array elements. We return a `script` tag with the public path of the JavaScript `bundle` for each array element so that the browser can download it. The `join` method is used to add a line break after each `script` tag.

The setup looks like it should be finished. However, why do we make a production build of the client-side code, and not the server-side code?

That is a good question. We will change that next. The reason that we should do so is that by bundling our server-side code, we will get rid of unnecessary loading times (when the import statements are processed, for example). Bundling our back end code will improve the performance. To bundle our back end, we are going to set up a new webpack configuration file. Create a `webpack.server.build.config.js` file next to the other webpack files with the following content:

```
const path = require('path');
var nodeExternals = require('webpack-node-externals');
const buildDirectory = 'dist/server';

module.exports = {
  mode: 'production',
  entry: [
    './src/server/index.js'
  ],
  output: {
    path: path.join(__dirname, buildDirectory),
    filename: 'bundle.js',
    publicPath: '/server'
  },
  module: {
    rules: [{
      test: /\.js$/,
      use: {
        loader: 'babel-loader',
        options: {
          plugins: ["@babel/plugin-transform-runtime"]
        }
      },
    }],
  },
  node: {
    __dirname: false,
    __filename: false,
  },
    target: 'node',
    externals: [nodeExternals()],
  plugins: [],
};
```

The preceding configuration file is very simple and not complex. Let's go through all of the settings that we use to configure webpack, as follows:

- We load our new `webpack-node-externals` package at the top.

- The `build` directory, where we save the bundle, is located in the `dist` folder, inside of a special `server` folder.
- The `mode` field is set to `'production'`.
- The `entry` point for webpack is the server's root `index.js` file.
- The `output` property holds the standard fields to bundle our code and save it inside of the folder specified through the `buildDirectory` variable.
- We use the previously installed `@babel/plugin-transform-runtime` plugin in the `module` property to reduce the file size for our bundle.
- Inside of the `node` property, you can set Node.js-specific configuration options. The `__dirname` field tells webpack that the global `__dirname` is used with its default settings, and is not customized by webpack. The same goes for the `__filename` property.
- The `target` field accepts multiple environments in which the generated bundle should work. For our case, we set it to `'node'`, as we want to run our back end in Node.js.
- The `externals` property gives us the possibility to exclude specific dependencies from our bundle. By using the `webpack-node-externals` package, we prevent all `node_modules` from being included in our bundle.

To make use of our new build configuration file, we have to add two new commands to the `scripts` field of our `package.json` file. As we are trying to generate a final production build that we can publicize, we have to build our client-side code in parallel. Add the following two lines to the `scripts` field of the `package.json` file:

```
"build": "npm run client:build && npm run server:build",
"server:build": "webpack --config webpack.server.build.config.js"
```

The `build` command uses the `&&` syntax to chain two `npm run` commands. It executes the build process for our client-side code first, and afterwards, it bundles the entire server-side code. The result is that we have a filled `dist` folder with a `client` and a `server` folder. Both can import components dynamically. To start our server with the new production code, we are going to add one further command to the `scripts` field. The old `npm run server` command would start the server-side code in the unbundled version, which is not what we want. Insert the following line into the `package.json` file:

```
"server:production": "node dist/server/bundle.js"
```

The preceding command simply executes the `bundle.js` file from the `dist/server` folder, using the plain `node` command to launch our back end.

Now, you should be able to generate your final build by running `npm run build`. Before starting the production server as a test, however, make sure that you have set all of the environment variables for your database correctly, or your `JWT_SECRET`, for example. Then, you can execute the `npm run server:production` command to launch the back end.

Because we have changed the way that our back end and front end load components, we have to adapt these changes to our development and testing commands. When trying to rerun them, the main problem is that the dynamic imports and React Loadable functionality are not supported.

Replace our `npm run server` command with the following line, in the `package.json` file:

```
"server": "nodemon --exec babel-node --plugins require-context-
hook,dynamic-import-node --watch src/server src/server/index.js",
```

The preceding command has one more plugin, which is the `dynamic-import-node` package. For our test, the only thing that we have to change is the `babel-hook.js` file to let Babel transpile everything correctly. Add the following plugins to the `babel-hook.js` file:

```
"react-loadable/babel", "dynamic-import-node"
```

Our test runs in the production environment, because only then can we verify that all features that are enabled in the live environment work correctly. Because we have just introduced React Loadable, which generates a JSON file when building the client-side code, we have to run a full build when we are testing our application. Edit the `test` command of the `package.json` file to reflect this change, as follows:

```
"test": "npm run build && mocha --exit test/ --require babel-hook --require
@babel/polyfill --recursive",
```

Now, you should be able to test your application again.

This entire setup allows us to render your complete application, but instead of one big bundle, we only load the chunks that are required to render the current page that's shown to the user. When a user navigates to a new page, only the chunks that are required are fetched from the server.

For the development environment, we stick with a simple setup, and we only include the `bundle.js` file. If necessary, the code that's included with the bundle will load all of the other files.

In the next section, we will cover how to use Docker to bundle your entire application.

# Setting up Docker

Publishing an application is a critical step that requires a lot of work and care. Many things can go wrong when releasing a new version.

We have already made sure that we can test our application before it goes live. After deployment, we will have Apollo Engine, which will inform us about anything that goes well and anything that goes wrong.

The real act of transforming our local files into a production-ready package, which is then uploaded to a server, is the most onerous task. Regular applications generally rely on a server that is preconfigured with all the packages that the application needs to run. For example, when looking at a standard PHP setup, most people rent a preconfigured server. This means that the PHP runtime, with all of the extensions, like the MySQL PHP library, are installed via the built-in package manager of the operating system. This procedure applies not only to PHP, but also to nearly any other programming language. This might be okay for general websites or applications that are not too complex, but for professional software development or deployment, this process can lead to issues, such as the following:

- The configuration needs to be done by someone that knows the requirements of the application, and the server itself.
- A second server needs the same configuration, in order to allow our application to run. While doing that configuration, we must ensure that all servers are standardized and consistent with one another.
- All of the servers have to be reconfigured when the runtime environment gets an update, either because the application requires it, or due to other reasons, such as security updates. In this case, everything must be tested again.
- Multiple applications running inside of the same server environment may require different package versions, or may interfere with each other.
- The deployment process must be executed by someone with the required knowledge.
- Starting an application directly on a server exposes it to all services running on your server. Other processes could take over your complete application, since they run within the same environment.
- Also, the application is not limited to using a specified maximum of the server's resources.

Many people have tried to figure out how to avoid these consequences by introducing a new containerization and deployment workflow.

# What is Docker?

One major trending price of software is called Docker. It was released in 2013, and its aim is at isolating the application within a container by offering its own runtime environment, without having access to the server itself.

The aim of a container is to isolate the application from the operating system of the server.

Standard virtual machines can also accomplish this by running a guest operating system for the application. Inside of the virtual machine, all packages and runtimes can be installed to prepare it for your application. This solution comes with significant overhead, of course, because we are running a second operating system that's just for our application. It is not scalable when many services or multiple applications are involved.

On the other hand, Docker containers work entirely differently. The application itself, and all of its dependencies, receive a segment of the operating system's resources. All processes are isolated by the host system inside of those resources.

Any server supporting the container runtime environment (which is Docker) can run your dockerized application. The great thing is that the actual operating system is abstracted away. Your operating system will be very slim, as nothing more than the kernel and Docker is required.

With Docker, the developer can specify how the container image is composed. They can directly test and deploy those images on their infrastructure.

To see the process and advantages that Docker provides, we are going to build a container image that includes our application and all of the dependencies it needs to run.

# Installing Docker

Like any virtualization software, Docker has to be installed via the regular package manager of your operating system.

I will assume that you are using a Debian-based system. If this is not the case, please get the correct instructions for your system at `https://docs.docker.com/install/overview/`.

Continue with the following instructions to get Docker up and running:

1. Update your system's package manager, as follows:

```
sudo apt-get update
```

2. Install all of the dependencies for Docker, as follows:

```
sudo apt-get install apt-transport-https ca-certificates curl
gnupg2 software-properties-common
```

3. Verify and add the **GNU Privacy Guard** (**GPG**) key for the Docker repository, as follows:

```
curl -fsSL https://download.docker.com/linux/debian/gpg | sudo apt-
key add -
```

   If you are using Ubuntu, add the separate GPG key from the official Docker documentation, or just replace the word `debian` with `ubuntu` in the preceding URL.

4. Now that the GPG key has been imported, we can add the repository to the package manager, as follows:

```
sudo add-apt-repository "deb [arch=amd64]
https://download.docker.com/linux/debian $(lsb_release -cs) stable"
```

   Again, if you use Ubuntu, please add the repository made for Ubuntu by replacing the word `debian` with `ubuntu`.

5. After adding the new repository, you must update the package manager's index again, as follows:

```
sudo apt-get update
```

6. Lastly, we can install the Docker package to our system, as follows:

```
sudo apt-get install docker-ce
```

   The `docker-ce` package stands for **Docker Community Edition**. There are two further versions, which include more features, but which are also meant for bigger teams. You can look at what makes them different from the Community Edition in the installation overview of the Docker documentation.

That's everything that is required to get a working copy of Docker on your system.

Next, you will learn how to use Docker by building your first Docker container image.

# Dockerizing your application

Many companies have adopted Docker and replaced their old infrastructure setup, thereby largely reducing system administration. Still, there is some work to do before deploying your application straight to production.

One primary task is to dockerize your application. The term **dockerize** means that you take care of wrapping your application inside of a valid Docker container.

There are many service providers that connect Docker with continuous integration or continuous deployment, because they work well together. In the last section of this chapter, you will learn what continuous deployment is, and how it can be implemented. We are going to rely on such a service provider. It will provide us with an automatic workflow for our continuous deployment process. As this book should teach you how to dockerize your application without relying on too many third parties, we are going to implement it in the official Docker way.

## Writing your first Dockerfile

The conventional approach to generating a Docker image of your application is to create a `Dockerfile` in the root of your project. But what does the `Dockerfile` stand for?

A `Dockerfile` is a series of commands that are run through the Docker CLI. The typical workflow in such a file looks as follows:

1. A `Dockerfile` starts from a base image, which is imported using the `FROM` command. This base image may include a runtime environment, like Node.js, or other things that your project can make use of. The container images are downloaded from the Docker Hub, which is a central container registry that you can find at `https://hub.docker.com/`. There is the option to download the images from custom registries, too.
2. Then, Docker offers many commands to interact with the image and your application code. Those commands can be looked up at `https://docs.docker.com/engine/reference/builder/`.
3. After the configuration of the image has finished and all of the build steps are complete, you will need to provide a command that will be executed when your application's Docker container starts.

4. The result of all of the build steps will be a new docker image. The image is saved on the machine where it was generated.
5. Optionally, you can now publish your new image to a registry, where other applications or users can pull your image. You can also upload them as private images or private registries.

We will start by generating a really simple Docker image. First, create the `Dockerfile` inside of the root of your project. The filename is written without any file extensions.

The first task is to find a matching base image that we can use for our project. The criteria by which we choose a base image are the dependencies and runtime environment. As we have mainly used Node.js without relying on any other server-side package that needs to be covered from our Docker container, we only need to find a base image that provides Node.js. For the moment, we will ignore the database, and we'll focus on it again in a later step.

Docker Hub is the official container image registry, providing many minimalistic images. Just insert the following line inside of our new `Dockerfile`, in the root of our project:

```
FROM node:10
```

As we mentioned before, we use the `FROM` command to download our base image. As the name of the preceding image states, it includes Node.js in version 10. There are numerous other versions that you can use. Beyond the different versions, you can also find different flavors (for example, a Node.js based on an Alpine Linux image). Take a look at the image's `readme` to get an overview of the available options, at `https://hub.docker.com/_/node/`.

I recommend that you read through the reference documentation of the `Dockerfile`. Many advanced commands and scenarios are explained there, which will help you to customize your Docker workflow. Just go to `https://docs.docker.com/engine/reference/builder/`.

After Docker has run the `FROM` command, you will be working directly within this base image, and all further commands will then run inside of this environment. You can access all of the features that the underlying operating system provides. Of course, the features are limited by the image that you have chosen. A `Dockerfile` is only valid if it starts with the `FROM` command.

The next step for our `Dockerfile` is to create a new folder, in which the application will be stored and run. Add the following line to the `Dockerfile`:

```
WORKDIR /usr/src/app
```

The `WORKDIR` command changes the directory to the specified path. The path that you enter lives inside of the filesystem of the image, which does not affect your computer's filesystem. From then on, the Docker commands `RUN`, `CMD`, `ENTRYPOINT`, `COPY`, and `ADD` will be executed in the new working directory. Furthermore, the `WORKDIR` command will create the new folder, if it does not exist yet.

Next, we need to get our application's code inside of the new folder. Until now, we have only made sure that the base image was loaded. The image that we are generating at the moment does not include our application yet. Docker provides a command to move our code into the final image.

As the third line of our `Dockerfile`, add the following code:

```
COPY . .
```

The `COPY` command accepts two parameters. The first one is the source, which can be a file or folder. The second parameter is the destination path inside of the image's filesystem. You can use a subset of regular expressions to filter the files or folders that you copy.

After Docker has executed the preceding command, all contents living in the current directory will be copied over to the `/usr/src/app` path. The current directory, in this case, is the root of our project folder. All of the files are now automatically inside of the final Docker image. You can interact with the files through all Docker commands, but also with the commands the shell provides.

One important task is that we install all of the npm packages that our application relies on. When running the `COPY` command, like in the preceding code, all of the files and folders are transferred, including the `node_modules` folder. This could lead to problems when trying to run the application, however. Many `npm` packages are compiled when they are being installed, or they differentiate between operating systems. We must make sure that the packages that we use are clean, and work in the environment that we want them to work in. We must do two things to accomplish this, as follows:

1. Create a `.dockerignore` file in the root of the project folder, next to the `Dockerfile`, and enter the following content:

```
node_modules
package-lock.json
```

The `.dockerignore` file is comparable to the `.gitignore` file, which excludes special files or folders from being tracked by Git. Docker reads the `.dockerignore` file before all files are sent to the Docker daemon. If it is able to read a valid `.dockerignore`, all specified files or folders are excluded. The preceding two lines exclude the whole `node_modules` folder and the `package-lock.json` file. The last one is critical, because the exact versions of all npm packages are saved in this file.

2. Install the npm packages inside of the Docker image that we are creating at the moment. Add the following line of code to the `Dockerfile`:

   ```
   RUN npm install
   ```

   The `RUN` command executes `npm install` inside of the current working directory. The related `package.json` file and `node_modules` folder are stored in the file system of the Docker image. Those files are directly committed, and are included in the final image. Docker's `RUN` command sends the command that we pass as the first parameter into the Bash and executes it. To avoid the problems of spaces in the shell commands, or other syntax problems, you can pass the command as an array of strings, which will be transformed by Docker into valid Bash syntax. Through `RUN`, you can interact with other system-level tools (like `apt-get` or `curl`, for example).

Now that all of the files and dependencies are in the correct filesystem, we can start Graphbook from our new Docker image. Before doing so, there are two things that we need to do: we have to allow for external access to the container via the IP, and define what the container should do when it has started.

Graphbook uses port `8000` by default, under which it listens for incoming requests, be it a GraphQL or a normal web request. When running a Docker container, it receives its own network, with IP and ports. We must make port 8000 available to the public, not only inside of the container itself. Insert the following line at the end of the `Dockerfile` to make the port accessible from outside of the container:

```
EXPOSE 8000
```

It is essential that you understand that the `EXPOSE` command does not map the inner port `8000` from the container to the matching port of our working machine. By writing the `EXPOSE` command, you give the developer using the image the option to publish port `8000` to any port of the real machine running the container. The mapping is done while starting the container, not when building the image. Later in this chapter, we will look at how to map port `8000` to a port of your local machine.

Finally, we have to tell Docker what our container should do once it has booted. In our case, we want to start our back end (including SSR, of course). Since this should be a simple example, we will start the development server.

Add the last line of the `Dockerfile`, as follows:

```
CMD [ "npm", "run", "server" ]
```

The `CMD` command defines the way that our container is booted, and which command to run. We are using the `exec` option of Docker to pass an array of strings. A `Dockerfile` can only have one `CMD` command. The `exec` format does not run a Bash or shell command when using `CMD`.

The container executes the `server` script of our `package.json` file, which has been copied into the Docker image.

At this point, everything is finished and prepared to generate a basic Docker image. Next, we will continue with getting a container up and running.

# Building and running Docker containers

The `Dockerfile` and `.dockerignore` files are ready. Docker provides us with the tools to generate a real image, which we can run or share with others. Having a `Dockerfile` on its own does not make an application dockerized.

Make sure that the database credentials specified in the `/server/config/index.js` file for the back end are valid for development, because they are statically saved there. Furthermore, the MySQL host must allow for remote connections from inside the container.

Execute the following command to build the Docker image on your local machine:

```
docker build -t sgrebe/graphbook .
```

This command requires you to have the Docker CLI and daemon installed.

The first option that we use is `-t`, following a string (in our case, `sgrebe/graphbook`). The finished build will be saved under the username `sgrebe` and the application name `graphbook`. This text is also called a `tag`. The only required parameter of the `docker build` command is the build context, or the set of files that Docker will use for the container. We specified the current directory as the build context by adding the dot at the end of the command. Furthermore, the `build` action expects the `Dockerfile` to be located within this folder. If you want the file to be taken from somewhere else, you can specify it with the `--file` option.

If the `docker build` command fails, it may be that some environment variables are missing. They usually include the IP and port of the Docker daemon. To look them up, execute the `docker-machine env` command, and set the environment variables as returned by the command.

When the command has finished generating the image, it should be available locally. To prove this, you can use the Docker CLI by running the following command:

```
docker images
```

The output from Docker should look as follows:

```
REPOSITORY          TAG         IMAGE ID        CREATED           SIZE
sgrebe/graphbook    latest      fe30bceb0268    27 minutes ago    1.22GB
node                10          75a3a4428e1d    3 days ago        894MB
```

You should see two containers; the first one is the `sgrebe/graphbook` container image, or whatever you used as a tag name. The second one should be the `node` image, which we used as the base for our custom Docker image. The size of the custom image should be much higher, because we installed all npm packages.

Now, we should be able to start our Docker container with this new image. The following command will launch your Docker container:

```
docker run -p 8000:8000 -d --env-file .env sgrebe/graphbook
```

The `docker run` command also has only one required parameter, which is the image to start the container with. In our case, this is `sgrebe/graphbook`, or whatever you specified as a tag name. Still, we define some optional parameters that we need to get our application working. You can find an explanation of each of them, as follows:

- We set the `-p` option to `8000:8000`. The parameter is used to map ports from the actual host operating system to a specific port inside of the Docker container. The first port is the port of the host machine, and the second one is the port of the container. This option gives us access to the exposed port 8000, where the application is running under the `http://localhost:8000` of our local machine.
- The `--env-file` parameter is required to pass environment variables to the container. Those can be used to hand over the `NODE_ENV` or `JWT_SECRET` variables, for example, which we require throughout our application. We will create this file in a second.

- You can also pass the environment variables one by one using the `-e` option. It is much easier to provide a file, however.
- The `-d` option sets the container to **detached mode**. This means that your container will not run in the foreground after executing it inside the shell. Instead, after running the command, you will have access to the shell again, and will see no output from the container. If you remove the option again, you will see all of the logs that our application triggers.

The `docker run` command provides many more options. It allows for various advanced setups. The link to the official documentation is `https://docs.docker.com/engine/reference/run/#general-form`.

Let's create the `.env` file in the root directory of our project. Insert the following content, replacing all placeholders with the correct value for every environment variable:

```
ENGINE_KEY=YOUR_APLLO_ENGINE_API_KEY
NODE_ENV=development
JWT_SECRET=YOUR_JWT_SECRET
AWS_ACCESS_KEY_ID=YOUR_AWS_KEY_ID
AWS_SECRET_ACCESS_KEY=YOUR_AWS_SECRET_ACCESS_KEY
```

The `.env` file is a simple key-value list, where you can specify one variable per line, which our application can access from its environment variables.

It is vital that you do not commit this file to the public at any stage. Please add this file directly to the `.gitignore` file.

If you have filled out this file, you will be able to start the Docker container with the previous command that I showed you. Now that the container is running in the detached mode, you will have the problem that you cannot be sure whether Graphbook has started to listen. Consequently, Docker also provides a command to test this, as follows:

```
docker ps
```

The `docker ps` command gives you a list of all running containers. You should find the Graphbook container in there, too. The output should appear as follows:

```
CONTAINER ID   IMAGE              COMMAND              CREATED          STATUS         PORTS                    NAMES
08499322a998   sgrebe/graphbook   "npm run server"     4 seconds ago    Up 3 seconds   0.0.0.0:8000->8000/tcp   dreamy_knuth
```

Like all commands that Docker provides, the `docker ps` command gives us many options to customize and filter the output. Read up on all of the features that it offers in the official documentation at `https://docs.docker.com/engine/reference/commandline/ps/`.

Our container is running, and it uses the database that we have specified. You should be able to use Graphbook as you know it by visiting `http://localhost:8000`.

If you take a look at the preceding image, you will see that all running containers receive their own ids. This id can be used in various situations to interact with the container.

In development, it makes sense to have access to the command-line printouts that our application generates. When running the container in the detached mode, you have to use the Docker CLI to see the printouts, using the following command. Replace the id at the end of the command with the id of your container:

```
docker logs 08499322a998
```

The `docker logs` command will show you all of the printouts that have been made by our application or container recently. Replace the preceding id with the one given to you by the `docker ps` command. If you want to see the logs in real time, while using Graphbook, you can add the `--follow` option.

As we are running the container in the detached mode, you will not be able to stop it by just using *Ctrl* + *C*, like before. Instead, you have to use the Docker CLI again.

To stop the container again, run the following command:

```
docker rm 08499322a998
```

The `docker rm` command stops and removes the container from the system. Any changes made to the filesystem inside of the container will be lost. If you start the image again, a new container will be created, with a clean filesystem. Alternatively, you can also use the `stop` command instead, which only shuts down the container.

When working and developing with Docker frequently, you will probably generate many images to test and verify the deployment of your application. These take up a lot of space on your local machine. To remove the images, you can execute the following command:

```
docker rmi fe30bceb0268
```

The id can be taken from the `docker images` command, the output of which you can see in the first image in this section. You can only remove an image if it is not used in a running container.

We have come far. We have successfully dockerized our application. However, it is still running in development mode, so there is a lot to do.

# Multi-stage Docker production builds

Our current Docker image, which we are creating from the `Dockerfile`, is already useful. We want our application to be transpiled and running in production mode, because many things are not optimized for the public when running in development mode.

Obviously, we have to run our build scripts for the back end and front end while generating the Docker image.

Up until now, we have installed all npm packages and copied all files and folders for our project to the container image. This is fine for development, because this image is not published or deployed to a production environment. When going live with your application, you will want your image to be as slim and efficient as possible. To achieve this, we will use a so-called **multi-stage build**.

Before Docker implemented the functionality to allow for multi-stage builds, you had to rely on tricks, like using shell commands to only keep the files that were really required in the container image. The problem that we have is that we copy all of the files that are used to build the actual distribution code from the project folder. Those files are not needed in the production Docker container, however.

Let's see how this looks in reality. You can back up or remove the first `Dockerfile` that we wrote, as we will start with a blank one now. The new file still needs to be called `Dockerfile`. All of the following lines of code go directly into this empty `Dockerfile`. Follow these instructions to get the multi-stage production build running:

1. Our new file starts with the `FROM` command again. We are going to have multiple `FROM` statements, because we are preparing a multi-stage build. The first one should look as follows:

   ```
   FROM node:10 AS build
   ```

We are introducing the first build stage here. Like before, we are using the `node` image in version 10. Furthermore, we append the `AS build` suffix, which tells Docker that this stage, or everything that we do in it, will be accessible under the name `build` later on. A new stage is started with every new `FROM` command.

2. Next, we initialize the working directory, like we did in our first `Dockerfile`, as follows:

```
WORKDIR /usr/src/app
```

3. It is essential to only copy the files that we really need. It hugely improves the performance if you reduce the amount of data/files that need to be processed:

```
COPY .babelrc ./
COPY package*.json ./
COPY webpack.server.build.config.js ./
COPY webpack.client.build.config.js ./
COPY src src
COPY assets assets
```

We copy the `.babelrc`, `package.json`, `package-lock.json`, and webpack files that are required for our application. These include all of the information we need to generate a production build for the front end and back end. Furthermore, we also copy the `src` and `assets` folders, because they include the code and CSS that will be transpiled and bundled.

4. Like in our first `Dockerfile`, we must install all npm packages; otherwise, our application won't work. We do this with the following line of code:

```
RUN npm install
```

5. After we have copied all of the files and installed all of the packages, we can start the production build. Before doing so, it would make sense to run our automated test. Add the test script to the `Dockerfile`, as follows:

```
ENV NODE_ENV production
ENV JWT_SECRET YOUR_SECRET
ENV username YOUR_USERNAME
ENV password YOUR_PASSWORD
ENV database YOUR_DATABASE
ENV host YOUR_HOST
RUN npm install -g mysql2 sequelize sequelize-cli
RUN sequelize db:migrate --migrations-path src/server/migrations --
config src/server/config/index.js --env production
RUN npm run test
```

We use the `ENV` command from Docker to fill the environment variables while building the image. This is needed to run our test, because this way, we can add the required variables, such as `NODE_ENV` and `JWT_SECRET`.

Before running a test, we have to migrate all database changes to the test database. We do this by installing Sequelize and using the `db:migrate` feature. You will see this command again later.

We are running our Mocha test, as we did before. The good thing here is that every time our application gets dockerized, the test will run automatically. If the test fails, the error will bubble up, and the complete build will fail. We will never launch the application if a test fails.

6. After all packages have been installed successfully, we can start the build process. We added the `build` script in the first section of this chapter. Add the following line to execute the script that will generate the production bundles in the Docker image:

```
RUN npm run build
```

The following command will generate a `dist` folder for us, where the runnable code (including CSS) will be stored. After the `dist` folder with all of the bundles has been created, we will no longer need most of the files that we initially copied over to the current build stage.

7. To get a clean Docker image that only contains the `dist` folder and the files that we need to run the application, we will introduce a new build stage that will generate the final image. The new stage is started with a second `FROM` statement, as follows:

```
FROM node:10
```

We are building the final image in this build step; therefore, it does not need its own name.

8. Again, we need to specify the working directory for the second stage, as the path is not copied from the first build stage:

```
WORKDIR /usr/src/app
```

9. Because we have given our first build stage a name, we can access the filesystem of this stage through that name. To copy the files from the first stage, we can add a parameter to the `COPY` statement. Add the following commands to the `Dockerfile`:

   ```
   COPY --from=build /usr/src/app/package.json package.json
   COPY --from=build /usr/src/app/dist dist
   ```

   As you should see in the preceding code, we are copying the `package.json` file and the `dist` folder. However, instead of copying the files from our original project folder, we are getting those files directly from the first build stage. For this, we use the `--from` option, following the name of the stage that we want to access; so, we enter the name `build`. The `package.json` file is needed because it includes all of the dependencies, and also the `scripts` field, which holds the information on how to run the application in production. The `dist` folder is, of course, our bundled application.

10. Notice that we only copy the `package.json` file and the `dist` folder. Our npm dependencies are not included in the application build inside of the `dist` folder. As a result, we need to install the `npm` packages in the second build stage, too:

    ```
    RUN npm install --only=production
    ```

    The production image should only hold npm packages that are really required; npm offers the `only` parameter, which lets you install only the production packages, as an example. It will exclude all of the `devDependecies` of your `package.json` file. This is really great for keeping your image size low.

11. The last two things to do here are to expose the container port to the public and to execute the `CMD` command, which will let the image run a command of our `package.json` file when the container has booted:

    ```
    EXPOSE 8000
    CMD [ "npm", "run", "server:production" ]
    ```

    You should have seen both of these commands in our first `Dockerfile`. The only difference is that we execute the `server:production` command from our `package.json` file. This will start our bundled application from the `dist` folder of the final image.

Now, you can execute the `docker build` command again, and try to start the container. There is only one problem: the database credentials are read from the environment variables when running in production. As the production setup for a database cannot be on our local machine, it needs to live somewhere on a real server. We could also accomplish this through Docker, but this would involve a very advanced Docker configuration. We would need to save the MySQL data in separate storage, because Docker does not persist data of any kind, by default.

I personally like to rely on a cloud host, which handles all of the database setup for me. It is not only great for the overall setup, but it also improves the scalability of our application. The next section will cover the Amazon Relational Database Service, and how to configure it for use with our application. You can, of course, use any database infrastructure that you like.

# Amazon Relational Database Service

AWS offers the Amazon **Relation Database Service (RDS)**, which is an easy tool for setting up a relational database in just a few clicks. Shortly, I will explain how to create your first database with RDS, and afterwards, we will look at how to insert environment variables correctly, in order to get a database connection going with our application.

The first step is to log in to the AWS Console, like we did in `Chapter 7`, *Handling Image Uploads*. You can find the service by clicking on the **Services** tab in the top bar and searching for `RDS`.

After navigating to **RDS**, you will see the dashboard for the Relational Database Service, as shown in the following screenshot:

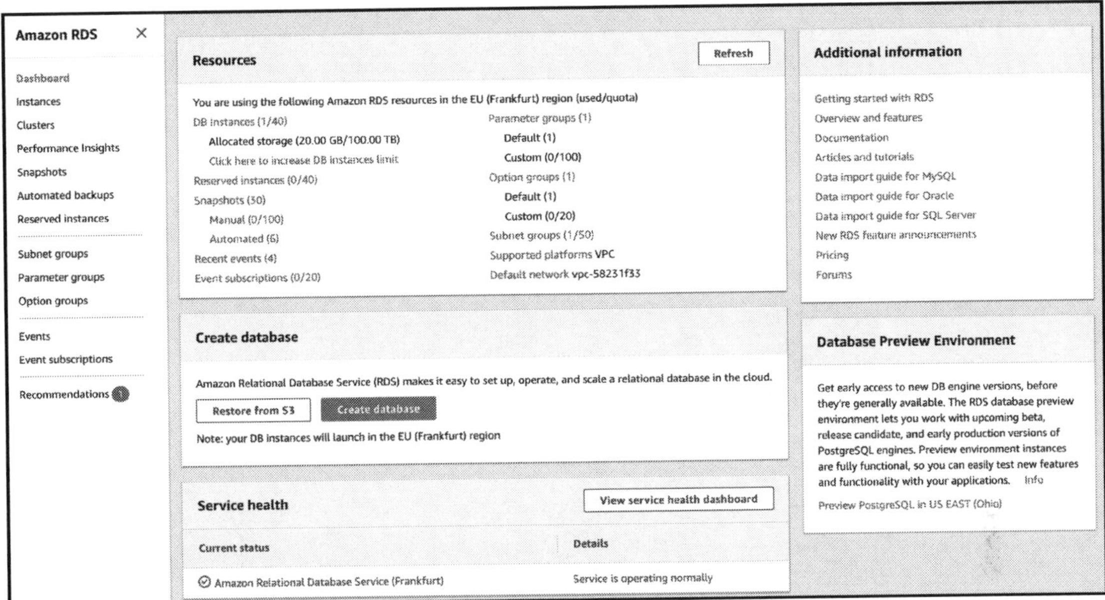


The first step is to initialize a new database by hitting the **Create database** button. You will be presented with a new screen, where you should select an engine for our new database. I recommend that you select **MySQL** here. You should also be able to select **Amazon Aurora** or **MariaDB**, as they are also MySQL compatible; for this book, I have chosen MySQL. Continue by clicking **Next**.

Then, you will need to specify the use case for your database. Both of the production options are very good for live applications, but generate real costs. Please be aware that this should only be used when going public with your application, and when you are able to pay the fees for the service.

If you want to try Amazon RDS, you can choose the third option, which should be the **Dev MySQL** database. In this case, it is not a production-ready database, but you will notice the advantages of a database inside of the cloud, anyway. For your first test, I recommend that you go on with this selection. Continue by clicking **Next**.

You will be asked for the database specification details. The first part of the screen will look as follows:

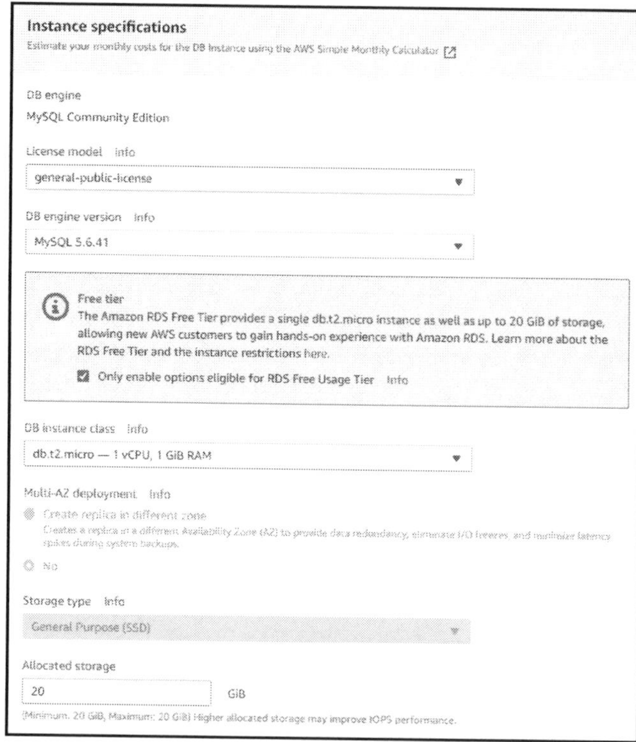


Make sure that you choose the same settings that are shown in the preceding screenshot. If you only want to use the free tier of Amazon, select the checkbox in the blue alert box. This option will set the **DB instance class** to **micro**, and the allocated storage amount to **20 GiB**, fixed.

Below the instance specifications, you have to enter the credential settings for your database. The credentials consist of a database identifier, a username, and a password. The database identifier must be unique to your AWS account. You will need to insert those credentials into the environment variables later on. You can continue by hitting **Next** again.

You will now be asked for advanced settings. The only thing that you need to specify is the database name, in the **Database options** box. It is important that you select **Public accessibility,** with **Yes** checked. This does not share your database to the public, but makes it accessible from other IPs and other EC2 instances, if you select them in your AWS Security Group. Finish the setup process for your first AWS RDS database by clicking on **Create database** at the bottom of the screen.

You should now be redirected to the dashboard of the new database instance.

Inside of the **Connect** box, you can find the security groups that have been applied to the instance. Click on the group with the type **CIDR/IP - Inbound**.

You will see a list of security groups and a small view with some tabs at the top, as follows:

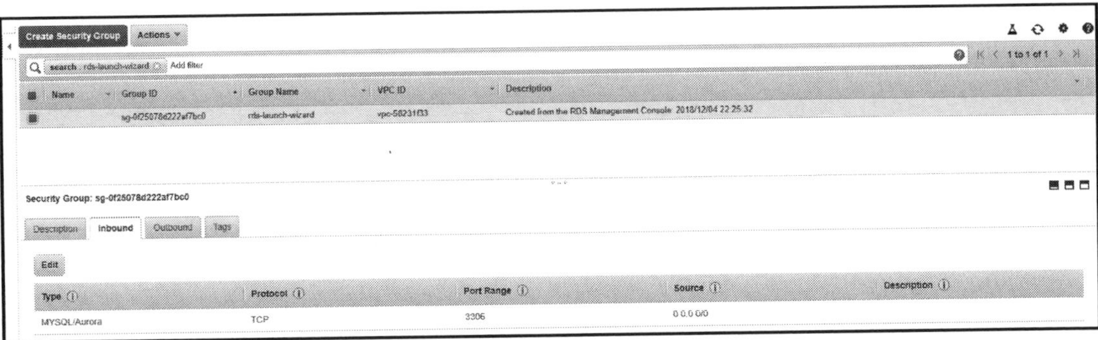

In the preceding screenshot, you can see how the security groups for your new database should look. At the bottom of the window, inside of the small view, select the **Inbound** tab. There, you will be able to insert the IP that is allowed to access the database. If you insert the `0.0.0.0` IP, it will allow any remote IP to access the database. This is not a recommended database setup for production use, but it makes it easier to test it with multiple environments in developmental use.

The credentials that you have specified for the database must be included in the `.env` file for running our Docker container, as follows:

```
username=YOUR_USERNAME
password=YOUR_PASSWORD
database=YOUR_DATABASE
host=YOUR_HOST
```

The `host` URL can be taken from the Amazon RDS instance dashboard. It should look something like `INSTANCE_NAME.xxxxxxxxxx.eu-central-1.rds.amazonaws.com`.

Now, you should be able to run the build for your Docker image again, without any problems. The database has been set up and is available.

If the test runs through, it will create a new user, as we have specified this in the Mocha test file. The user will be inserted into the database that has been set in the `Dockerfile`, via the `ENV` command. You have to ensure that this database is cleaned after each test is run; otherwise, the second test will fail, because we are trying to create a new user that already exists after running the test for the first time. By using the `ENV` commands, we can set a special test database that will be used while generating the Docker image.

Next, we will look at how we can automate the process of generating the Docker image through continuous integration.

# Configuring Continuous Integration

Many people (especially developers) will have heard of **continuous integration** (**CI**) or **continuous deployment** (**CD**). However, most of them cannot explain their meanings and the differences between the two terms. So, what is continuous integration and deployment, in reality?

When it comes to going live with your application, it might seem easy to upload some files to a server and then start the application through a simple command in the shell, via SSH.

This approach might be a solution for many developers, or for small applications that are not updated often. For most scenarios, it is not a good approach, however. The word **continuous** represents the fact that all changes or updates are continuously reflected by our application to the user. This would be a lot of work, and it would be tough to do if we stayed with a simple file upload and took a manual approach. Automating this workflow makes it convenient to update your application at any time.

Continuous integration is the development practice where all developers commit their code to the central project repository at least once a day to bring their changes to the mainline stream of code. The integrated code will be verified by automated test cases. This will avoid problems when trying to go live at a specific time.

Continuous deployment goes further; it's based on the main principles of continuous integration. Every time the application is successfully built and tested, the changes are directly released to the customer. This is what we are going to implement.

Our automation process will be based on CircleCI. It is a third-party service offering a continuous integration and delivery platform, with a massive amount of features.

To sign up for CircleCI, visit `https://circleci.com/signup/`.

You will need to have a Bitbucket or GitHub account in order to sign up. This will also be the source from which the repositories of your application will be taken, for which we can begin using CI or CD.

To get your project running with CircleCI, you will need to click on the **Add Projects** button in the left-hand panel, or you will be redirected there because you have no projects setup yet. After signing up, you should see all of your repositories inside of CircleCI.

Select the project that you want to process with CircleCI by hitting **Set up Project** on the right-hand side of the project. You will then be confronted with the following screenshot:

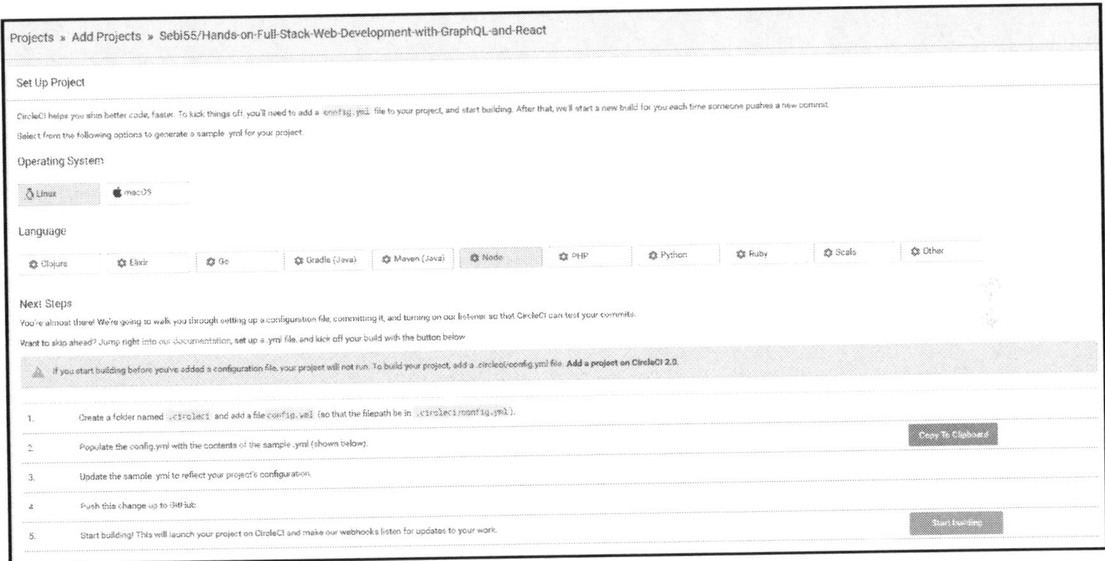


Select the **Operating System** as **Linux** and the **Language** as **Node**. The final step will be to hit the **Start building** button at the bottom of the window.

The problem is that you have not configured your repository or application accordingly. You are required to create a folder called `.circleci`, and a file inside of it, called `config.yml`, which tells CircleCI what to do when a new commit is pushed to the repository.

We will create a straightforward first CircleCI configuration so that we can test that everything is working. The final configuration will be done at a later step, when we have configured Heroku.

So, create a `.circleci` folder in the root of our project and a `config.yml` file inside of this new folder. The `.yml` file extension stands for YAML, which is a file format for saving various configurations or data. What is important here is that all `.yml` files need a correct indentation. Otherwise, they will not be valid files, and cannot be understood by CircleCI.

Insert the following code into the `config.yml` file:

```
version: 2
jobs:
  build:
    docker:
      - image: circleci/node:10
    steps:
      - checkout
      - setup_remote_docker:
          docker_layer_caching: true
      - run:
          command: echo "This is working"
```

Let's quickly go through all of the steps in the file, as follows:

1. The file starts with a `version` specification. We are using version 2, as this is the current version of CircleCI.
2. Then, we will have a list of `jobs` that get executed in parallel. As we only have one thing that we want to do, we can only see the `build` job that we are running. Later, we will add the whole docker build and publish the functionality here.
3. Each job receives an executor type, which needs to be `machine`, `docker`, or `macos`. We are using the `docker` type, because we can rely on many prebuilt images of CircleCI. The image is specified in a separate `image` property. There, I have specified `node` in version 10, because we need Node.js for our CI workflow.
4. Each job then receives a number of steps that are executed with every commit that is pushed to the Git repository.
5. The first step is the `checkout` command, which clones the current version of our repository, so that we can use it in any further steps.
6. The second `setup_remote_docker` command will create a remote environment, in which we can run docker commands, like `docker build`. We will use this later, when we are building our application automatically. The `docker_layer_caching` property enables the caching of each Docker command that we run. This will make our build time much faster, because we are saving each layer or command that we run through Docker. Only the Docker commands are executed, which follow a change in the `Dockerfile`.

7. Lastly, to test that everything has worked, we use the `run` step. It lets us execute a command directly in the Docker `node:10` image that we have started with CircleCI. Each command that you want to execute must be prefixed with `command`.

The result of this config file should be that we have pulled the current master branch of our application and printed the text `This is working` at the end. To test the CircleCI setup, commit and push this file to your GitHub or Bitbucket repository.

CircleCI should automatically notify you that it has started a new **continuous integration** job for our repository. You can find the job by hitting the **Jobs** button in the left-hand panel of CircleCI. The newest job should be at the top of the list. Click on the job to see the details. They should look as follows:

In the preceding screenshot, each step is represented in a separate row, at the bottom of the window. You can expand each row to see the logs that printed while executing the specific command shown in the current row. The preceding screenshot shows that the job has been successful.

Now that we have configured CircleCI to process our repository on each push, we must take a look at how to host and deploy our application directly, after finishing the build.

# Deploying applications to Heroku

CircleCI executes our build steps each time we push a new commit. Now, we want to build our Docker image and deploy it automatically to a machine that will serve our application to the public.

Our database and files are hosted on Amazon Web Services already, so we could also use AWS to serve our application. The problem is that setting up AWS correctly is a significant task, and it takes a large amount of time. We could use AWS ECS or EC2 to run our Docker image. Still, to correctly set up the network, security, and container registry is too complex to be explained in just one chapter. I recommend that you take a course or pick up a separate book, to understand and learn advanced setups with AWS, and the configuration that is needed to get a production-ready hosting.

We will use Heroku to host and deploy our application, as it is much more user-friendly and easier to set up. To get started, you must sign up for a free Heroku account. You can do this at `https://signup.heroku.com/`.

After logging in, you will be redirected to the apps list for Heroku, as shown in the following screenshot:

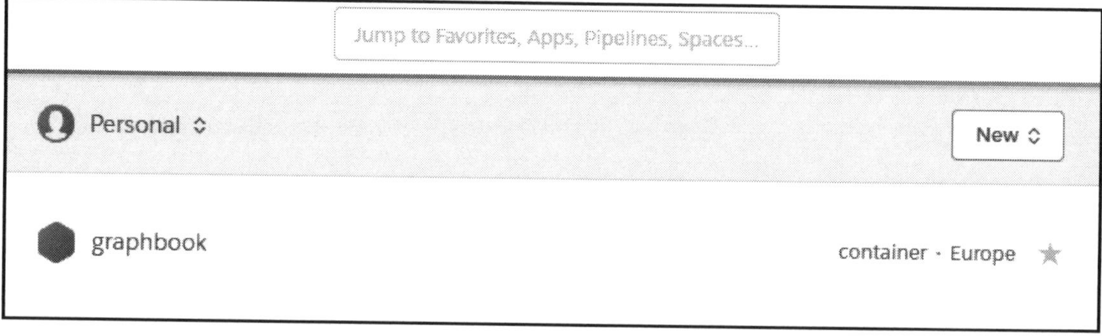


As you can see, I have already created an app called **graphbook**. You should do so, too, by hitting the **New** button in the top-right corner, and then clicking on **Create new app**.

You will be asked for the name of your application. The name of the application must be unique across Heroku, as it will be used as the subdomain under which your application will be accessible. That is all we have to do to set up our Heroku app correctly.

You will be redirected to the app dashboard, as follows:

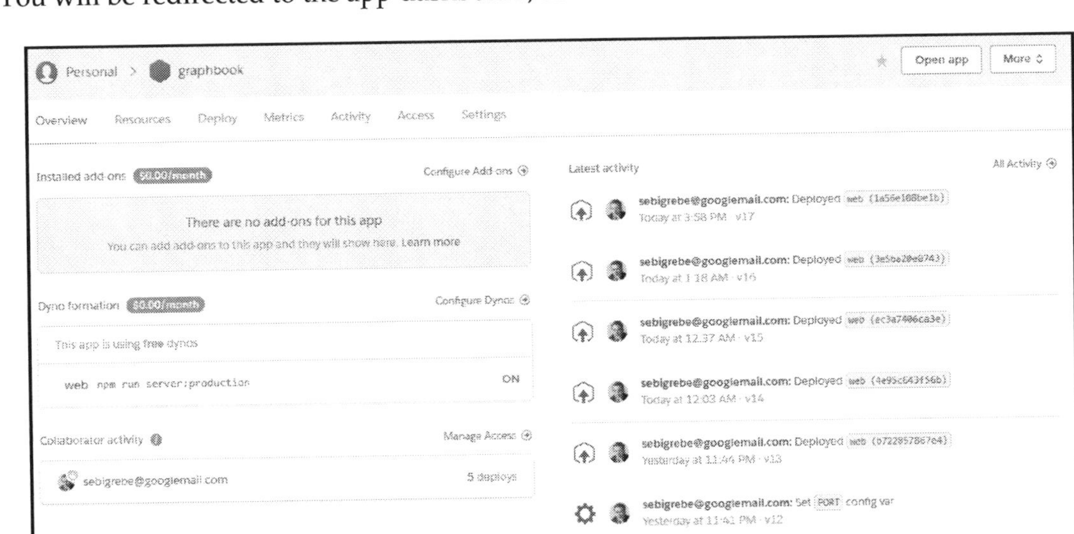


You can find the different Heroku features at the top of the window, in different tabs, as follows:

- The current one, which we can see in the preceding screenshot, is the **Overview**, which shows us the latest activity and the current Dynos that we are using on the left-hand side. You can see that I am already running the Docker image successfully, with the `npm run server:production` command. Dyno is a kind of flexible computing time, which represents the basis on which Heroku's system and pricing work.
- The **Resources** tab shows you information about the Dynos that we are using, as well as **add-ons** that Heroku provides. They provide a dozen **add-ons**, which includes a MySQL database, a CMS system, and many others.
- The **Deploy** tab shows you information about the deployment process. Here, you can find information on how deploying through Git, GitHub, or the Docker Registry works. Furthermore, you can also set up a CI/CD pipeline, like we did manually through CircleCI.

- The **Metrics** tab provides analytics on CPU usage and other things. This could be helpful for seeing the workload in production.
- The **Activity** tab shows you the latest things that have happened with the Heroku app.
- The **Access** tab gives you the option to share your Heroku app with other colleagues so that they can work together with you as a team.
- The **Settings** tab shows you basic information and configuration options that can be used to customize your application. You can find the current Heroku URL, under which your application is served. You can also add custom domains, under which it will be served. More advanced options, like adding environment variables, can also be found here.

Now that our Heroku app has been set up, we can prepare our CD workflow. Before going over to our CircleCI configuration file, we should verify that the new Heroku app can run our application as planned. We are going to test this manually, via the Terminal. Later, CircleCI will automate this process for us.

We should add all of the environment variables that we are using throughout our application first. Our application has to know the credentials for the database, the AWS API keys, and much more. Go to the **Settings** tab and hit **Reveal Config Vars**, under **Config Vars**. You can add each variable by clicking the **Add** button, as shown in the following screenshot:

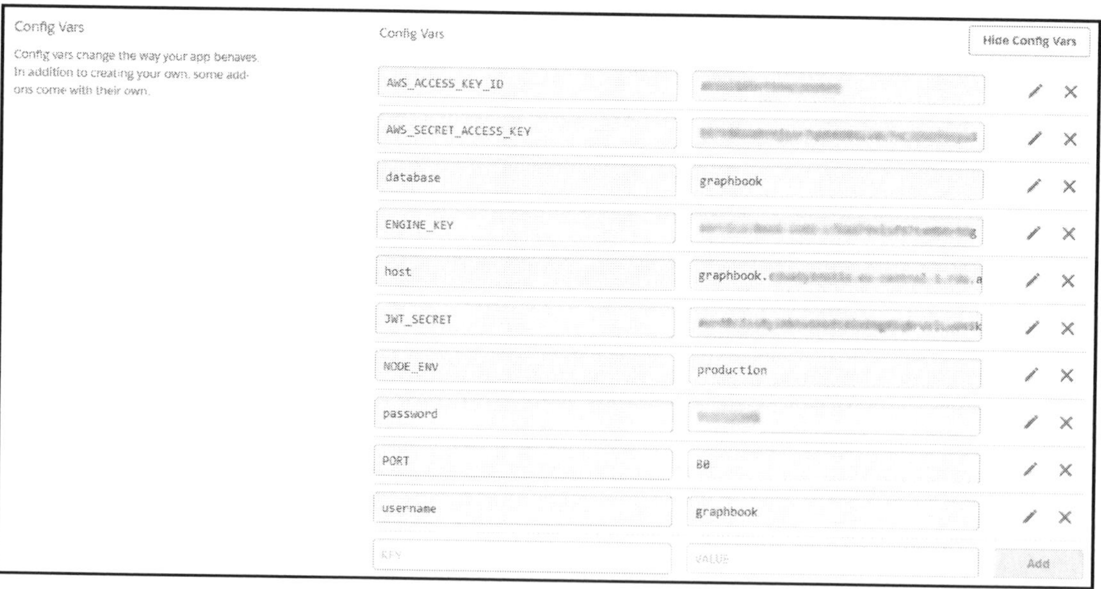

All of the environment variables can be taken from the preceding screenshot. Otherwise, our application will not run as expected.

Continue by installing the Heroku CLI on your local machine to test the workflow manually. The instructions can be found at `https://devcenter.heroku.com/articles/heroku-cli`.

If you have Snap installed on your system, you can run the following command:

```
sudo snap install --classic heroku
```

If this is not the case, manually install the Heroku CLI by using the following command:

```
curl https://cli-assets.heroku.com/install.sh | sh
```

Make sure that the installation has worked by verifying the version number, using the `heroku` command, as follows:

```
heroku --version
```

From now on, you can follow these instructions to test that your workflow works as expected:

1. The Heroku CLI offers a `login` method. Otherwise, you cannot access your Heroku app and deploy images to it. Execute the following command:

   ```
   heroku login
   ```

   The `login` function will open a browser window for you, where you can log in like before. You will be logged in directly inside of your Terminal through the Heroku web page.

2. Heroku offers a private Docker image registry, like Docker Hub, which was specially made for use with Heroku. We will publish our image to this registry, because we can rely on the automatic deployment feature. You can deploy images from this repository to your Heroku app automatically. To authorize yourself at the registry, you can use the following command:

   ```
   heroku container:login
   ```

   You should be directly logged in, without further ado.

3. Now that we are authorized in all services, we can build our Docker image again. We are using a different tag now, because we will publish the image to the Heroku registry, which is not possible with the old tag name. We are using the image name `web`, as it is the default name provided by Heroku.

Replace the name `graphbook` with the name of your app. Run the following command to build the Docker image:

```
docker build -t registry.heroku.com/graphbook/web .
```

4. In the previous tests in this chapter, we did not publish the generated images to any registry. Replace the `graphbook` name with your app's name. We will use the `docker push` command to upload our image to Heroku, as follows:

```
docker push registry.heroku.com/graphbook/web:latest
```

This is nothing complicated; we upload the latest version of our Docker image to the registry.

5. Still, nothing has gone live yet. There is only one command that we must run to make our application go live, as follows:

```
heroku container:release web --app graphbook
```

The `container:release` command deploys our new `web` image to our Heroku app. The `--app` parameter needs to be filled in with the name of the Heroku app that we want to deploy to.

After running the preceding commands, your application should launch. We have tested the complete routine manually, so we should translate this to a CircleCI config, which will do this for us automatically.

We will start with a blank CircleCI config again; so, empty the old `config.yml` file, and then follow these steps:

1. The beginning of our configuration should be the same as before. Insert it into our `config.yml` file, as follows:

```
version: 2
jobs:
  build:
    docker:
      - image: circleci/node:10
    steps:
      - checkout
      - setup_remote_docker:
          docker_layer_caching: true
```

I have just removed the echo command from our config.yml. Next, we must add all of the single steps to build, migrate, and deploy our application. The important thing here is that the indentation is correct.

2. Before building and deploying our application, we have to ensure that everything works as planned. We can use the tests we built in the previous chapter using Mocha. Add a second image to the docker section of the preceding code like so:

```
- image: tkuchiki/delayed-mysql
  environment:
    MYSQL_ALLOW_EMPTY_PASSWORD: yes
    MYSQL_ROOT_PASSWORD: ''
    MYSQL_DATABASE: graphbook_test
```

We add this second image because it launches an empty MySQL database for us. Our test will use this database to run all tests. The great thing about it is that our tests can run multiple times without failing. Normally, when running our tests locally, we had to remove all test data that was created, otherwise a second test would have failed. Since CircleCI spawns a new database with every job, there won't be such problems.

The image we use allows us to wait for the MySQL server to start and furthermore to specify the credentials using the MYSQL_ROOT_PASSWORD field for example. Our test can use the aforementioned defined credentials to connect to the database.

3. Instead of building and deploying the Docker image straight away, we first have to run our automated test. We have to install all dependencies from our package.json file directly within the CircleCI job's container. Add the following lines to the configuration file:

```
- run:
    name: "Install dependencies"
    command: npm install
```

The name property is the text that is displayed inside of CircleCI, next to each row of our job's details.

4. Our test relies on the fact that the back end and front end code is working. This includes the fact that our database is also correctly structured with the newest migrations applied. We can apply the migrations using Sequelize which we are going to install with the following lines of code::

```
- run:
    name: "Install Sequelize"
    command: sudo npm install -g mysql2 sequelize sequelize-cli
```

   We migrate all of the database changes, like new fields or tables. To do this, we will install the Sequelize CLI, which will run all of the migrations for us, We install the `mysql2`, `sequelize`, and `sequelize-cli` packages, which are the only required ones. Do not forget to prefix the command with `sudo`. Otherwise, you will get an **Access denied error** alert.

5. Everything that we need to run our test is now prepared. All of the packages are installed, so, we just have to migrate the database and run the tests. To make sure that the database has been started though, we have to add one further command, which lets the CircleCI job wait until the database is started. Insert the following lines:

```
- run:
    name: Wait for DB
    command: dockerize -wait tcp://127.0.0.1:3306 -timeout 120s
```

   The `dockerize` command is a small tool featuring some functionalities that make your work easier in an environment with Docker images. The `-wait` option tells `dockerize` to poll the MySQL database port 3306 of the CircleCI container. Until a successful response is received, all later commands from our configuration file are not executed.

6. The next task of our CircleCI workflow is, of course, to apply all migrations to the test database. Add the following lines:

```
- run:
    name: "Run migrations for test DB"
    command: sequelize db:migrate --migrations-path
    src/server/migrations --config src/server/config/index.js --env
    production
    environment:
      NODE_ENV: production
      password: ''
      database: graphbook_test
      username: root
      host: localhost
```

What's important here is that you add the `--env` option with `production` to apply the changes to the database we have in the environment variables. To overwrite the default environment variables in our CircleCI project settings, we can specify the environment property under which we can define environment variables that only take action in the command we execute. They are not taken over to later commands. It is a great way to overwrite default variables with the credentials that work for the test database within CircleCI. The command we execute is the same one we already used for our application.

7. Now that the database has been updated, we can execute the test. Insert the following lines to run our `npm` run test script with the correct environment variables, as before:

```
- run:
    name: "Run tests"
    command: npm run test
    environment:
      NODE_ENV: production
      password: ''
      database: graphbook_test
      username: root
      host: localhost
      JWT_SECRET: 1234
```

Beyond the database credentials, we also have to specify the `JWT_SECRET` for the automated test. Our back end assumes that it is set to verify the signup process for the users.

8. Because we release our container image to our Heroku app, we also need the Heroku CLI installed inside of the deployment job that was started by CircleCI. Add the following lines to our `config.yml` file to install the Heroku CLI:

```
- run:
    name: "Install Heroku CLI"
    command: curl https://cli-assets.heroku.com/install.sh | sh
```

The preceding command will install the Heroku CLI, like we did before on our local machine.

9. We must log in to the Heroku Image Registry to push our Docker image after the image has been built. Add the following lines of code to our configuration file:

```
- run:
    name: "Login to Docker"
    command: docker login -u $HEROKU_LOGIN -p $HEROKU_API_KEY
    registry.heroku.com
```

The `docker login` command takes a `-u` or `--user` parameter with the username for our Heroku account. You have to specify a second option, using the `-p` parameter, which is the password for our Heroku account. However, instead of the password, we will provide a Heroku API key here. You can find your API key at `https://dashboard.heroku.com/account`. You can click on **reveal** or **regenerate** to get a new API key.

The `HEROKU_LOGIN` and `HEROKU_API_KEY` variables must be set inside of CircleCI's environment variables. Go to the project settings by hitting the settings icon in the top-right of your CircleCI job, and add the environment variables, as follows:

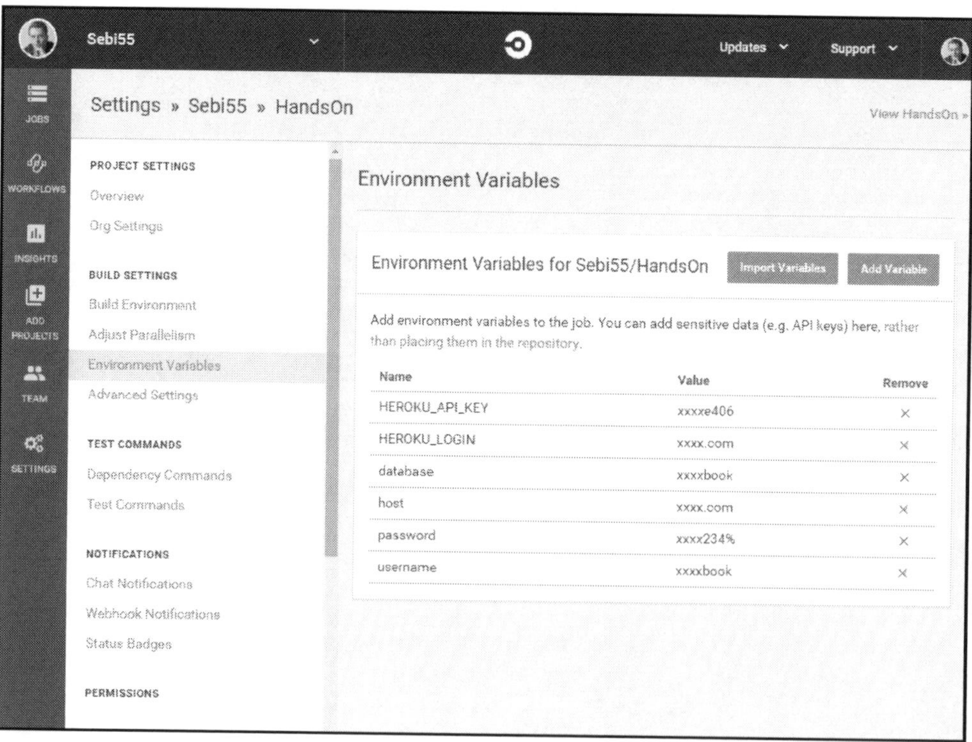

The first two variables are required to upload the final image to the Heroku registry. The last four variables store the database credentials for our production database. We already specified them on Heroku, but we will also need them while migrating all of the database changes in a later step.

The database credentials will automatically be used for migrating database changes to the production database. If you want to use a different database for testing and production, you will need to define them separately here, and apply them in the `Dockerfile`. The best approach is to have a separate testing database that is cleaned after running the automated tests. You can add another CircleCI task to create a new database whenever a new build job is started. Please remember to edit the `ENV` statements and add a special test database for the testing procedure when going live with this workflow.

10. Now, we can start building our Docker image, like we did previously in our manual test. Add the following step to the `config.yml` file:

```
- run:
    name: "Build Docker Image"
    command: docker build -t registry.heroku.com/graphbook/web .
```

11. After building the image with the preceding command, we can push the image to the Heroku registry. Add the following lines to the configuration file:

```
- run:
    name: "Push Docker Image to Heroku registry"
    command: docker push registry.heroku.com/graphbook/web:latest
```

12. Next, we will migrate the changes to the database structures with the command that we covered in `Chapter 3`, *Connecting to The Database*:

```
- run:
    name: "Run migrations for production DB"
    command: sequelize db:migrate --migrations-path
    src/server/migrations --config src/server/config/index.js --env
    production
```

What's important here is that you add the `--env` option with `production` to apply the changes to the production database. The environment variables from the CircleCI project settings are used to apply those migrations.

13. Finally, we can deploy our new application, as follows:

```
- run:
    name: "Deploy image to Heroku App"
    command: heroku container:release web --app graphbook
```

    This is the same command that we used before, when we manually tested the workflow. The preceding command uses the Heroku CLI, which we installed in an earlier step.

You can commit and push this new config file into your Git repository, and CircleCI should automatically process it and create a new job for you.

The resulting job should look like as follows:

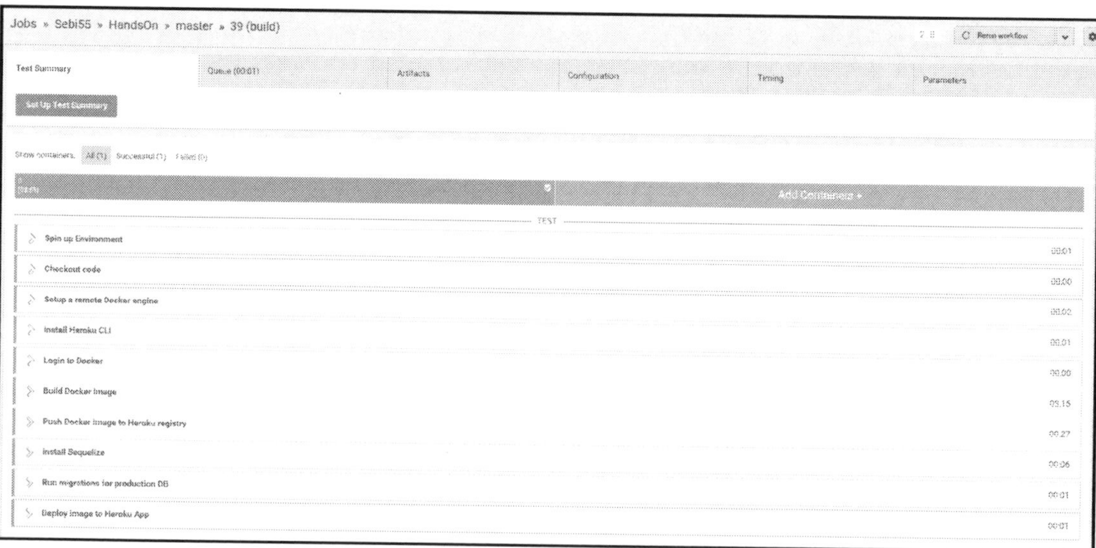


As you can see in the preceding screenshot, all of the steps of our `config.yml` file are listed with their names and were successfully executed. Your application should be running now. The image was pushed to the Heroku image registry, which directly deployed the latest version of our image to the Heroku app.

If you want to know whether everything is working as expected, you can run the `logs` function of Heroku CLI on your local machine, as follows:

```
heroku logs --app graphbook
```

This command will show you the latest logs in the command line of our application's container.

The automated deployment of our application is finished now, and we will be able to release new versions of our application continuously.

# Summary

In this chapter, you learned how to dockerize your application using a normal Dockerfile and a multi-stage build.

Furthermore, I have shown you how to set up an exemplary continuous deployment workflow using CircleCI and Heroku. You can replace the deployment process with a more complex setup by using AWS, but continue using our Docker image.

Having read this chapter, you have learned everything from developing a complete application to deploying it to a production environment. Your application should now be running on Heroku.

# Other Books You May Enjoy

If you enjoyed this book, you may be interested in these other books by Packt:

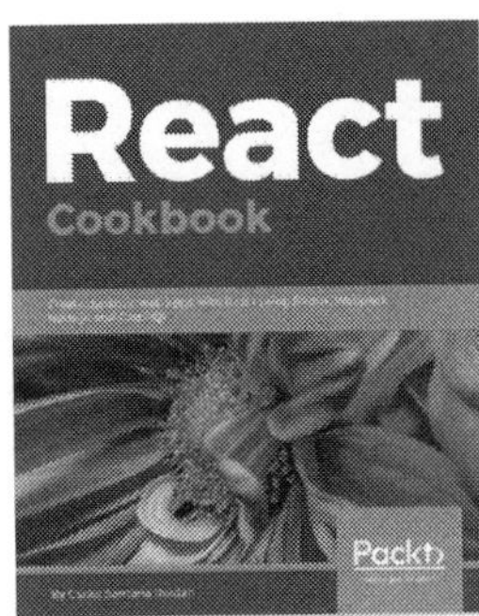


**React Cookbook**
Carlos Santana Roldan

ISBN: 9781783980727

- Gain the ability to wield complex topics such as Webpack and server-side rendering
- Implement an API using Node.js, Firebase, and GraphQL
- Learn to maximize the performance of React applications
- Create a mobile application using React Native
- Deploy a React application on Digital Ocean
- Get to know the best practices when organizing and testing a large React application

**Learn React with TypeScript 3**
Carl Rippon

ISBN: 9781789610253

- Gain a first-hand experience of TypeScript and its productivity features
- Transpile your TypeScript code into JavaScript for it to run in a browser
- Learn relevant advanced types in TypeScript for creating strongly typed and reusable components.
- Create stateful function-based components that handle lifecycle events using hooks
- Get to know what GraphQL is and how to work with it by executing basic queries to get familiar with the syntax
- Become confident in getting good unit testing coverage on your components using Jest

## Leave a review - let other readers know what you think

Please share your thoughts on this book with others by leaving a review on the site that you bought it from. If you purchased the book from Amazon, please leave us an honest review on this book's Amazon page. This is vital so that other potential readers can see and use your unbiased opinion to make purchasing decisions, we can understand what our customers think about our products, and our authors can see your feedback on the title that they have worked with Packt to create. It will only take a few minutes of your time, but is valuable to other potential customers, our authors, and Packt. Thank you!

# Index

## A

advanced routing, with React Router
about 283
parameters, adding in routes 284, 286, 287, 288
programmatic navigation 292, 293, 294
redirect location 295, 296
user profile, querying 290, 291
Amazon Relation Database Service (RDS) 416, 417, 418, 419, 420
Amazon S3
images, uploading to 259
Amazon Web Services (AWS)
about 44
setting up 251, 252
Apollo cache
updating 134, 135
Apollo Client Developer Tools
about 160
debugging with 161, 163
Apollo Client
binding, to React 122
caching with 387, 389
dependencies 116, 117
installing 116, 117
mutations 128
optimistic UI 135, 136
queries, refetching 134
Query component, polling 138
querying, in React 124
React component, connecting with 123
setting up 115, 116
subscriptions 334, 335, 336, 338, 339, 340, 341, 343, 344, 346, 347
testing 119, 120
UI, updating 133
using, in React 122
Apollo Consumer
about 210, 211
versus React Context API 207
Apollo documentation
reference 117
Apollo Engine
error tracking 383, 385, 386
performance metrics 380, 381, 382
reference 377
schemas, analyzing 378, 379, 380
setting up 375, 376, 377
Apollo HoC query 124, 125
Apollo Mutation component 131, 180, 182, 184
Apollo Mutation HoC 129, 130
Apollo queries
running, with server-side rendering (SSR) 320, 321, 322, 323, 324
Apollo Query component 126, 176, 178, 180
Apollo React components 176
Apollo Server
caching with 387, 389
subscriptions 328, 329, 330, 332, 333, 334
Apollo Subscriptions
about 139, 326, 327, 328
reference 327
used, for authentication 347, 348, 350, 351, 352
used, for notifications 352, 353, 354, 356
Apollo
about 63
Express.js, combining with 46, 47, 48
Sequelize, using with 82
application architecture 8
applications
deploying, to Heroku 424, 426, 427, 428, 429, 430, 431, 432, 433, 434, 435

arrays
rendering, from React state 20, 21, 22
AsyncIterable 333
AsyncIterator 331
authentication, with GraphQL
about 223, 224
Apollo login mutation 225, 226, 228
Apollo sign up mutation 233, 234, 235
React login form 228, 229, 231, 232, 233
React sign up form 235, 236, 237
React, used for logging out 246, 247, 248
user context, resolving from resolver functions 243
authentication
with Apollo Subscriptions 347, 348, 350, 351, 352
with server-side rendering (SSR) 314, 315, 316, 317, 318, 319
Automatic Persisted Queries (APQ) 387
AWS access keys
generating 257, 258, 259
AWS Identity and Access Management (IAM) 257
AWS S3 bucket
creating 253, 254, 255, 256

# B

backend debugging 56
backend
starting, with Mocha 362, 363
bundle size
analyzing 34, 35

# C

caching
with Apollo Client 389
with Apollo Server 387, 389
catch-all routes
in React Router 282
Chat model 98, 100
chats
about 102
creating 110
displaying 139, 140, 142, 143, 144, 145
fetching 139, 140, 142, 143, 144
implementing 139
resolver functions 243
child components
rendering 172
children pass-through pattern 177
CircleCI
reference 420
code-splitting
with react loadable 392, 393, 394
with SSR 395, 396, 397, 398, 399, 400
with webpack 392, 393, 394
conditional rendering 171
configuration file
using, with Sequelize 71
Content Security Policy (CSP)
reference 45
continuous deployment (CD) 420
continuous integration (CI)
about 420
configuring 420, 421, 422, 423
controlled components 26, 167, 168
cookies
advantages 222
disadvantages 223
versus localStorage 221
CORS(Cross-origin resource sharing) 46
CSRF
reference 314
CurrentUser GraphQL query 244, 245

# D

database migration 75
database models
importing, with Sequelize 77, 78
writing 73
database query
running 85, 86
database
connecting, with Sequelize 69, 70
creating, in MySQL 67
using, in GraphQL 63
debugging
with Postman 58, 60
detached mode 410
development tools 32, 33, 34
Docker Community Edition 403

Docker containers
building 408, 409, 410, 411
running 408, 409, 410, 411
docker ps
reference 411
Docker run
reference 410
Docker
about 402
application, deploying 404
installing 402, 404
multi-stage Docker production builds 412, 413, 414, 415
reference 402
setting up 401
Dockerfile
reference 404, 405
writing 404, 405, 406, 407, 408
dockerize 404
document heads
controlling, with React Helmet 30
DOM
reference 189
dynamic routing 276

# E

Enzyme
used, for testing React 369, 370, 371, 372, 373
error tracking
with Apollo Engine 383, 385, 386
event handling
with React 26, 27, 28, 29
Express Helmet 44, 45
Express.js middleware
compression, enabling 45
CORS 45, 46
Helmet 44, 45
installing 43
using 42, 43
Express.js
about 37
combining, with Apollo 46, 47, 48
production build, serving 41, 42
routing 40, 41
running, in development 39, 40
server-side rendering (SSR) 299, 300, 302, 303, 305, 307, 308, 309, 310, 311, 312, 313
setting up 38, 39

# F

FontAwesome
reference 186
foreign key data
seeding 91

# G

global database instance 82, 84
GNU Privacy Guard (GPG) 403
graphbook app 424
Graphbook
about 7, 350
basic setup 10, 11
extending 185
React application bar 200, 202, 203, 204, 205, 206
React Context API, versus Apollo Consumer 207
React context menu 185
GraphQL mutation
writing 54, 56
GraphQL queries
sending 51, 52
GraphQL requests
authenticating 238, 239, 240, 241, 242
GraphQL resolvers
implementing 50, 51
GraphQL schemas
types, using 53
writing 49, 50
GraphQL Voyager
reference 379
GraphQL
about 8, 9, 63, 325, 326
authenticated requests, testing 367, 368
authentication, testing 366, 367
databases, using 63
image upload mutation 260, 262, 263
pagination 155, 158
testing, with Mocha 365

## H

helper components 187
Heroku API key
  reference 432
Heroku CLI
  reference 427
Heroku
  applications, deploying to 424, 426, 427, 428, 429, 430, 431, 432, 433, 434, 435
  features 425
  reference 424
higher-order component (HoC)
  about 124
  reference 124
Hot Module Replace (HMR) 302
HTTP 9

## I

images
  uploading, to Amazon S3 259

## J

join tables 97
JSON Web Tokens (JWTs)
  about 219
  reference 220

## L

localStorage
  advantages 222
  disadvantages 221
  versus cookies 221
logging
  about 56
  in Node.js 57

## M

many-to-many data
  seeding 105, 108, 109
many-to-many relationships 97
Message model 100
messages
  about 102
  creating 112
  displaying 147
  fetching 147
  implementing 139
  sending, through mutations 152, 153, 154, 155
migration file
  advantages 75
migrations
  properties 76
  table structure, updating 87, 89
Mocha test 358, 359, 360, 361
Mocha
  correct routing, verifying 364, 365
  used, for starting backend 362, 363
  used, for testing 357
  used, for testing GraphQL 365
model associations, Sequelize 90
multi-stage Docker production builds 412, 413, 414, 415
mutations, with Apollo Client
  about 128
  Apollo Mutation component 131
  Apollo Mutation HoC 129, 130
mutations
  messages, sending through 152, 153, 155
MySQL
  database, creating 67
  installing 64, 66

## N

Node Version Manager (NVM) 11
Node.js web server
  setting up 37
Node.js
  configuring 11, 12
  installing 11, 12
  logging in 57, 58
  reference, for Downloads section 11
notifications
  with Apollo Subscriptions 352, 353, 354, 356

## O

one-to-one relationships, Sequelize 86

# P


packages, GraphQL
  reference 116
pagination
  about 155
  in GraphQL 155, 159
  in React 155, 159
performance metrics
  with Apollo Engine 380, 381, 382
polling 138
Postman
  download link 58
  used, for debugging 58, 60
preflight request 46
production build
  preparing 391, 392
  serving, through Express.js 41, 42
PropTypes
  reference 216


# Q


querying, in React
  with Apollo Client 124


# R


React applications
  documenting 212
  PropTypes 214, 215, 216, 218
  structuring 173
  Styleguidist, setting up 212, 214
React component
  connecting, with Apollo Client 123
  rendering 19
React Context API
  about 208, 209, 210
  methods 208
  versus Apollo Consumer 207
React context menu
  about 185
  Apollo deletePost mutation 199, 200
  FontAwesome 186, 187
  GraphQL updatePost mutation 190, 191, 193, 194, 195, 196
  helper components 187, 188, 190
React Developer Tools
  installation link 32
React Helmet
  document heads, controlling 30
react loadable
  used, for code-splitting 392, 393, 394
React patterns
  about 165
  child components, rendering 172
  conditional rendering 171
  controlled components 166, 167, 168
  reference 166
  stateless functions 168, 169, 170
React Router
  advanced routing 283
  catch-all routes 282
  components 280
  installing 277, 278
  parameters, adding in routes 289
  reference 282
  route, implementing 278, 279
  secured routes 281, 282
  setting up 275, 276
React setup
  arrays, rendering from React state 20, 21, 22
  CSS with Webpack 24, 26
  production build, with Webpack 30, 31, 32
  React component, rendering 18, 20
  Webpack, configuring 15, 16
  Webpack, preparing 14, 16
React state
  arrays, rendering from 20, 21, 22
React
  about 9
  Apollo Client, binding to 122
  Apollo Client, using in 122
  event handling 26, 27, 28, 29
  file structure 173, 175
  image, cropping 263, 264, 265, 266, 267, 268, 269, 271
  image, uploading 263, 264, 265, 266, 267, 268, 269, 271
  pagination 155, 158
  setting up 12, 13, 14
  state updates 26, 27, 28, 29

testing, with Enzyme 369, 370, 371, 372, 373
render props, React
reference 126
Requests Per Minute (rpm) 381
Resolver functions 8
resolver functions
for chats 243
routing, Express.js 40, 41

# S

schema directives
reference 241
schemas
analyzing, with Apollo Engine 378, 380
search engine optimization (SEO) 275
secured routes 281, 282
Sequelize
about 68
configuration file, using with 71
data mutating 95, 96
data seeding 80, 82
database models, importing 77, 78
database, connecting with 69, 70
integrating, into stack 68
model associations 90, 91
one-to-one relationships 87
reference 68
using, with Apollo 82
server package, react-dom
reference 309
server-sent events 139
server-side rendering (SSR)
about 297, 298
Apollo queries, running with 320, 321, 322, 323, 324
in Express.js 299, 302, 303, 305, 306, 308, 309, 310, 311, 312, 313
used, for code-splitting 395, 396, 397, 398, 399, 400
using, for authentication 314, 315, 316, 317, 318, 319
SQL 9
state updates
with React 26, 27, 28, 29
stateless functions 168, 169, 170
static routing 276
subscriptions
on Apollo Client 334, 335, 336, 337, 339, 340, 341, 343, 344, 346, 347
on Apollo Server 328, 329, 330, 332, 333, 334

# T

table structure
updating, with migrations 87, 89
template literal 120
test-driven development (TDD) 357
testing
with Mocha 357
types
using, in GraphQL schemas 53

# U

universal rendering 298

# W

webpack
used, for code-splitting 392, 393, 394
WebSockets
about 139, 326
disadvantages 326
withFilter function
properties 351

Made in the USA
San Bernardino, CA
11 June 2019